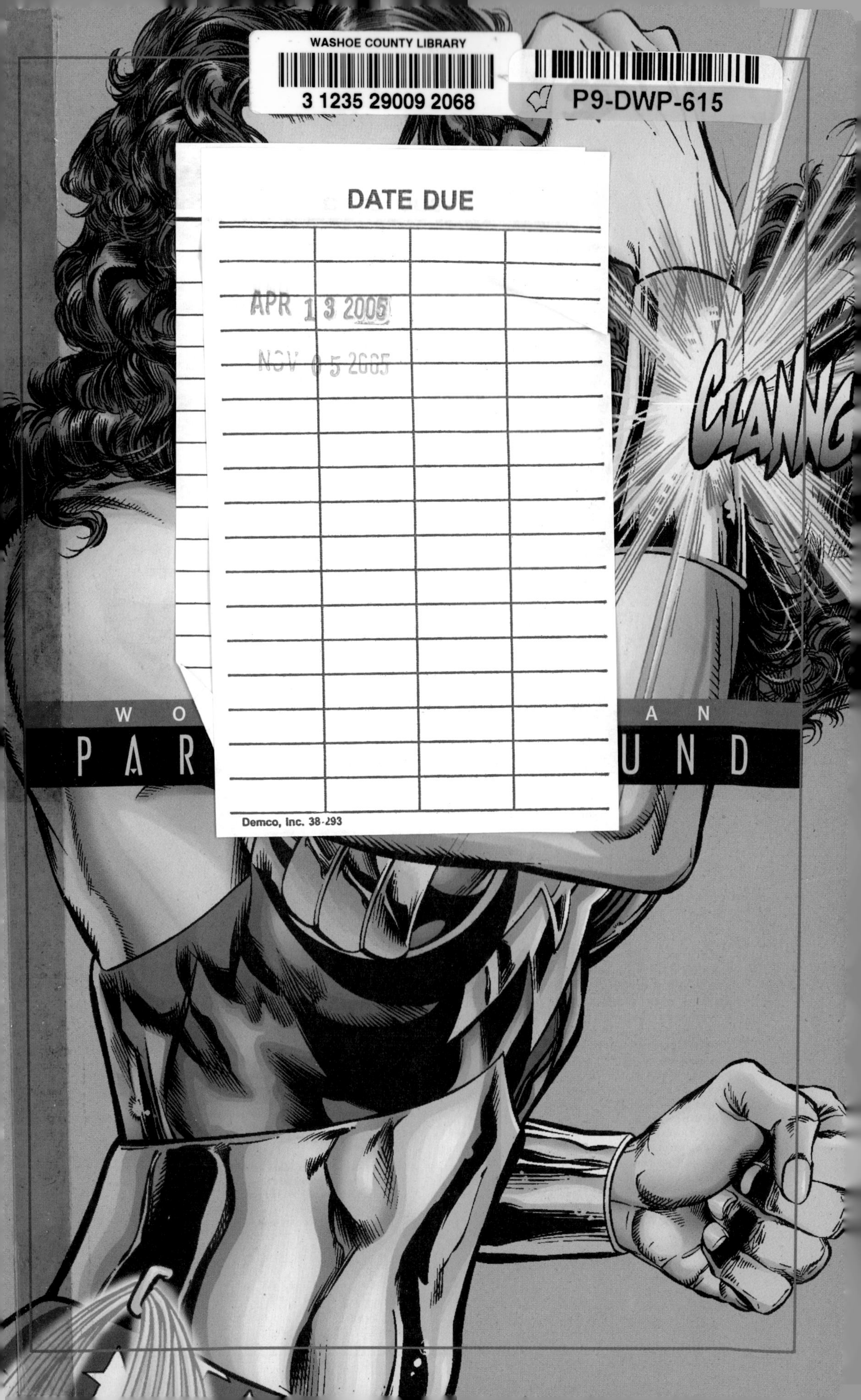

MIKE CARLIN VP-EXECUTIVE EDITOR
EDDIE BERGANZA EDITOR-ORIGINAL SERIES
ANTON KAWASAKI EDITOR-COLLECTED EDITION
ROBBIN BROSTERMAN SENIOR ART DIRECTOR
PAUL LEVITZ PRESIDENT & PUBLISHER
GEORG BREWER VP-DESIGN & RETAIL PRODUCT DEVELOPMENT
RICHARD BRUNING VP-CREATIVE DIRECTOR
PATRICK CALDON SENIOR VP-FINANCE & OPERATIONS
CHRIS CARAMALIS VP-FINANCE
TERRI CUNNINGHAM VP-MANAGING EDITOR
DAN DIDIO VP-EDITORIAL
JOEL EHRLICH SENIOR VP-ADVERTISING & PROMOTIONS
ALISON GILL VP-MANUFACTURING
LILLIAN LASERSON SENIOR VP & GENERAL COUNSEL
DAVID MCKILLIPS VP-ADVERTISING
JOHN NEE VP-BUSINESS DEVELOPMENT
CHERYL RUBIN VP-LICENSING & MERCHANDISING
BOB WAYNE VP-SALES & MARKETING

WONDER WOMAN: PARADISE FOUND

PUBLISHED BY DC COMICS.
COVER AND COMPILATION COPYRIGHT © 2003 DC COMICS.
ALL RIGHTS RESERVED.

ORIGINALLY PUBLISHED IN SINGLE MAGAZINE FORM IN WONDER WOMAN #171-177
AND WONDER WOMAN SECRET FILES #3.
COPYRIGHT © 2001-2002 DC COMICS. ALL RIGHTS RESERVED.
ALL CHARACTERS, THEIR DISTINCTIVE LIKENESSES AND RELATED INDICIA FEATURED
IN THIS PUBLICATION ARE TRADEMARKS OF DC COMICS.
THE STORIES, CHARACTERS, AND INCIDENTS FEATURED IN. THIS PUBLICATION ARE
ENTIRELY FICTIONAL. DC COMICS DOES NOT READ OR ACCEPT
UNSOLICITED SUBMISSIONS OF IDEAS, STORIES, OR ARTWORK.

DC COMICS, 1700 BROADWAY, NEW YORK, NY 10019
A DIVISION OF WARNER BROS. — AN AOL TIME WARNER COMPANY
PRINTED IN CANADA. FIRST PRINTING.
ISBN: 1-56389-956-6
COVER ILLUSTRATIONS BY ADAM HUGHES.

WONDER WOMAN
PARADISE FOUND

★ ★ ★ ✶ ★ ★ ★

PHIL JIMENEZ WRITER

PHIL JIMENEZ TRAVIS MOORE BRANDON BADEAUX PENCILLERS

ANDY LANNING MARLO ALQUIZA LARY STUCKER

KEVIN CONRAD JOSÉ MARZAN JR. INKERS

PATRICIA MULVIHILL TOM MCCRAW COLORISTS

COMICRAFT LETTERER

ADAM HUGHES JIM LEE ORIGINAL SERIES COVERS

WONDER WOMAN CREATED BY WILLIAM MOULTON MARSTON

WONDER WOMAN

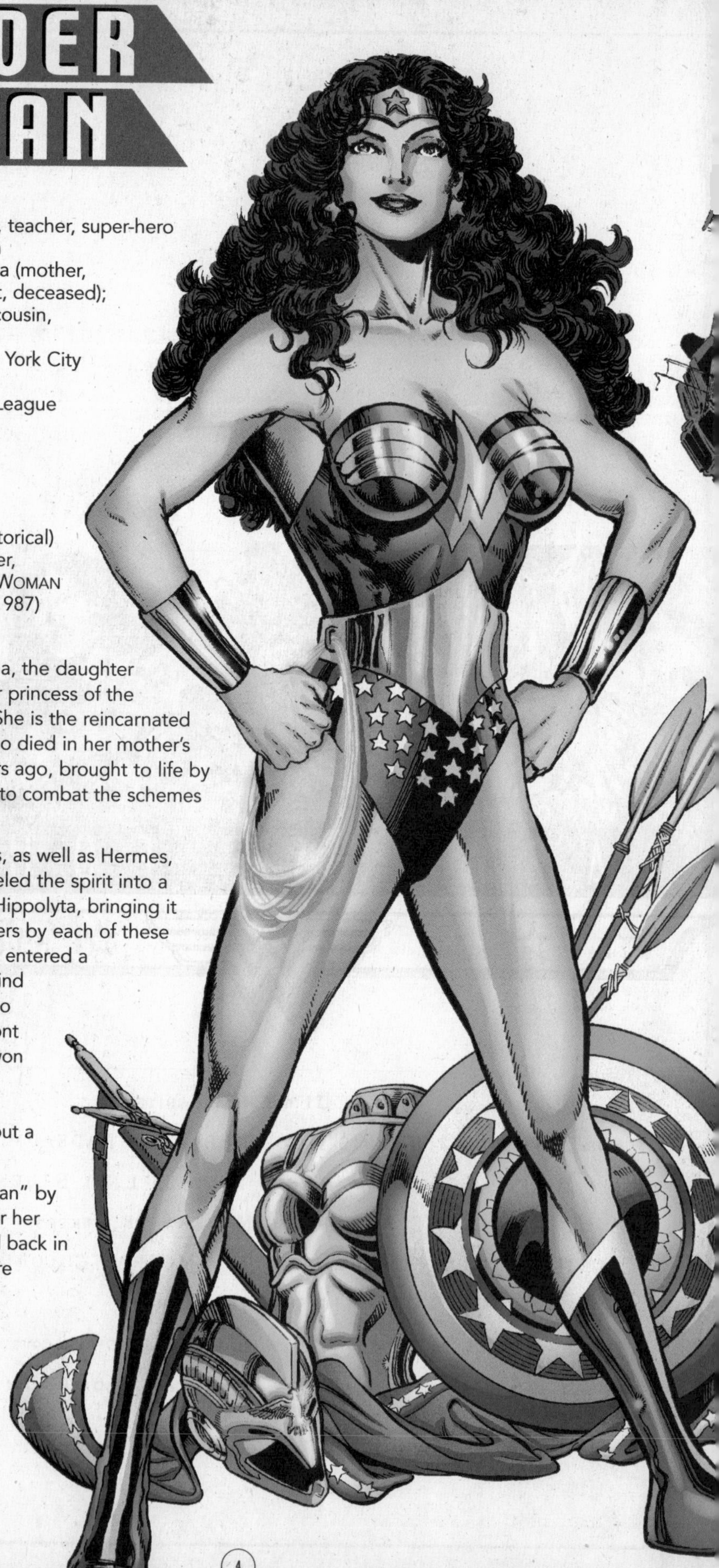

Real name: Diana
Occupation: Ambassador, teacher, super-hero
Place of birth: Themyscira
Known relatives: Hippolyta (mother, deceased) ; Antiope (aunt, deceased); Donna ("sister"); Phthia (cousin, deceased)
Bases of operations: New York City and Themyscira
Group affiliation: Justice League of America
Height: 5' 11"
Weight: 140 lbs.
Eyes: Blue
Hair: Black
FIRST APPEARANCE: (historical) ALL STAR COMICS #8 (Winter, 1941); (current) WONDER WOMAN (2nd series) #1(February, 1987)

Wonder Woman is Diana, the daughter of Hippolyta and a former princess of the Amazons of Themyscira. She is the reincarnated spirit of a human child who died in her mother's womb almost 30,000 years ago, brought to life by several Greek goddesses to combat the schemes of Ares, God of War.

These Greek goddesses, as well as Hermes, the messenger god, funneled the spirit into a clay sculpture crafted by Hippolyta, bringing it to life. Given special powers by each of these Olympians, Diana secretly entered a tournament designed to find the worthiest Amazon, who would go forth and confront the War God's evil. She won and, as Themyscira's champion, defeated Ares before he could bring about a nuclear holocaust.

Dubbed "Wonder Woman" by the press (and named after her mother, who later traveled back in time to World War II, where she used the name and garb of Wonder Woman), Diana became Themyscira's ambassador to the outside world, called "Patriarch's World" by the Amazons.

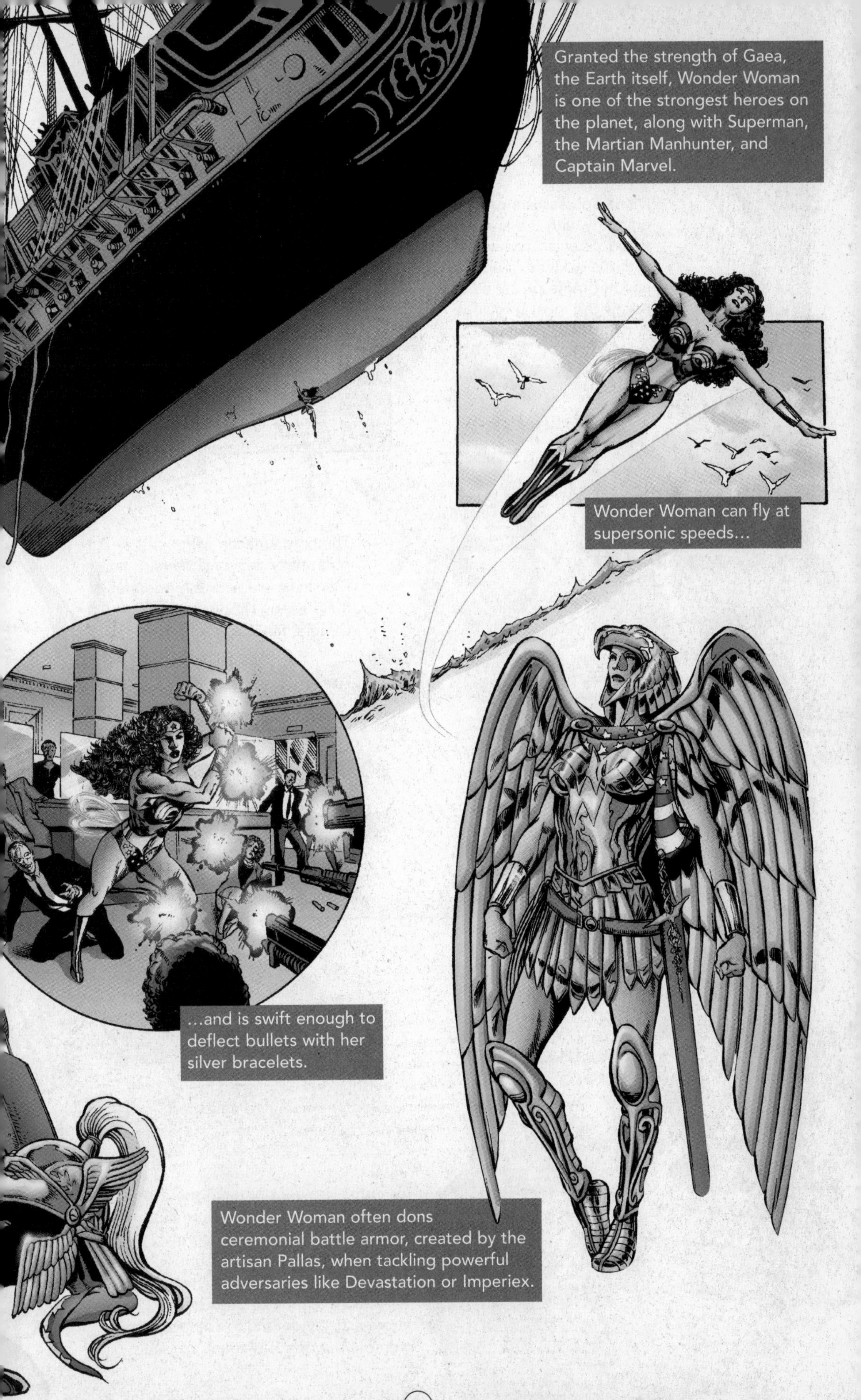
Granted the strength of Gaea, the Earth itself, Wonder Woman is one of the strongest heroes on the planet, along with Superman, the Martian Manhunter, and Captain Marvel.
Wonder Woman can fly at supersonic speeds…
…and is swift enough to deflect bullets with her silver bracelets.
Wonder Woman often dons ceremonial battle armor, created by the artisan Pallas, when tackling powerful adversaries like Devastation or Imperiex.

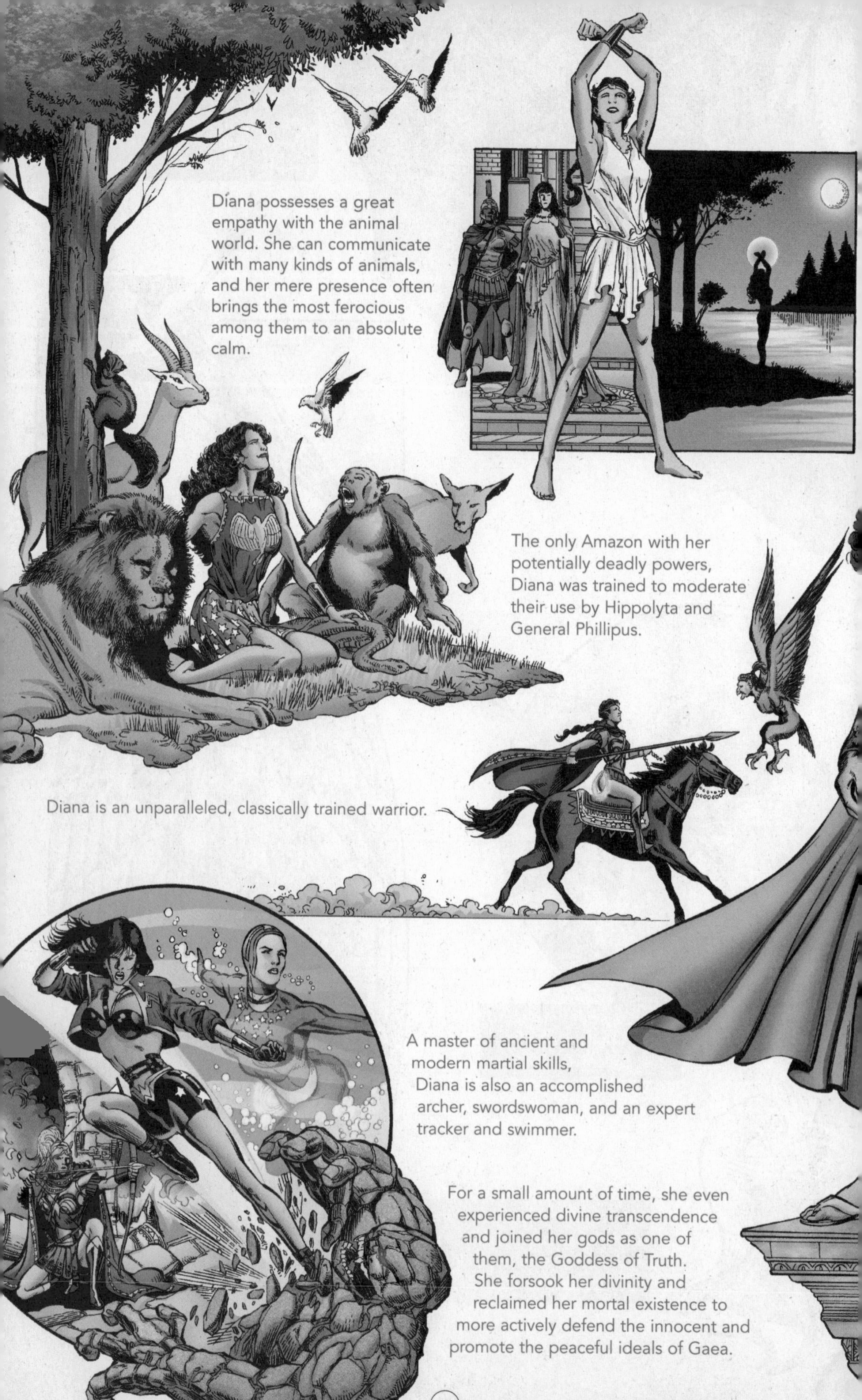

Diana possesses a great empathy with the animal world. She can communicate with many kinds of animals, and her mere presence often brings the most ferocious among them to an absolute calm.

The only Amazon with her potentially deadly powers, Diana was trained to moderate their use by Hippolyta and General Phillipus.

Diana is an unparalleled, classically trained warrior.

A master of ancient and modern martial skills, Diana is also an accomplished archer, swordswoman, and an expert tracker and swimmer.

For a small amount of time, she even experienced divine transcendence and joined her gods as one of them, the Goddess of Truth. She forsook her divinity and reclaimed her mortal existence to more actively defend the innocent and promote the peaceful ideals of Gaea.

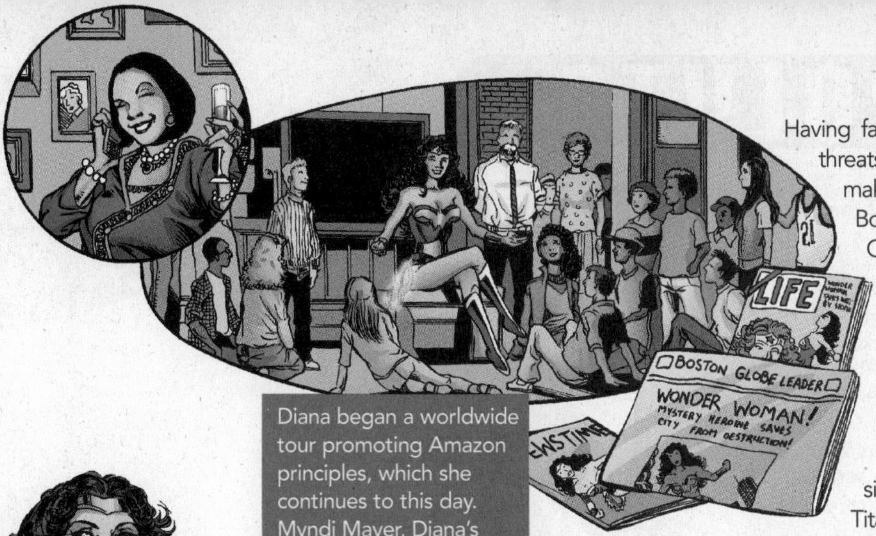
LIFE
BOSTON GLOBE LEADER
WONDER WOMAN!
MYSTERY HEROINE SAVES CITY FROM DESTRUCTION!

Having faced countless mystical threats and super-villains, and making her home first in Boston and later Gateway City, Wonder Woman became a member of the Justice League of America. She moved to New York City to be closer to her work at the United Nations and now lives with her sister Donna (a.k.a. the Titan Troia) in a penthouse on Fifth Avenue.

Diana began a worldwide tour promoting Amazon principles, which she continues to this day. Myndi Mayer, Diana's bawdy celebrity publicist, plastered "Wonder Woman's" image across every newspaper and TV talk show in the nation, before her unexpected death from a drug overdose.

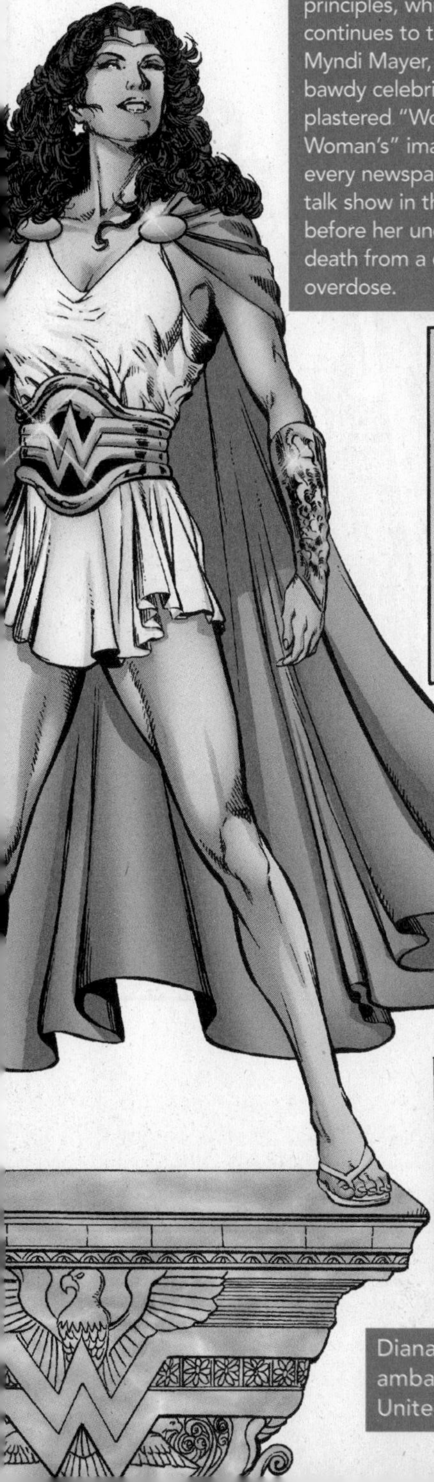

In a bid to end the recent civil war on Themyscira, Hippolyta abolished the monarchy, ending Diana's royal status as a princess. Hippolyta then returned to Patriarch's World as Wonder Woman, a role Diana secretly resented. As Wonder Woman, Diana remains Themyscira's ambassador to the world beyond its shores, promoting the ideals of equality and peace.

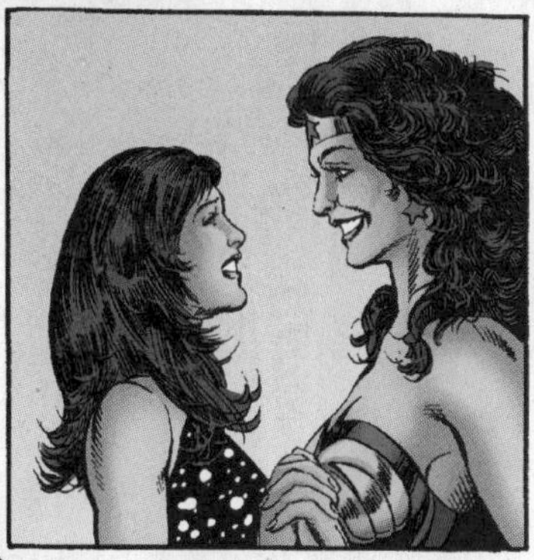

Diana and her younger sister, Donna.

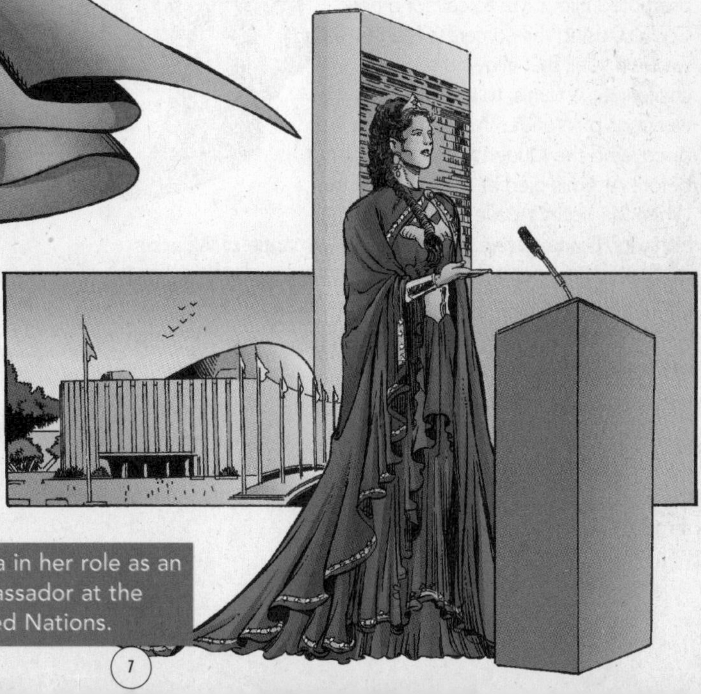

Diana in her role as an ambassador at the United Nations.

HIPPOLYTA

Full name: Hippolyta
Occupation: Queen of the Amazons; adventurer
Place of birth: A grove in ancient Greece
Height: 5' 9"   Weight: 138 lbs.
Eyes: Blue   Hair: Black
FIRST APPEARANCE: (historical) ALL STAR COMICS #8 (Winter, 1941); (current): WONDER WOMAN (2nd series) #1 (February, 1987); (as Wonder Woman) WONDER WOMAN (2nd series) #128 (December, 1997)

Hippolyta, the former queen of the Amazons, and her sister Antiope ruled the nation of Themyscira until their city was razed by Theseus and the ransacking demigod Heracles. Raped and humiliated by Heracles, Hippolyta led her Amazons to freedom. She and her followers were led by the Olympian goddesses to an island paradise, where they rebuilt the nation of Themyscira.

Queen of Themyscira for 3,000 years, Hippolyta yearned for a child, and created a sculpture of an infant girl from the clay of Paradise Island. The goddesses and Hermes, the messenger god, brought the clay figure to life. This child was named Diana, after a great and holy Amazon warrior. Diana won the sacred Contest and went forth into Man's World, becoming Wonder Woman.

Antiope and her daughter, Phthia.

Years later, a mystic vision foretelling the death of Wonder Woman prompted Hippolyta to call for a new Contest, using the sorceress Magala to weave a spell that allowed a challenger, Artemis, to win the title and weapons of Wonder Woman. Diana discovered the Queen's duplicity, but not before Artemis died at the hands of the White Magician. Apalled by Hippolyta's behavior, Diana once again claimed the mantle of Wonder Woman, mother and daughter alike believing the threat to her life had passed. But soon after, Hippolyta witnessed the mystic vision she so feared. The demon Neron attacked Wonder Woman and killed her.

The Amazons decreed that Hippolyta should do penance for abusing her royal power. Seeking retribution in her late daughter's eyes, Hippolyta became the new Wonder Woman. After Diana's resurrection Hippolyta continued to don her own Wonder Woman armor.

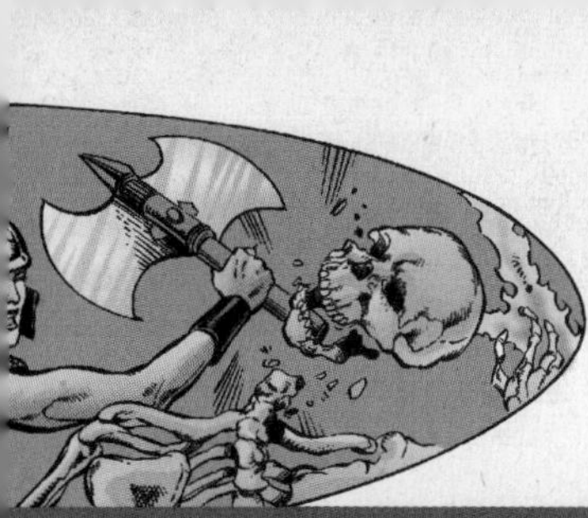

A fierce, aggressive warrior, Hippolyta was also a decisive leader. Having been blessed by the gods with her daughter Diana, Hippolyta was a doting mother who loved her child more than life itself and always acted, sometimes irresponsibly, to defend her.

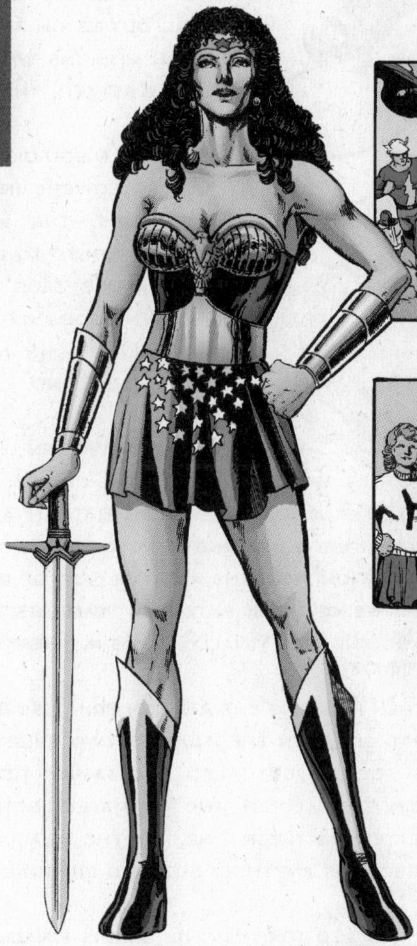

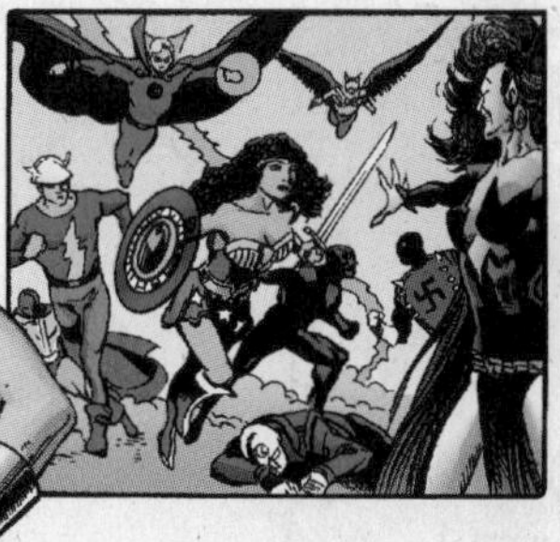

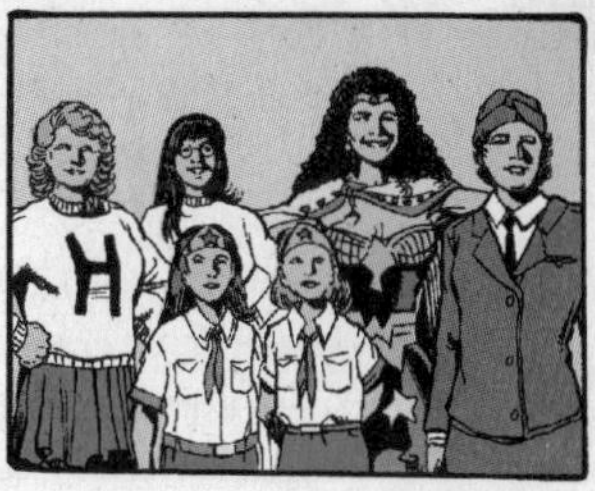

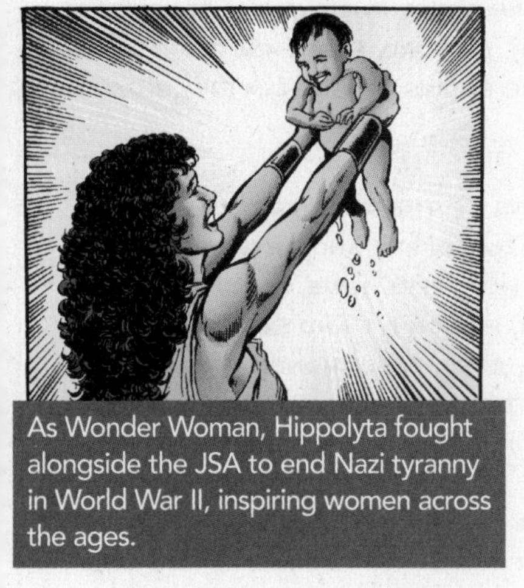

As Wonder Woman, Hippolyta fought alongside the JSA to end Nazi tyranny in World War II, inspiring women across the ages.

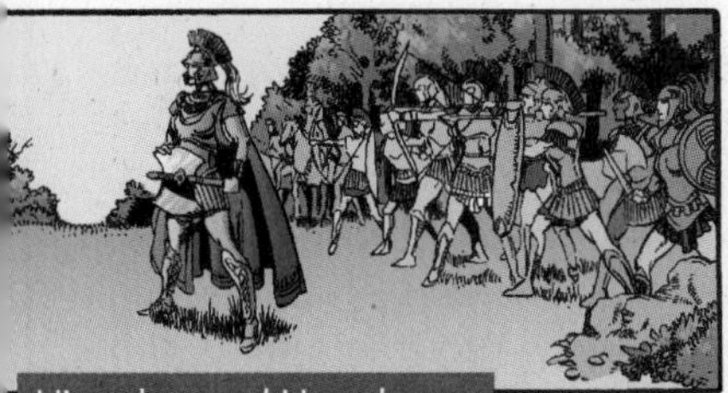

Hippolyta and Heracles face off in ancient Greece.

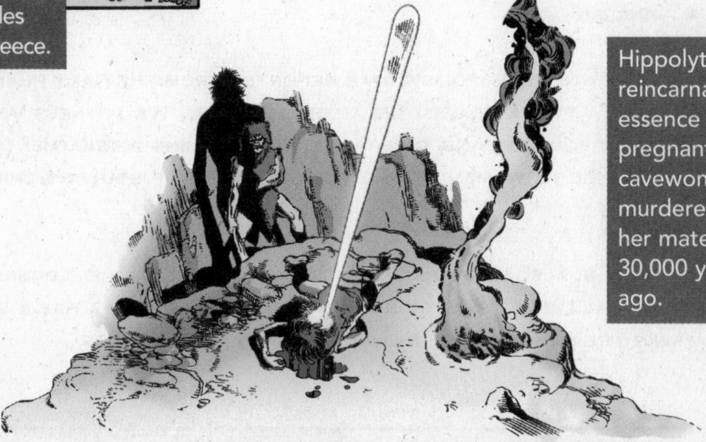

Hippolyta is the reincarnated essence of a pregnant cavewoman murdered by her mate over 30,000 years ago.

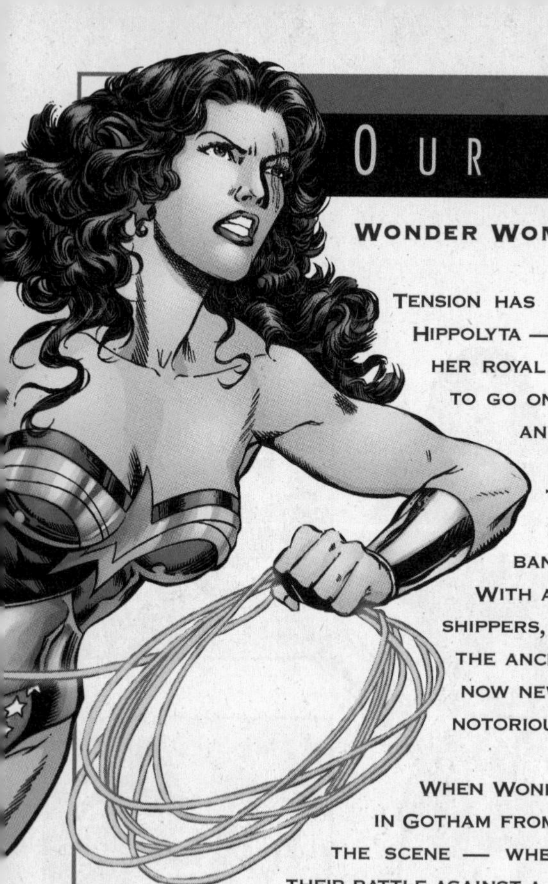

Our Story So Far...

Wonder Woman's life hasn't been easy lately.

Tension has been mounting between Diana and her mother Hippolyta — as Diana feels the Queen has been neglecting her royal duties on the legendary island of Themyscira to go on missions with the JSA. But before things get any better, they're about to get far worse...

The misguided Maxie Zeus has built a church of followers in Gotham City composed of gang-bangers, the homeless, and religious zealots. With a promise to usher in a new age for these worshippers, Maxie Zeus manipulates their faith to revive the ancient gods of War, Discord, Fear, and Terror — now newly reborn in the bodies of Gotham City's most notorious villains!

When Wonder Woman learns of the dark forces brewing in Gotham from the oracle Penelope, she and Artemis race to the scene — where Batman and Huntress have already begun their battle against a possessed Joker, Poison Ivy and Scarecrow. As the situation worsens and the God of War, Ares, is summoned, the heroes are joined by more of their extended "families" — Troia, Nightwing, Wonder Girl and Robin — and the tide finally turns in their favor with the villains defeated.

But conflict then follows the Amazon Princess back to her home of Themyscira, as civil war erupts between the island's two tribes of Amazons, tearing at not only the bonds of society but also the family ties of Diana, Troia and Hippolyta. Misunderstandings, jealousy and ultimately betrayal lead to the Amazons' home becoming a heated battleground, as the place often referred to as "Paradise Island" soon becomes anything but, and several Amazons are slain.

The true evil that led to this civil war is finally revealed as Ariadne (now in the body of the Themysciran witch Magala), who murdered Hippolyta's sister some three thousand years ago. Diana's efforts to end the matter peacefully are thwarted by the Golden Age Fury, who rips out the witch's heart and brings it to the Queen. Feeling that she has failed her subjects in recent years, Hippolyta forsakes her crown and throne, abolishing the monarchy — leaving Diana without her tiara and no longer a princess.

As things settle down, Metropolis's star reporter from the Daily Planet, Lois Lane, follows Diana for a typical day in the heroine's life. We witness Wonder Woman giving a lecture on equality and tolerance, researching a treatment for diabetes, teaching self-defense to women, easing the suffering of starving children, and so much more.

It is here that we are also introduced to Trevor Barnes — a field director for the United Nations Rural Development Organization — whom Diana has a crush on. But when Diana asks Trevor out on a dinner date, Trevor declines...

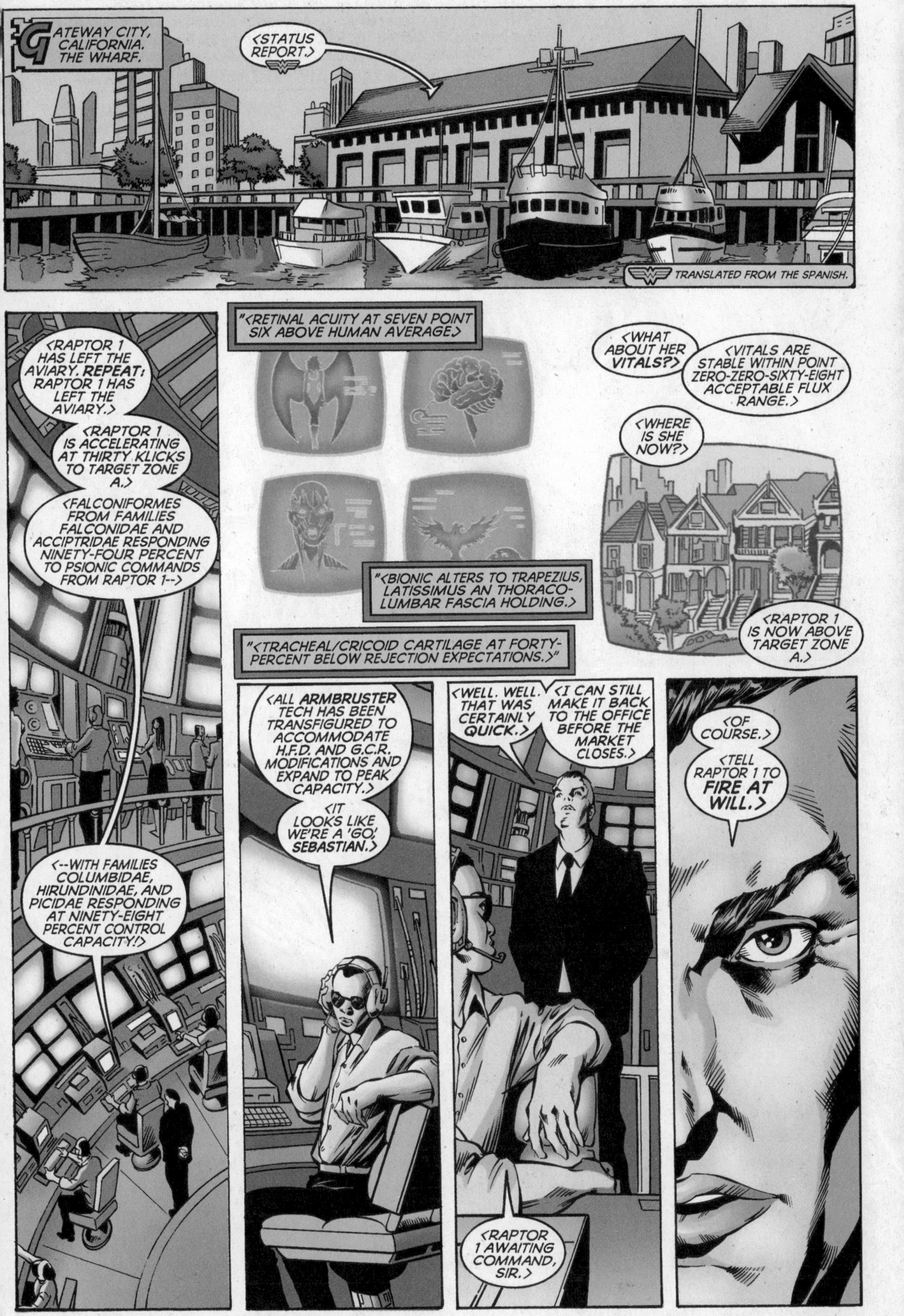
GATEWAY CITY, CALIFORNIA. THE WHARF.
<STATUS REPORT.>
TRANSLATED FROM THE SPANISH.
<RAPTOR 1 HAS LEFT THE AVIARY. REPEAT: RAPTOR 1 HAS LEFT THE AVIARY.>
<RAPTOR 1 IS ACCELERATING AT THIRTY KLICKS TO TARGET ZONE A.>
<FALCONIFORMES FROM FAMILIES FALCONIDAE AND ACCIPTRIDAE RESPONDING NINETY-FOUR PERCENT TO PSIONIC COMMANDS FROM RAPTOR 1-->
<--WITH FAMILIES COLUMBIDAE, HIRUNDINIDAE, AND PICIDAE RESPONDING AT NINETY-EIGHT PERCENT CONTROL CAPACITY!>
"<RETINAL ACUITY AT SEVEN POINT SIX ABOVE HUMAN AVERAGE.>
"<BIONIC ALTERS TO TRAPEZIUS, LATISSIMUS AN THORACO-LUMBAR FASCIA HOLDING.>
"<TRACHEAL/CRICOID CARTILAGE AT FORTY-PERCENT BELOW REJECTION EXPECTATIONS.>"
<WHAT ABOUT HER VITALS?>
<VITALS ARE STABLE WITHIN POINT ZERO-ZERO-SIXTY-EIGHT ACCEPTABLE FLUX RANGE.>
<WHERE IS SHE NOW?>
<RAPTOR 1 IS NOW ABOVE TARGET ZONE A.>
<ALL ARMBRUSTER TECH HAS BEEN TRANSFIGURED TO ACCOMMODATE H.F.D. AND G.C.R. MODIFICATIONS AND EXPAND TO PEAK CAPACITY.>
<IT LOOKS LIKE WE'RE A 'GO,' SEBASTIAN.>
<WELL. WELL. THAT WAS CERTAINLY QUICK.>
<I CAN STILL MAKE IT BACK TO THE OFFICE BEFORE THE MARKET CLOSES.>
<RAPTOR 1 AWAITING COMMAND, SIR.>
<OF COURSE.>
<TELL RAPTOR 1 TO FIRE AT WILL.>

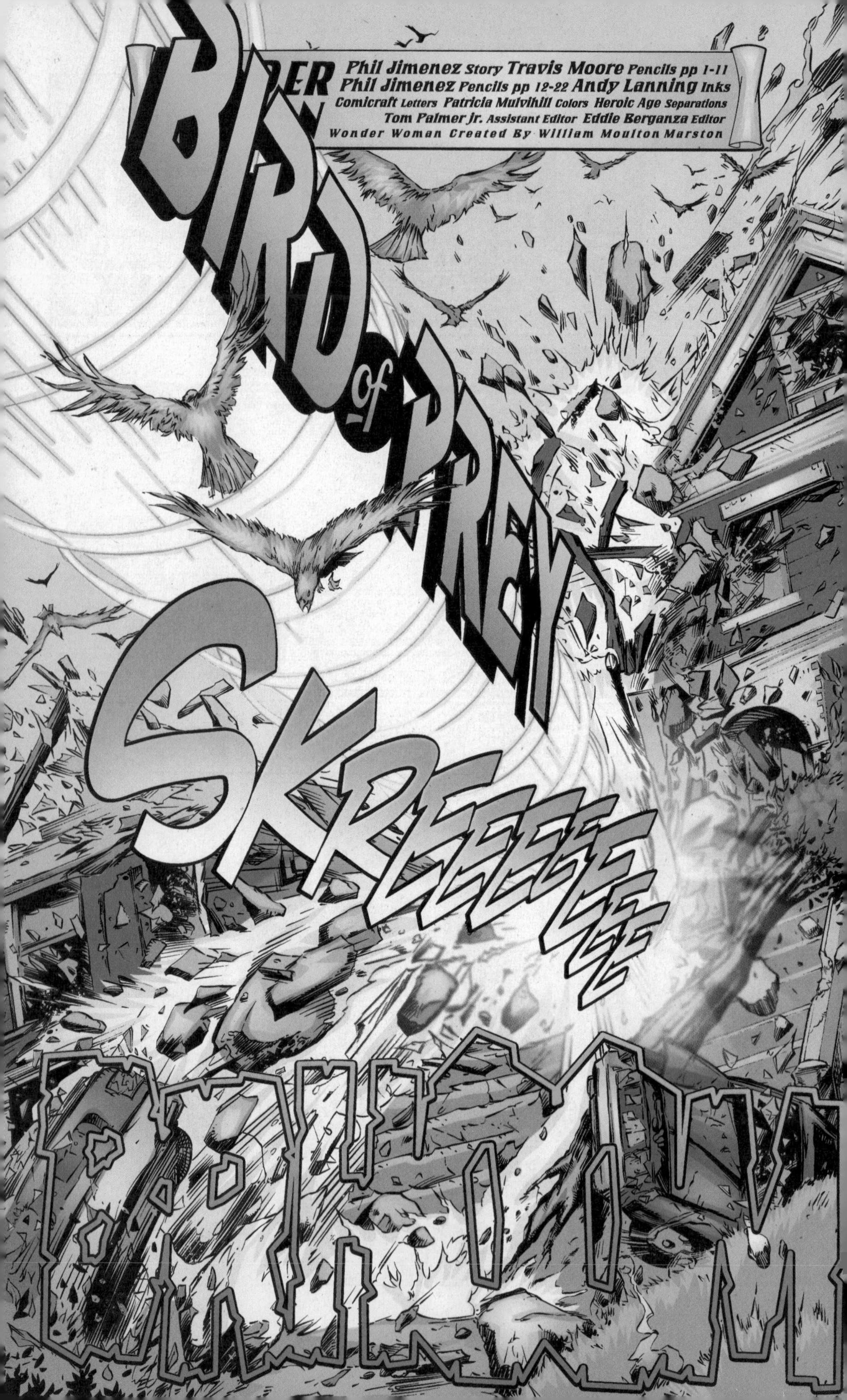
BIRD of PREY
Phil Jimenez Story Travis Moore Pencils pp 1-11
Phil Jimenez Pencils pp 12-22 Andy Lanning Inks
Comicraft Letters Patricia Mulvihill Colors Heroic Age Separations
Tom Palmer jr. Assistant Editor Eddie Berganza Editor
Wonder Woman Created By William Moulton Marston

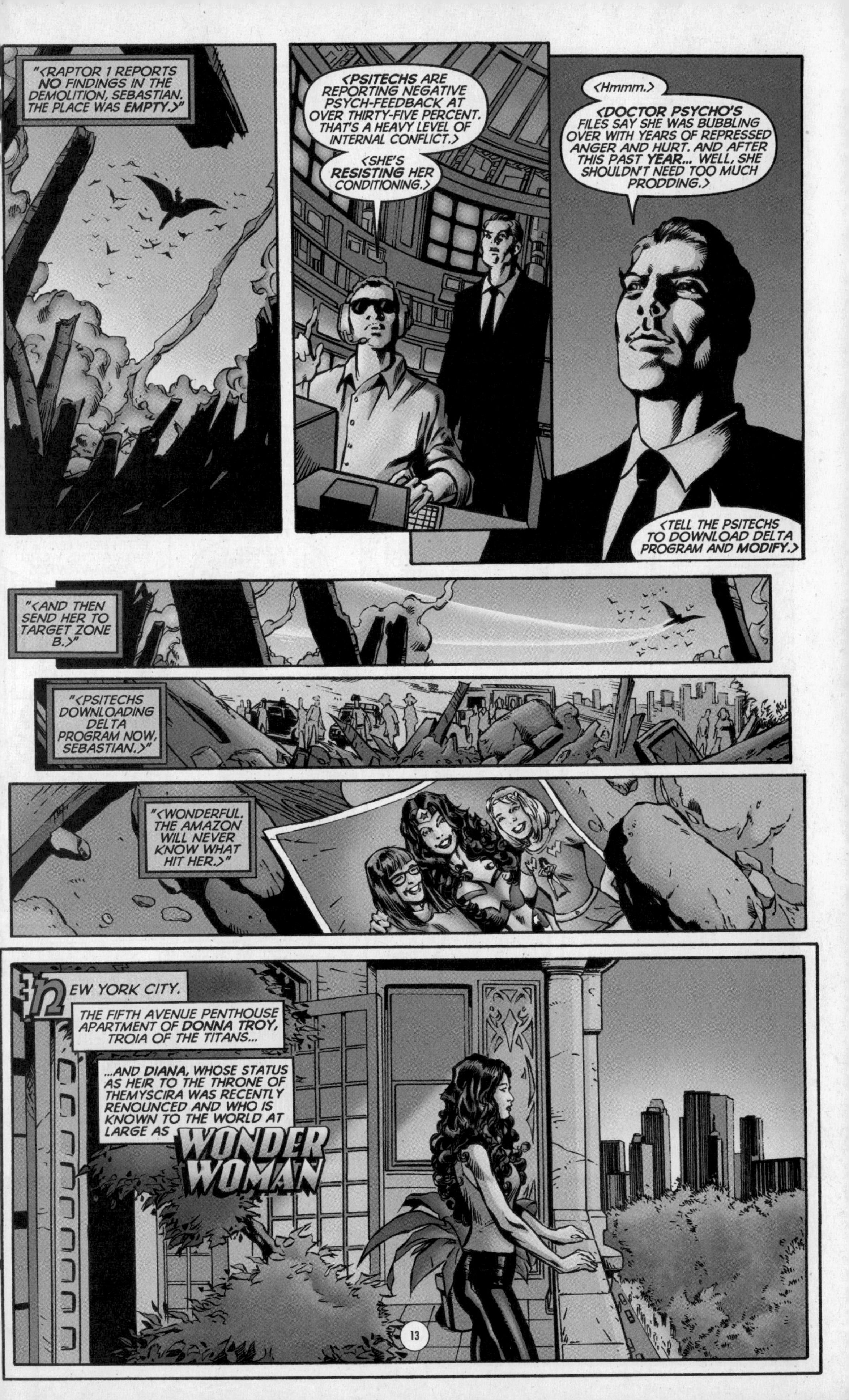
"<RAPTOR 1 REPORTS NO FINDINGS IN THE DEMOLITION, SEBASTIAN. THE PLACE WAS EMPTY.>"
<PSITECHS ARE REPORTING NEGATIVE PSYCH-FEEDBACK AT OVER THIRTY-FIVE PERCENT. THAT'S A HEAVY LEVEL OF INTERNAL CONFLICT.>
<SHE'S RESISTING HER CONDITIONING.>
<Hmmm.>
<DOCTOR PSYCHO'S FILES SAY SHE WAS BUBBLING OVER WITH YEARS OF REPRESSED ANGER AND HURT. AND AFTER THIS PAST YEAR... WELL, SHE SHOULDN'T NEED TOO MUCH PRODDING.>
<TELL THE PSITECHS TO DOWNLOAD DELTA PROGRAM AND MODIFY.>
"<AND THEN SEND HER TO TARGET ZONE B.>"
"<PSITECHS DOWNLOADING DELTA PROGRAM NOW, SEBASTIAN.>"
"<WONDERFUL. THE AMAZON WILL NEVER KNOW WHAT HIT HER.>"
NEW YORK CITY.
THE FIFTH AVENUE PENTHOUSE APARTMENT OF DONNA TROY, TROIA OF THE TITANS...
...AND DIANA, WHOSE STATUS AS HEIR TO THE THRONE OF THEMYSCIRA WAS RECENTLY RENOUNCED AND WHO IS KNOWN TO THE WORLD AT LARGE AS
WONDER WOMAN

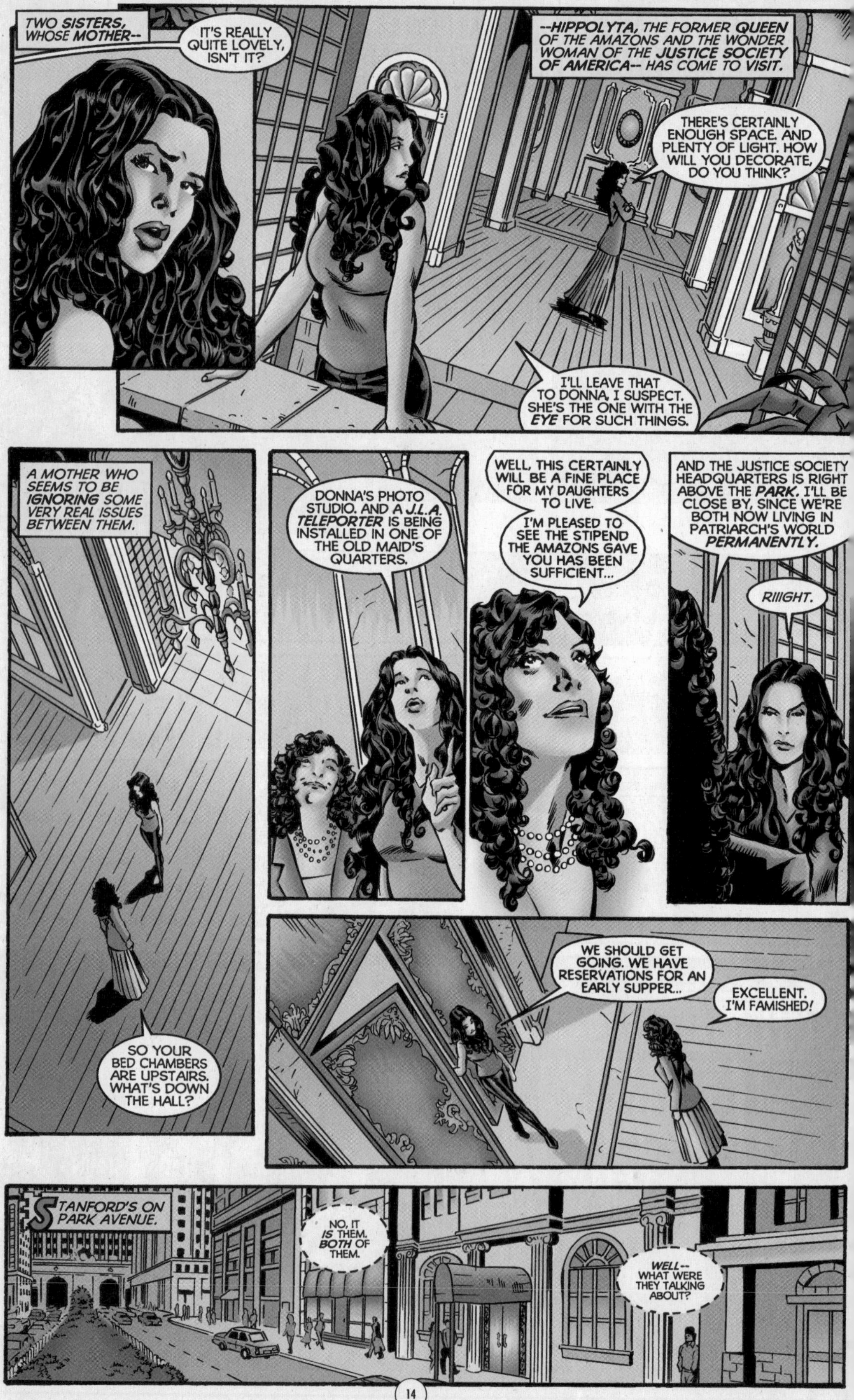
TWO SISTERS, WHOSE MOTHER--
IT'S REALLY QUITE LOVELY, ISN'T IT?
--HIPPOLYTA, THE FORMER QUEEN OF THE AMAZONS AND THE WONDER WOMAN OF THE JUSTICE SOCIETY OF AMERICA-- HAS COME TO VISIT.
THERE'S CERTAINLY ENOUGH SPACE. AND PLENTY OF LIGHT. HOW WILL YOU DECORATE, DO YOU THINK?
I'LL LEAVE THAT TO DONNA, I SUSPECT. SHE'S THE ONE WITH THE EYE FOR SUCH THINGS.
A MOTHER WHO SEEMS TO BE IGNORING SOME VERY REAL ISSUES BETWEEN THEM.
SO YOUR BED CHAMBERS ARE UPSTAIRS. WHAT'S DOWN THE HALL?
DONNA'S PHOTO STUDIO. AND A J.L.A. TELEPORTER IS BEING INSTALLED IN ONE OF THE OLD MAID'S QUARTERS.
WELL, THIS CERTAINLY WILL BE A FINE PLACE FOR MY DAUGHTERS TO LIVE.
I'M PLEASED TO SEE THE STIPEND THE AMAZONS GAVE YOU HAS BEEN SUFFICIENT...
AND THE JUSTICE SOCIETY HEADQUARTERS IS RIGHT ABOVE THE PARK. I'LL BE CLOSE BY, SINCE WE'RE BOTH NOW LIVING IN PATRIARCH'S WORLD PERMANENTLY.
RIIIGHT.
WE SHOULD GET GOING. WE HAVE RESERVATIONS FOR AN EARLY SUPPER...
EXCELLENT. I'M FAMISHED!
STANFORD'S ON PARK AVENUE.
NO, IT IS THEM. BOTH OF THEM.
WELL-- WHAT WERE THEY TALKING ABOUT?

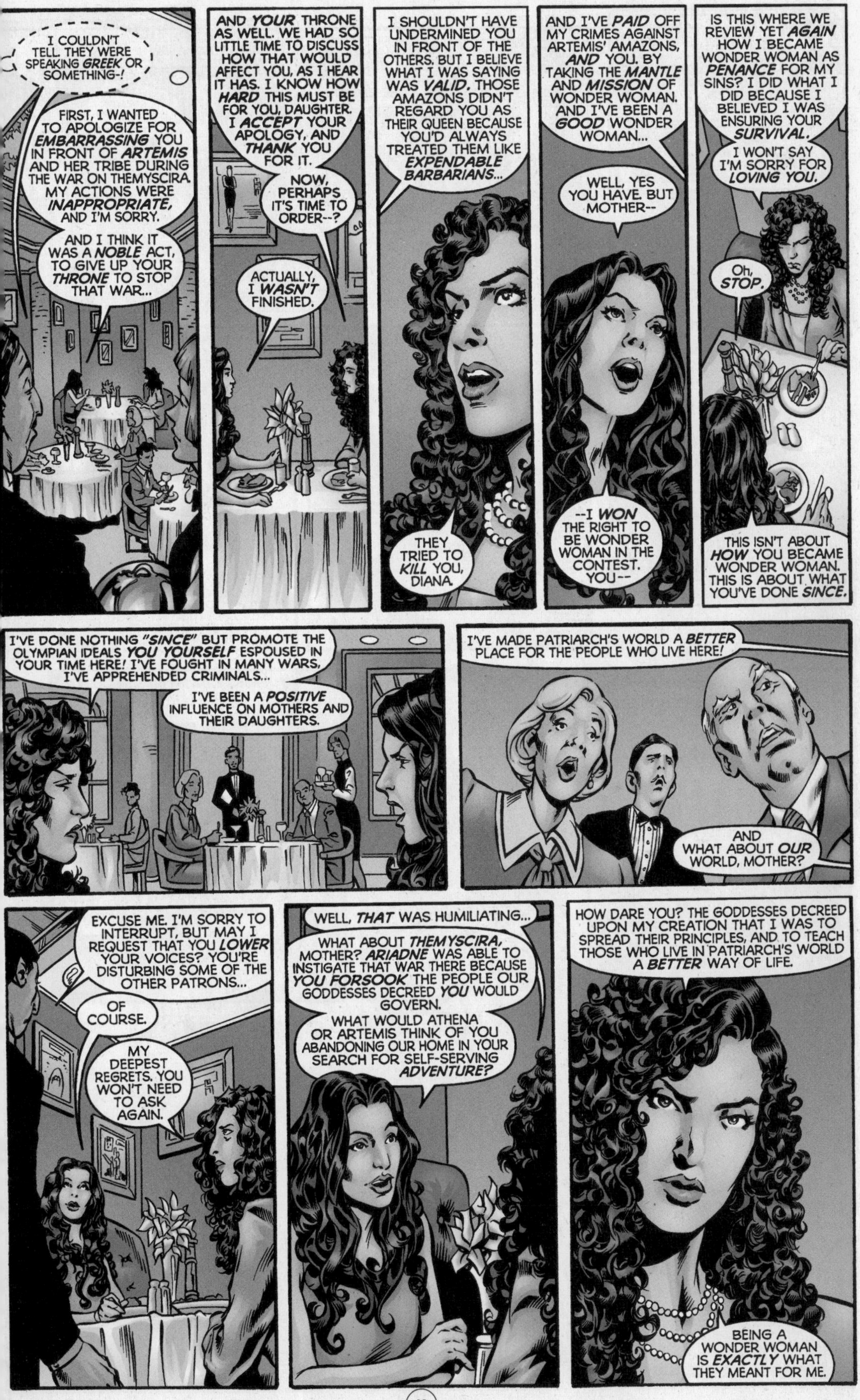

I COULDN'T TELL. THEY WERE SPEAKING GREEK OR SOMETHING-!
FIRST, I WANTED TO APOLOGIZE FOR EMBARRASSING YOU IN FRONT OF ARTEMIS AND HER TRIBE DURING THE WAR ON THEMYSCIRA. MY ACTIONS WERE INAPPROPRIATE, AND I'M SORRY.
AND I THINK IT WAS A NOBLE ACT, TO GIVE UP YOUR THRONE TO STOP THAT WAR...
AND YOUR THRONE AS WELL. WE HAD SO LITTLE TIME TO DISCUSS HOW THAT WOULD AFFECT YOU, AS I HEAR IT HAS. I KNOW HOW HARD THIS MUST BE FOR YOU, DAUGHTER. I ACCEPT YOUR APOLOGY, AND THANK YOU FOR IT.
NOW, PERHAPS IT'S TIME TO ORDER--?
ACTUALLY, I WASN'T FINISHED.
I SHOULDN'T HAVE UNDERMINED YOU IN FRONT OF THE OTHERS. BUT I BELIEVE WHAT I WAS SAYING WAS VALID. THOSE AMAZONS DIDN'T REGARD YOU AS THEIR QUEEN BECAUSE YOU'D ALWAYS TREATED THEM LIKE EXPENDABLE BARBARIANS...
THEY TRIED TO KILL YOU, DIANA.
AND I'VE PAID OFF MY CRIMES AGAINST ARTEMIS' AMAZONS, AND YOU. BY TAKING THE MANTLE AND MISSION OF WONDER WOMAN. AND I'VE BEEN A GOOD WONDER WOMAN...
WELL, YES YOU HAVE. BUT MOTHER--
--I WON THE RIGHT TO BE WONDER WOMAN IN THE CONTEST. YOU--
IS THIS WHERE WE REVIEW YET AGAIN HOW I BECAME WONDER WOMAN AS PENANCE FOR MY SINS? I DID WHAT I DID BECAUSE I BELIEVED I WAS ENSURING YOUR SURVIVAL.
I WON'T SAY I'M SORRY FOR LOVING YOU.
Oh, STOP.
THIS ISN'T ABOUT HOW YOU BECAME WONDER WOMAN. THIS IS ABOUT WHAT YOU'VE DONE SINCE.
I'VE DONE NOTHING "SINCE" BUT PROMOTE THE OLYMPIAN IDEALS YOU YOURSELF ESPOUSED IN YOUR TIME HERE! I'VE FOUGHT IN MANY WARS, I'VE APPREHENDED CRIMINALS...
I'VE BEEN A POSITIVE INFLUENCE ON MOTHERS AND THEIR DAUGHTERS.
I'VE MADE PATRIARCH'S WORLD A BETTER PLACE FOR THE PEOPLE WHO LIVE HERE!
AND WHAT ABOUT OUR WORLD, MOTHER?
EXCUSE ME. I'M SORRY TO INTERRUPT, BUT MAY I REQUEST THAT YOU LOWER YOUR VOICES? YOU'RE DISTURBING SOME OF THE OTHER PATRONS...
OF COURSE.
MY DEEPEST REGRETS. YOU WON'T NEED TO ASK AGAIN.
WELL, THAT WAS HUMILIATING...
WHAT ABOUT THEMYSCIRA, MOTHER? ARIADNE WAS ABLE TO INSTIGATE THAT WAR THERE BECAUSE YOU FORSOOK THE PEOPLE OUR GODDESSES DECREED YOU WOULD GOVERN.
WHAT WOULD ATHENA OR ARTEMIS THINK OF YOU ABANDONING OUR HOME IN YOUR SEARCH FOR SELF-SERVING ADVENTURE?
HOW DARE YOU? THE GODDESSES DECREED UPON MY CREATION THAT I WAS TO SPREAD THEIR PRINCIPLES, AND TO TEACH THOSE WHO LIVE IN PATRIARCH'S WORLD A BETTER WAY OF LIFE.
BEING A WONDER WOMAN IS EXACTLY WHAT THEY MEANT FOR ME.

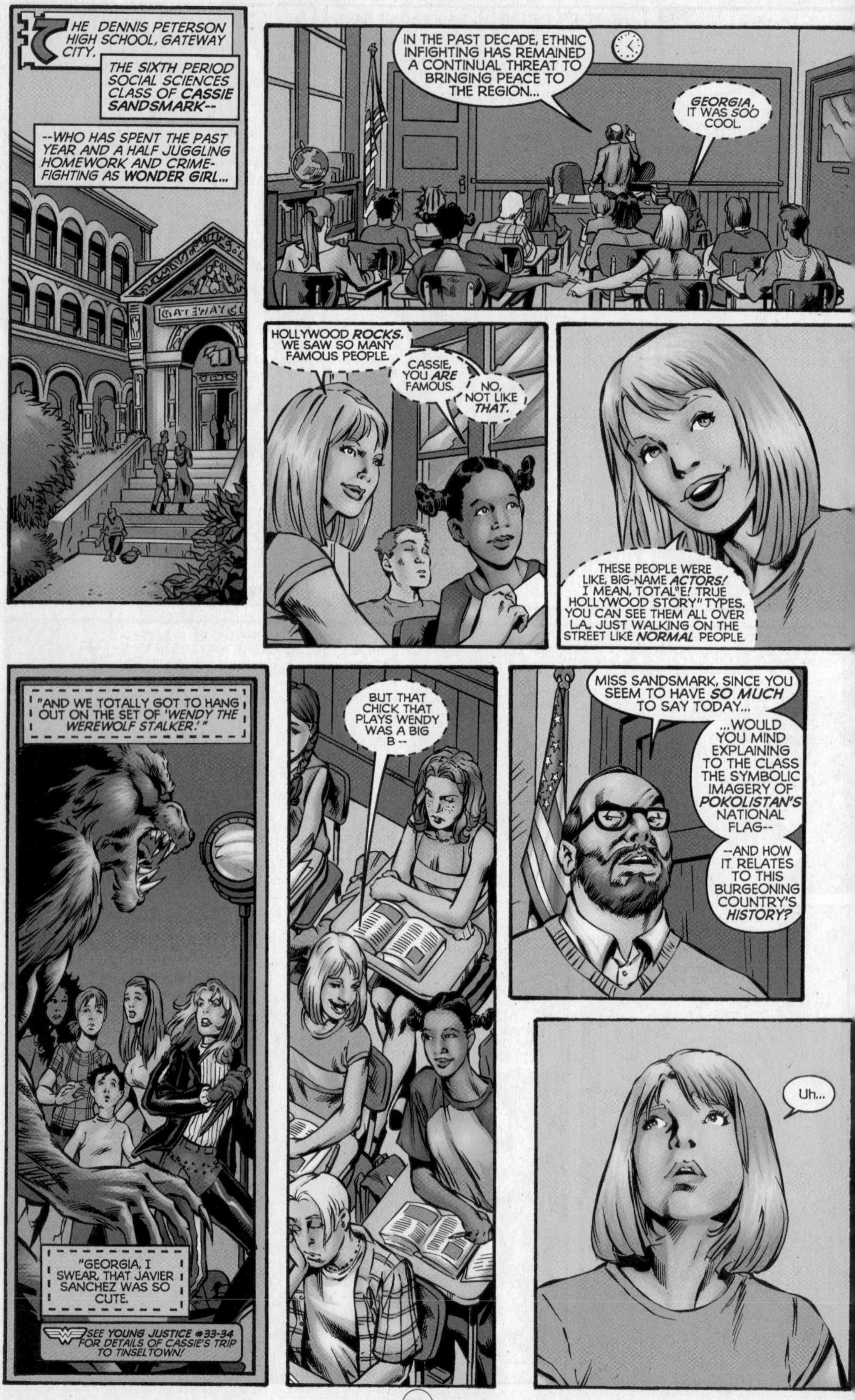
THE DENNIS PETERSON HIGH SCHOOL, GATEWAY CITY.
THE SIXTH PERIOD SOCIAL SCIENCES CLASS OF CASSIE SANDSMARK--
--WHO HAS SPENT THE PAST YEAR AND A HALF JUGGLING HOMEWORK AND CRIME-FIGHTING AS WONDER GIRL...
GATEWAY C
IN THE PAST DECADE, ETHNIC INFIGHTING HAS REMAINED A CONTINUAL THREAT TO BRINGING PEACE TO THE REGION...
GEORGIA, IT WAS SOO COOL.
HOLLYWOOD ROCKS. WE SAW SO MANY FAMOUS PEOPLE.
CASSIE, YOU ARE FAMOUS.
NO, NOT LIKE THAT.
THESE PEOPLE WERE LIKE, BIG-NAME ACTORS! I MEAN, TOTAL "E! TRUE HOLLYWOOD STORY" TYPES. YOU CAN SEE THEM ALL OVER L.A., JUST WALKING ON THE STREET LIKE NORMAL PEOPLE.
"AND WE TOTALLY GOT TO HANG OUT ON THE SET OF 'WENDY THE WEREWOLF STALKER.'"
"GEORGIA, I SWEAR, THAT JAVIER SANCHEZ WAS SO CUTE.
SEE YOUNG JUSTICE #33-34 FOR DETAILS OF CASSIE'S TRIP TO TINSELTOWN!
BUT THAT CHICK THAT PLAYS WENDY WAS A BIG B --
MISS SANDSMARK, SINCE YOU SEEM TO HAVE SO MUCH TO SAY TODAY...
...WOULD YOU MIND EXPLAINING TO THE CLASS THE SYMBOLIC IMAGERY OF POKOLISTAN'S NATIONAL FLAG--
--AND HOW IT RELATES TO THIS BURGEONING COUNTRY'S HISTORY?
Uh...

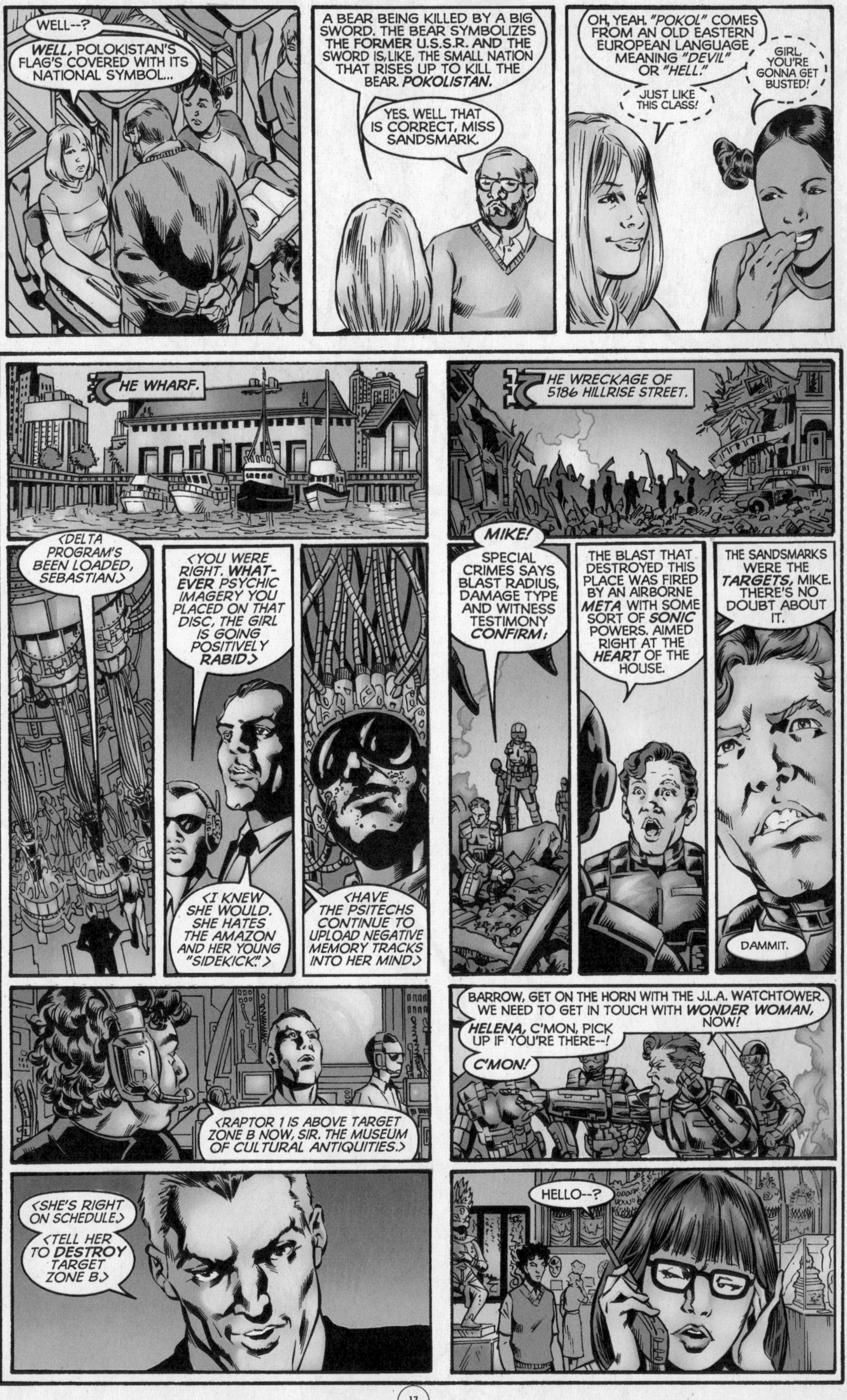
WELL--?
WELL, POLOKISTAN'S FLAG'S COVERED WITH ITS NATIONAL SYMBOL...
A BEAR BEING KILLED BY A BIG SWORD. THE BEAR SYMBOLIZES THE FORMER U.S.S.R. AND THE SWORD IS, LIKE, THE SMALL NATION THAT RISES UP TO KILL THE BEAR. POKOLISTAN.
YES. WELL. THAT IS CORRECT, MISS SANDSMARK.
OH, YEAH. "POKOL" COMES FROM AN OLD EASTERN EUROPEAN LANGUAGE MEANING "DEVIL" OR "HELL."
JUST LIKE THIS CLASS!
GIRL, YOU'RE GONNA GET BUSTED!
THE WHARF.
THE WRECKAGE OF 5186 HILLRISE STREET.
<DELTA PROGRAM'S BEEN LOADED, SEBASTIAN.>
<YOU WERE RIGHT. WHATEVER PSYCHIC IMAGERY YOU PLACED ON THAT DISC, THE GIRL IS GOING POSITIVELY RABID.>
<I KNEW SHE WOULD. SHE HATES THE AMAZON AND HER YOUNG "SIDEKICK.">
<HAVE THE PSITECHS CONTINUE TO UPLOAD NEGATIVE MEMORY TRACKS INTO HER MIND.>
MIKE!
SPECIAL CRIMES SAYS BLAST RADIUS, DAMAGE TYPE AND WITNESS TESTIMONY CONFIRM:
THE BLAST THAT DESTROYED THIS PLACE WAS FIRED BY AN AIRBORNE META WITH SOME SORT OF SONIC POWERS. AIMED RIGHT AT THE HEART OF THE HOUSE.
THE SANDSMARKS WERE THE TARGETS, MIKE. THERE'S NO DOUBT ABOUT IT.
DAMMIT.
<RAPTOR 1 IS ABOVE TARGET ZONE B NOW, SIR. THE MUSEUM OF CULTURAL ANTIQUITIES.>
BARROW, GET ON THE HORN WITH THE J.L.A. WATCHTOWER. WE NEED TO GET IN TOUCH WITH WONDER WOMAN, NOW!
HELENA, C'MON, PICK UP IF YOU'RE THERE--!
C'MON!
<SHE'S RIGHT ON SCHEDULE.>
<TELL HER TO DESTROY TARGET ZONE B.>
HELLO--?

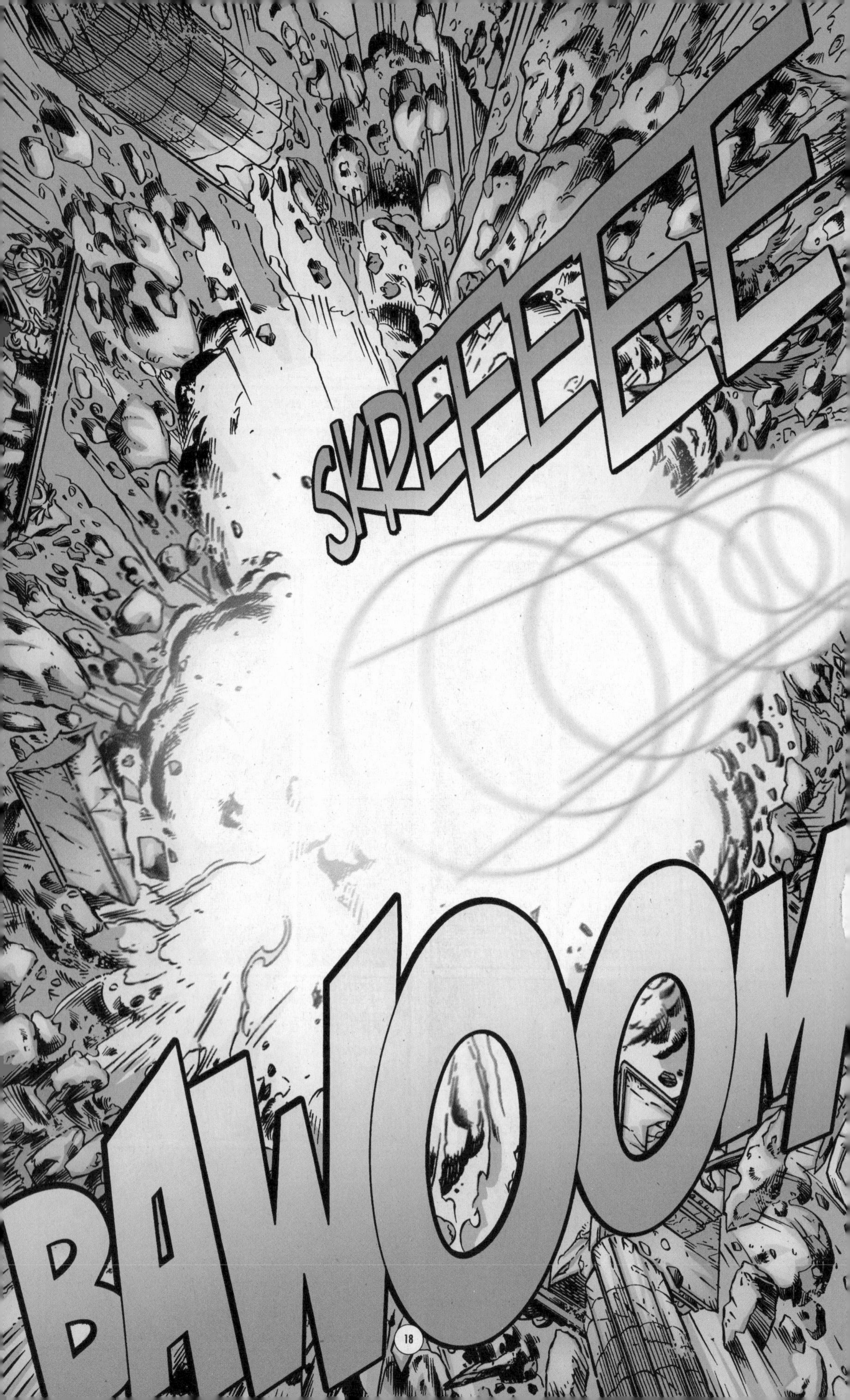
SKREEEEEE
BAWOOM

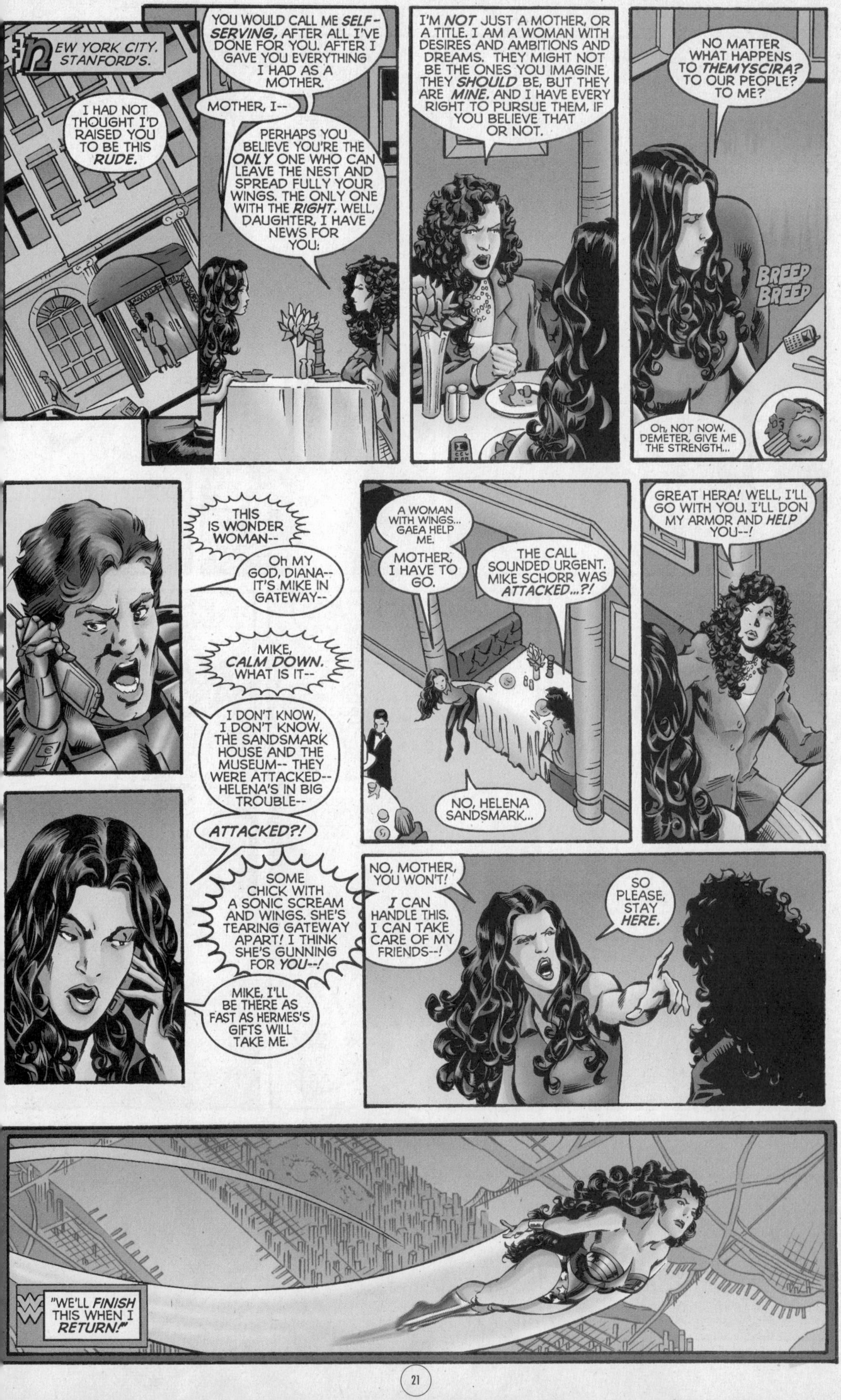
NEW YORK CITY. STANFORD'S.
I HAD NOT THOUGHT I'D RAISED YOU TO BE THIS RUDE.
YOU WOULD CALL ME SELF-SERVING, AFTER ALL I'VE DONE FOR YOU. AFTER I GAVE YOU EVERYTHING I HAD AS A MOTHER.
MOTHER, I--
PERHAPS YOU BELIEVE YOU'RE THE ONLY ONE WHO CAN LEAVE THE NEST AND SPREAD FULLY YOUR WINGS. THE ONLY ONE WITH THE RIGHT. WELL, DAUGHTER, I HAVE NEWS FOR YOU:
I'M NOT JUST A MOTHER, OR A TITLE. I AM A WOMAN WITH DESIRES AND AMBITIONS AND DREAMS. THEY MIGHT NOT BE THE ONES YOU IMAGINE THEY SHOULD BE, BUT THEY ARE MINE. AND I HAVE EVERY RIGHT TO PURSUE THEM, IF YOU BELIEVE THAT OR NOT.
NO MATTER WHAT HAPPENS TO THEMYSCIRA? TO OUR PEOPLE? TO ME?
BREEP BREEP
Oh, NOT NOW. DEMETER, GIVE ME THE STRENGTH...
THIS IS WONDER WOMAN--
Oh MY GOD, DIANA-- IT'S MIKE IN GATEWAY--
MIKE, CALM DOWN. WHAT IS IT--
I DON'T KNOW, I DON'T KNOW. THE SANDSMARK HOUSE AND THE MUSEUM-- THEY WERE ATTACKED-- HELENA'S IN BIG TROUBLE--
ATTACKED?!
SOME CHICK WITH A SONIC SCREAM AND WINGS. SHE'S TEARING GATEWAY APART! I THINK SHE'S GUNNING FOR YOU--!
MIKE, I'LL BE THERE AS FAST AS HERMES'S GIFTS WILL TAKE ME.
A WOMAN WITH WINGS... GAEA HELP ME.
MOTHER, I HAVE TO GO.
THE CALL SOUNDED URGENT. MIKE SCHORR WAS ATTACKED...?!
NO, HELENA SANDSMARK...
GREAT HERA! WELL, I'LL GO WITH YOU. I'LL DON MY ARMOR AND HELP YOU--!
NO, MOTHER, YOU WON'T!
I CAN HANDLE THIS. I CAN TAKE CARE OF MY FRIENDS--!
SO PLEASE, STAY HERE.
"WE'LL FINISH THIS WHEN I RETURN!"

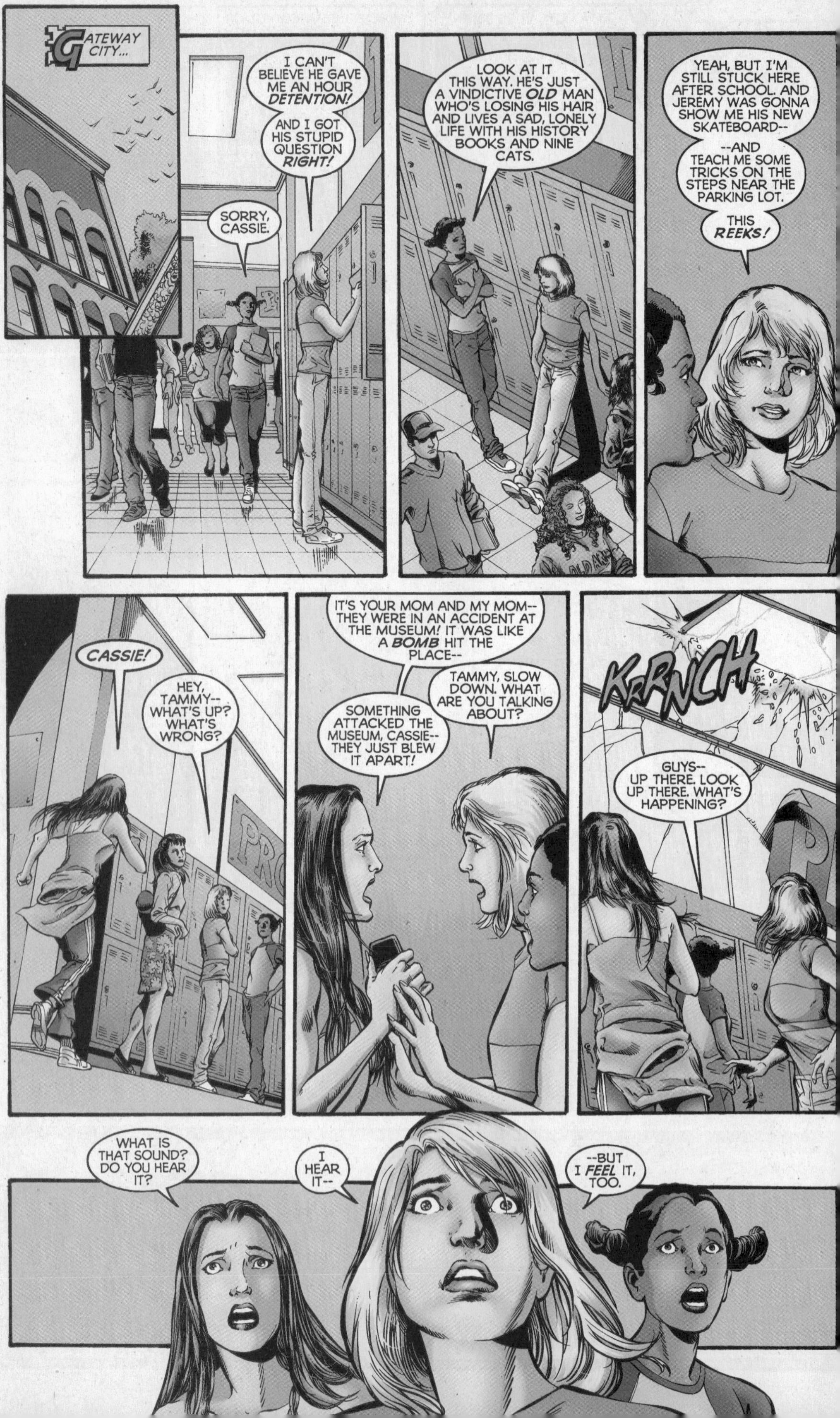
GATEWAY CITY...
I CAN'T BELIEVE HE GAVE ME AN HOUR DETENTION!
AND I GOT HIS STUPID QUESTION RIGHT!
SORRY, CASSIE.
LOOK AT IT THIS WAY. HE'S JUST A VINDICTIVE OLD MAN WHO'S LOSING HIS HAIR AND LIVES A SAD, LONELY LIFE WITH HIS HISTORY BOOKS AND NINE CATS.
YEAH, BUT I'M STILL STUCK HERE AFTER SCHOOL. AND JEREMY WAS GONNA SHOW ME HIS NEW SKATEBOARD--
--AND TEACH ME SOME TRICKS ON THE STEPS NEAR THE PARKING LOT.
THIS REEKS!
CASSIE!
HEY, TAMMY-- WHAT'S UP? WHAT'S WRONG?
IT'S YOUR MOM AND MY MOM-- THEY WERE IN AN ACCIDENT AT THE MUSEUM! IT WAS LIKE A BOMB HIT THE PLACE--
TAMMY, SLOW DOWN. WHAT ARE YOU TALKING ABOUT?
SOMETHING ATTACKED THE MUSEUM, CASSIE-- THEY JUST BLEW IT APART!
KRRNCH
GUYS-- UP THERE. LOOK UP THERE. WHAT'S HAPPENING?
WHAT IS THAT SOUND? DO YOU HEAR IT?
I HEAR IT--
--BUT I FEEL IT, TOO.

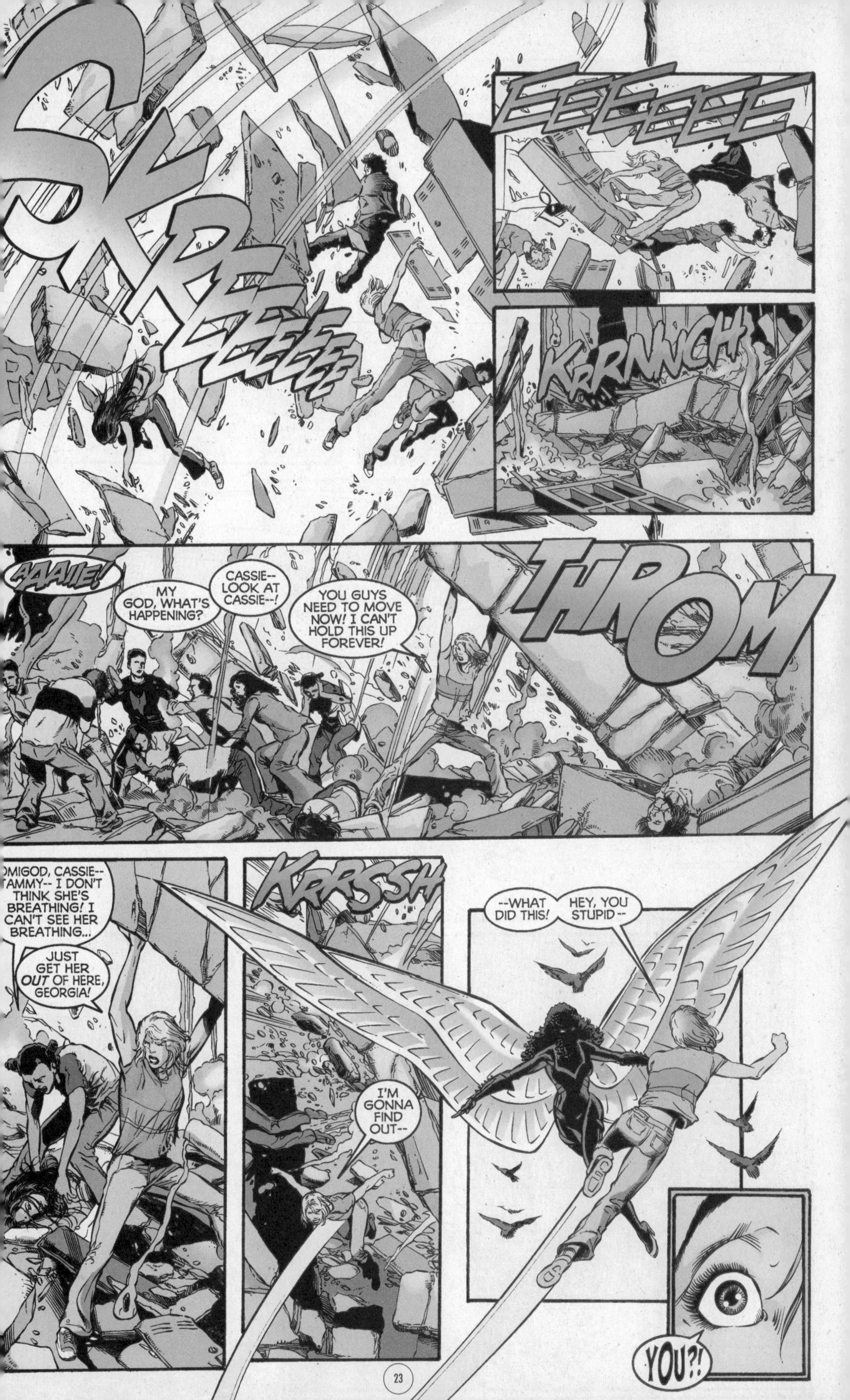
SKREEEEEE
EEEEEEE
KRRNNCH
AAAIIIE!
MY GOD, WHAT'S HAPPENING?
CASSIE-- LOOK AT CASSIE--!
YOU GUYS NEED TO MOVE NOW! I CAN'T HOLD THIS UP FOREVER!
THROM
OMIGOD, CASSIE-- TAMMY-- I DON'T THINK SHE'S BREATHING! I CAN'T SEE HER BREATHING...
JUST GET HER OUT OF HERE, GEORGIA!
KRRSSH
I'M GONNA FIND OUT--
--WHAT DID THIS!
HEY, YOU STUPID --
YOU?!

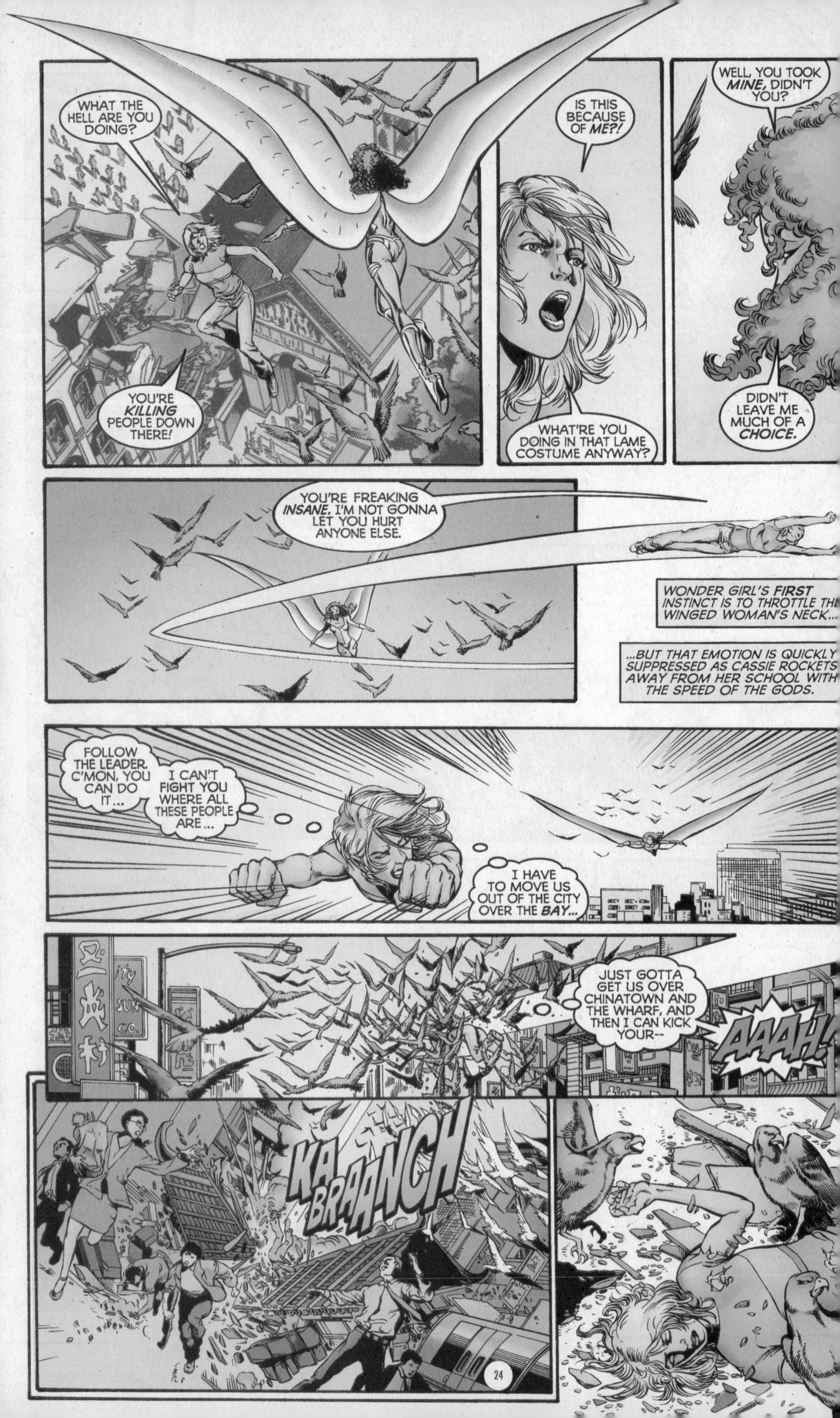

WHAT THE HELL ARE YOU DOING?
YOU'RE KILLING PEOPLE DOWN THERE!
IS THIS BECAUSE OF ME?!
WHAT'RE YOU DOING IN THAT LAME COSTUME ANYWAY?
WELL, YOU TOOK MINE, DIDN'T YOU?
DIDN'T LEAVE ME MUCH OF A CHOICE.
YOU'RE FREAKING INSANE. I'M NOT GONNA LET YOU HURT ANYONE ELSE.
WONDER GIRL'S FIRST INSTINCT IS TO THROTTLE THE WINGED WOMAN'S NECK...
...BUT THAT EMOTION IS QUICKLY SUPPRESSED AS CASSIE ROCKETS AWAY FROM HER SCHOOL WITH THE SPEED OF THE GODS.
FOLLOW THE LEADER. C'MON, YOU CAN DO IT...
I CAN'T FIGHT YOU WHERE ALL THESE PEOPLE ARE...
I HAVE TO MOVE US OUT OF THE CITY OVER THE BAY...
JUST GOTTA GET US OVER CHINATOWN AND THE WHARF, AND THEN I CAN KICK YOUR--
AAAH!
KA BRAAANCH

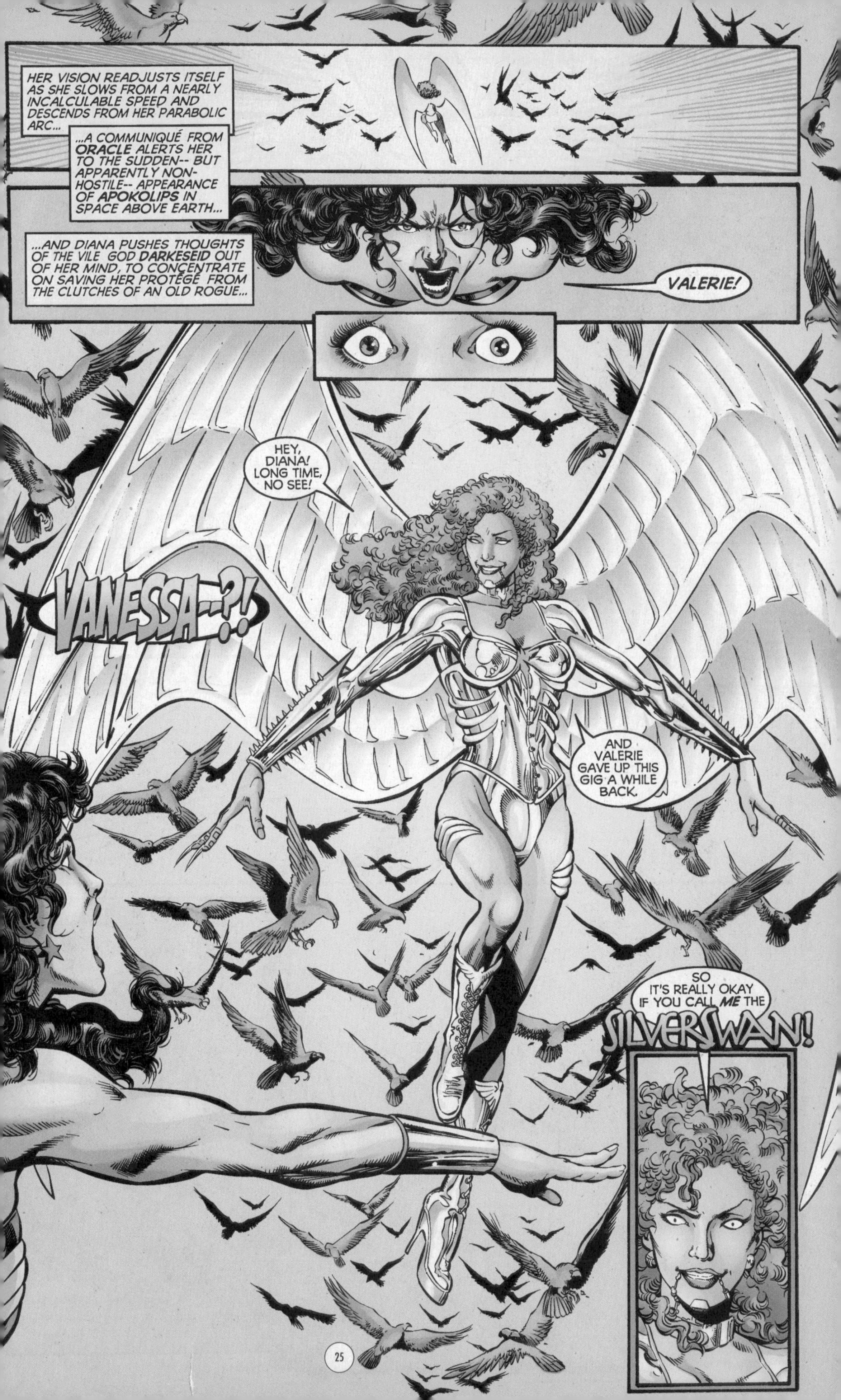

HER VISION READJUSTS ITSELF AS SHE SLOWS FROM A NEARLY INCALCULABLE SPEED AND DESCENDS FROM HER PARABOLIC ARC...
...A COMMUNIQUÉ FROM ORACLE ALERTS HER TO THE SUDDEN-- BUT APPARENTLY NON-HOSTILE-- APPEARANCE OF APOKOLIPS IN SPACE ABOVE EARTH...
...AND DIANA PUSHES THOUGHTS OF THE VILE GOD DARKESEID OUT OF HER MIND, TO CONCENTRATE ON SAVING HER PROTÉGÉ FROM THE CLUTCHES OF AN OLD ROGUE...
VALERIE!
HEY, DIANA! LONG TIME, NO SEE!
VANESSA--?!
AND VALERIE GAVE UP THIS GIG A WHILE BACK.
SO IT'S REALLY OKAY IF YOU CALL ME THE SILVER SWAN!

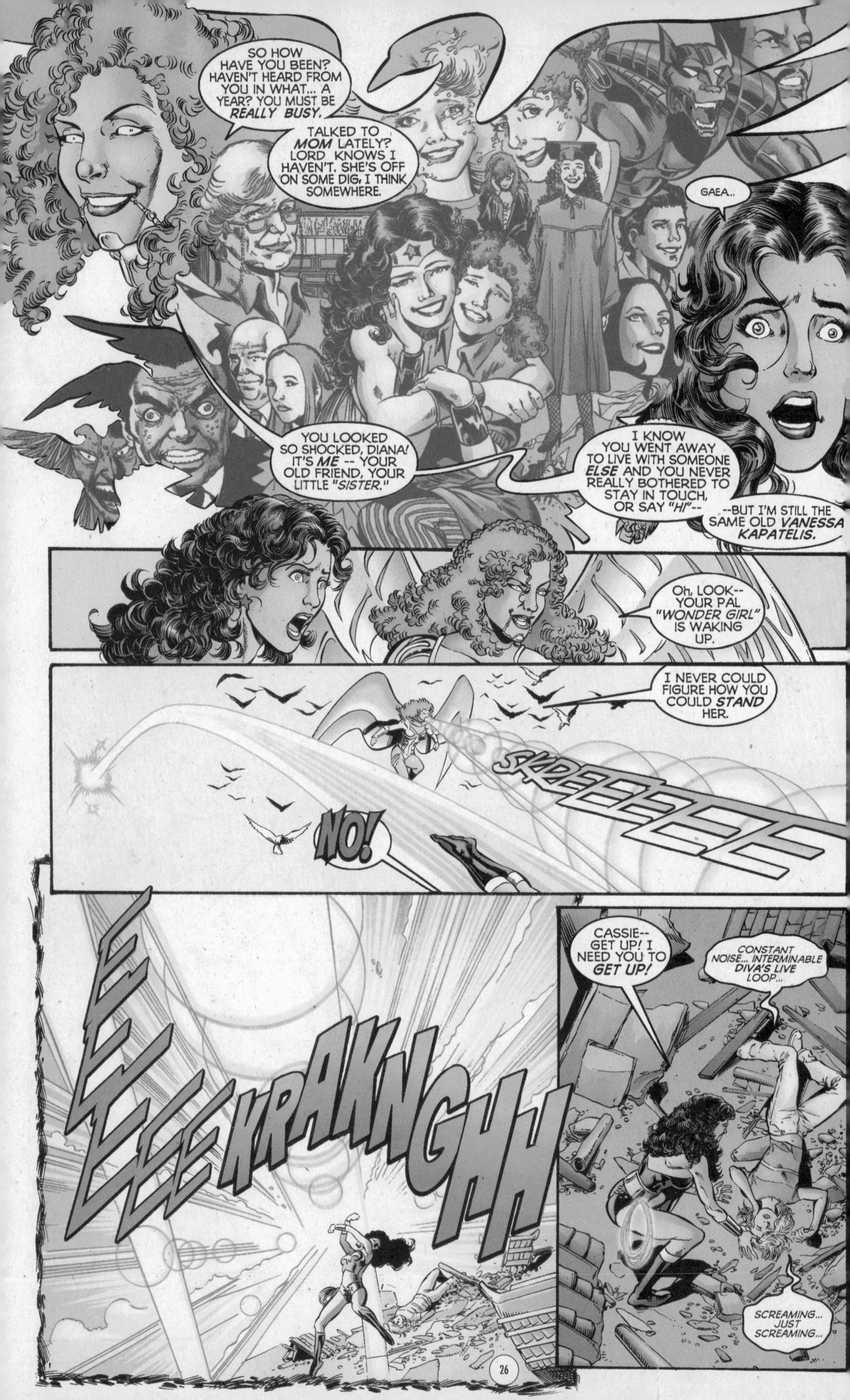
SO HOW HAVE YOU BEEN? HAVEN'T HEARD FROM YOU IN WHAT... A YEAR? YOU MUST BE REALLY BUSY.
TALKED TO MOM LATELY? LORD KNOWS I HAVEN'T. SHE'S OFF ON SOME DIG, I THINK. SOMEWHERE.
GAEA..
YOU LOOKED SO SHOCKED, DIANA! IT'S ME -- YOUR OLD FRIEND, YOUR LITTLE "SISTER."
I KNOW YOU WENT AWAY TO LIVE WITH SOMEONE ELSE AND YOU NEVER REALLY BOTHERED TO STAY IN TOUCH, OR SAY "HI"--
--BUT I'M STILL THE SAME OLD VANESSA KAPATELIS.
Oh, LOOK-- YOUR PAL "WONDER GIRL" IS WAKING UP.
I NEVER COULD FIGURE HOW YOU COULD STAND HER.
SKREEEEEEE
NO!
EEEKRAKNGHH
CASSIE-- GET UP! I NEED YOU TO GET UP!
CONSTANT NOISE... INTERMINABLE DIVA'S LIVE LOOP...
SCREAMING... JUST SCREAMING...

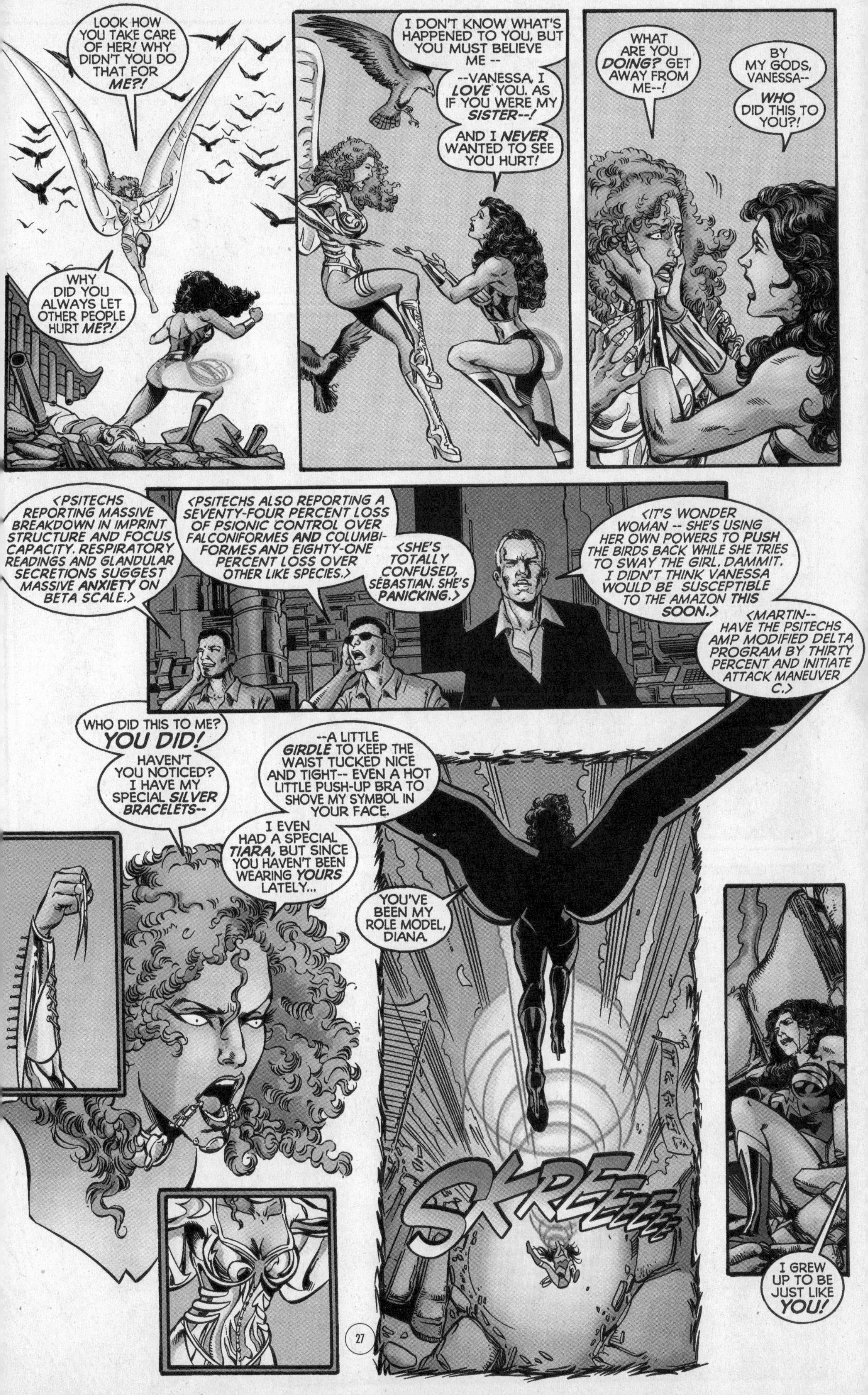
LOOK HOW YOU TAKE CARE OF HER! WHY DIDN'T YOU DO THAT FOR ME?!
WHY DID YOU ALWAYS LET OTHER PEOPLE HURT ME?!
I DON'T KNOW WHAT'S HAPPENED TO YOU, BUT YOU MUST BELIEVE ME --
--VANESSA, I LOVE YOU. AS IF YOU WERE MY SISTER--!
AND I NEVER WANTED TO SEE YOU HURT!
WHAT ARE YOU DOING? GET AWAY FROM ME--!
BY MY GODS, VANESSA-- WHO DID THIS TO YOU?!
<PSITECHS REPORTING MASSIVE BREAKDOWN IN IMPRINT STRUCTURE AND FOCUS CAPACITY. RESPIRATORY READINGS AND GLANDULAR SECRETIONS SUGGEST MASSIVE ANXIETY ON BETA SCALE.>
<PSITECHS ALSO REPORTING A SEVENTY-FOUR PERCENT LOSS OF PSIONIC CONTROL OVER FALCONIFORMES AND COLUMBIFORMES AND EIGHTY-ONE PERCENT LOSS OVER OTHER LIKE SPECIES.>
<SHE'S TOTALLY CONFUSED, SÉBASTIAN. SHE'S PANICKING.>
<IT'S WONDER WOMAN -- SHE'S USING HER OWN POWERS TO PUSH THE BIRDS BACK WHILE SHE TRIES TO SWAY THE GIRL. DAMMIT. I DIDN'T THINK VANESSA WOULD BE SUSCEPTIBLE TO THE AMAZON THIS SOON.>
<MARTIN-- HAVE THE PSITECHS AMP MODIFIED DELTA PROGRAM BY THIRTY PERCENT AND INITIATE ATTACK MANEUVER C.>
WHO DID THIS TO ME? YOU DID!
HAVEN'T YOU NOTICED? I HAVE MY SPECIAL SILVER BRACELETS--
--A LITTLE GIRDLE TO KEEP THE WAIST TUCKED NICE AND TIGHT-- EVEN A HOT LITTLE PUSH-UP BRA TO SHOVE MY SYMBOL IN YOUR FACE.
I EVEN HAD A SPECIAL TIARA, BUT SINCE YOU HAVEN'T BEEN WEARING YOURS LATELY...
YOU'VE BEEN MY ROLE MODEL, DIANA.
SKREEEEEE
I GREW UP TO BE JUST LIKE YOU!

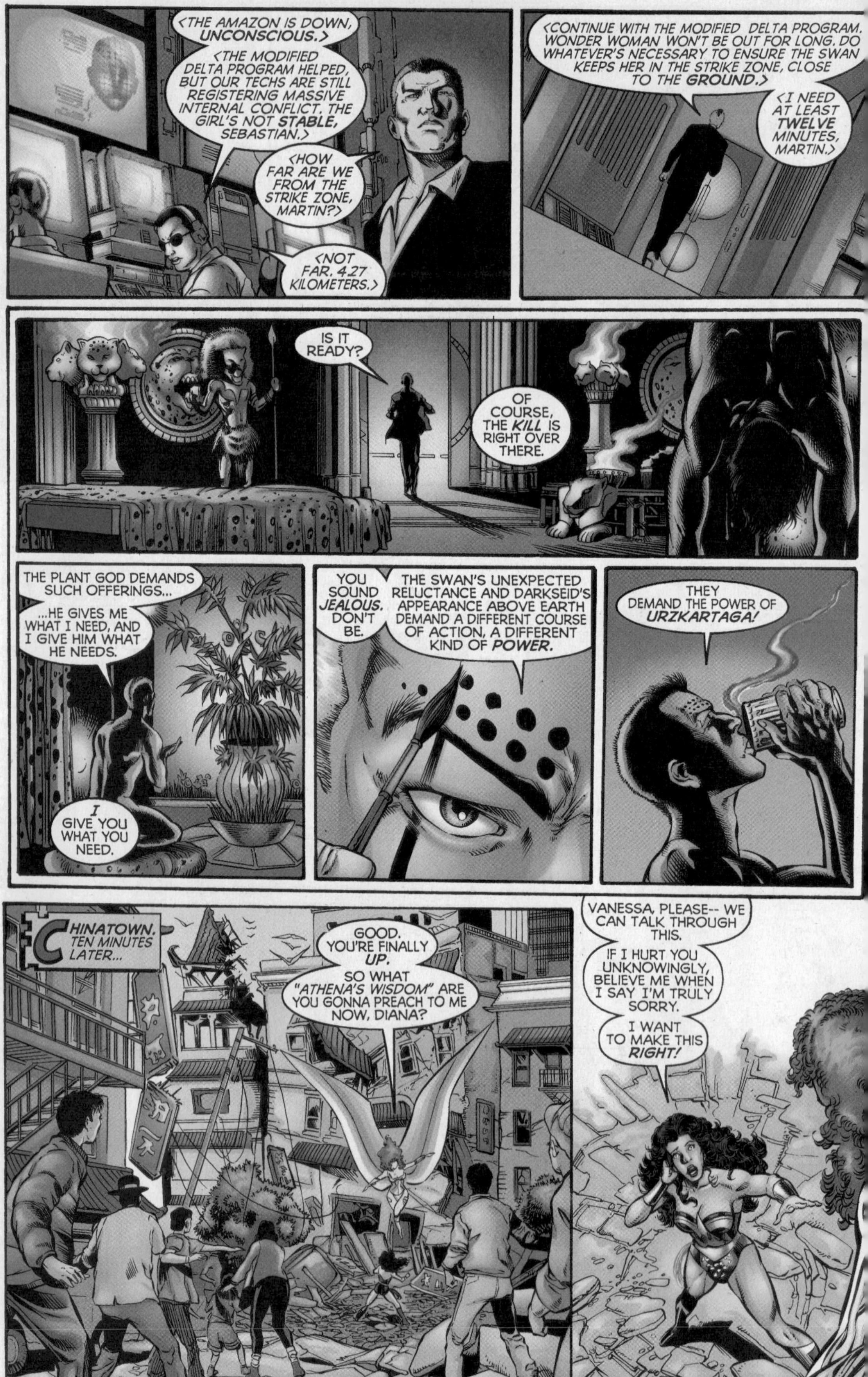
<THE AMAZON IS DOWN, UNCONSCIOUS.>
<THE MODIFIED DELTA PROGRAM HELPED, BUT OUR TECHS ARE STILL REGISTERING MASSIVE INTERNAL CONFLICT. THE GIRL'S NOT STABLE, SEBASTIAN.>
<HOW FAR ARE WE FROM THE STRIKE ZONE, MARTIN?>
<NOT FAR. 4.27 KILOMETERS.>
<CONTINUE WITH THE MODIFIED DELTA PROGRAM. WONDER WOMAN WON'T BE OUT FOR LONG. DO WHATEVER'S NECESSARY TO ENSURE THE SWAN KEEPS HER IN THE STRIKE ZONE, CLOSE TO THE GROUND.>
<I NEED AT LEAST TWELVE MINUTES, MARTIN.>
IS IT READY?
OF COURSE, THE KILL IS RIGHT OVER THERE.
THE PLANT GOD DEMANDS SUCH OFFERINGS...
...HE GIVES ME WHAT I NEED, AND I GIVE HIM WHAT HE NEEDS.
I GIVE YOU WHAT YOU NEED.
YOU SOUND JEALOUS. DON'T BE.
THE SWAN'S UNEXPECTED RELUCTANCE AND DARKSEID'S APPEARANCE ABOVE EARTH DEMAND A DIFFERENT COURSE OF ACTION, A DIFFERENT KIND OF POWER.
THEY DEMAND THE POWER OF URZKARTAGA!
CHINATOWN. TEN MINUTES LATER...
GOOD. YOU'RE FINALLY UP.
SO WHAT "ATHENA'S WISDOM" ARE YOU GONNA PREACH TO ME NOW, DIANA?
VANESSA, PLEASE-- WE CAN TALK THROUGH THIS.
IF I HURT YOU UNKNOWINGLY, BELIEVE ME WHEN I SAY I'M TRULY SORRY.
I WANT TO MAKE THIS RIGHT!

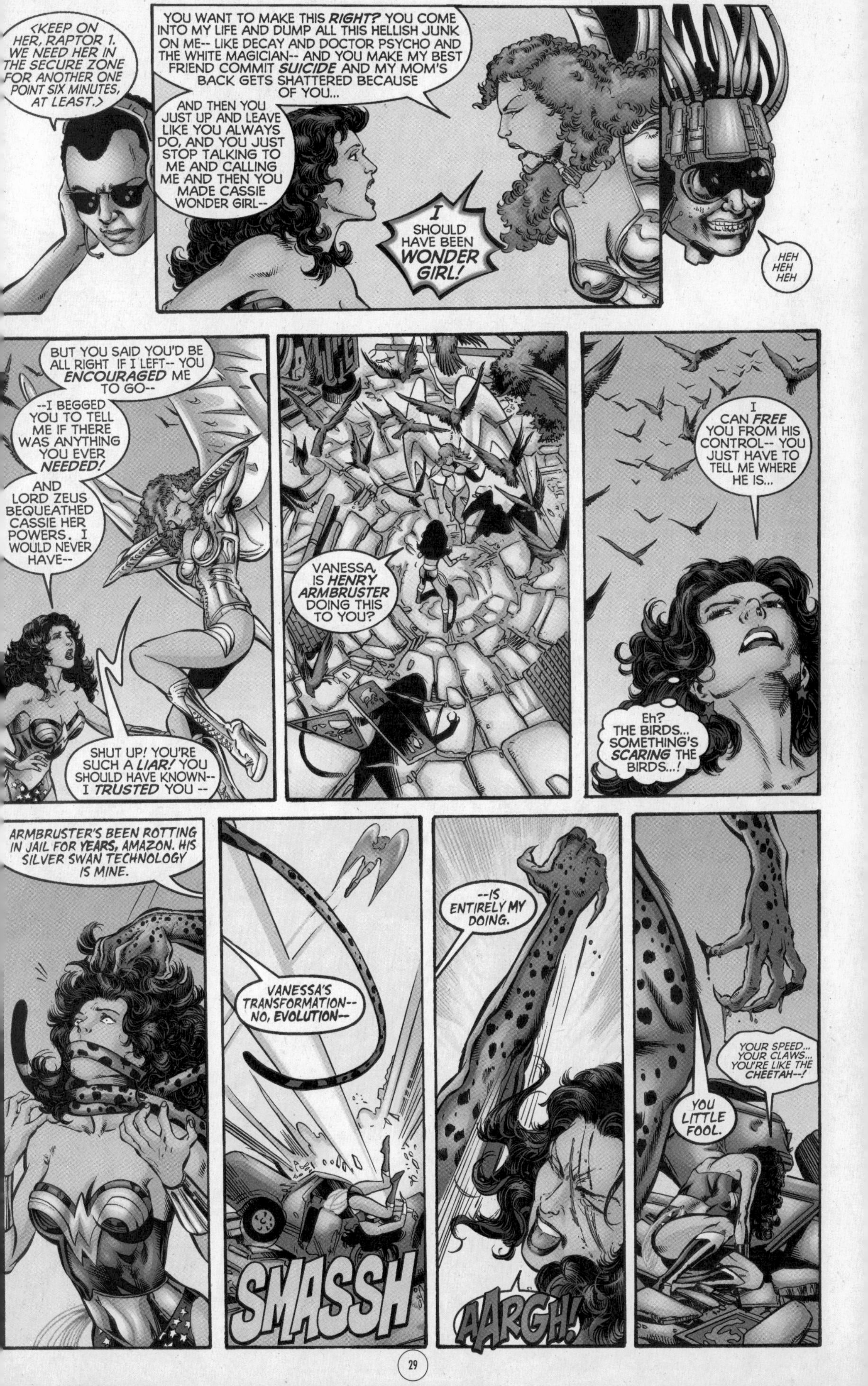

<KEEP ON HER, RAPTOR 1. WE NEED HER IN THE SECURE ZONE FOR ANOTHER ONE POINT SIX MINUTES, AT LEAST.>
YOU WANT TO MAKE THIS RIGHT? YOU COME INTO MY LIFE AND DUMP ALL THIS HELLISH JUNK ON ME-- LIKE DECAY AND DOCTOR PSYCHO AND THE WHITE MAGICIAN-- AND YOU MAKE MY BEST FRIEND COMMIT SUICIDE AND MY MOM'S BACK GETS SHATTERED BECAUSE OF YOU...
AND THEN YOU JUST UP AND LEAVE LIKE YOU ALWAYS DO, AND YOU JUST STOP TALKING TO ME AND CALLING ME AND THEN YOU MADE CASSIE WONDER GIRL--
I SHOULD HAVE BEEN WONDER GIRL!
HEH HEH HEH
BUT YOU SAID YOU'D BE ALL RIGHT IF I LEFT-- YOU ENCOURAGED ME TO GO--
--I BEGGED YOU TO TELL ME IF THERE WAS ANYTHING YOU EVER NEEDED!
AND LORD ZEUS BEQUEATHED CASSIE HER POWERS. I WOULD NEVER HAVE--
SHUT UP! YOU'RE SUCH A LIAR! YOU SHOULD HAVE KNOWN-- I TRUSTED YOU --
VANESSA, IS HENRY ARMBRUSTER DOING THIS TO YOU?
I CAN FREE YOU FROM HIS CONTROL-- YOU JUST HAVE TO TELL ME WHERE HE IS...
Eh? THE BIRDS... SOMETHING'S SCARING THE BIRDS...!
ARMBRUSTER'S BEEN ROTTING IN JAIL FOR YEARS, AMAZON. HIS SILVER SWAN TECHNOLOGY IS MINE.
VANESSA'S TRANSFORMATION-- NO, EVOLUTION--
--IS ENTIRELY MY DOING.
SMASSH
AARGH!
YOUR SPEED... YOUR CLAWS... YOU'RE LIKE THE CHEETAH--!
YOU LITTLE FOOL.

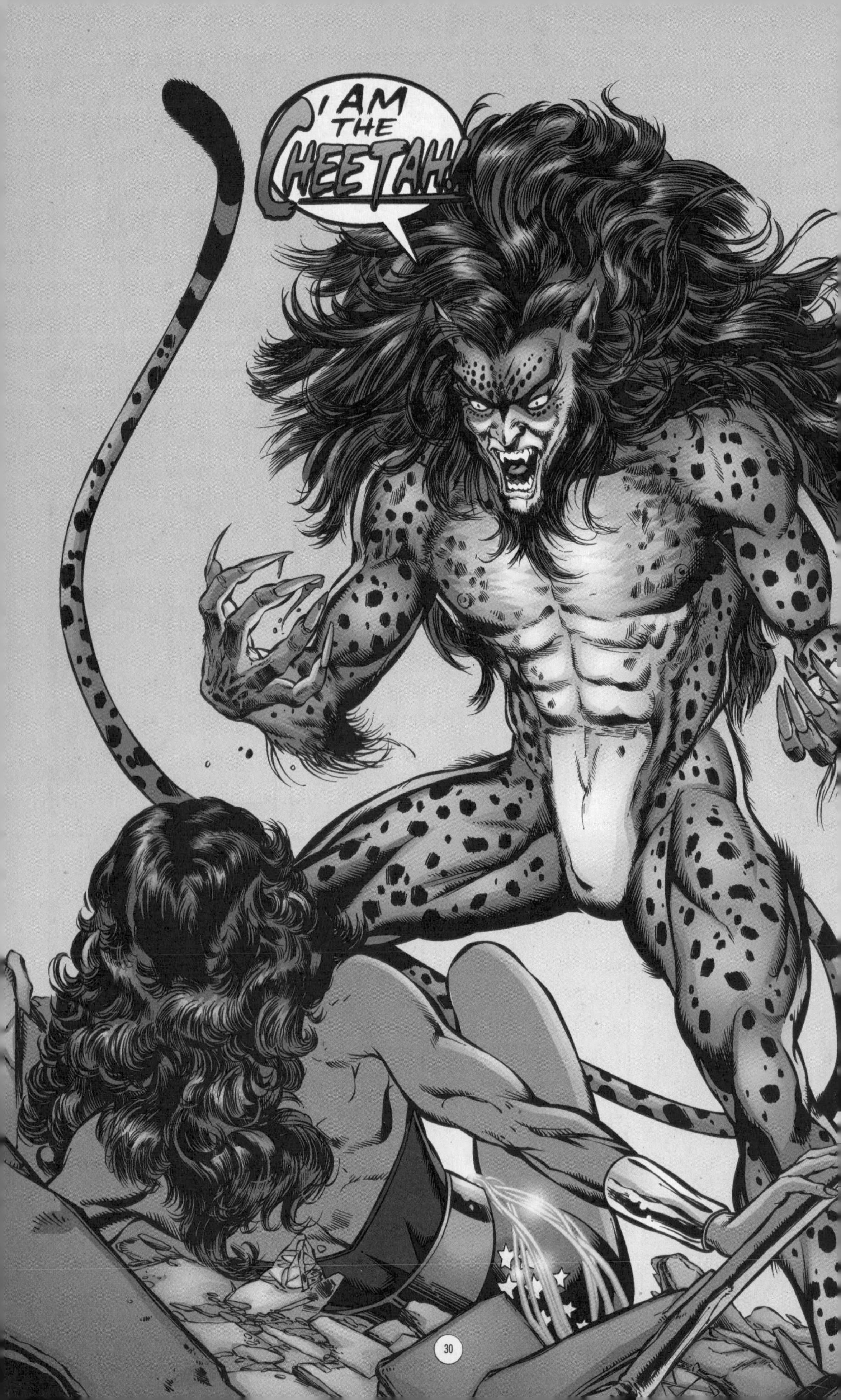
I AM THE CHEETAH!

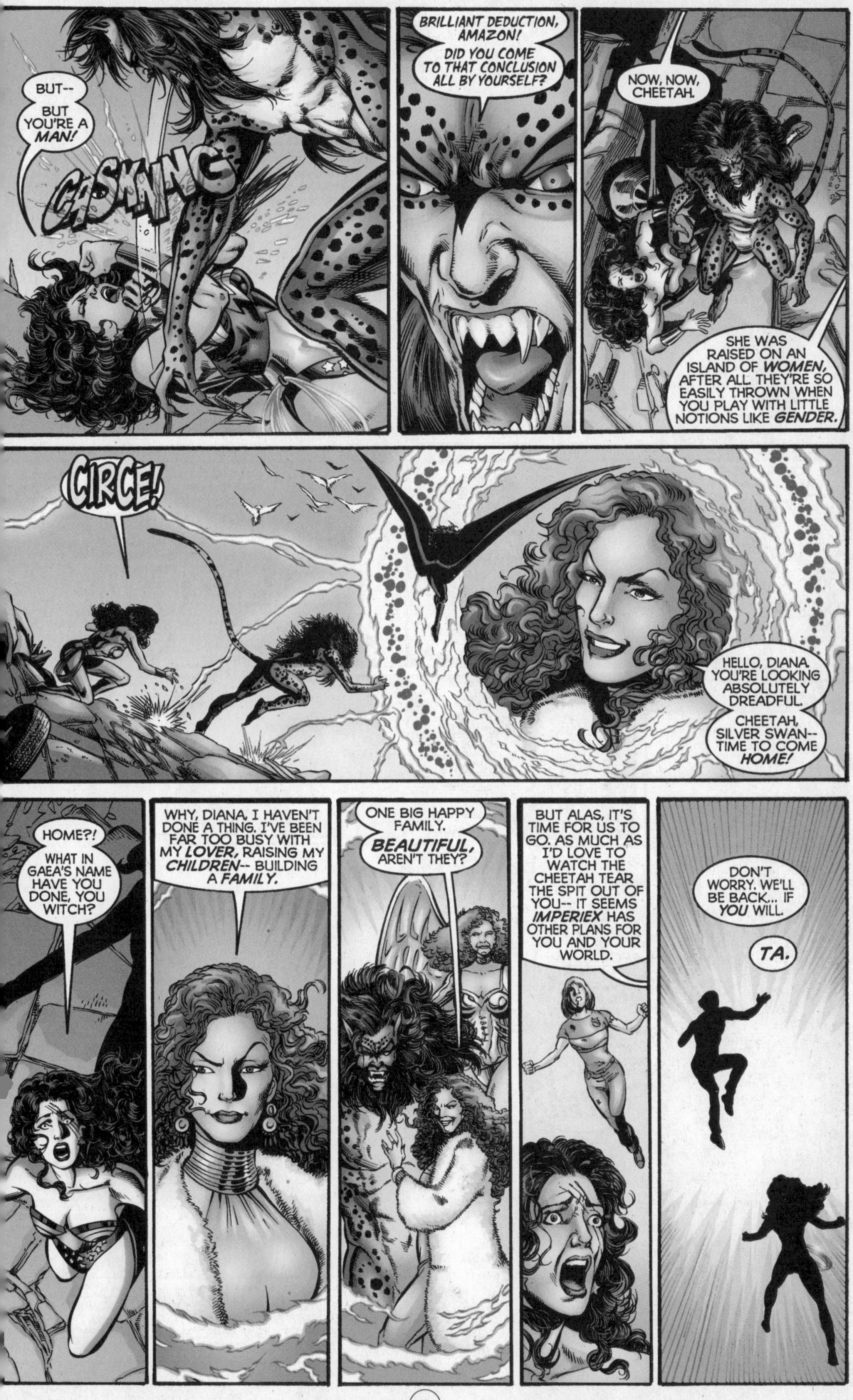

BUT-- BUT YOU'RE A MAN!
CHSKNNG
BRILLIANT DEDUCTION, AMAZON!
DID YOU COME TO THAT CONCLUSION ALL BY YOURSELF?
NOW, NOW, CHEETAH.
SHE WAS RAISED ON AN ISLAND OF WOMEN, AFTER ALL. THEY'RE SO EASILY THROWN WHEN YOU PLAY WITH LITTLE NOTIONS LIKE GENDER.
CIRCE!
HELLO, DIANA. YOU'RE LOOKING ABSOLUTELY DREADFUL.
CHEETAH, SILVER SWAN-- TIME TO COME HOME!
HOME?!
WHAT IN GAEA'S NAME HAVE YOU DONE, YOU WITCH?
WHY, DIANA, I HAVEN'T DONE A THING. I'VE BEEN FAR TOO BUSY WITH MY LOVER, RAISING MY CHILDREN-- BUILDING A FAMILY.
ONE BIG HAPPY FAMILY.
BEAUTIFUL, AREN'T THEY?
BUT ALAS, IT'S TIME FOR US TO GO. AS MUCH AS I'D LOVE TO WATCH THE CHEETAH TEAR THE SPIT OUT OF YOU-- IT SEEMS IMPERIEX HAS OTHER PLANS FOR YOU AND YOUR WORLD.
DON'T WORRY. WE'LL BE BACK... IF YOU WILL.
TA.

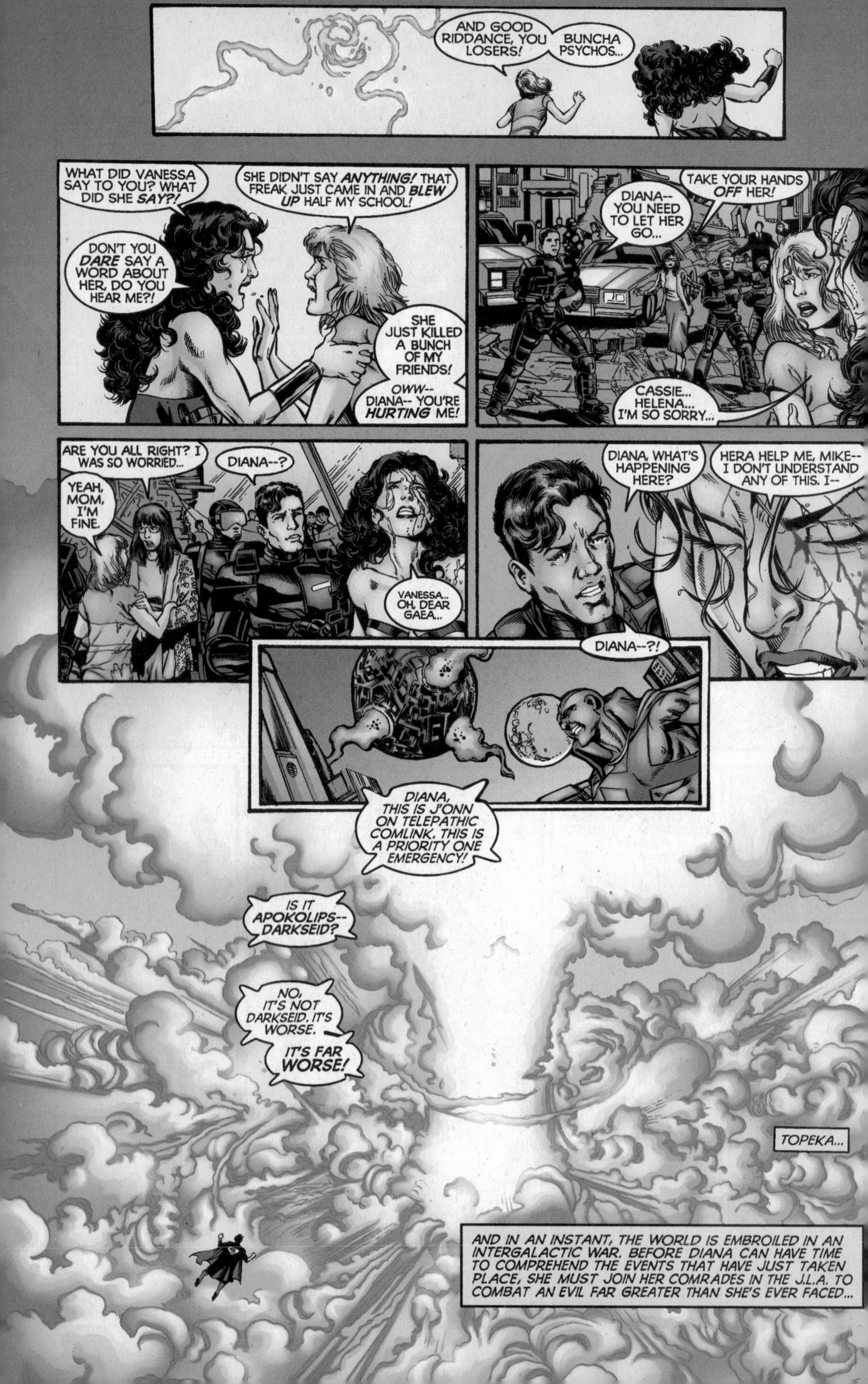
AND GOOD RIDDANCE, YOU LOSERS!
BUNCHA PSYCHOS...
WHAT DID VANESSA SAY TO YOU? WHAT DID SHE SAY?!
SHE DIDN'T SAY ANYTHING! THAT FREAK JUST CAME IN AND BLEW UP HALF MY SCHOOL!
DON'T YOU DARE SAY A WORD ABOUT HER, DO YOU HEAR ME?!
SHE JUST KILLED A BUNCH OF MY FRIENDS!
OWW-- DIANA-- YOU'RE HURTING ME!
TAKE YOUR HANDS OFF HER!
DIANA-- YOU NEED TO LET HER GO...
CASSIE... HELENA... I'M SO SORRY...
ARE YOU ALL RIGHT? I WAS SO WORRIED...
DIANA--?
YEAH, MOM, I'M FINE.
VANESSA... OH, DEAR GAEA...
DIANA, WHAT'S HAPPENING HERE?
HERA HELP ME, MIKE-- I DON'T UNDERSTAND ANY OF THIS. I--
DIANA--?!
DIANA, THIS IS J'ONN ON TELEPATHIC COMLINK. THIS IS A PRIORITY ONE EMERGENCY!
IS IT APOKOLIPS-- DARKSEID?
NO, IT'S NOT DARKSEID. IT'S WORSE.
IT'S FAR WORSE!
TOPEKA...
AND IN AN INSTANT, THE WORLD IS EMBROILED IN AN INTERGALACTIC WAR. BEFORE DIANA CAN HAVE TIME TO COMPREHEND THE EVENTS THAT HAVE JUST TAKEN PLACE, SHE MUST JOIN HER COMRADES IN THE J.L.A. TO COMBAT AN EVIL FAR GREATER THAN SHE'S EVER FACED...

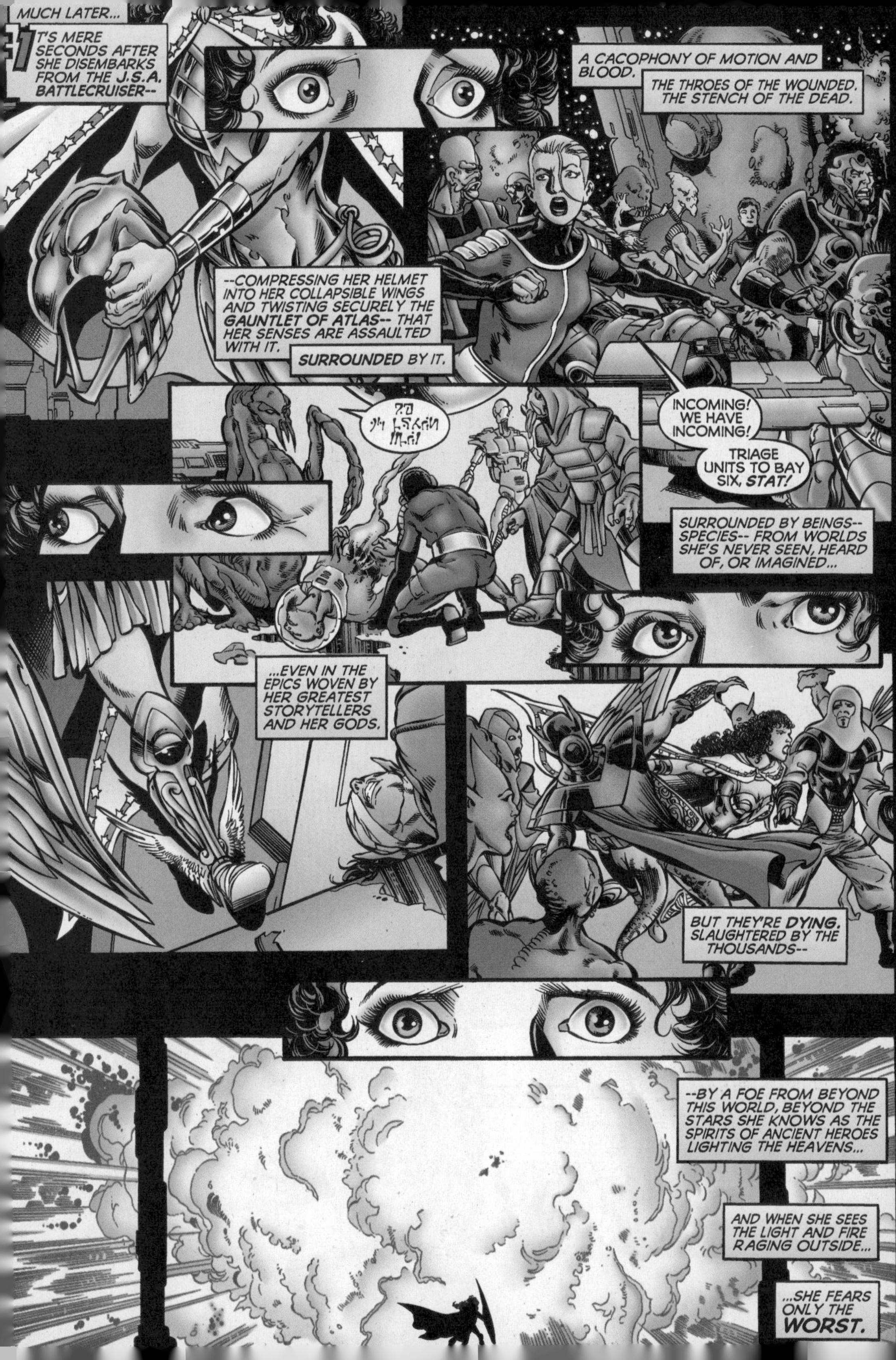
MUCH LATER...
IT'S MERE SECONDS AFTER SHE DISEMBARKS FROM THE J.S.A. BATTLECRUISER--
A CACOPHONY OF MOTION AND BLOOD.
THE THROES OF THE WOUNDED. THE STENCH OF THE DEAD.
--COMPRESSING HER HELMET INTO HER COLLAPSIBLE WINGS AND TWISTING SECURELY THE GAUNTLET OF ATLAS-- THAT HER SENSES ARE ASSAULTED WITH IT.
SURROUNDED BY IT.
INCOMING! WE HAVE INCOMING!
TRIAGE UNITS TO BAY SIX, STAT!
SURROUNDED BY BEINGS-- SPECIES-- FROM WORLDS SHE'S NEVER SEEN, HEARD OF, OR IMAGINED...
...EVEN IN THE EPICS WOVEN BY HER GREATEST STORYTELLERS AND HER GODS.
BUT THEY'RE DYING. SLAUGHTERED BY THE THOUSANDS--
--BY A FOE FROM BEYOND THIS WORLD, BEYOND THE STARS SHE KNOWS AS THE SPIRITS OF ANCIENT HEROES LIGHTING THE HEAVENS...
AND WHEN SHE SEES THE LIGHT AND FIRE RAGING OUTSIDE...
...SHE FEARS ONLY THE WORST.

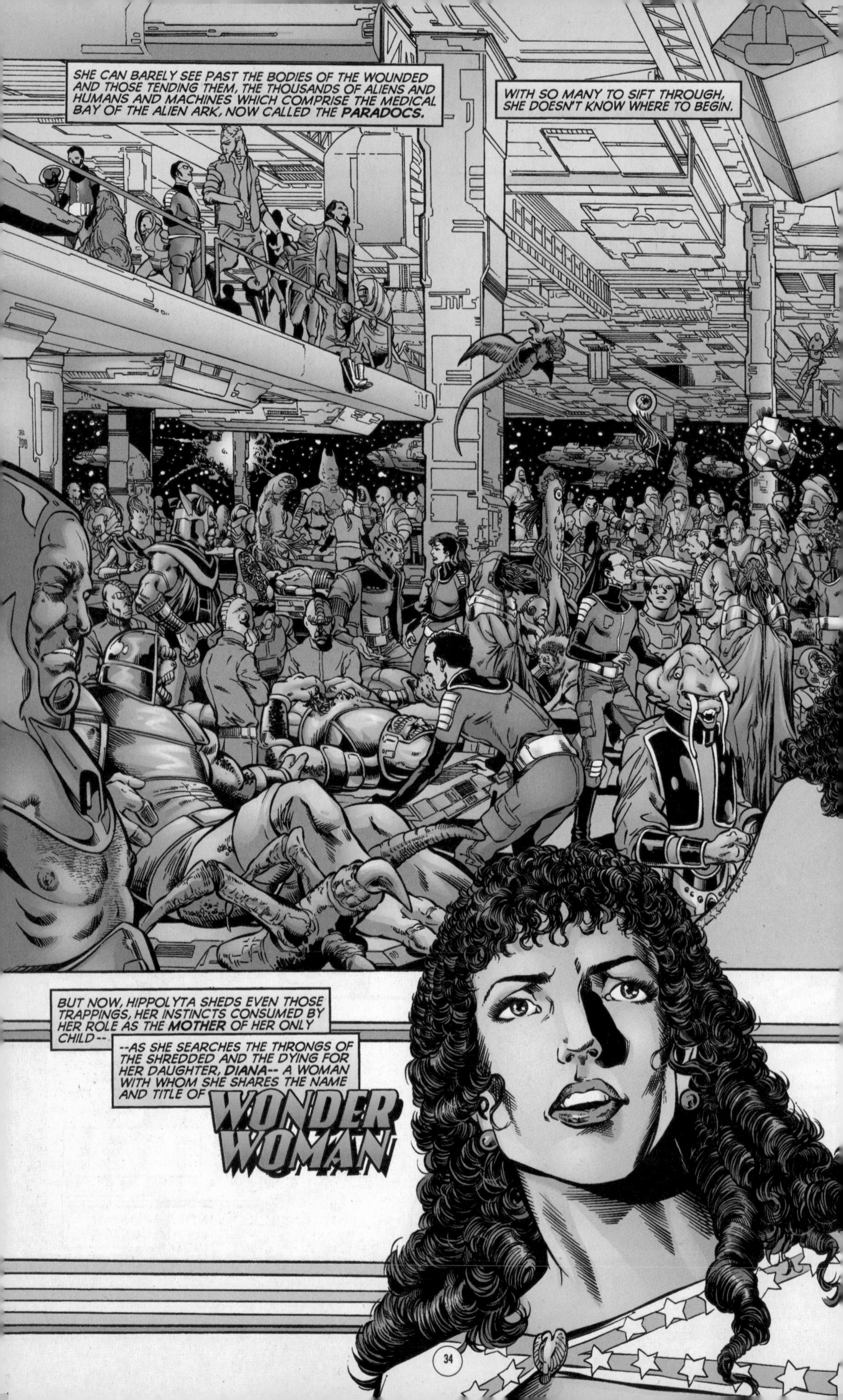

SHE CAN BARELY SEE PAST THE BODIES OF THE WOUNDED AND THOSE TENDING THEM, THE THOUSANDS OF ALIENS AND HUMANS AND MACHINES WHICH COMPRISE THE MEDICAL BAY OF THE ALIEN ARK, NOW CALLED THE PARADOCS.
WITH SO MANY TO SIFT THROUGH, SHE DOESN'T KNOW WHERE TO BEGIN.
BUT NOW, HIPPOLYTA SHEDS EVEN THOSE TRAPPINGS, HER INSTINCTS CONSUMED BY HER ROLE AS THE MOTHER OF HER ONLY CHILD--
--AS SHE SEARCHES THE THRONGS OF THE SHREDDED AND THE DYING FOR HER DAUGHTER, DIANA-- A WOMAN WITH WHOM SHE SHARES THE NAME AND TITLE OF
WONDER WOMAN

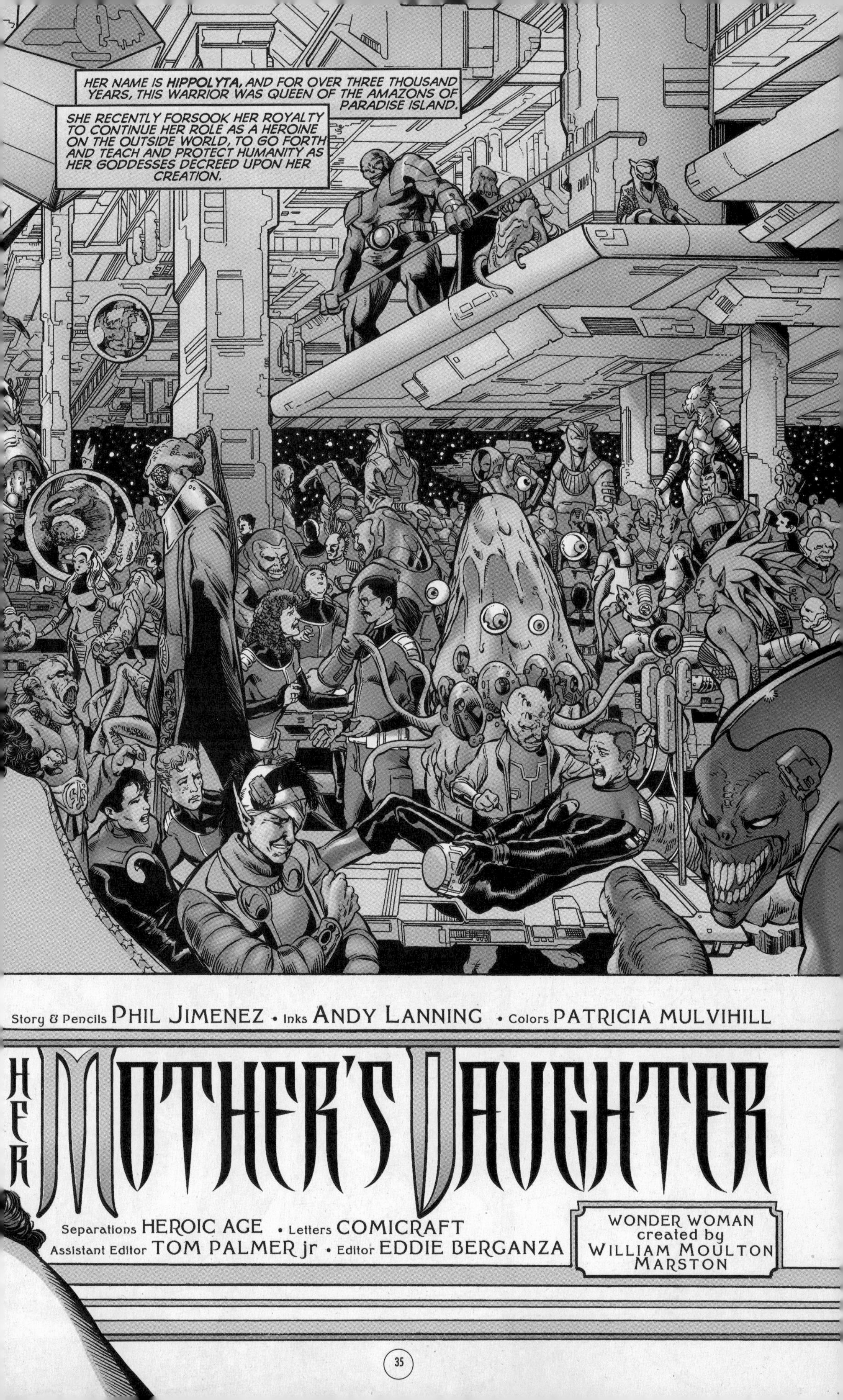
HER NAME IS HIPPOLYTA, AND FOR OVER THREE THOUSAND YEARS, THIS WARRIOR WAS QUEEN OF THE AMAZONS OF PARADISE ISLAND.
SHE RECENTLY FORSOOK HER ROYALTY TO CONTINUE HER ROLE AS A HEROINE ON THE OUTSIDE WORLD, TO GO FORTH AND TEACH AND PROTECT HUMANITY AS HER GODDESSES DECREED UPON HER CREATION.

Story & Pencils PHIL JIMENEZ • Inks ANDY LANNING • Colors PATRICIA MULVIHILL

HER MOTHER'S DAUGHTER

Separations HEROIC AGE • Letters COMICRAFT
Assistant Editor TOM PALMER jr • Editor EDDIE BERGANZA

WONDER WOMAN created by WILLIAM MOULTON MARSTON

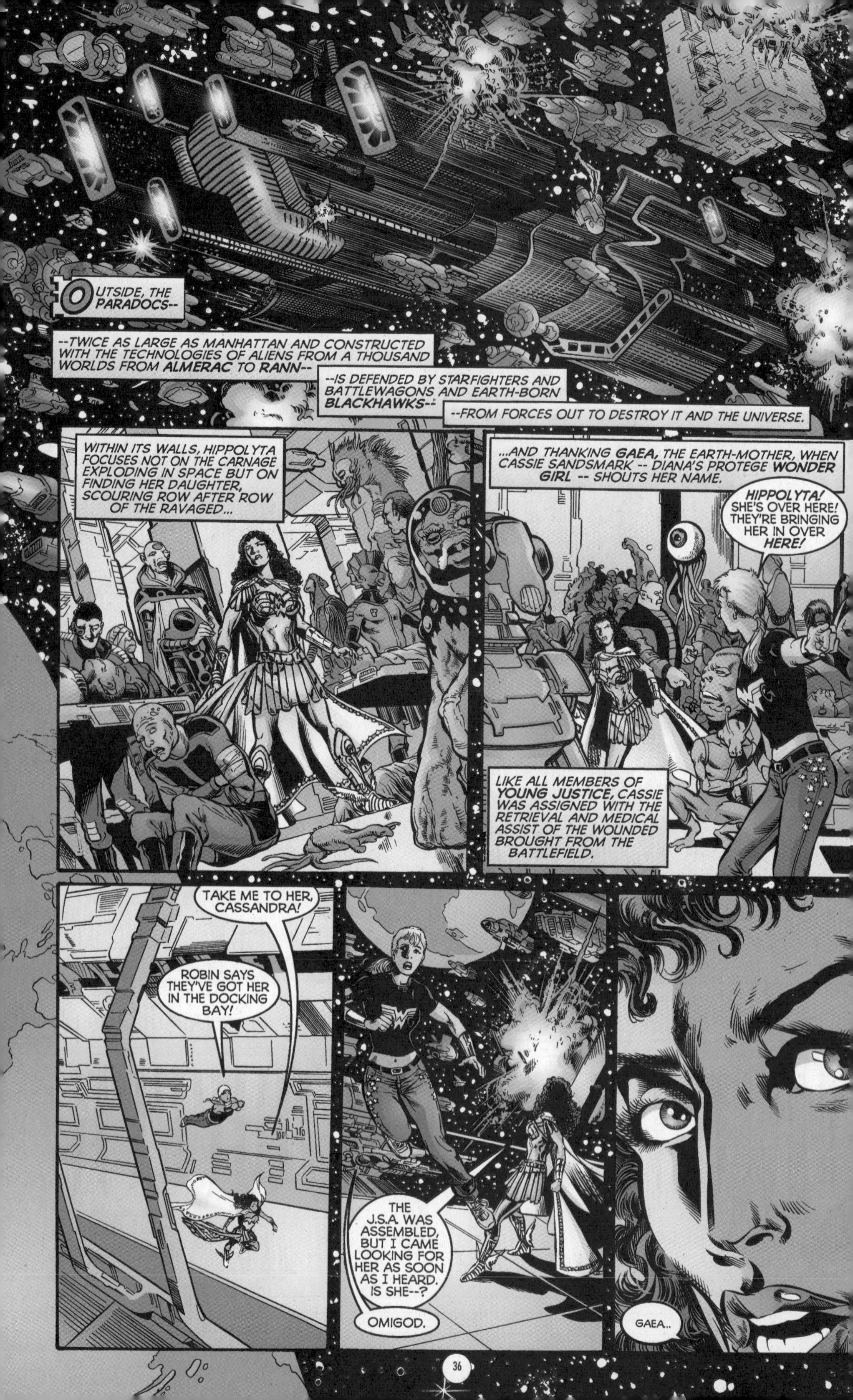
OUTSIDE, THE PARADOCS--
--TWICE AS LARGE AS MANHATTAN AND CONSTRUCTED WITH THE TECHNOLOGIES OF ALIENS FROM A THOUSAND WORLDS FROM ALMERAC TO RANN--
--IS DEFENDED BY STARFIGHTERS AND BATTLEWAGONS AND EARTH-BORN BLACKHAWKS--
--FROM FORCES OUT TO DESTROY IT AND THE UNIVERSE.
WITHIN ITS WALLS, HIPPOLYTA FOCUSES NOT ON THE CARNAGE EXPLODING IN SPACE BUT ON FINDING HER DAUGHTER, SCOURING ROW AFTER ROW OF THE RAVAGED...
...AND THANKING GAEA, THE EARTH-MOTHER, WHEN CASSIE SANDSMARK -- DIANA'S PROTEGE WONDER GIRL -- SHOUTS HER NAME.
HIPPOLYTA! SHE'S OVER HERE! THEY'RE BRINGING HER IN OVER HERE!
LIKE ALL MEMBERS OF YOUNG JUSTICE, CASSIE WAS ASSIGNED WITH THE RETRIEVAL AND MEDICAL ASSIST OF THE WOUNDED BROUGHT FROM THE BATTLEFIELD.
TAKE ME TO HER, CASSANDRA!
ROBIN SAYS THEY'VE GOT HER IN THE DOCKING BAY!
THE J.S.A. WAS ASSEMBLED, BUT I CAME LOOKING FOR HER AS SOON AS I HEARD. IS SHE--?
OMIGOD.
GAEA..

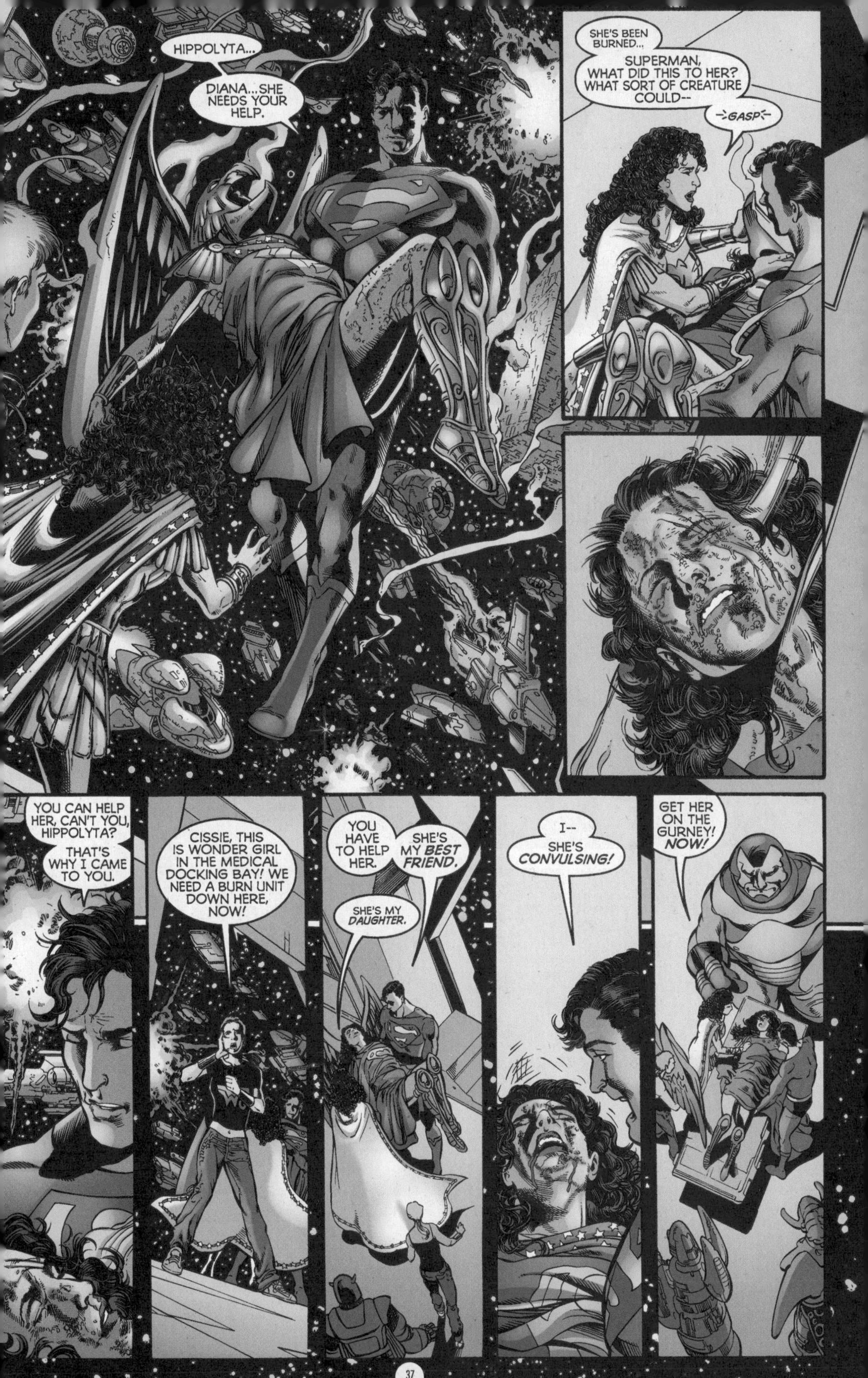

HIPPOLYTA...
DIANA...SHE NEEDS YOUR HELP.
SHE'S BEEN BURNED...
SUPERMAN, WHAT DID THIS TO HER? WHAT SORT OF CREATURE COULD--
GASP
YOU CAN HELP HER, CAN'T YOU, HIPPOLYTA?
THAT'S WHY I CAME TO YOU.
CISSIE, THIS IS WONDER GIRL IN THE MEDICAL DOCKING BAY! WE NEED A BURN UNIT DOWN HERE, NOW!
YOU HAVE TO HELP HER.
SHE'S MY *BEST FRIEND.*
SHE'S MY *DAUGHTER.*
I--
SHE'S *CONVULSING!*
GET HER ON THE GURNEY! *NOW!*

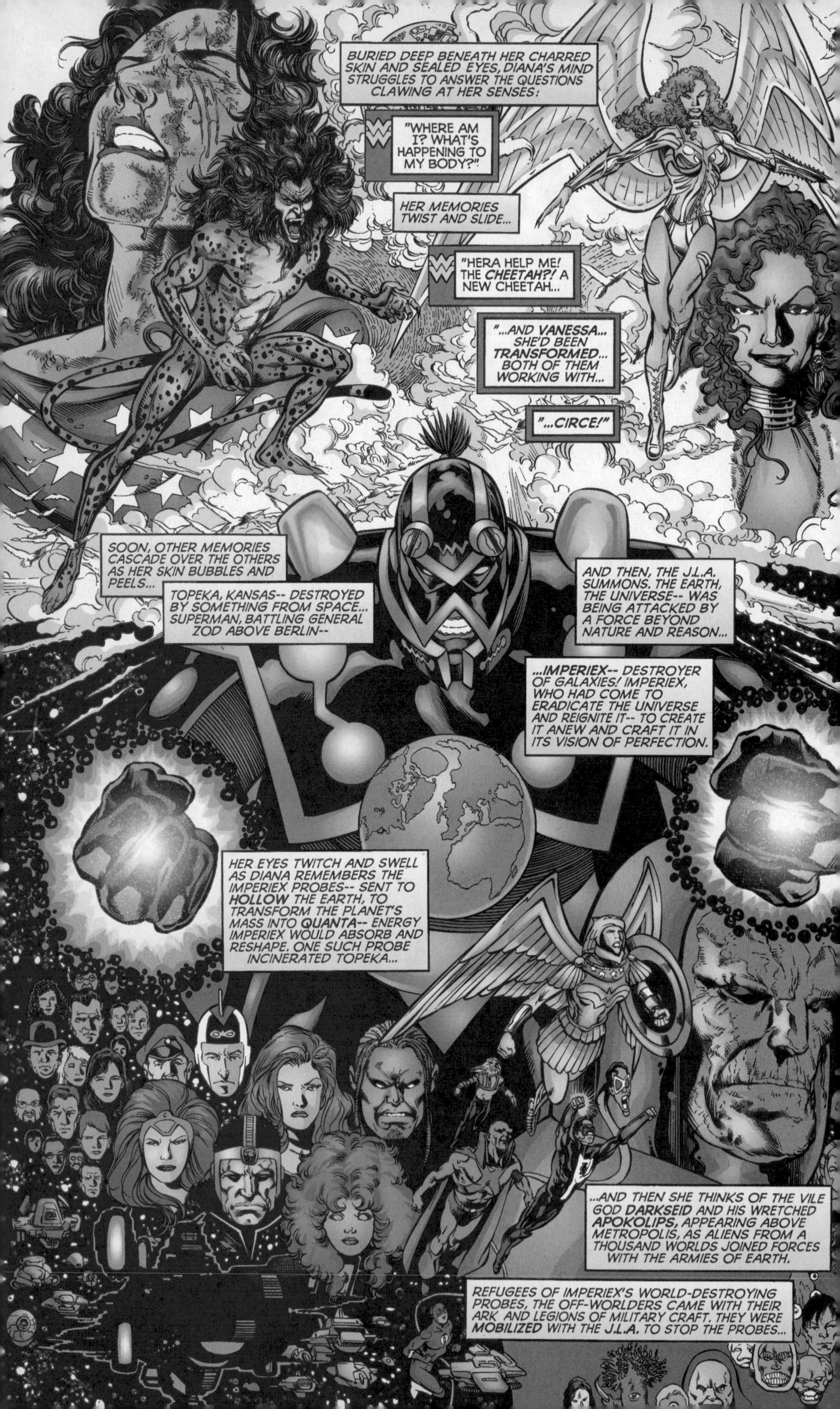

BURIED DEEP BENEATH HER CHARRED SKIN AND SEALED EYES, DIANA'S MIND STRUGGLES TO ANSWER THE QUESTIONS CLAWING AT HER SENSES:
"WHERE AM I? WHAT'S HAPPENING TO MY BODY?"
HER MEMORIES TWIST AND SLIDE...
"HERA HELP ME! THE CHEETAH?! A NEW CHEETAH...
"...AND VANESSA... SHE'D BEEN TRANSFORMED... BOTH OF THEM WORKING WITH...
"...CIRCE!"
SOON, OTHER MEMORIES CASCADE OVER THE OTHERS AS HER SKIN BUBBLES AND PEELS...
TOPEKA, KANSAS-- DESTROYED BY SOMETHING FROM SPACE... SUPERMAN, BATTLING GENERAL ZOD ABOVE BERLIN--
AND THEN, THE J.L.A. SUMMONS. THE EARTH, THE UNIVERSE-- WAS BEING ATTACKED BY A FORCE BEYOND NATURE AND REASON...
...IMPERIEX-- DESTROYER OF GALAXIES! IMPERIEX, WHO HAD COME TO ERADICATE THE UNIVERSE AND REIGNITE IT-- TO CREATE IT ANEW AND CRAFT IT IN ITS VISION OF PERFECTION.
HER EYES TWITCH AND SWELL AS DIANA REMEMBERS THE IMPERIEX PROBES-- SENT TO HOLLOW THE EARTH, TO TRANSFORM THE PLANET'S MASS INTO QUANTA-- ENERGY IMPERIEX WOULD ABSORB AND RESHAPE. ONE SUCH PROBE INCINERATED TOPEKA...
...AND THEN SHE THINKS OF THE VILE GOD DARKSEID AND HIS WRETCHED APOKOLIPS, APPEARING ABOVE METROPOLIS, AS ALIENS FROM A THOUSAND WORLDS JOINED FORCES WITH THE ARMIES OF EARTH.
REFUGEES OF IMPERIEX'S WORLD-DESTROYING PROBES, THE OFF-WORLDERS CAME WITH THEIR ARK AND LEGIONS OF MILITARY CRAFT. THEY WERE MOBILIZED WITH THE J.L.A. TO STOP THE PROBES...

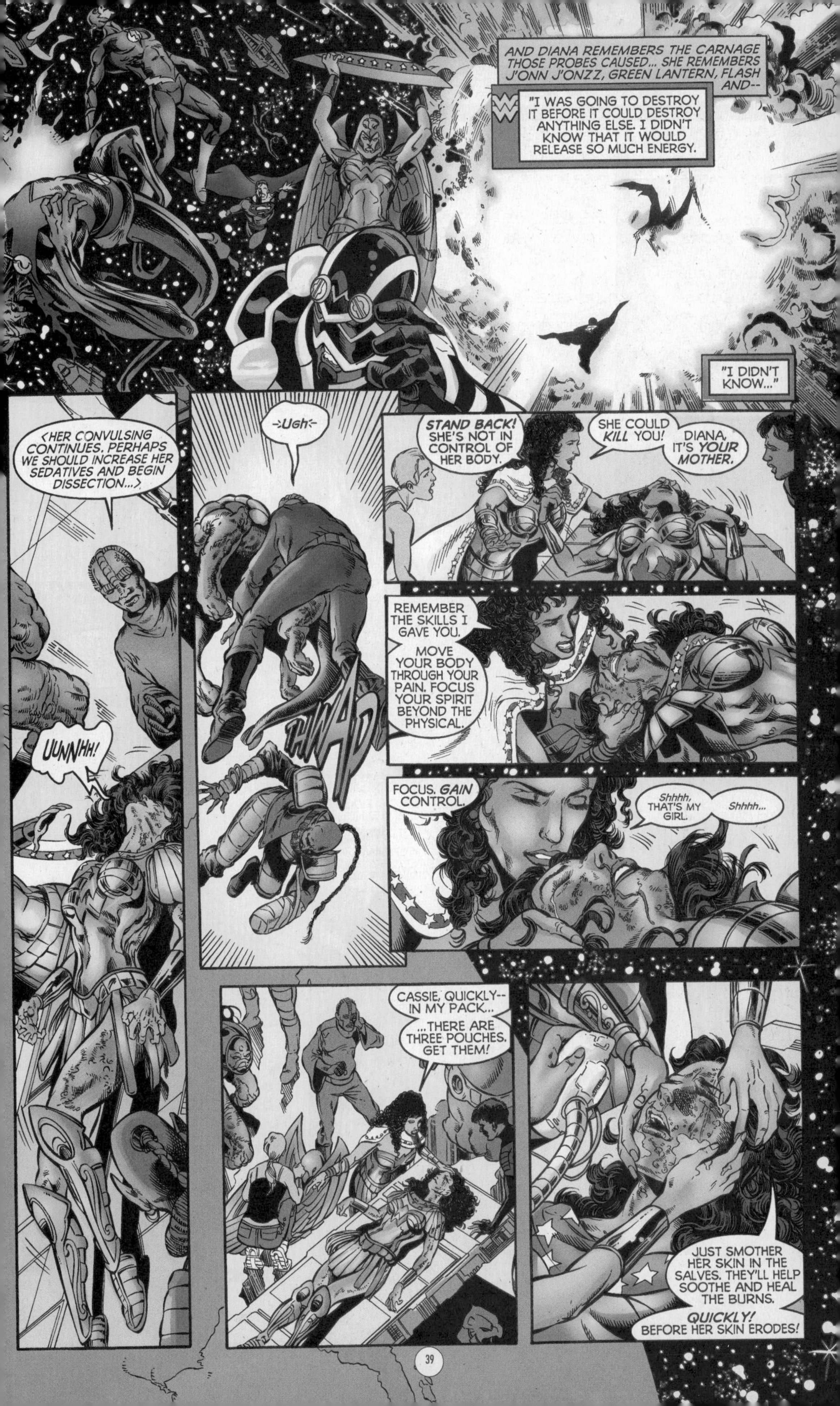
AND DIANA REMEMBERS THE CARNAGE THOSE PROBES CAUSED... SHE REMEMBERS J'ONN J'ONZZ, GREEN LANTERN, FLASH AND--
"I WAS GOING TO DESTROY IT BEFORE IT COULD DESTROY ANYTHING ELSE. I DIDN'T KNOW THAT IT WOULD RELEASE SO MUCH ENERGY.
"I DIDN'T KNOW..."
<HER CONVULSING CONTINUES. PERHAPS WE SHOULD INCREASE HER SEDATIVES AND BEGIN DISSECTION...>
UUNNHH!
-Ugh-
THWAD
STAND BACK! SHE'S NOT IN CONTROL OF HER BODY.
SHE COULD KILL YOU!
DIANA, IT'S YOUR MOTHER.
REMEMBER THE SKILLS I GAVE YOU.
MOVE YOUR BODY THROUGH YOUR PAIN. FOCUS YOUR SPIRIT BEYOND THE PHYSICAL.
FOCUS. GAIN CONTROL.
Shhhh, THAT'S MY GIRL.
Shhhh...
CASSIE, QUICKLY-- IN MY PACK...
...THERE ARE THREE POUCHES. GET THEM!
JUST SMOTHER HER SKIN IN THE SALVES. THEY'LL HELP SOOTHE AND HEAL THE BURNS.
QUICKLY! BEFORE HER SKIN ERODES!

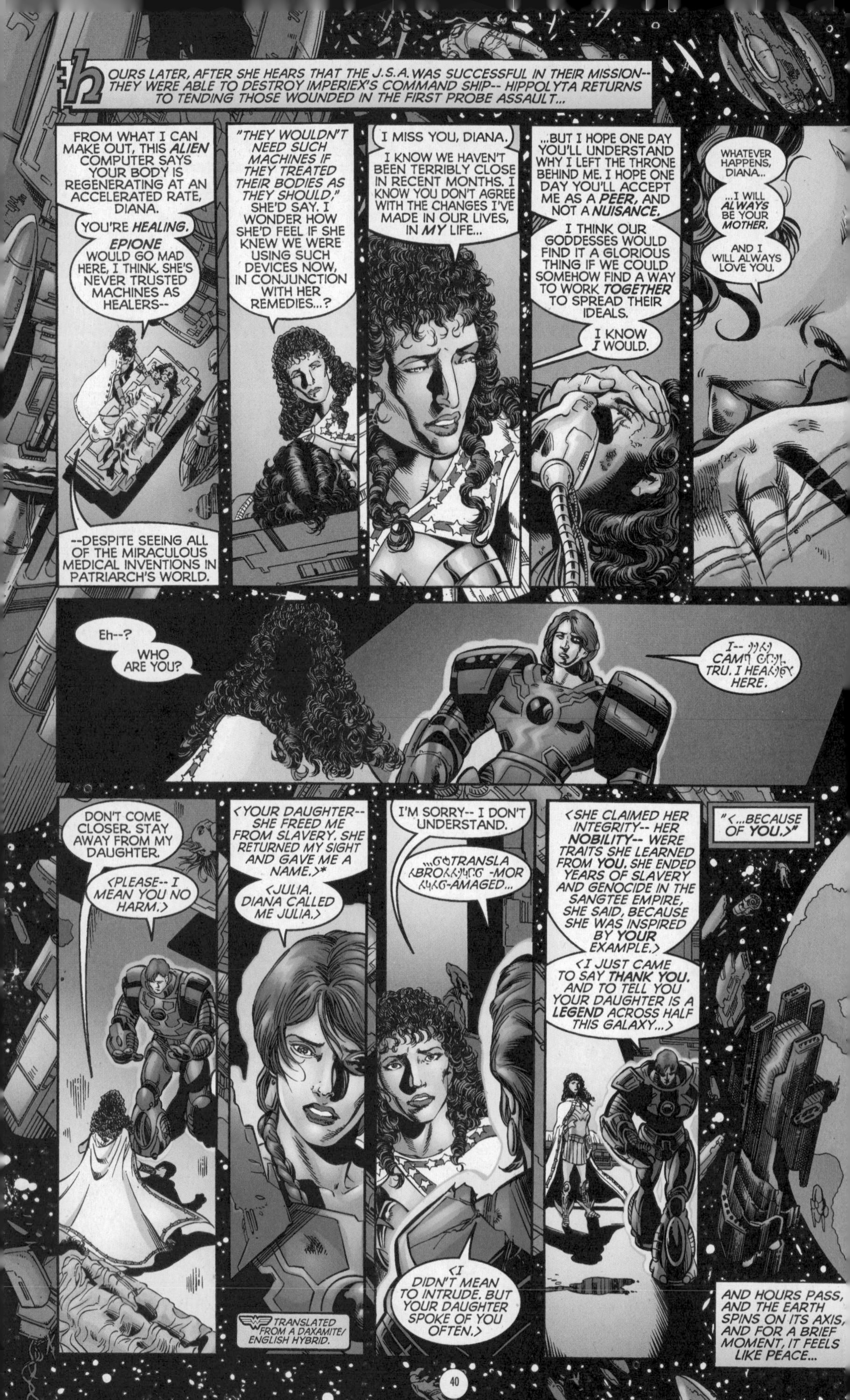
HOURS LATER, AFTER SHE HEARS THAT THE J.S.A. WAS SUCCESSFUL IN THEIR MISSION-- THEY WERE ABLE TO DESTROY IMPERIEX'S COMMAND SHIP-- HIPPOLYTA RETURNS TO TENDING THOSE WOUNDED IN THE FIRST PROBE ASSAULT...
FROM WHAT I CAN MAKE OUT, THIS ALIEN COMPUTER SAYS YOUR BODY IS REGENERATING AT AN ACCELERATED RATE, DIANA.
YOU'RE HEALING.
EPIONE WOULD GO MAD HERE, I THINK. SHE'S NEVER TRUSTED MACHINES AS HEALERS--
--DESPITE SEEING ALL OF THE MIRACULOUS MEDICAL INVENTIONS IN PATRIARCH'S WORLD.
"THEY WOULDN'T NEED SUCH MACHINES IF THEY TREATED THEIR BODIES AS THEY SHOULD," SHE'D SAY. I WONDER HOW SHE'D FEEL IF SHE KNEW WE WERE USING SUCH DEVICES NOW, IN CONJUNCTION WITH HER REMEDIES...?
I MISS YOU, DIANA.
I KNOW WE HAVEN'T BEEN TERRIBLY CLOSE IN RECENT MONTHS. I KNOW YOU DON'T AGREE WITH THE CHANGES I'VE MADE IN OUR LIVES, IN MY LIFE...
...BUT I HOPE ONE DAY YOU'LL UNDERSTAND WHY I LEFT THE THRONE BEHIND ME. I HOPE ONE DAY YOU'LL ACCEPT ME AS A PEER, AND NOT A NUISANCE.
I THINK OUR GODDESSES WOULD FIND IT A GLORIOUS THING IF WE COULD SOMEHOW FIND A WAY TO WORK TOGETHER TO SPREAD THEIR IDEALS.
I KNOW I WOULD.
WHATEVER HAPPENS, DIANA...
...I WILL ALWAYS BE YOUR MOTHER.
AND I WILL ALWAYS LOVE YOU.
Eh--? WHO ARE YOU?
I-- CAM TRU. I HEA HERE.
DON'T COME CLOSER. STAY AWAY FROM MY DAUGHTER.
<PLEASE-- I MEAN YOU NO HARM.>
<YOUR DAUGHTER-- SHE FREED ME FROM SLAVERY. SHE RETURNED MY SIGHT AND GAVE ME A NAME.>*
<JULIA. DIANA CALLED ME JULIA.>
*TRANSLATED FROM A DAXAMITE/ ENGLISH HYBRID.
I'M SORRY-- I DON'T UNDERSTAND.
...TRANSLA -MOR -AMAGED...
<I DIDN'T MEAN TO INTRUDE. BUT YOUR DAUGHTER SPOKE OF YOU OFTEN.>
<SHE CLAIMED HER INTEGRITY-- HER NOBILITY-- WERE TRAITS SHE LEARNED FROM YOU. SHE ENDED YEARS OF SLAVERY AND GENOCIDE IN THE SANGTEE EMPIRE, SHE SAID, BECAUSE SHE WAS INSPIRED BY YOUR EXAMPLE.>
<I JUST CAME TO SAY THANK YOU. AND TO TELL YOU YOUR DAUGHTER IS A LEGEND ACROSS HALF THIS GALAXY...>
"<...BECAUSE OF YOU.>"
AND HOURS PASS, AND THE EARTH SPINS ON ITS AXIS, AND FOR A BRIEF MOMENT, IT FEELS LIKE PEACE...

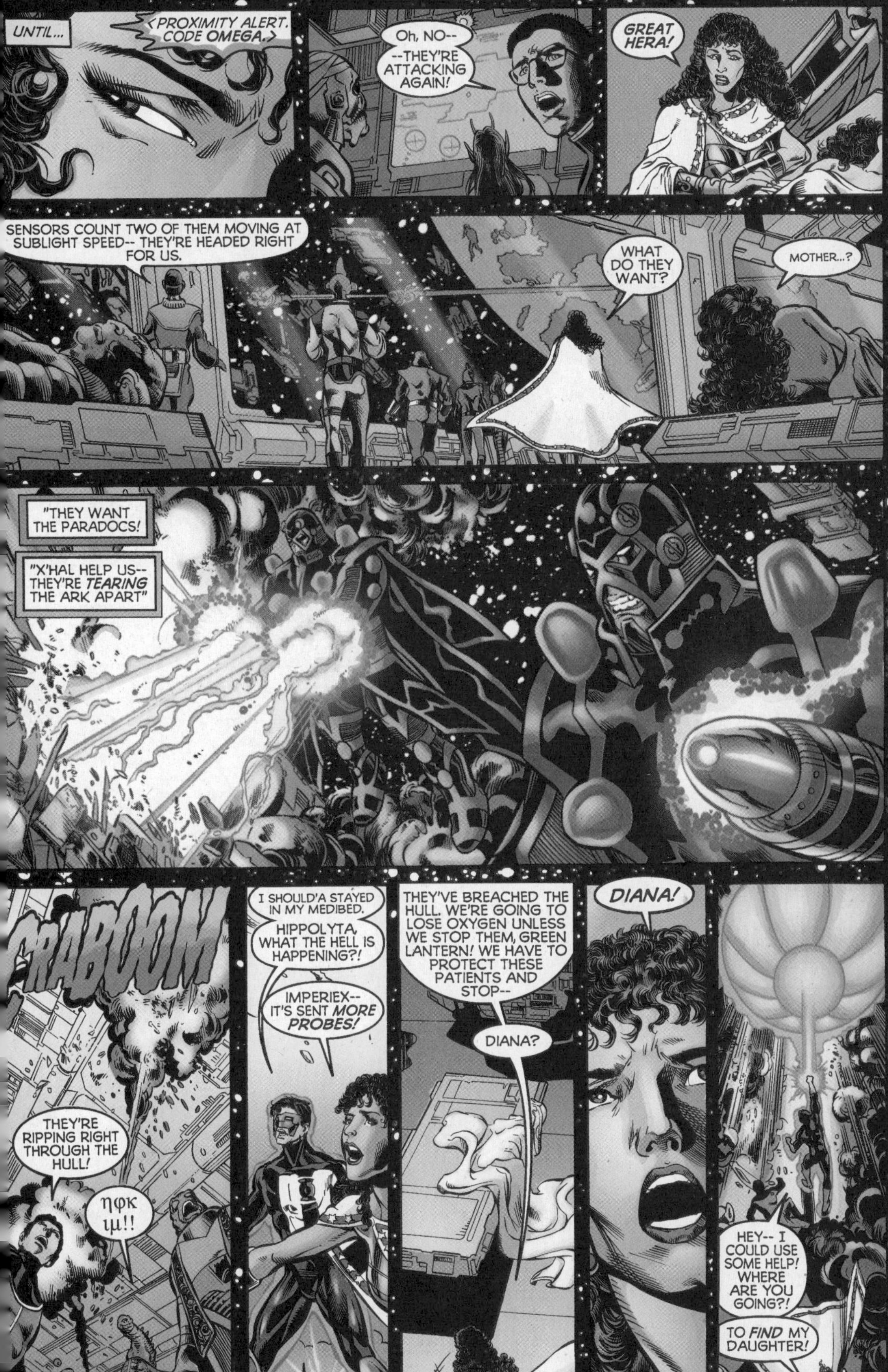
UNTIL...
<PROXIMITY ALERT. CODE OMEGA.>
Oh, NO-- --THEY'RE ATTACKING AGAIN!
GREAT HERA!
SENSORS COUNT TWO OF THEM MOVING AT SUBLIGHT SPEED-- THEY'RE HEADED RIGHT FOR US.
WHAT DO THEY WANT?
MOTHER...?
"THEY WANT THE PARADOCS!
"X'HAL HELP US-- THEY'RE TEARING THE ARK APART"
CRABOOM
THEY'RE RIPPING RIGHT THROUGH THE HULL!
ηφκ ιμ!!
I SHOULD'A STAYED IN MY MEDIBED.
HIPPOLYTA, WHAT THE HELL IS HAPPENING?!
IMPERIEX-- IT'S SENT MORE PROBES!
GREAT...
THEY'VE BREACHED THE HULL. WE'RE GOING TO LOSE OXYGEN UNLESS WE STOP THEM, GREEN LANTERN! WE HAVE TO PROTECT THESE PATIENTS AND STOP--
DIANA?
DIANA!
HEY-- I COULD USE SOME HELP! WHERE ARE YOU GOING?!
TO FIND MY DAUGHTER!

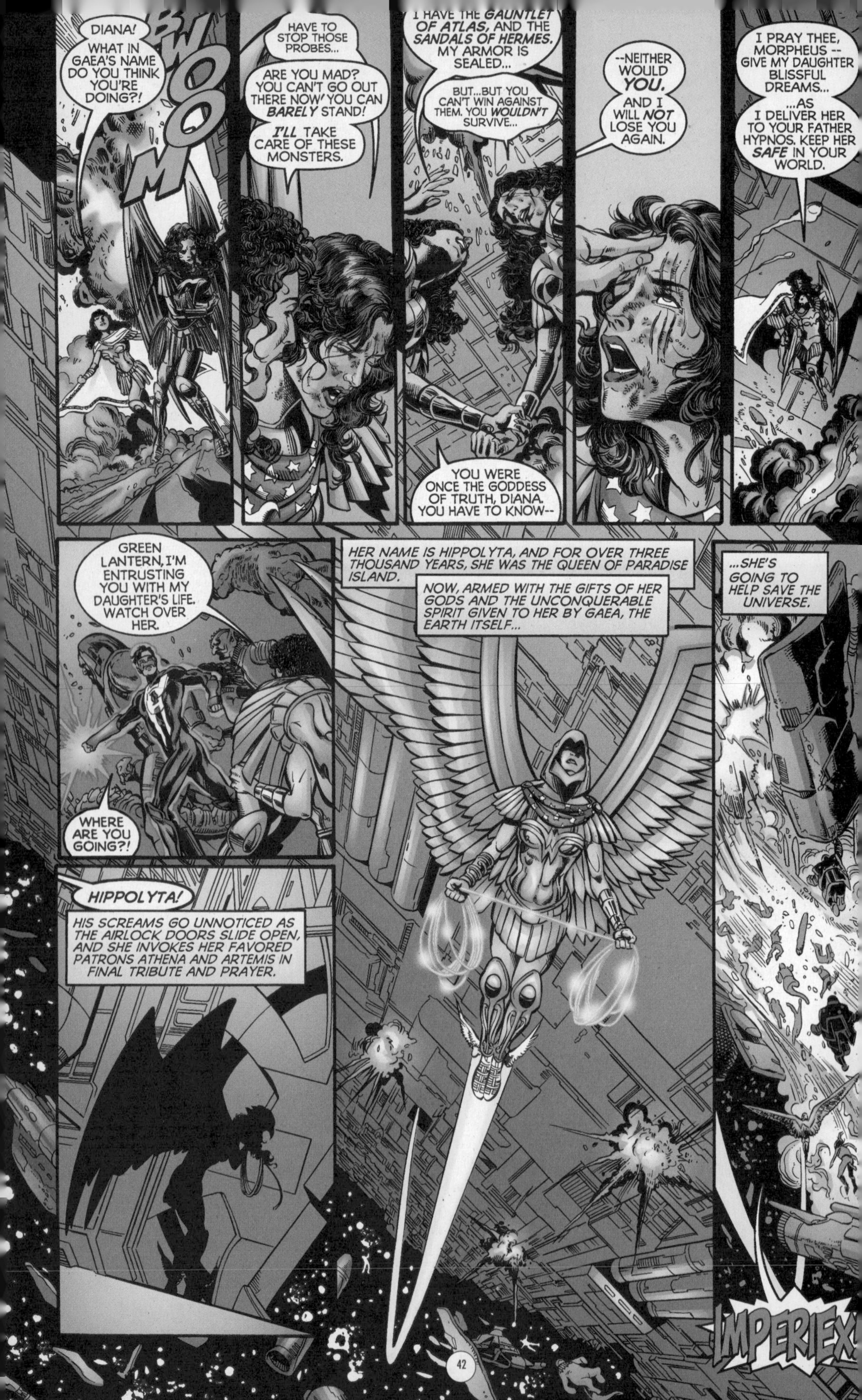
DIANA! WHAT IN GAEA'S NAME DO YOU THINK YOU'RE DOING?!
BWOOOM
HAVE TO STOP THOSE PROBES...
ARE YOU MAD? YOU CAN'T GO OUT THERE NOW! YOU CAN BARELY STAND!
I'LL TAKE CARE OF THESE MONSTERS.
I HAVE THE GAUNTLET OF ATLAS, AND THE SANDALS OF HERMES. MY ARMOR IS SEALED...
BUT...BUT YOU CAN'T WIN AGAINST THEM. YOU WOULDN'T SURVIVE...
YOU WERE ONCE THE GODDESS OF TRUTH, DIANA. YOU HAVE TO KNOW--
--NEITHER WOULD YOU.
AND I WILL NOT LOSE YOU AGAIN.
I PRAY THEE, MORPHEUS -- GIVE MY DAUGHTER BLISSFUL DREAMS...
...AS I DELIVER HER TO YOUR FATHER HYPNOS. KEEP HER SAFE IN YOUR WORLD.
GREEN LANTERN, I'M ENTRUSTING YOU WITH MY DAUGHTER'S LIFE. WATCH OVER HER.
WHERE ARE YOU GOING?!
HIPPOLYTA!
HIS SCREAMS GO UNNOTICED AS THE AIRLOCK DOORS SLIDE OPEN, AND SHE INVOKES HER FAVORED PATRONS ATHENA AND ARTEMIS IN FINAL TRIBUTE AND PRAYER.
HER NAME IS HIPPOLYTA, AND FOR OVER THREE THOUSAND YEARS, SHE WAS THE QUEEN OF PARADISE ISLAND.
NOW, ARMED WITH THE GIFTS OF HER GODS AND THE UNCONQUERABLE SPIRIT GIVEN TO HER BY GAEA, THE EARTH ITSELF...
...SHE'S GOING TO HELP SAVE THE UNIVERSE.
IMPERIEX

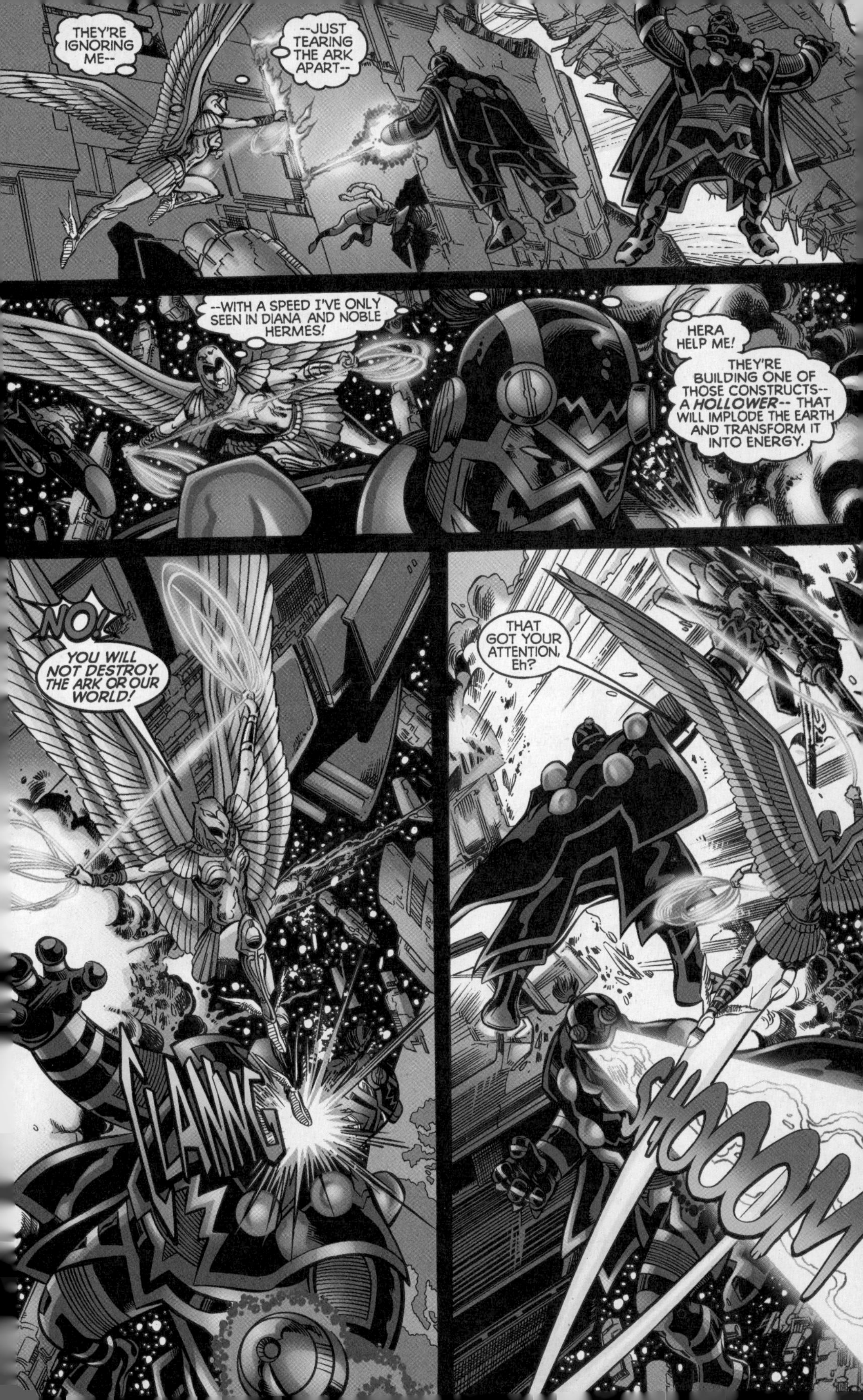
THEY'RE IGNORING ME--
--JUST TEARING THE ARK APART--
--WITH A SPEED I'VE ONLY SEEN IN DIANA AND NOBLE HERMES!
HERA HELP ME!
THEY'RE BUILDING ONE OF THOSE CONSTRUCTS-- A HOLLOWER-- THAT WILL IMPLODE THE EARTH AND TRANSFORM IT INTO ENERGY.
NO!
YOU WILL NOT DESTROY THE ARK OR OUR WORLD!
CLANNG
THAT GOT YOUR ATTENTION, Eh?
SHOOOM

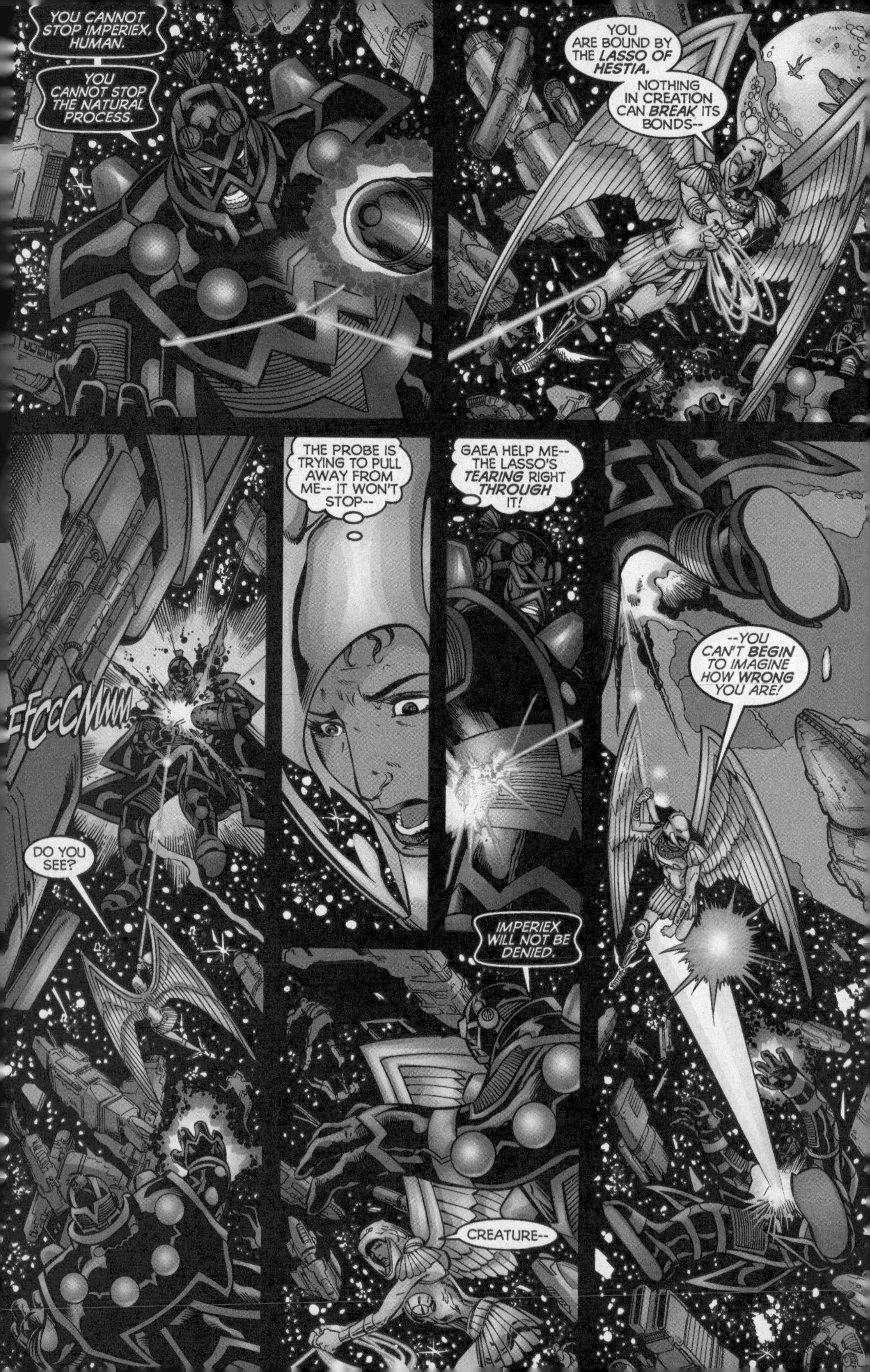
YOU CANNOT STOP IMPERIEX, HUMAN.
YOU CANNOT STOP THE NATURAL PROCESS.
YOU ARE BOUND BY THE LASSO OF HESTIA.
NOTHING IN CREATION CAN BREAK ITS BONDS--
FFCCCMMM
DO YOU SEE?
THE PROBE IS TRYING TO PULL AWAY FROM ME-- IT WON'T STOP--
GAEA HELP ME-- THE LASSO'S TEARING RIGHT THROUGH IT!
IMPERIEX WILL NOT BE DENIED.
CREATURE--
--YOU CAN'T BEGIN TO IMAGINE HOW WRONG YOU ARE!

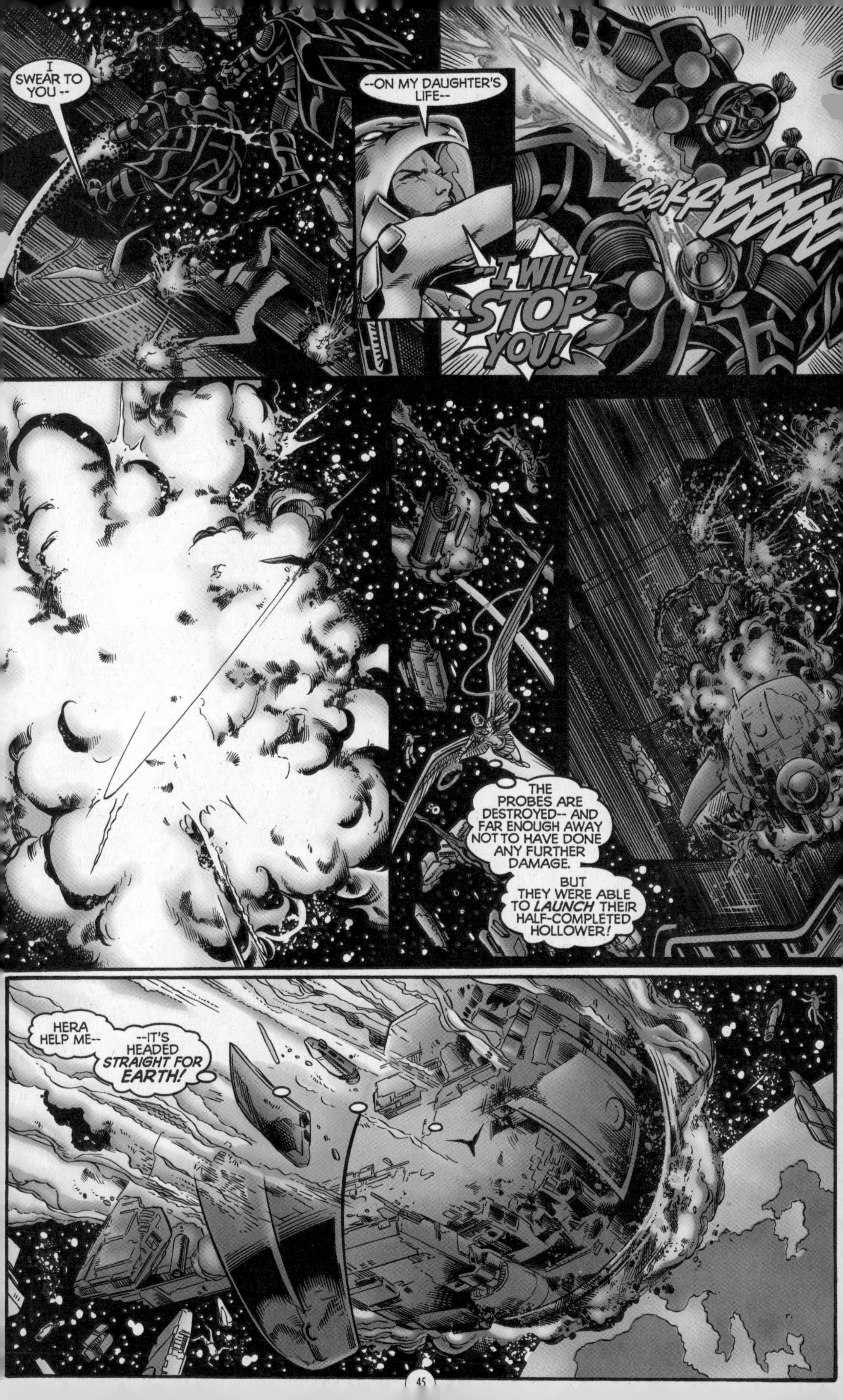
I SWEAR TO YOU --
--ON MY DAUGHTER'S LIFE--
--I WILL STOP YOU!
SSKREEEEE
THE PROBES ARE DESTROYED-- AND FAR ENOUGH AWAY NOT TO HAVE DONE ANY FURTHER DAMAGE.
BUT THEY WERE ABLE TO *LAUNCH* THEIR HALF-COMPLETED HOLLOWER!
HERA HELP ME--
--IT'S HEADED *STRAIGHT FOR EARTH!*

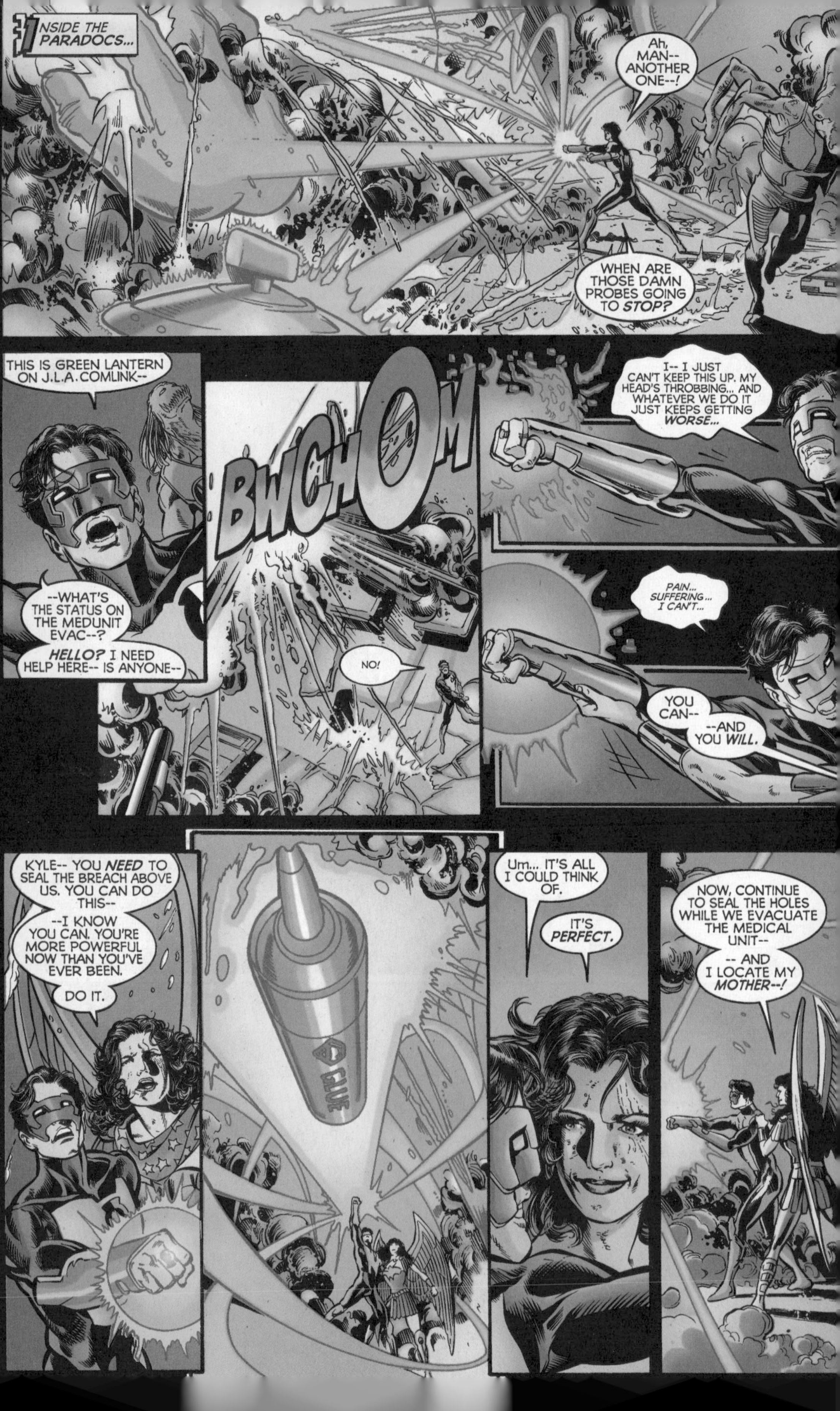
INSIDE THE PARADOCS...
Ah, MAN-- ANOTHER ONE--!
WHEN ARE THOSE DAMN PROBES GOING TO STOP?
THIS IS GREEN LANTERN ON J.L.A. COMLINK--
--WHAT'S THE STATUS ON THE MEDUNIT EVAC--?
HELLO? I NEED HELP HERE-- IS ANYONE--
BWCHOOM
NO!
I-- I JUST CAN'T KEEP THIS UP. MY HEAD'S THROBBING... AND WHATEVER WE DO IT JUST KEEPS GETTING WORSE...
PAIN... SUFFERING... I CAN'T...
YOU CAN--
--AND YOU WILL.
KYLE-- YOU NEED TO SEAL THE BREACH ABOVE US. YOU CAN DO THIS--
--I KNOW YOU CAN. YOU'RE MORE POWERFUL NOW THAN YOU'VE EVER BEEN.
DO IT.
GLUE
Um... IT'S ALL I COULD THINK OF.
IT'S PERFECT.
NOW, CONTINUE TO SEAL THE HOLES WHILE WE EVACUATE THE MEDICAL UNIT--
-- AND I LOCATE MY MOTHER--!

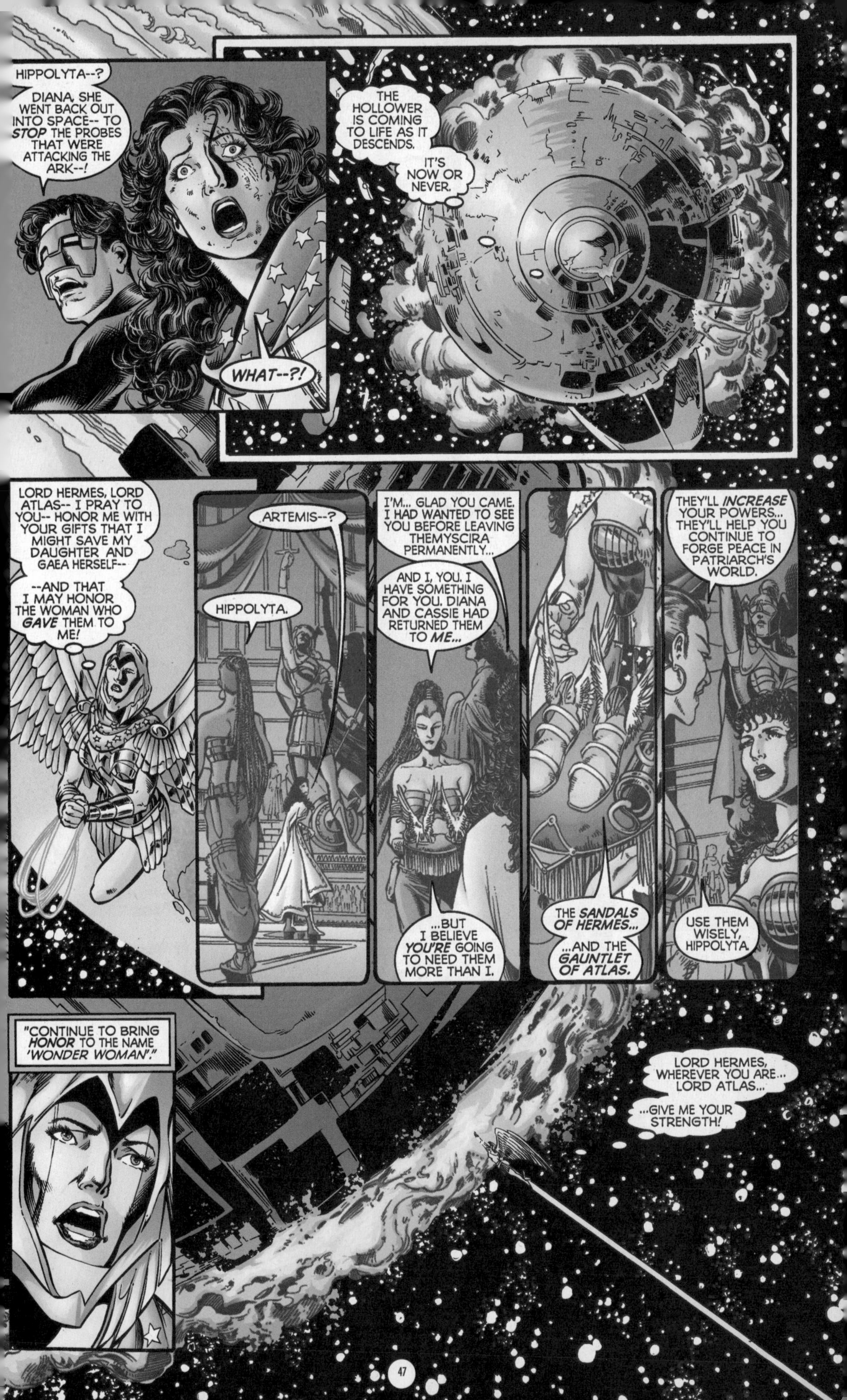
HIPPOLYTA--?
DIANA, SHE WENT BACK OUT INTO SPACE-- TO STOP THE PROBES THAT WERE ATTACKING THE ARK--!
WHAT--?!
THE HOLLOWER IS COMING TO LIFE AS IT DESCENDS.
IT'S NOW OR NEVER.
LORD HERMES, LORD ATLAS-- I PRAY TO YOU-- HONOR ME WITH YOUR GIFTS THAT I MIGHT SAVE MY DAUGHTER AND GAEA HERSELF--
--AND THAT I MAY HONOR THE WOMAN WHO GAVE THEM TO ME!
ARTEMIS--?
HIPPOLYTA.
I'M... GLAD YOU CAME. I HAD WANTED TO SEE YOU BEFORE LEAVING THEMYSCIRA PERMANENTLY...
AND I, YOU. I HAVE SOMETHING FOR YOU. DIANA AND CASSIE HAD RETURNED THEM TO ME...
...BUT I BELIEVE YOU'RE GOING TO NEED THEM MORE THAN I.
THE SANDALS OF HERMES...
...AND THE GAUNTLET OF ATLAS.
THEY'LL INCREASE YOUR POWERS... THEY'LL HELP YOU CONTINUE TO FORGE PEACE IN PATRIARCH'S WORLD.
USE THEM WISELY, HIPPOLYTA.
"CONTINUE TO BRING HONOR TO THE NAME 'WONDER WOMAN'."
LORD HERMES, WHEREVER YOU ARE... LORD ATLAS...
...GIVE ME YOUR STRENGTH!

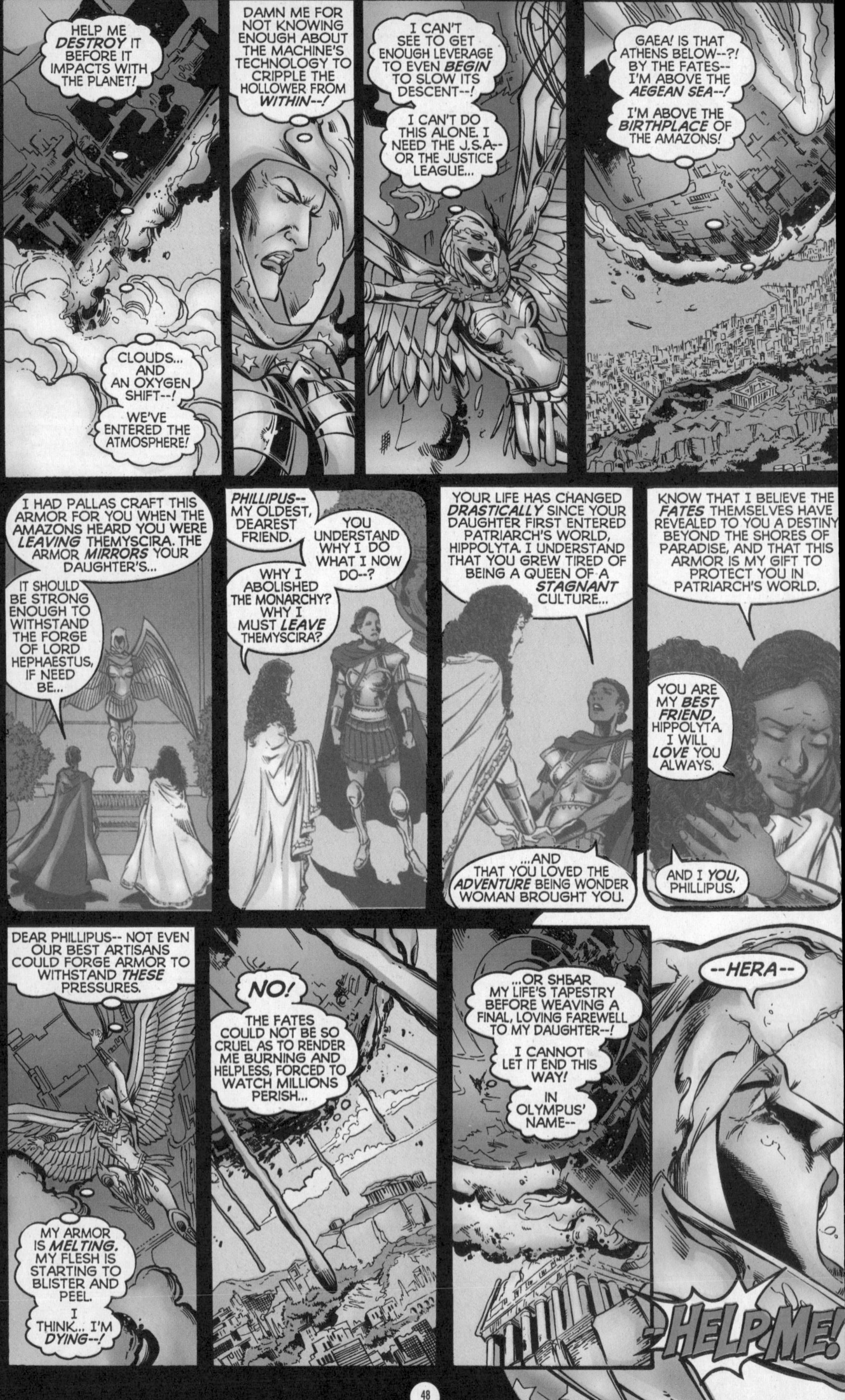

HELP ME *DESTROY* IT BEFORE IT IMPACTS WITH THE PLANET!
CLOUDS... AND AN OXYGEN SHIFT--!
WE'VE ENTERED THE ATMOSPHERE!
DAMN ME FOR NOT KNOWING ENOUGH ABOUT THE MACHINE'S TECHNOLOGY TO CRIPPLE THE HOLLOWER FROM *WITHIN*--!
I CAN'T SEE TO GET ENOUGH LEVERAGE TO EVEN *BEGIN* TO SLOW ITS DESCENT--!
I CAN'T DO THIS ALONE. I NEED THE J.S.A.-- OR THE JUSTICE LEAGUE...
GAEA! IS THAT ATHENS BELOW--?! BY THE FATES-- I'M ABOVE THE *AEGEAN SEA*--!
I'M ABOVE THE *BIRTHPLACE* OF THE AMAZONS!
I HAD PALLAS CRAFT THIS ARMOR FOR YOU WHEN THE AMAZONS HEARD YOU WERE *LEAVING* THEMYSCIRA. THE ARMOR *MIRRORS* YOUR DAUGHTER'S...
IT SHOULD BE STRONG ENOUGH TO WITHSTAND THE FORGE OF LORD HEPHAESTUS, IF NEED BE...
PHILLIPUS-- MY OLDEST, DEAREST FRIEND.
YOU UNDERSTAND WHY I DO WHAT I NOW DO--?
WHY I ABOLISHED THE MONARCHY? WHY I MUST *LEAVE* THEMYSCIRA?
YOUR LIFE HAS CHANGED *DRASTICALLY* SINCE YOUR DAUGHTER FIRST ENTERED PATRIARCH'S WORLD, HIPPOLYTA. I UNDERSTAND THAT YOU GREW TIRED OF BEING A QUEEN OF A *STAGNANT* CULTURE...
...AND THAT YOU LOVED THE *ADVENTURE* BEING WONDER WOMAN BROUGHT YOU.
KNOW THAT I BELIEVE THE *FATES* THEMSELVES HAVE REVEALED TO YOU A DESTINY BEYOND THE SHORES OF PARADISE, AND THAT THIS ARMOR IS MY GIFT TO PROTECT YOU IN PATRIARCH'S WORLD.
YOU ARE MY *BEST FRIEND*, HIPPOLYTA. I WILL *LOVE* YOU ALWAYS.
AND I *YOU*, PHILLIPUS.
DEAR PHILLIPUS-- NOT EVEN OUR BEST ARTISANS COULD FORGE ARMOR TO WITHSTAND *THESE* PRESSURES.
MY ARMOR IS *MELTING*. MY FLESH IS STARTING TO BLISTER AND PEEL.
I THINK... I'M *DYING*--!
NO!
THE FATES COULD NOT BE SO CRUEL AS TO RENDER ME BURNING AND HELPLESS, FORCED TO WATCH MILLIONS PERISH...
...OR SHEAR MY LIFE'S TAPESTRY BEFORE WEAVING A FINAL, LOVING FAREWELL TO MY DAUGHTER--!
I CANNOT LET IT END THIS WAY!
IN OLYMPUS' NAME--
--HERA--
--HELP ME!

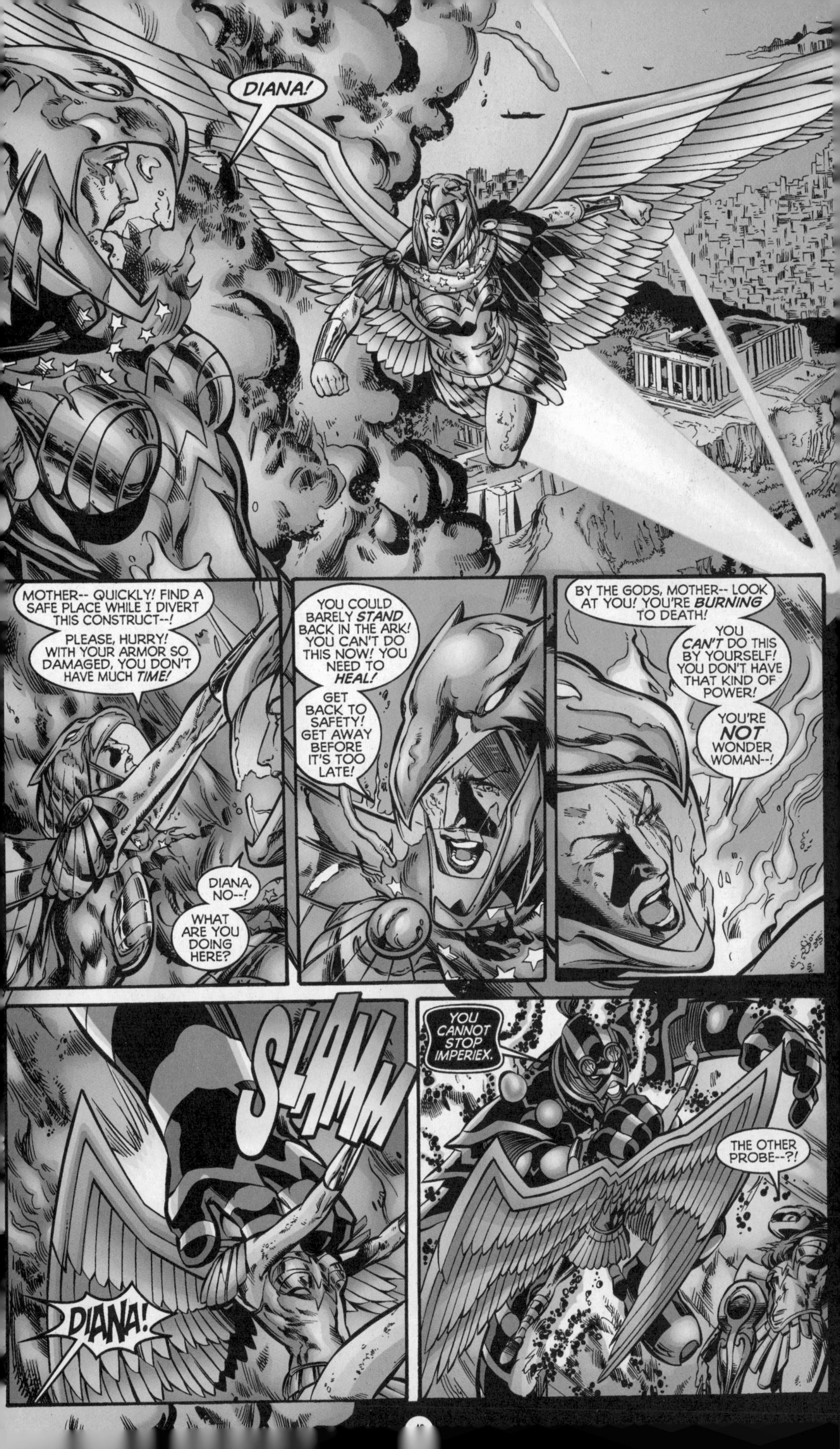
DIANA!
MOTHER-- QUICKLY! FIND A SAFE PLACE WHILE I DIVERT THIS CONSTRUCT--!
PLEASE, HURRY! WITH YOUR ARMOR SO DAMAGED, YOU DON'T HAVE MUCH TIME!
DIANA, NO--!
WHAT ARE YOU DOING HERE?
YOU COULD BARELY STAND BACK IN THE ARK! YOU CAN'T DO THIS NOW! YOU NEED TO HEAL!
GET BACK TO SAFETY! GET AWAY BEFORE IT'S TOO LATE!
BY THE GODS, MOTHER-- LOOK AT YOU! YOU'RE BURNING TO DEATH!
YOU CAN'T DO THIS BY YOURSELF! YOU DON'T HAVE THAT KIND OF POWER!
YOU'RE NOT WONDER WOMAN--!
SLAMM
DIANA!
YOU CANNOT STOP IMPERIEX.
THE OTHER PROBE--?!

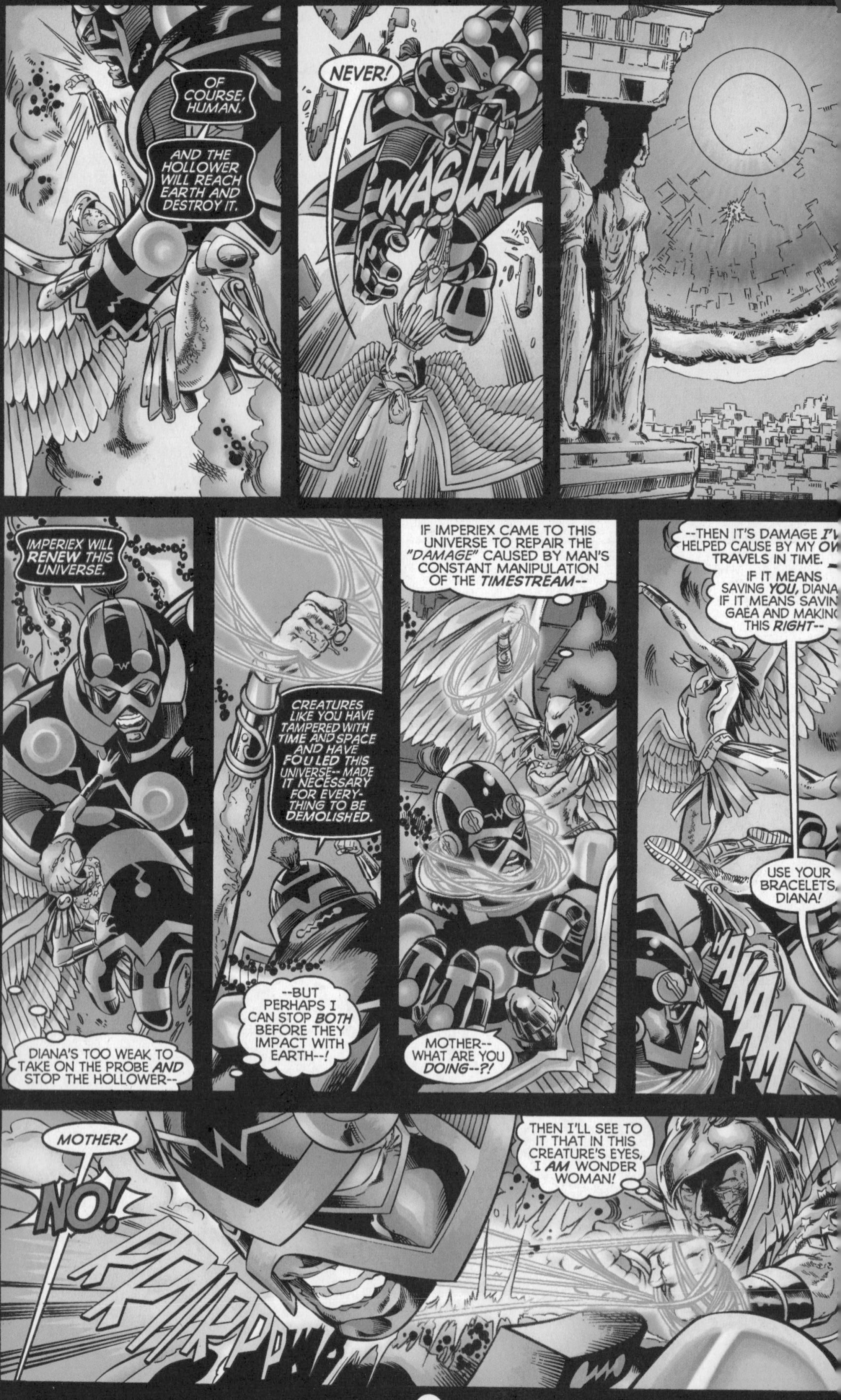

OF COURSE, HUMAN.
AND THE HOLLOWER WILL REACH EARTH AND DESTROY IT.
NEVER!
WASLAM
IMPERIEX WILL RENEW THIS UNIVERSE.
DIANA'S TOO WEAK TO TAKE ON THE PROBE AND STOP THE HOLLOWER--
CREATURES LIKE YOU HAVE TAMPERED WITH TIME AND SPACE AND HAVE FOULED THIS UNIVERSE-- MADE IT NECESSARY FOR EVERYTHING TO BE DEMOLISHED.
--BUT PERHAPS I CAN STOP BOTH BEFORE THEY IMPACT WITH EARTH--!
IF IMPERIEX CAME TO THIS UNIVERSE TO REPAIR THE "DAMAGE" CAUSED BY MAN'S CONSTANT MANIPULATION OF THE TIMESTREAM--
MOTHER-- WHAT ARE YOU DOING--?!
--THEN IT'S DAMAGE I'VE HELPED CAUSE BY MY OWN TRAVELS IN TIME.
IF IT MEANS SAVING YOU, DIANA IF IT MEANS SAVING GAEA AND MAKING THIS RIGHT--
USE YOUR BRACELETS, DIANA!
WAKAM
MOTHER!
NO!
THEN I'LL SEE TO IT THAT IN THIS CREATURE'S EYES, I AM WONDER WOMAN!

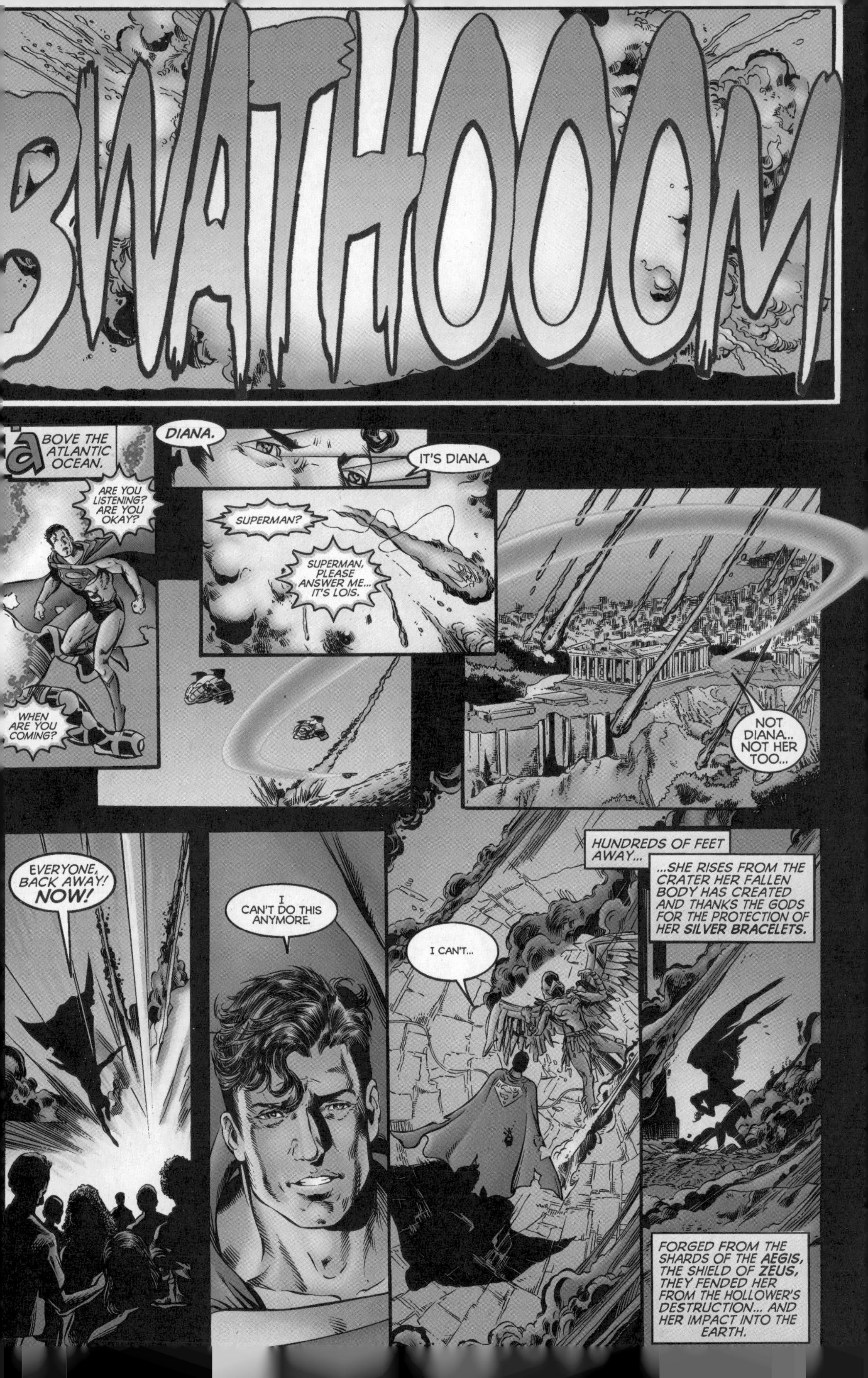
BWATHOOOM
ABOVE THE ATLANTIC OCEAN.
DIANA.
IT'S DIANA.
ARE YOU LISTENING? ARE YOU OKAY?
SUPERMAN?
SUPERMAN, PLEASE ANSWER ME... IT'S LOIS.
WHEN ARE YOU COMING?
NOT DIANA... NOT HER TOO...
EVERYONE, BACK AWAY! NOW!
I CAN'T DO THIS ANYMORE.
HUNDREDS OF FEET AWAY...
...SHE RISES FROM THE CRATER HER FALLEN BODY HAS CREATED AND THANKS THE GODS FOR THE PROTECTION OF HER SILVER BRACELETS.
I CAN'T...
FORGED FROM THE SHARDS OF THE AEGIS, THE SHIELD OF ZEUS, THEY FENDED HER FROM THE HOLLOWER'S DESTRUCTION... AND HER IMPACT INTO THE EARTH.

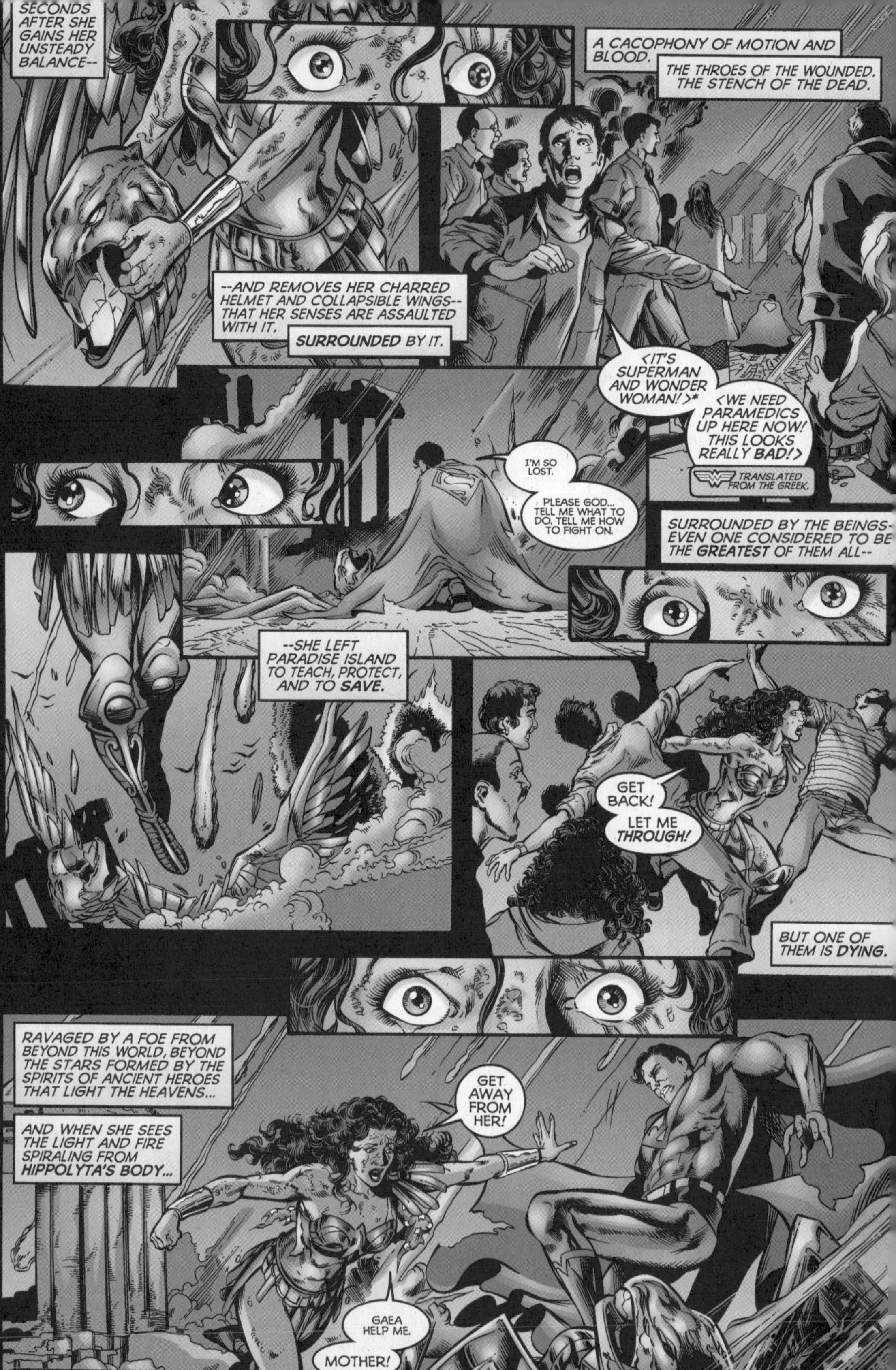

SECONDS AFTER SHE GAINS HER UNSTEADY BALANCE--
--AND REMOVES HER CHARRED HELMET AND COLLAPSIBLE WINGS--THAT HER SENSES ARE ASSAULTED WITH IT.
SURROUNDED BY IT.
A CACOPHONY OF MOTION AND BLOOD.
THE THROES OF THE WOUNDED. THE STENCH OF THE DEAD.
<IT'S SUPERMAN AND WONDER WOMAN!>*
<WE NEED PARAMEDICS UP HERE NOW! THIS LOOKS REALLY BAD!>
*TRANSLATED FROM THE GREEK.
I'M SO LOST.
PLEASE GOD... TELL ME WHAT TO DO. TELL ME HOW TO FIGHT ON.
SURROUNDED BY THE BEINGS-EVEN ONE CONSIDERED TO BE THE GREATEST OF THEM ALL--
--SHE LEFT PARADISE ISLAND TO TEACH, PROTECT, AND TO SAVE.
GET BACK!
LET ME THROUGH!
BUT ONE OF THEM IS DYING.
RAVAGED BY A FOE FROM BEYOND THIS WORLD, BEYOND THE STARS FORMED BY THE SPIRITS OF ANCIENT HEROES THAT LIGHT THE HEAVENS...
AND WHEN SHE SEES THE LIGHT AND FIRE SPIRALING FROM HIPPOLYTA'S BODY...
GET AWAY FROM HER!
GAEA HELP ME.
MOTHER!
...DIANA FEARS ONLY THE WORST.

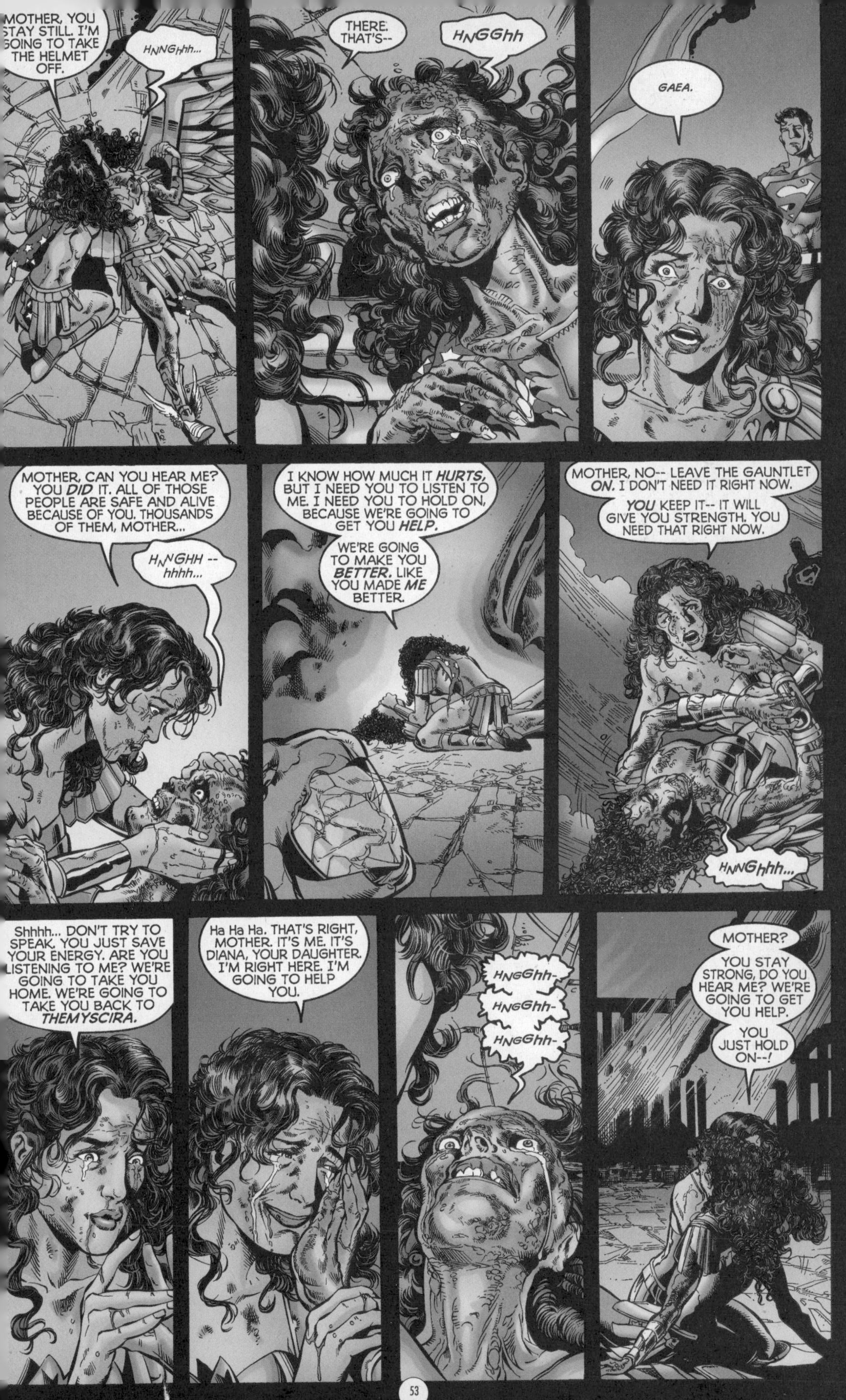
MOTHER, YOU STAY STILL. I'M GOING TO TAKE THE HELMET OFF.
HNNGhhh...
THERE. THAT'S--
HNGGhh
GAEA.
MOTHER, CAN YOU HEAR ME? YOU DID IT. ALL OF THOSE PEOPLE ARE SAFE AND ALIVE BECAUSE OF YOU. THOUSANDS OF THEM, MOTHER...
HNNGHH -- hhhh...
I KNOW HOW MUCH IT HURTS, BUT I NEED YOU TO LISTEN TO ME. I NEED YOU TO HOLD ON, BECAUSE WE'RE GOING TO GET YOU HELP.
WE'RE GOING TO MAKE YOU BETTER. LIKE YOU MADE ME BETTER.
MOTHER, NO-- LEAVE THE GAUNTLET ON. I DON'T NEED IT RIGHT NOW.
YOU KEEP IT-- IT WILL GIVE YOU STRENGTH. YOU NEED THAT RIGHT NOW.
HNNGhhh...
Shhhh... DON'T TRY TO SPEAK. YOU JUST SAVE YOUR ENERGY. ARE YOU LISTENING TO ME? WE'RE GOING TO TAKE YOU HOME. WE'RE GOING TO TAKE YOU BACK TO THEMYSCIRA.
Ha Ha Ha. THAT'S RIGHT, MOTHER. IT'S ME. IT'S DIANA, YOUR DAUGHTER. I'M RIGHT HERE. I'M GOING TO HELP YOU.
HNGGhh-
HNGGhh-
HNGGhh-
MOTHER?
YOU STAY STRONG, DO YOU HEAR ME? WE'RE GOING TO GET YOU HELP.
YOU JUST HOLD ON--!

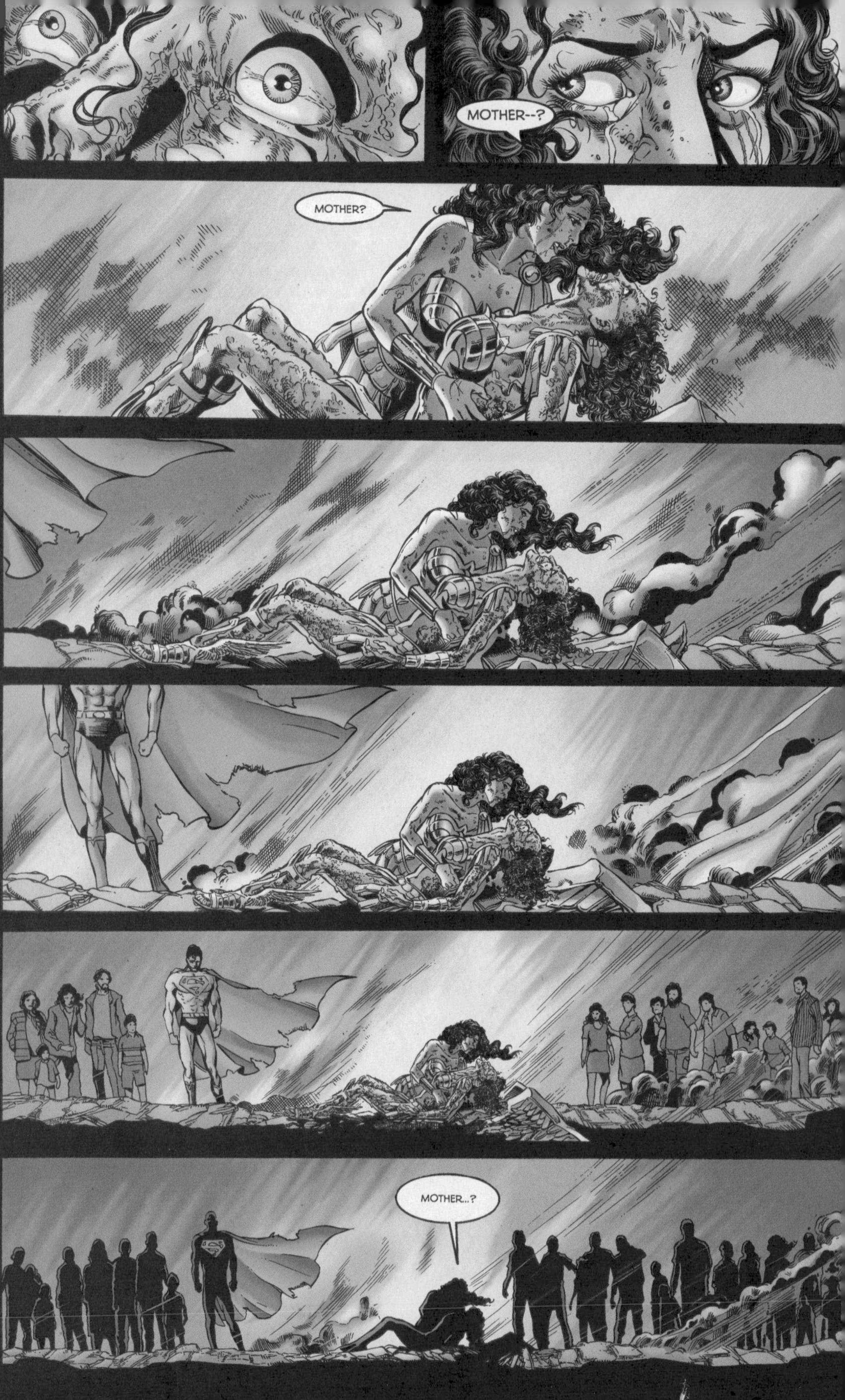
MOTHER--?
MOTHER?
MOTHER...?

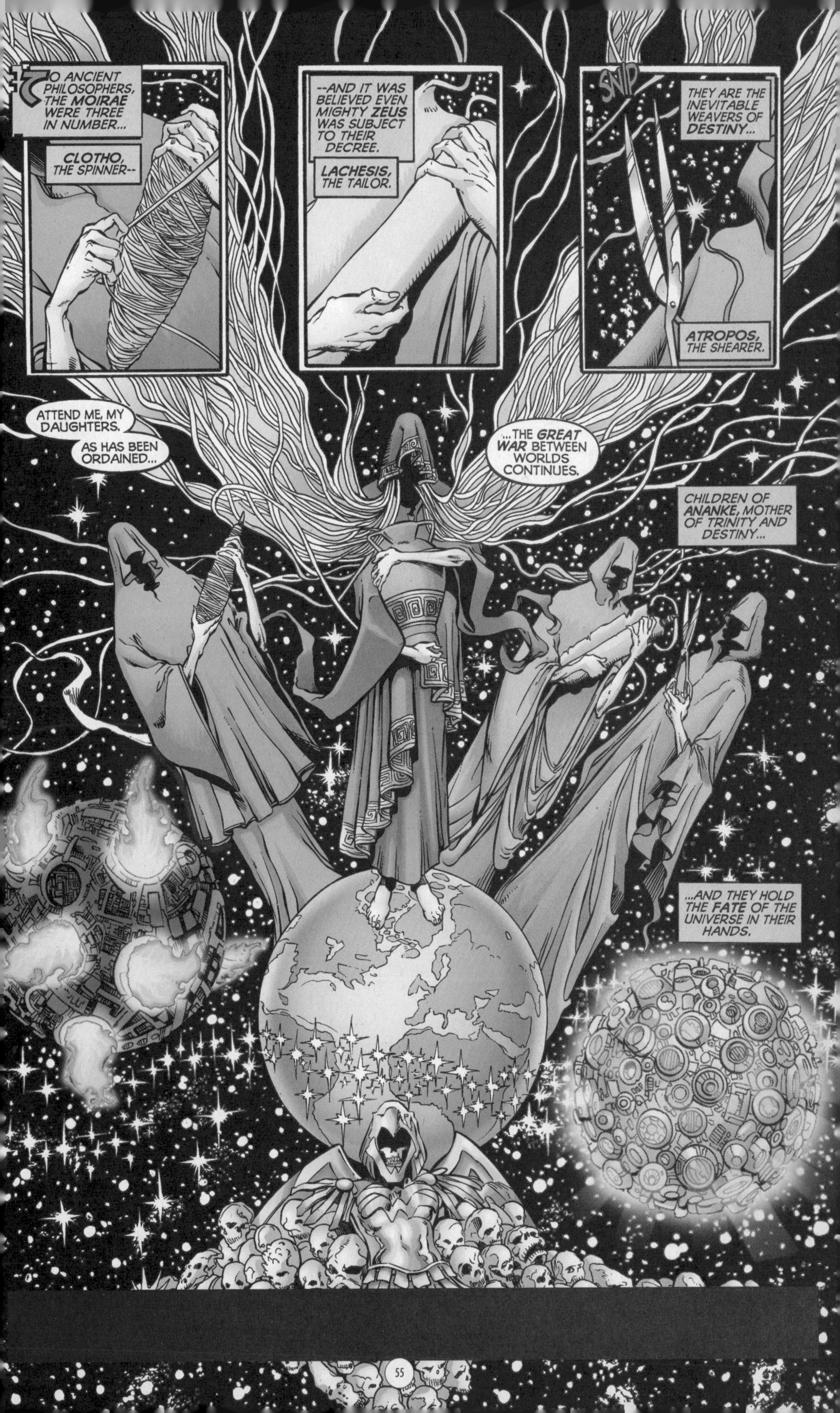
TO ANCIENT PHILOSOPHERS, THE MOIRAE WERE THREE IN NUMBER...
CLOTHO, THE SPINNER--
--AND IT WAS BELIEVED EVEN MIGHTY ZEUS WAS SUBJECT TO THEIR DECREE.
LACHESIS, THE TAILOR.
SNIP
THEY ARE THE INEVITABLE WEAVERS OF DESTINY...
ATROPOS, THE SHEARER.
ATTEND ME, MY DAUGHTERS.
AS HAS BEEN ORDAINED...
...THE GREAT WAR BETWEEN WORLDS CONTINUES.
CHILDREN OF ANANKE, MOTHER OF TRINITY AND DESTINY...
...AND THEY HOLD THE FATE OF THE UNIVERSE IN THEIR HANDS.
[redacted]

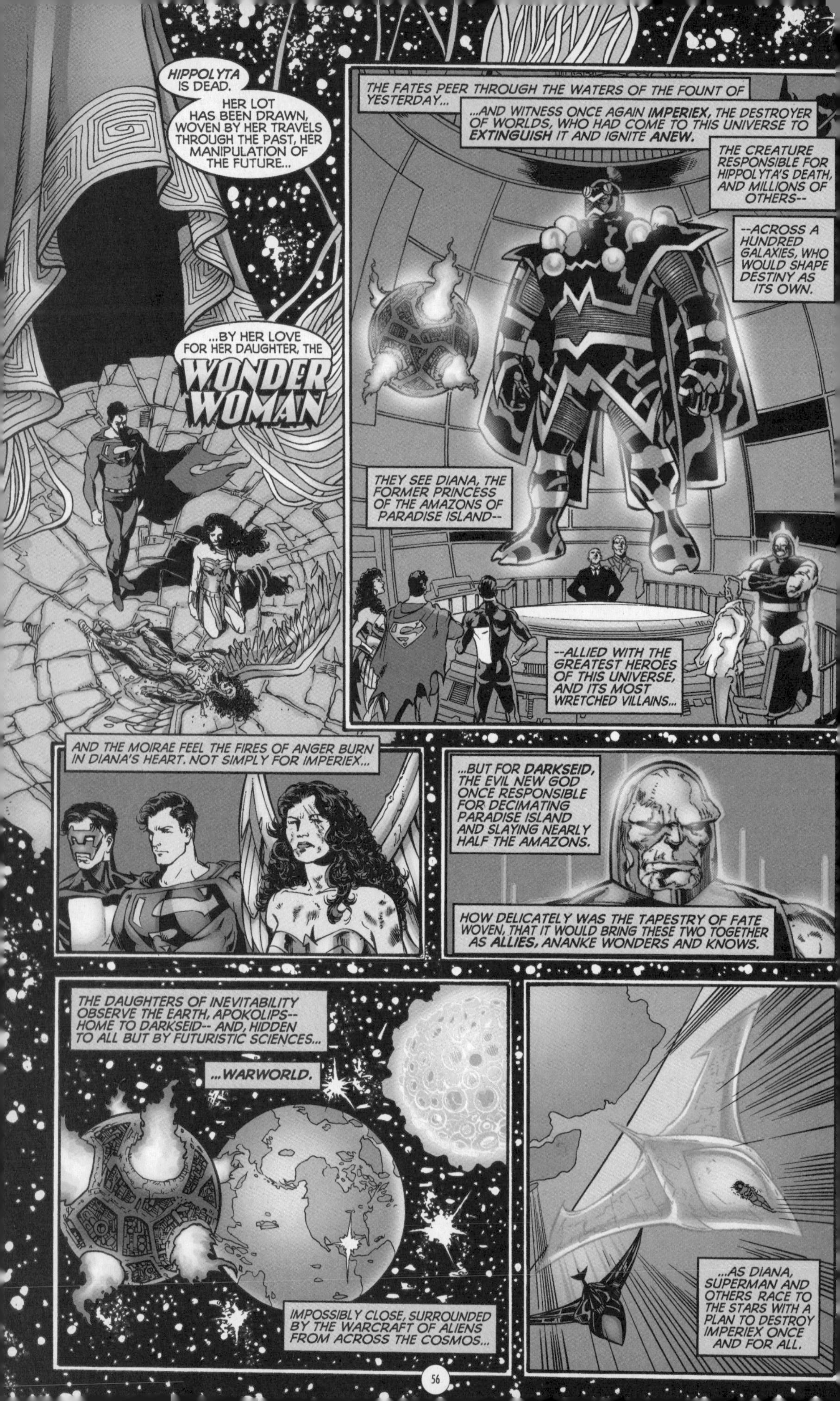
HIPPOLYTA IS DEAD.
HER LOT HAS BEEN DRAWN, WOVEN BY HER TRAVELS THROUGH THE PAST, HER MANIPULATION OF THE FUTURE...
...BY HER LOVE FOR HER DAUGHTER, THE
WONDER WOMAN
THE FATES PEER THROUGH THE WATERS OF THE FOUNT OF YESTERDAY...
...AND WITNESS ONCE AGAIN IMPERIEX, THE DESTROYER OF WORLDS, WHO HAD COME TO THIS UNIVERSE TO EXTINGUISH IT AND IGNITE ANEW.
THE CREATURE RESPONSIBLE FOR HIPPOLYTA'S DEATH, AND MILLIONS OF OTHERS--
--ACROSS A HUNDRED GALAXIES, WHO WOULD SHAPE DESTINY AS ITS OWN.
THEY SEE DIANA, THE FORMER PRINCESS OF THE AMAZONS OF PARADISE ISLAND--
--ALLIED WITH THE GREATEST HEROES OF THIS UNIVERSE, AND ITS MOST WRETCHED VILLAINS...
AND THE MOIRAE FEEL THE FIRES OF ANGER BURN IN DIANA'S HEART. NOT SIMPLY FOR IMPERIEX...
...BUT FOR DARKSEID, THE EVIL NEW GOD ONCE RESPONSIBLE FOR DECIMATING PARADISE ISLAND AND SLAYING NEARLY HALF THE AMAZONS.
HOW DELICATELY WAS THE TAPESTRY OF FATE WOVEN, THAT IT WOULD BRING THESE TWO TOGETHER AS ALLIES, ANANKE WONDERS AND KNOWS.
THE DAUGHTERS OF INEVITABILITY OBSERVE THE EARTH, APOKOLIPS-- HOME TO DARKSEID-- AND, HIDDEN TO ALL BUT BY FUTURISTIC SCIENCES...
...WARWORLD.
IMPOSSIBLY CLOSE, SURROUNDED BY THE WARCRAFT OF ALIENS FROM ACROSS THE COSMOS...
...AS DIANA, SUPERMAN AND OTHERS RACE TO THE STARS WITH A PLAN TO DESTROY IMPERIEX ONCE AND FOR ALL.

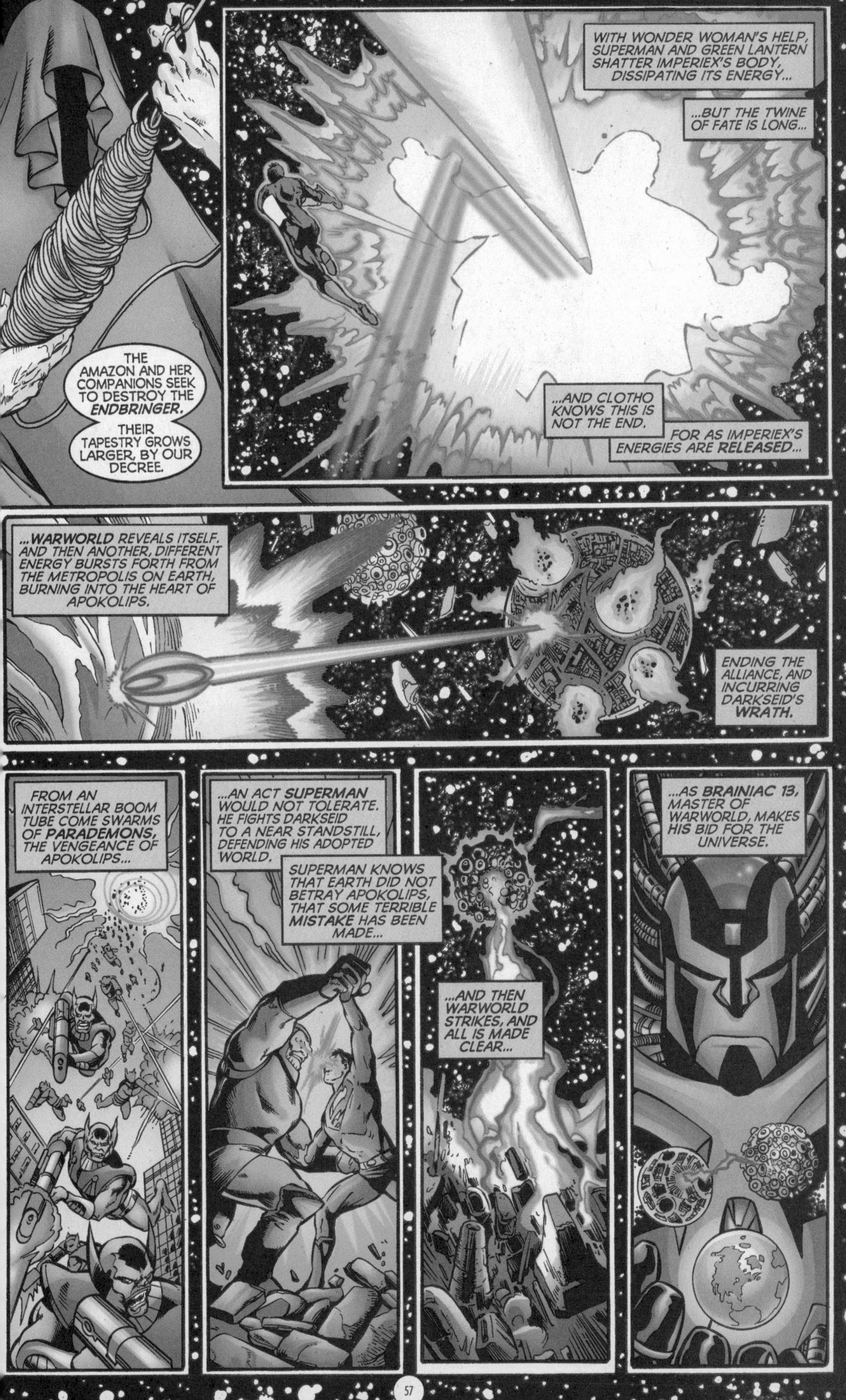
THE AMAZON AND HER COMPANIONS SEEK TO DESTROY THE ENDBRINGER.
THEIR TAPESTRY GROWS LARGER, BY OUR DECREE.
WITH WONDER WOMAN'S HELP, SUPERMAN AND GREEN LANTERN SHATTER IMPERIEX'S BODY, DISSIPATING ITS ENERGY...
...BUT THE TWINE OF FATE IS LONG...
...AND CLOTHO KNOWS THIS IS NOT THE END.
FOR AS IMPERIEX'S ENERGIES ARE RELEASED...
...WARWORLD REVEALS ITSELF, AND THEN ANOTHER, DIFFERENT ENERGY BURSTS FORTH FROM THE METROPOLIS ON EARTH, BURNING INTO THE HEART OF APOKOLIPS.
ENDING THE ALLIANCE, AND INCURRING DARKSEID'S WRATH.
FROM AN INTERSTELLAR BOOM TUBE COME SWARMS OF PARADEMONS, THE VENGEANCE OF APOKOLIPS...
...AN ACT SUPERMAN WOULD NOT TOLERATE. HE FIGHTS DARKSEID TO A NEAR STANDSTILL, DEFENDING HIS ADOPTED WORLD.
SUPERMAN KNOWS THAT EARTH DID NOT BETRAY APOKOLIPS, THAT SOME TERRIBLE MISTAKE HAS BEEN MADE...
...AND THEN WARWORLD STRIKES, AND ALL IS MADE CLEAR...
...AS BRAINIAC 13, MASTER OF WARWORLD, MAKES HIS BID FOR THE UNIVERSE.

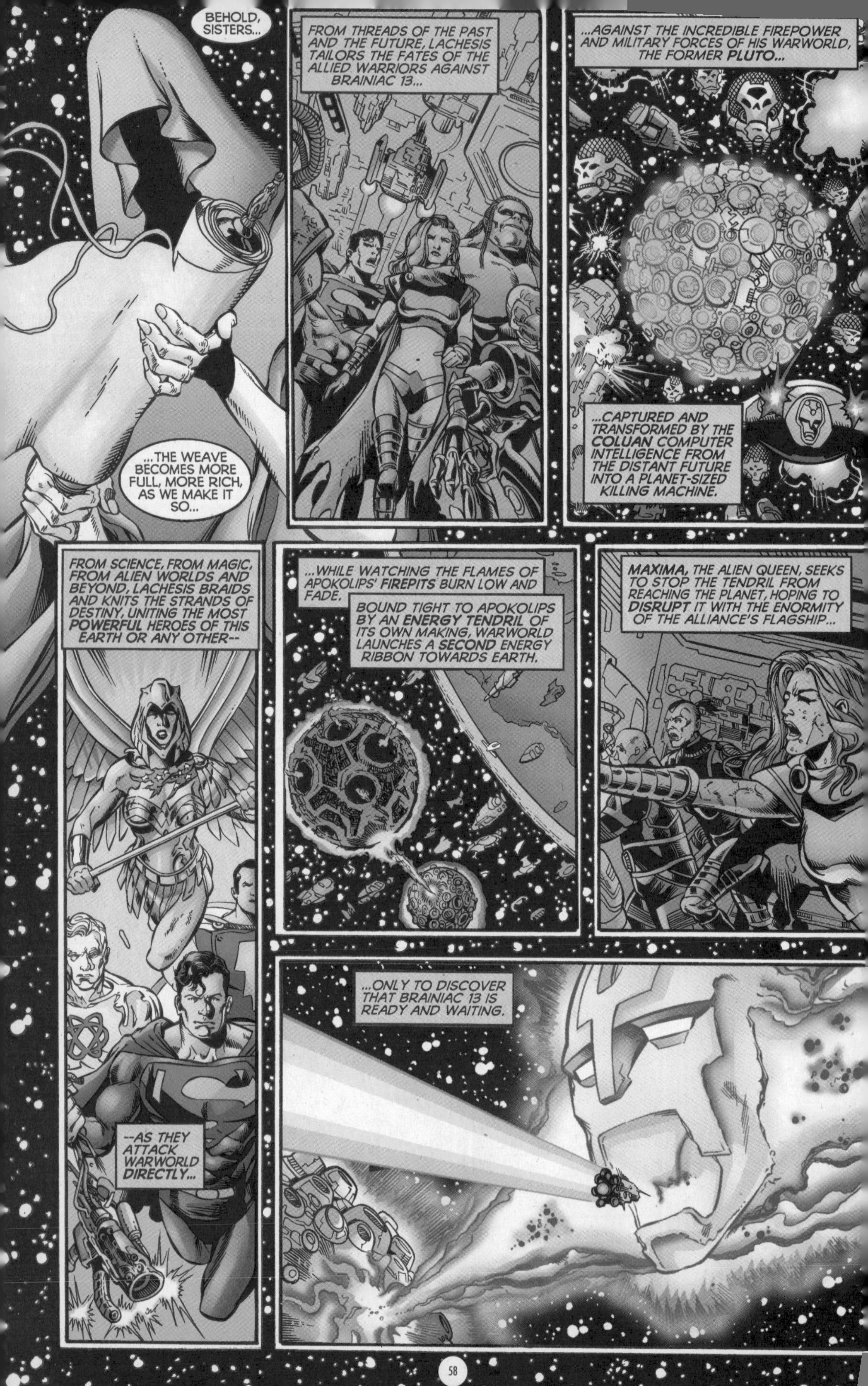
BEHOLD, SISTERS...
FROM THREADS OF THE PAST AND THE FUTURE, LACHESIS TAILORS THE FATES OF THE ALLIED WARRIORS AGAINST BRAINIAC 13...
...AGAINST THE INCREDIBLE FIREPOWER AND MILITARY FORCES OF HIS WARWORLD, THE FORMER PLUTO...
...CAPTURED AND TRANSFORMED BY THE COLUAN COMPUTER INTELLIGENCE FROM THE DISTANT FUTURE INTO A PLANET-SIZED KILLING MACHINE.
...THE WEAVE BECOMES MORE FULL, MORE RICH, AS WE MAKE IT SO...
FROM SCIENCE, FROM MAGIC, FROM ALIEN WORLDS AND BEYOND, LACHESIS BRAIDS AND KNITS THE STRANDS OF DESTINY, UNITING THE MOST POWERFUL HEROES OF THIS EARTH OR ANY OTHER--
--AS THEY ATTACK WARWORLD DIRECTLY...
...WHILE WATCHING THE FLAMES OF APOKOLIPS' FIREPITS BURN LOW AND FADE.
BOUND TIGHT TO APOKOLIPS BY AN ENERGY TENDRIL OF ITS OWN MAKING, WARWORLD LAUNCHES A SECOND ENERGY RIBBON TOWARDS EARTH.
MAXIMA, THE ALIEN QUEEN, SEEKS TO STOP THE TENDRIL FROM REACHING THE PLANET, HOPING TO DISRUPT IT WITH THE ENORMITY OF THE ALLIANCE'S FLAGSHIP...
...ONLY TO DISCOVER THAT BRAINIAC 13 IS READY AND WAITING.

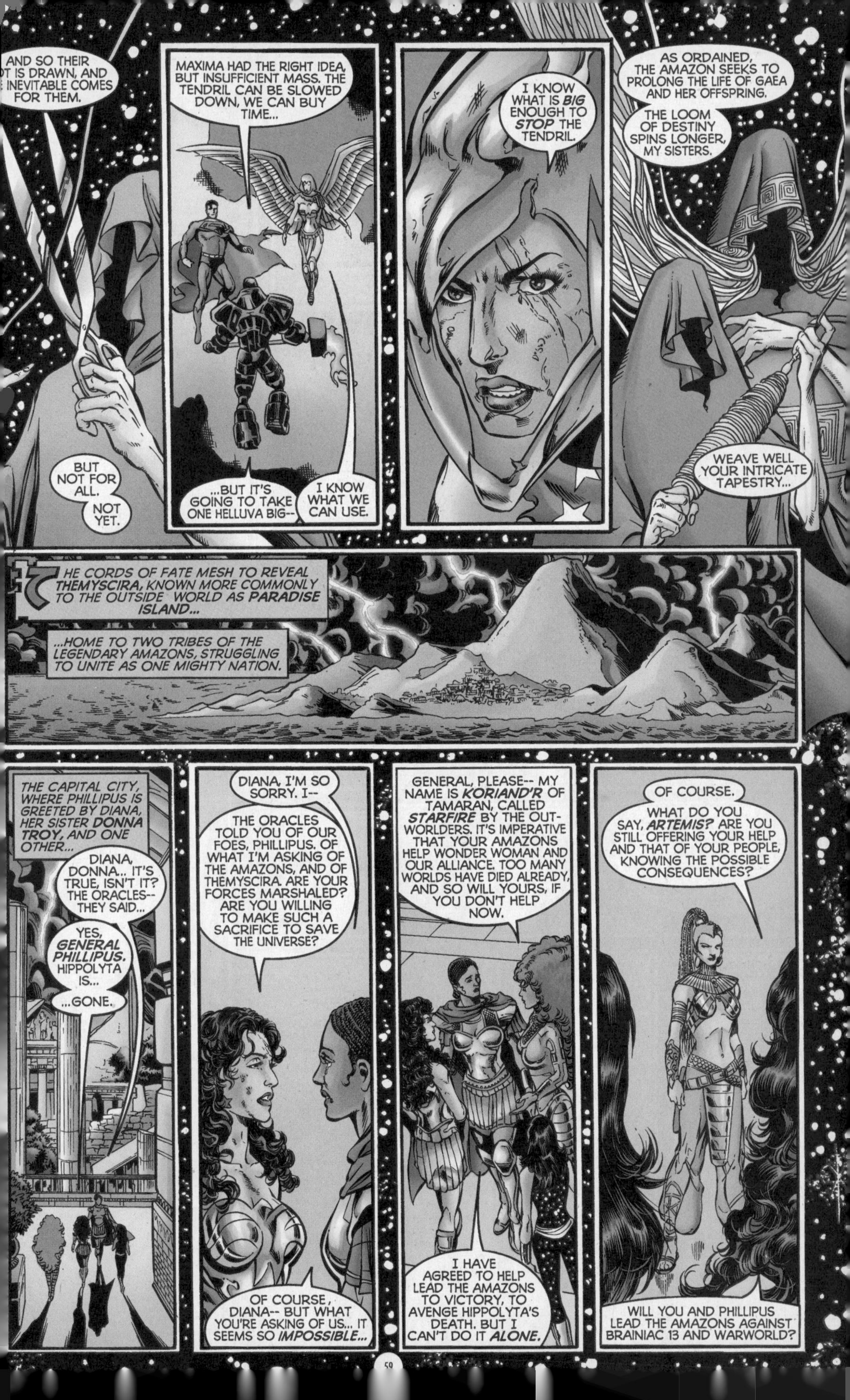
AND SO THEIR
...OT IS DRAWN, AND
...E INEVITABLE COMES FOR THEM.
BUT NOT FOR ALL.
NOT YET.
MAXIMA HAD THE RIGHT IDEA, BUT INSUFFICIENT MASS. THE TENDRIL CAN BE SLOWED DOWN, WE CAN BUY TIME...
...BUT IT'S GOING TO TAKE ONE HELLUVA BIG--
I KNOW WHAT WE CAN USE.
I KNOW WHAT IS BIG ENOUGH TO STOP THE TENDRIL.
AS ORDAINED, THE AMAZON SEEKS TO PROLONG THE LIFE OF GAEA AND HER OFFSPRING.
THE LOOM OF DESTINY SPINS LONGER, MY SISTERS.
WEAVE WELL YOUR INTRICATE TAPESTRY...
THE CORDS OF FATE MESH TO REVEAL THEMYSCIRA, KNOWN MORE COMMONLY TO THE OUTSIDE WORLD AS PARADISE ISLAND...
...HOME TO TWO TRIBES OF THE LEGENDARY AMAZONS, STRUGGLING TO UNITE AS ONE MIGHTY NATION.
THE CAPITAL CITY, WHERE PHILLIPUS IS GREETED BY DIANA, HER SISTER DONNA TROY, AND ONE OTHER...
DIANA, DONNA... IT'S TRUE, ISN'T IT? THE ORACLES-- THEY SAID...
YES, GENERAL PHILLIPUS. HIPPOLYTA IS...
...GONE.
DIANA, I'M SO SORRY. I--
THE ORACLES TOLD YOU OF OUR FOES, PHILLIPUS. OF WHAT I'M ASKING OF THE AMAZONS, AND OF THEMYSCIRA. ARE YOUR FORCES MARSHALED? ARE YOU WILLING TO MAKE SUCH A SACRIFICE TO SAVE THE UNIVERSE?
OF COURSE, DIANA-- BUT WHAT YOU'RE ASKING OF US... IT SEEMS SO IMPOSSIBLE...
GENERAL, PLEASE-- MY NAME IS KORIAND'R OF TAMARAN, CALLED STARFIRE BY THE OUT-WORLDERS. IT'S IMPERATIVE THAT YOUR AMAZONS HELP WONDER WOMAN AND OUR ALLIANCE. TOO MANY WORLDS HAVE DIED ALREADY, AND SO WILL YOURS, IF YOU DON'T HELP NOW.
I HAVE AGREED TO HELP LEAD THE AMAZONS TO VICTORY, TO AVENGE HIPPOLYTA'S DEATH. BUT I CAN'T DO IT ALONE.
OF COURSE.
WHAT DO YOU SAY, ARTEMIS? ARE YOU STILL OFFERING YOUR HELP AND THAT OF YOUR PEOPLE, KNOWING THE POSSIBLE CONSEQUENCES?
WILL YOU AND PHILLIPUS LEAD THE AMAZONS AGAINST BRAINIAC 13 AND WARWORLD?

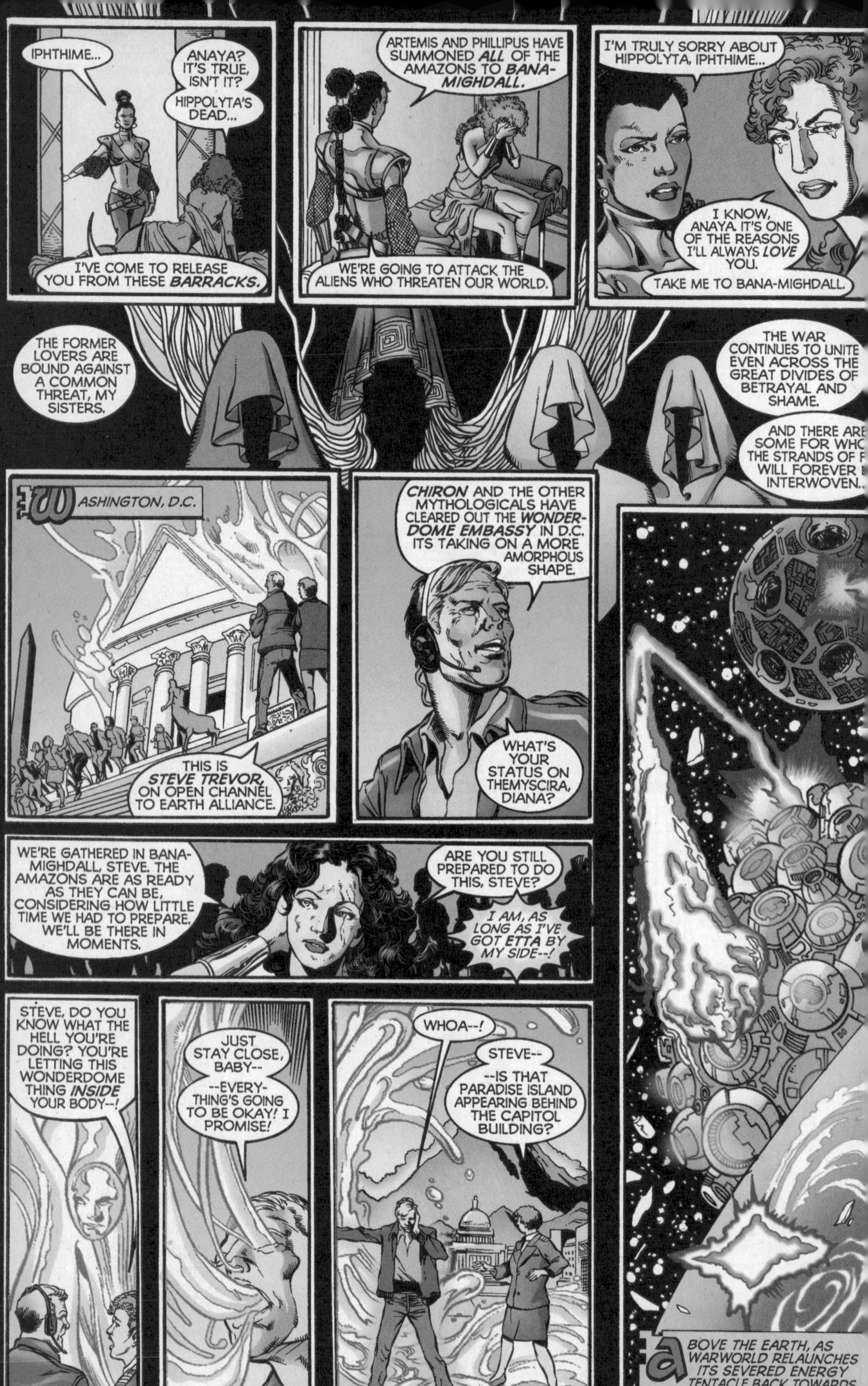
IPHTHIME...
ANAYA? IT'S TRUE, ISN'T IT?
HIPPOLYTA'S DEAD...
I'VE COME TO RELEASE YOU FROM THESE *BARRACKS.*
ARTEMIS AND PHILLIPUS HAVE SUMMONED *ALL* OF THE AMAZONS TO *BANA-MIGHDALL.*
WE'RE GOING TO ATTACK THE ALIENS WHO THREATEN OUR WORLD.
I'M TRULY SORRY ABOUT HIPPOLYTA, IPHTHIME...
I KNOW, ANAYA. IT'S ONE OF THE REASONS I'LL ALWAYS *LOVE* YOU.
TAKE ME TO BANA-MIGHDALL.
THE FORMER LOVERS ARE BOUND AGAINST A COMMON THREAT, MY SISTERS.
THE WAR CONTINUES TO UNITE EVEN ACROSS THE GREAT DIVIDES OF BETRAYAL AND SHAME.
AND THERE ARE SOME FOR WHO THE STRANDS OF F WILL FOREVER INTERWOVEN.
WASHINGTON, D.C.
THIS IS *STEVE TREVOR,* ON OPEN CHANNEL TO EARTH ALLIANCE.
CHIRON AND THE OTHER MYTHOLOGICALS HAVE CLEARED OUT THE *WONDER-DOME EMBASSY* IN D.C. ITS TAKING ON A MORE AMORPHOUS SHAPE.
WHAT'S YOUR STATUS ON THEMYSCIRA, DIANA?
WE'RE GATHERED IN BANA-MIGHDALL, STEVE. THE AMAZONS ARE AS READY AS THEY CAN BE, CONSIDERING HOW LITTLE TIME WE HAD TO PREPARE. WE'LL BE THERE IN MOMENTS.
ARE YOU STILL PREPARED TO DO THIS, STEVE?
I AM, AS LONG AS I'VE GOT ETTA BY MY SIDE--!
STEVE, DO YOU KNOW WHAT THE HELL YOU'RE DOING? YOU'RE LETTING THIS WONDERDOME THING *INSIDE* YOUR BODY--!
JUST STAY CLOSE, BABY--
--EVERY-THING'S GOING TO BE OKAY! I PROMISE!
WHOA--!
STEVE--
--IS THAT PARADISE ISLAND APPEARING BEHIND THE CAPITOL BUILDING?
ABOVE THE EARTH, AS WARWORLD RELAUNCHES ITS SEVERED ENERGY TENTACLE BACK TOWARDS THE BESIEGED PLANET...

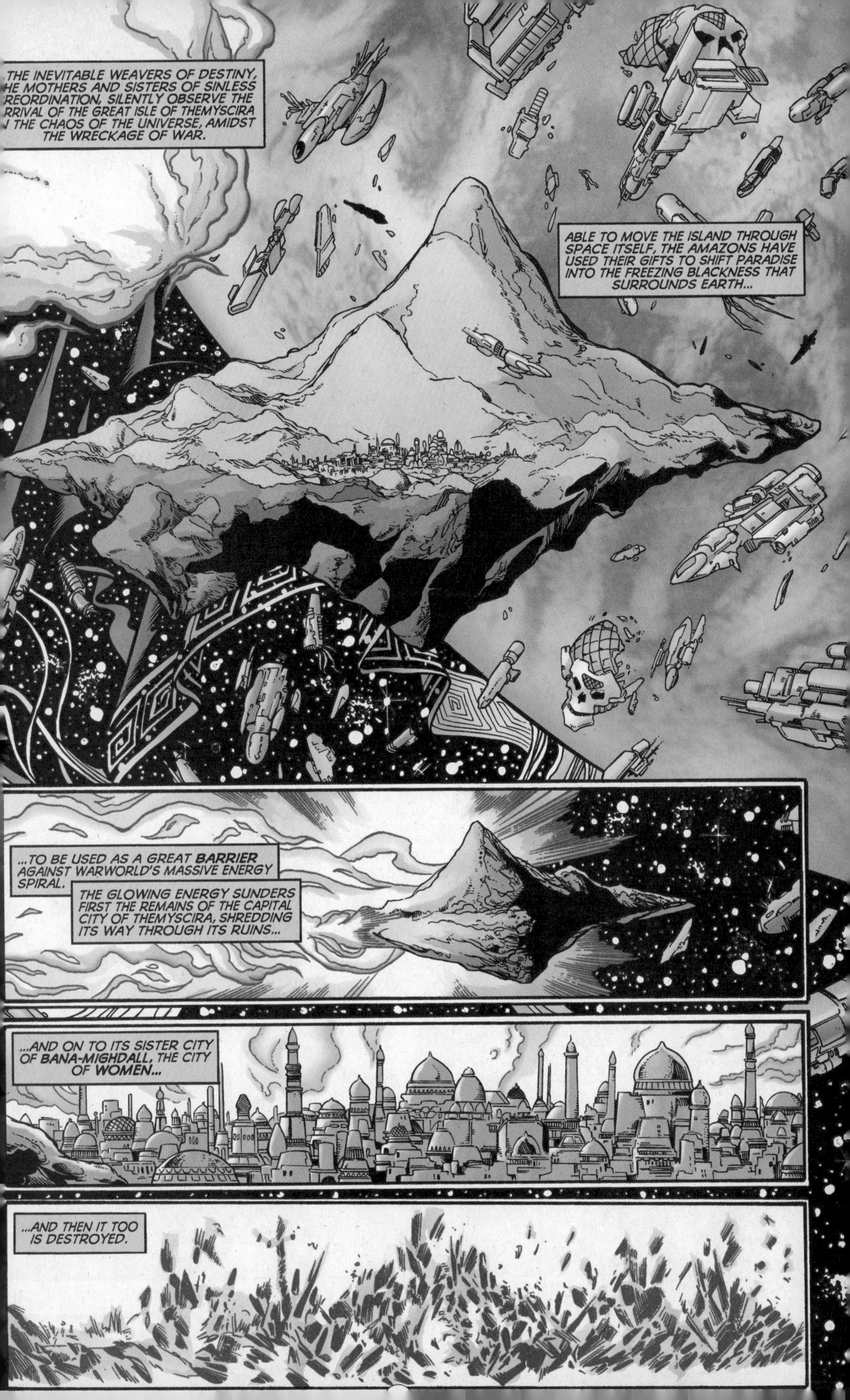
THE INEVITABLE WEAVERS OF DESTINY, HE MOTHERS AND SISTERS OF SINLESS REORDINATION, SILENTLY OBSERVE THE RRIVAL OF THE GREAT ISLE OF THEMYSCIRA N THE CHAOS OF THE UNIVERSE, AMIDST THE WRECKAGE OF WAR.
ABLE TO MOVE THE ISLAND THROUGH SPACE ITSELF, THE AMAZONS HAVE USED THEIR GIFTS TO SHIFT PARADISE INTO THE FREEZING BLACKNESS THAT SURROUNDS EARTH...
...TO BE USED AS A GREAT BARRIER AGAINST WARWORLD'S MASSIVE ENERGY SPIRAL.
THE GLOWING ENERGY SUNDERS FIRST THE REMAINS OF THE CAPITAL CITY OF THEMYSCIRA, SHREDDING ITS WAY THROUGH ITS RUINS...
...AND ON TO ITS SISTER CITY OF BANA-MIGHDALL, THE CITY OF WOMEN...
...AND THEN IT TOO IS DESTROYED.

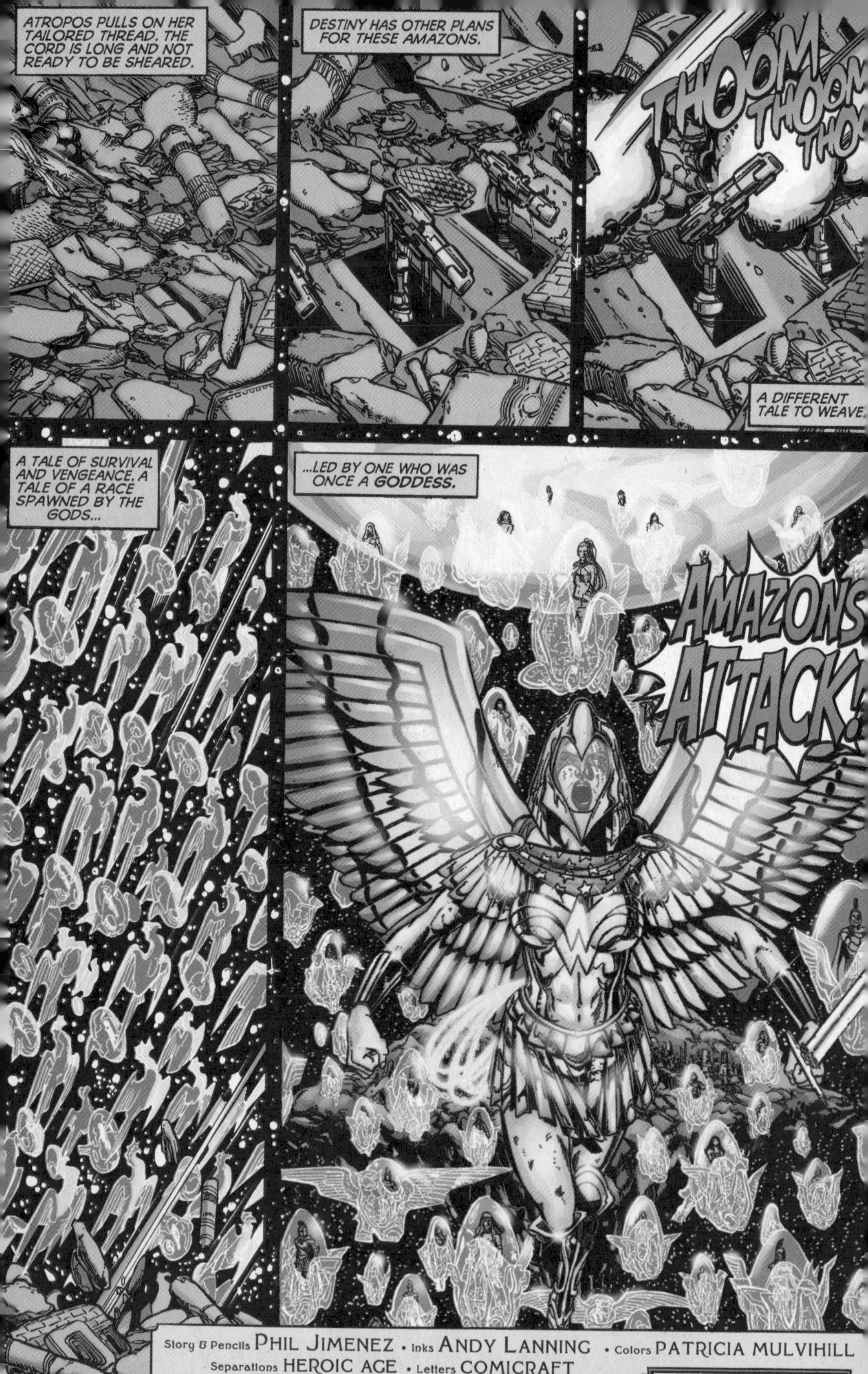
ATROPOS PULLS ON HER TAILORED THREAD. THE CORD IS LONG AND NOT READY TO BE SHEARED.
DESTINY HAS OTHER PLANS FOR THESE AMAZONS.
THOOM THOOM THO
A DIFFERENT TALE TO WEAVE.
A TALE OF SURVIVAL AND VENGEANCE. A TALE OF A RACE SPAWNED BY THE GODS...
...LED BY ONE WHO WAS ONCE A GODDESS.
AMAZONS ATTACK!
Story & Pencils PHIL JIMENEZ • Inks ANDY LANNING • Colors PATRICIA MULVIHILL
Separations HEROIC AGE • Letters COMICRAFT
Assistant Editor TOM PALMER jr • Editor EDDIE BERGANZA
WONDER WOMAN created by WILLIAM MOULTON MARSTON

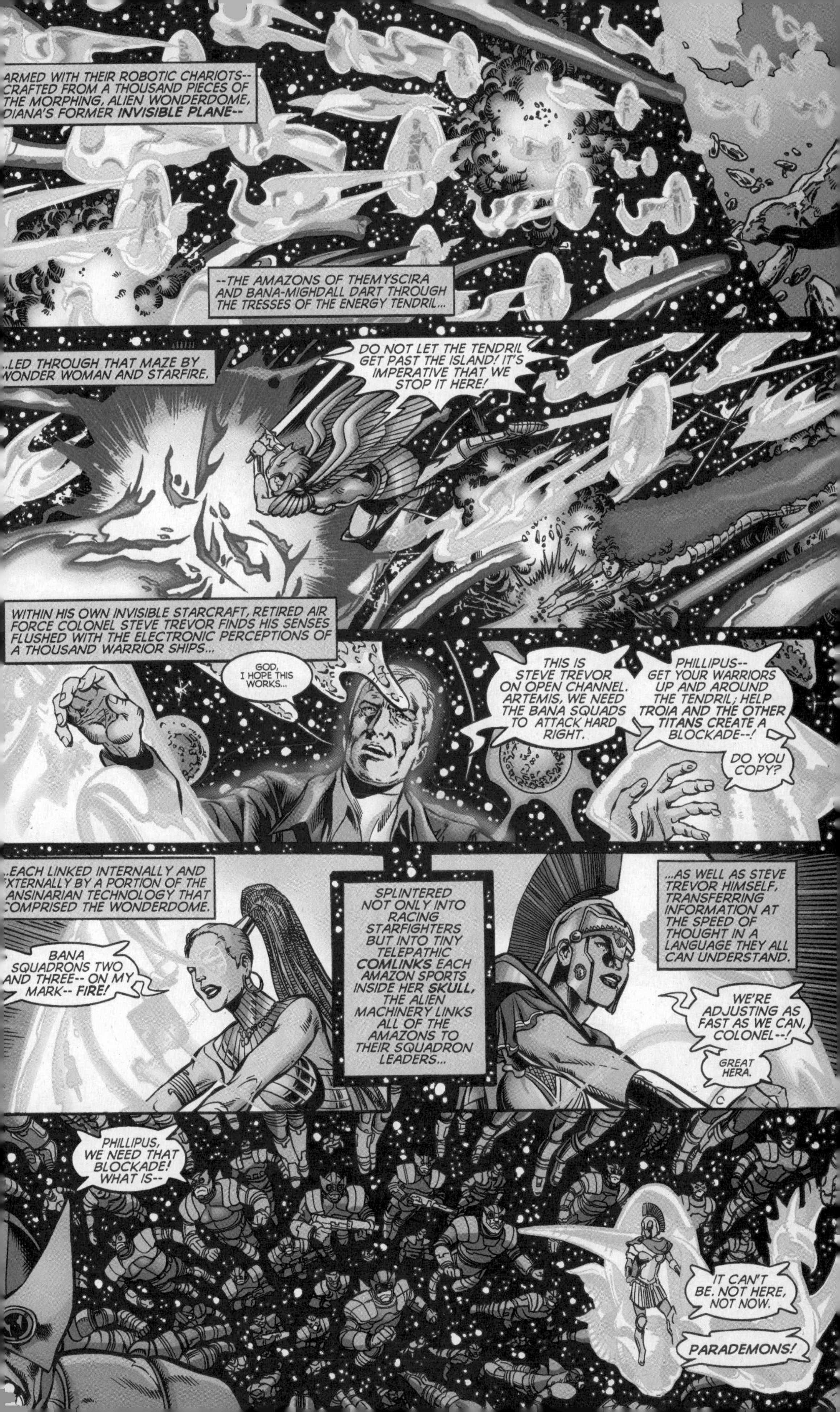
ARMED WITH THEIR ROBOTIC CHARIOTS-- CRAFTED FROM A THOUSAND PIECES OF THE MORPHING, ALIEN WONDERDOME, DIANA'S FORMER INVISIBLE PLANE--
--THE AMAZONS OF THEMYSCIRA AND BANA-MIGHDALL DART THROUGH THE TRESSES OF THE ENERGY TENDRIL...
..LED THROUGH THAT MAZE BY WONDER WOMAN AND STARFIRE.
DO NOT LET THE TENDRIL GET PAST THE ISLAND! IT'S IMPERATIVE THAT WE STOP IT HERE!
WITHIN HIS OWN INVISIBLE STARCRAFT, RETIRED AIR FORCE COLONEL STEVE TREVOR FINDS HIS SENSES FLUSHED WITH THE ELECTRONIC PERCEPTIONS OF A THOUSAND WARRIOR SHIPS...
GOD, I HOPE THIS WORKS...
THIS IS STEVE TREVOR ON OPEN CHANNEL. ARTEMIS, WE NEED THE BANA SQUADS TO ATTACK HARD RIGHT.
PHILLIPUS-- GET YOUR WARRIORS UP AND AROUND THE TENDRIL; HELP TROIA AND THE OTHER TITANS CREATE A BLOCKADE--!
DO YOU COPY?
..EACH LINKED INTERNALLY AND EXTERNALLY BY A PORTION OF THE ANSINARIAN TECHNOLOGY THAT COMPRISED THE WONDERDOME.
SPLINTERED NOT ONLY INTO RACING STARFIGHTERS BUT INTO TINY TELEPATHIC COMLINKS EACH AMAZON SPORTS INSIDE HER SKULL, THE ALIEN MACHINERY LINKS ALL OF THE AMAZONS TO THEIR SQUADRON LEADERS...
...AS WELL AS STEVE TREVOR HIMSELF, TRANSFERRING INFORMATION AT THE SPEED OF THOUGHT IN A LANGUAGE THEY ALL CAN UNDERSTAND.
BANA SQUADRONS TWO AND THREE-- ON MY MARK-- FIRE!
WE'RE ADJUSTING AS FAST AS WE CAN, COLONEL--!
GREAT HERA.
PHILLIPUS, WE NEED THAT BLOCKADE! WHAT IS--
IT CAN'T BE. NOT HERE, NOT NOW.
PARADEMONS!

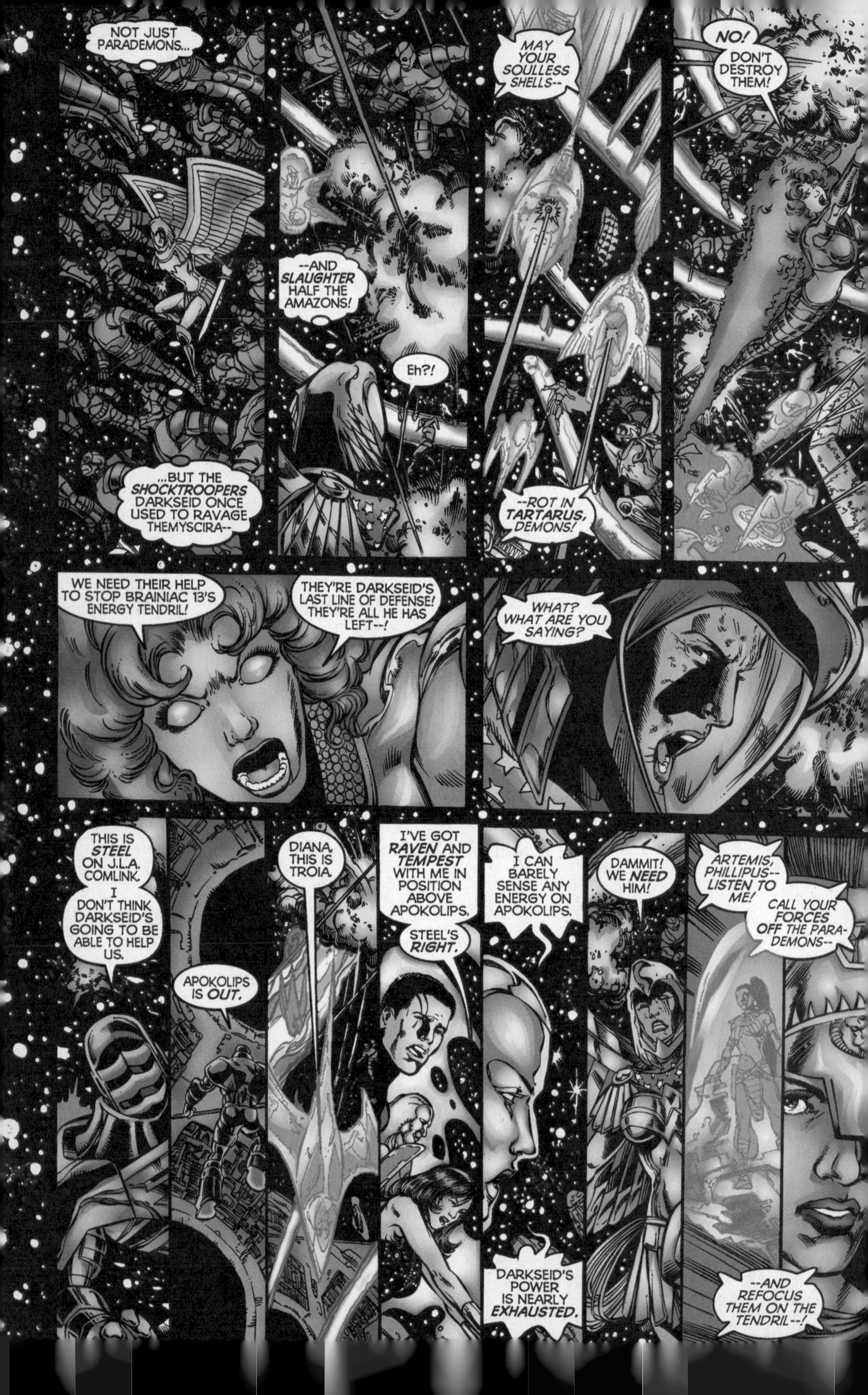

NOT JUST PARADEMONS...
...BUT THE SHOCKTROOPERS DARKSEID ONCE USED TO RAVAGE THEMYSCIRA--
--AND SLAUGHTER HALF THE AMAZONS!
Eh?!
MAY YOUR SOULLESS SHELLS--
--ROT IN TARTARUS, DEMONS!
NO! DON'T DESTROY THEM!
WE NEED THEIR HELP TO STOP BRAINIAC 13'S ENERGY TENDRIL!
THEY'RE DARKSEID'S LAST LINE OF DEFENSE! THEY'RE ALL HE HAS LEFT--!
WHAT? WHAT ARE YOU SAYING?
THIS IS STEEL ON J.L.A. COMLINK.
I DON'T THINK DARKSEID'S GOING TO BE ABLE TO HELP US.
APOKOLIPS IS OUT.
DIANA, THIS IS TROIA.
I'VE GOT RAVEN AND TEMPEST WITH ME IN POSITION ABOVE APOKOLIPS.
STEEL'S RIGHT.
I CAN BARELY SENSE ANY ENERGY ON APOKOLIPS.
DARKSEID'S POWER IS NEARLY EXHAUSTED.
DAMMIT! WE NEED HIM!
ARTEMIS, PHILLIPUS-- LISTEN TO ME!
CALL YOUR FORCES OFF THE PARADEMONS--
--AND REFOCUS THEM ON THE TENDRIL--!

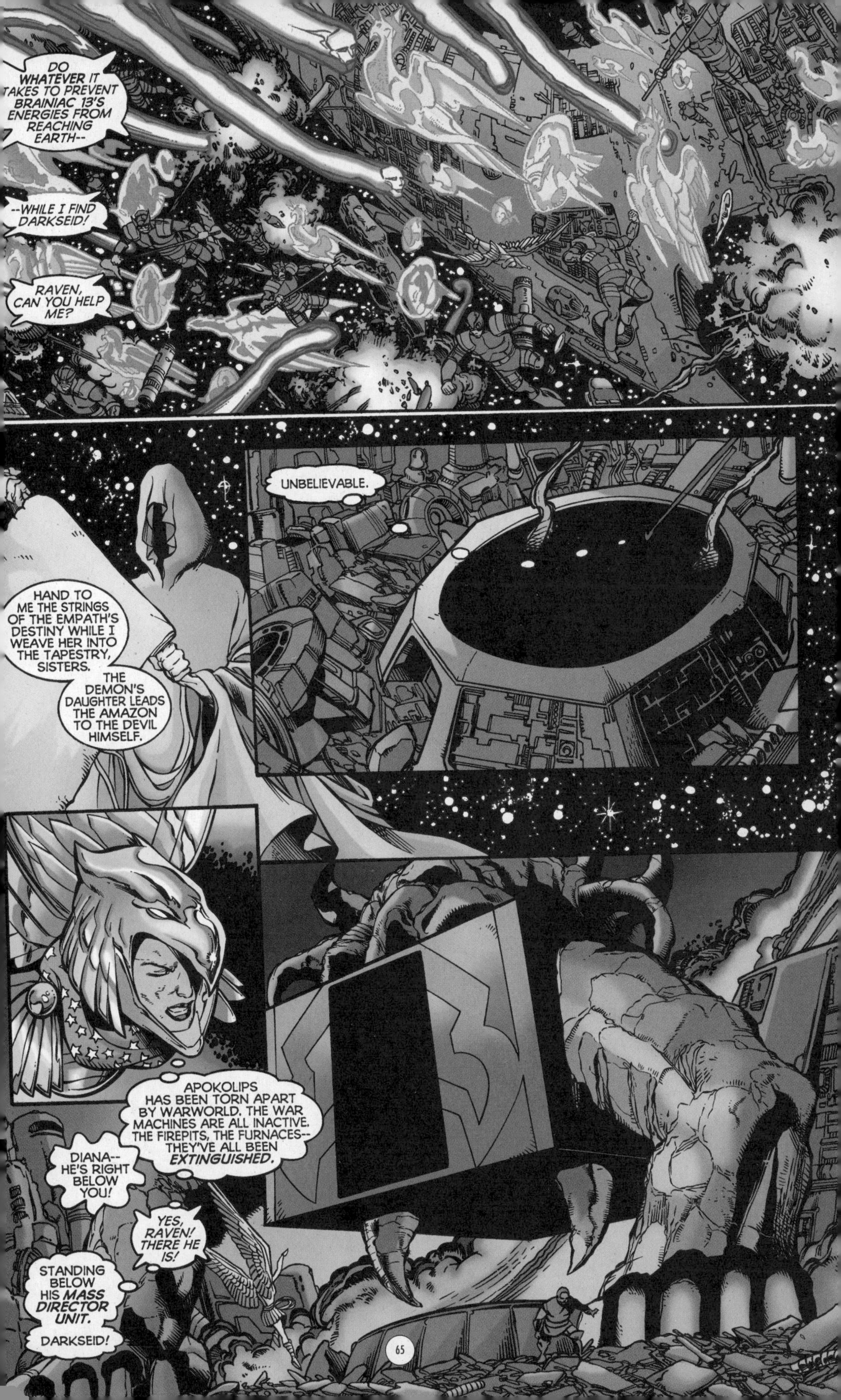
DO *WHATEVER* IT TAKES TO PREVENT BRAINIAC 13'S ENERGIES FROM REACHING EARTH--
--WHILE I FIND DARKSEID!
RAVEN, CAN YOU HELP ME?
UNBELIEVABLE.
HAND TO ME THE STRINGS OF THE EMPATH'S DESTINY WHILE I WEAVE HER INTO THE TAPESTRY, SISTERS.
THE DEMON'S DAUGHTER LEADS THE AMAZON TO THE DEVIL HIMSELF.
APOKOLIPS HAS BEEN TORN APART BY WARWORLD. THE WAR MACHINES ARE ALL INACTIVE. THE FIREPITS, THE FURNACES-- THEY'VE ALL BEEN ***EXTINGUISHED.***
DIANA-- HE'S RIGHT BELOW YOU!
YES, RAVEN! THERE HE IS!
STANDING BELOW HIS ***MASS DIRECTOR UNIT.***
DARKSEID!

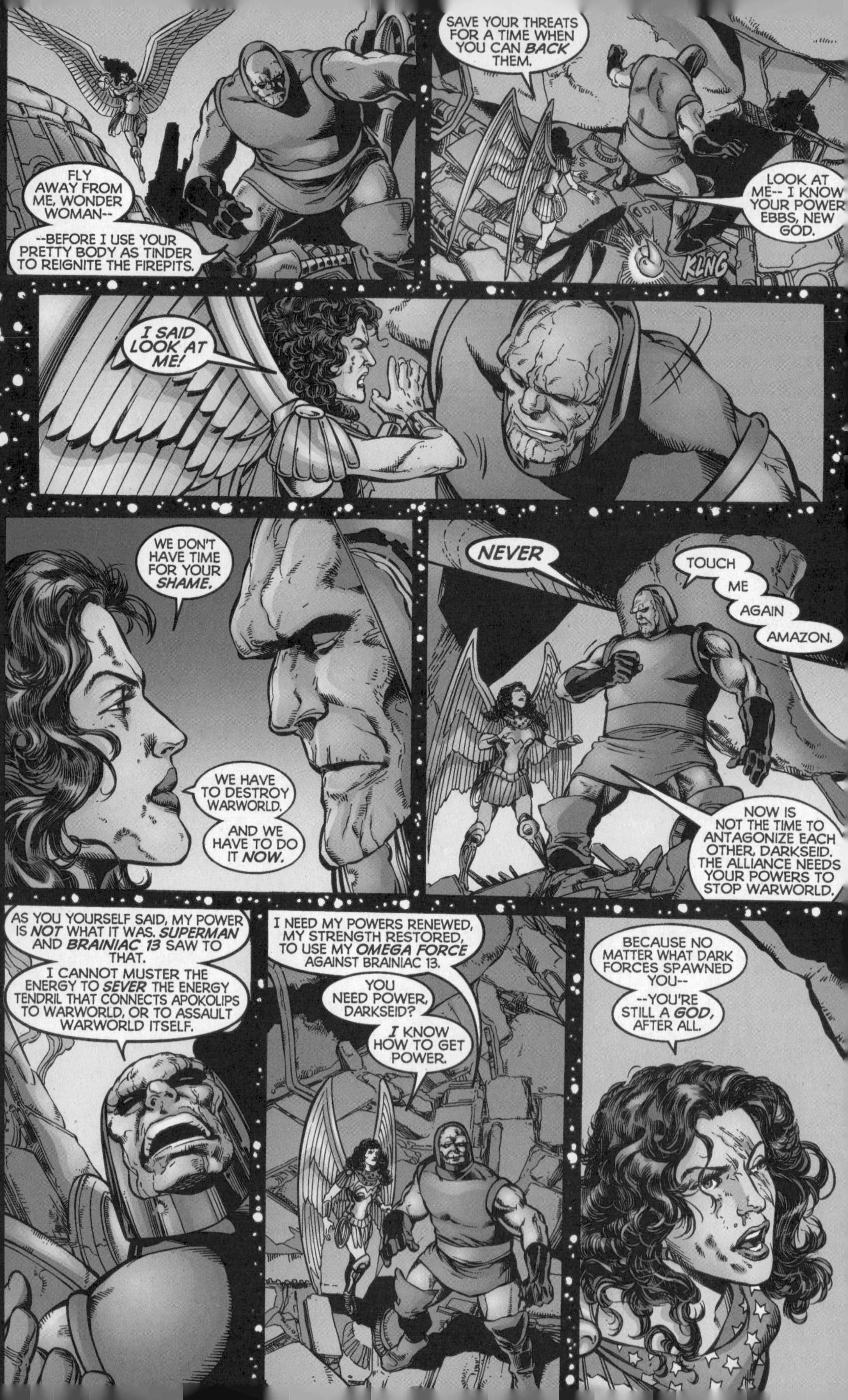
FLY AWAY FROM ME, WONDER WOMAN--
--BEFORE I USE YOUR PRETTY BODY AS TINDER TO REIGNITE THE FIREPITS.
SAVE YOUR THREATS FOR A TIME WHEN YOU CAN *BACK* THEM.
LOOK AT ME-- I KNOW YOUR POWER EBBS, NEW GOD.
KLNG
I SAID LOOK AT ME!
WE DON'T HAVE TIME FOR YOUR *SHAME.*
WE HAVE TO DESTROY WARWORLD.
AND WE HAVE TO DO IT *NOW.*
NEVER
TOUCH
ME
AGAIN
AMAZON.
NOW IS NOT THE TIME TO ANTAGONIZE EACH OTHER, DARKSEID. THE ALLIANCE NEEDS YOUR POWERS TO STOP WARWORLD.
AS YOU YOURSELF SAID, MY POWER IS *NOT* WHAT IT WAS. *SUPERMAN* AND *BRAINIAC 13* SAW TO THAT.
I CANNOT MUSTER THE ENERGY TO *SEVER* THE ENERGY TENDRIL THAT CONNECTS APOKOLIPS TO WARWORLD, OR TO ASSAULT WARWORLD ITSELF.
I NEED MY POWERS RENEWED, MY STRENGTH RESTORED, TO USE MY *OMEGA FORCE* AGAINST BRAINIAC 13.
YOU NEED POWER, DARKSEID?
I KNOW HOW TO GET POWER.
BECAUSE NO MATTER WHAT DARK FORCES SPAWNED YOU--
--YOU'RE STILL A *GOD,* AFTER ALL.

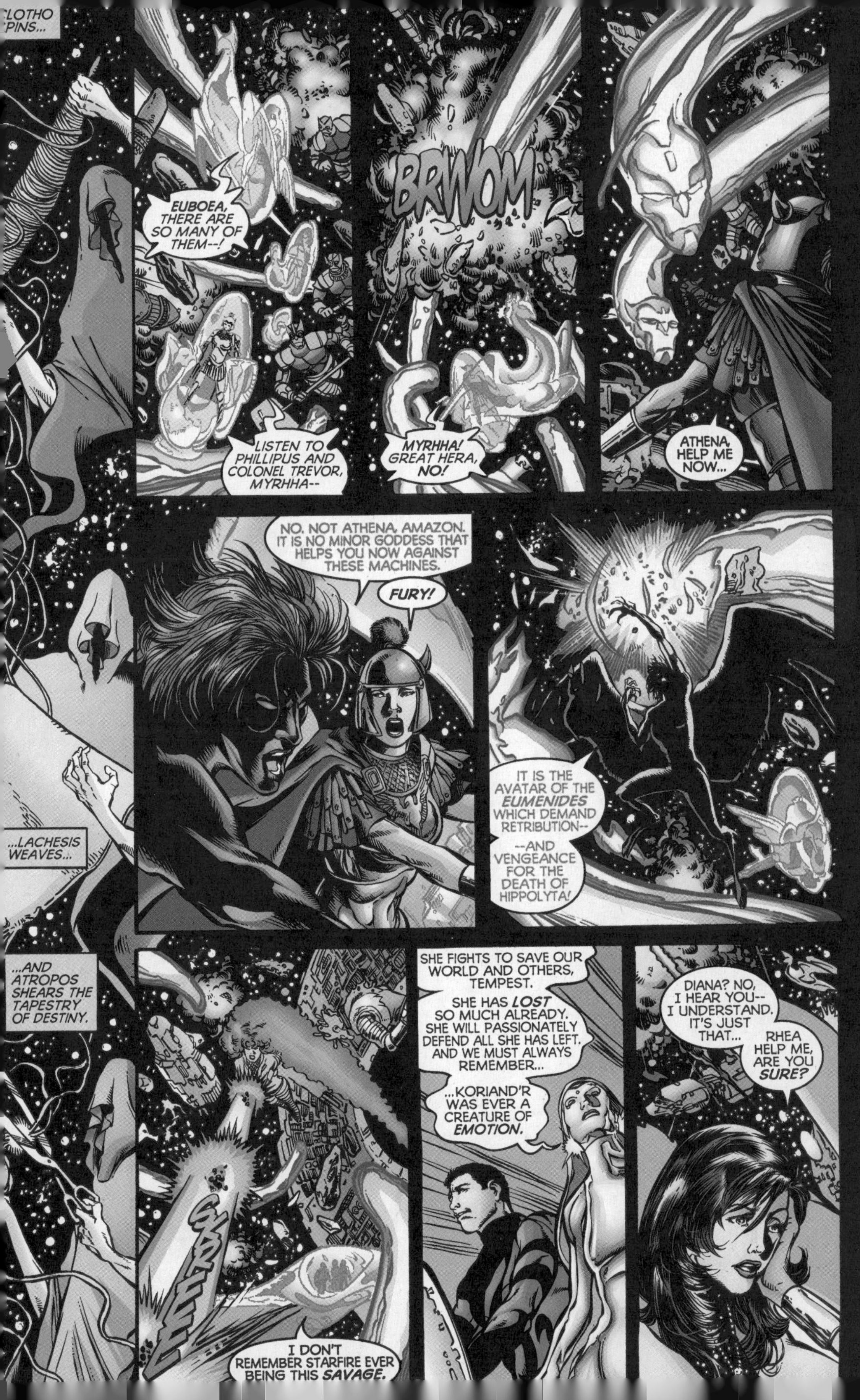
CLOTHO SPINS...
EUBOEA, THERE ARE SO MANY OF THEM--!
LISTEN TO PHILLIPUS AND COLONEL TREVOR, MYRHHA--
BRWOM
MYRHHA! GREAT HERA, NO!
ATHENA, HELP ME NOW...
NO. NOT ATHENA, AMAZON. IT IS NO MINOR GODDESS THAT HELPS YOU NOW AGAINST THESE MACHINES.
FURY!
IT IS THE AVATAR OF THE EUMENIDES WHICH DEMAND RETRIBUTION--
--AND VENGEANCE FOR THE DEATH OF HIPPOLYTA!
...LACHESIS WEAVES...
...AND ATROPOS SHEARS THE TAPESTRY OF DESTINY.
I DON'T REMEMBER STARFIRE EVER BEING THIS SAVAGE.
SHE FIGHTS TO SAVE OUR WORLD AND OTHERS, TEMPEST.
SHE HAS LOST SO MUCH ALREADY. SHE WILL PASSIONATELY DEFEND ALL SHE HAS LEFT. AND WE MUST ALWAYS REMEMBER...
...KORIAND'R WAS EVER A CREATURE OF EMOTION.
DIANA? NO, I HEAR YOU-- I UNDERSTAND. IT'S JUST THAT...
RHEA HELP ME, ARE YOU SURE?

DIANA HEAVES A MASSIVE SIGH AND GENTLY NODS HER HEAD. FOR SHE ALMOST CAN'T BELIEVE SHE SAYS "YES."

AND THEN DIANA'S THOUGHTS FILTER NOT JUST THROUGH THE PSYCHIC LINK SHE SHARES WITH HER SISTER, BUT INTO THE MINDS OF ALL OF THE AMAZONS-- COMMUNICATING TELEPATHICALLY THROUGH THE BIOTECH LINK OF THE LANSANARIAN WONDERDOME.

AT THE SPEED OF THOUGHT, DIANA TELLS THE AMAZONS OF DARKSEID'S PLIGHT, AND HOW HE NEEDS POWER TO END THE THREAT OF WARWORLD.

HER MIND RECOILS AT THE RAGE OF A THOUSAND AMAZONS AND MORE, AT THE MERE MENTION OF DARKSEID'S NAME. RECOILING AT FIRST FROM THE AMAZONS' THOUGHTS OF BLOODY VENGEANCE, DIANA STEELS HERSELF AND SIFTS THROUGH THE HATE AND BEGS THE AMAZONS TO DO THE SAME.

AS THE WAR RAGES BEYOND THEM, SHE IMPLORES THE AMAZONS TO FORSAKE THEIR RIGHTFUL GRIEVANCES AGAINST THE EVIL GOD, TO HELP SAVE THE UNIVERSE.

AND THEN DIANA ASKS THEM TO PRAY TO BRING ALL THEIR SPIRITUAL FOCUS TO BEAR.

TO SET ASIDE ALL OTHER EMOTIONS AND CENTER ON THAT INTENSE CORE OF BELIEF WITHIN THEM, TO LOOK INWARD TOWARDS THE ONE ENERGY THAT CONSTANTLY NOURISHES THEM, AND RENEWS THEM, AND GIVES THEM THE POWER AND REASON TO LIVE...

...TO FOCUS THAT ENERGY, THAT SPIRITUAL POWER, THAT FAITH...

...AND PREPARE TO HAVE IT CHANNELED...

...INTO DARKSEID.

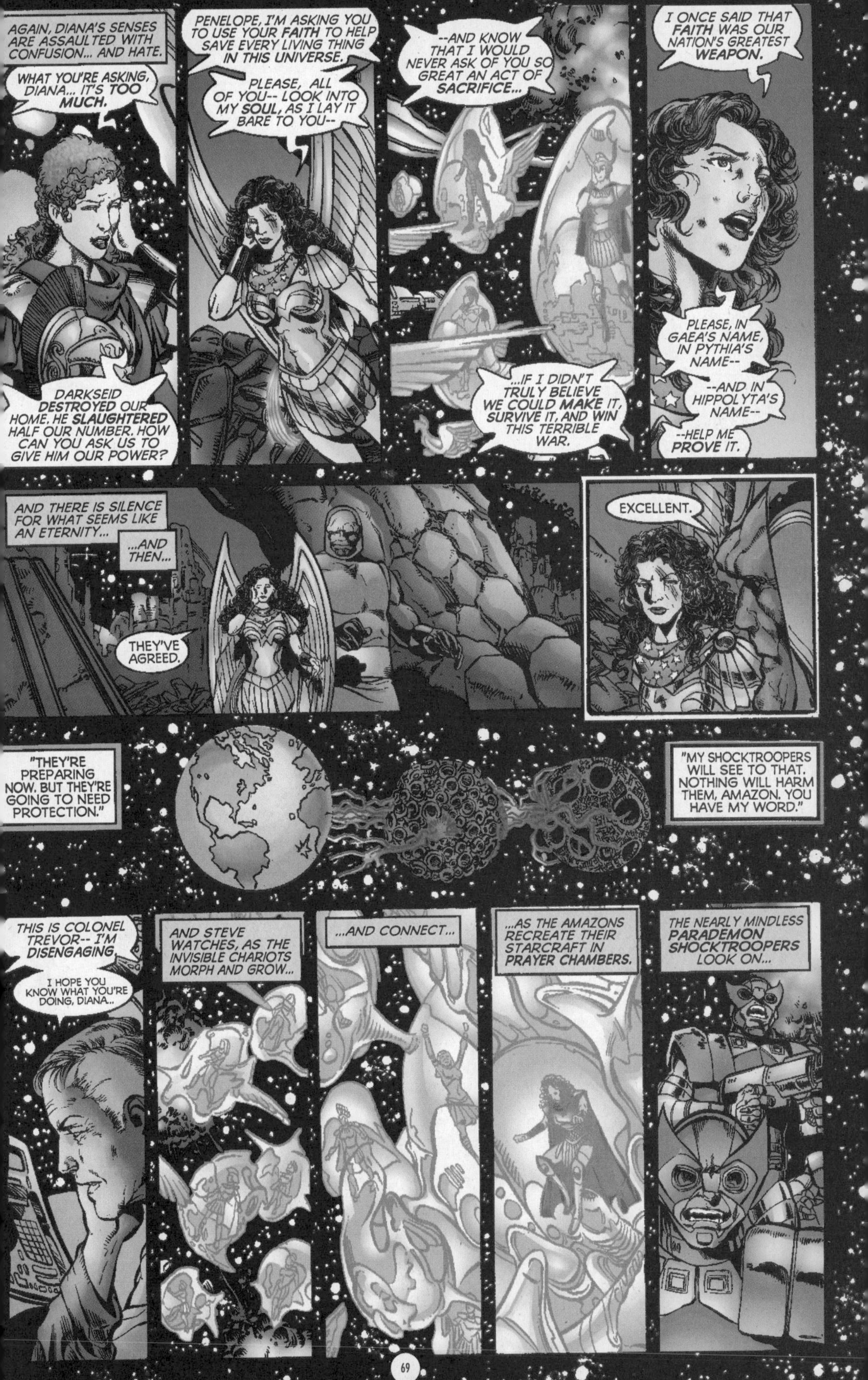
AGAIN, DIANA'S SENSES ARE ASSAULTED WITH CONFUSION... AND HATE.
WHAT YOU'RE ASKING, DIANA... IT'S TOO MUCH.
DARKSEID DESTROYED OUR HOME. HE SLAUGHTERED HALF OUR NUMBER. HOW CAN YOU ASK US TO GIVE HIM OUR POWER?
PENELOPE, I'M ASKING YOU TO USE YOUR FAITH TO HELP SAVE EVERY LIVING THING IN THIS UNIVERSE.
PLEASE, ALL OF YOU-- LOOK INTO MY SOUL, AS I LAY IT BARE TO YOU--
--AND KNOW THAT I WOULD NEVER ASK OF YOU SO GREAT AN ACT OF SACRIFICE...
...IF I DIDN'T TRULY BELIEVE WE COULD MAKE IT, SURVIVE IT, AND WIN THIS TERRIBLE WAR.
I ONCE SAID THAT FAITH WAS OUR NATION'S GREATEST WEAPON.
PLEASE, IN GAEA'S NAME, IN PYTHIA'S NAME--
--AND IN HIPPOLYTA'S NAME--
--HELP ME PROVE IT.
AND THERE IS SILENCE FOR WHAT SEEMS LIKE AN ETERNITY...
...AND THEN...
THEY'VE AGREED.
EXCELLENT.
"THEY'RE PREPARING NOW. BUT THEY'RE GOING TO NEED PROTECTION."
"MY SHOCKTROOPERS WILL SEE TO THAT. NOTHING WILL HARM THEM, AMAZON. YOU HAVE MY WORD."
THIS IS COLONEL TREVOR-- I'M DISENGAGING.
I HOPE YOU KNOW WHAT YOU'RE DOING, DIANA...
AND STEVE WATCHES, AS THE INVISIBLE CHARIOTS MORPH AND GROW...
...AND CONNECT...
...AS THE AMAZONS RECREATE THEIR STARCRAFT IN PRAYER CHAMBERS.
THE NEARLY MINDLESS PARADEMON SHOCKTROOPERS LOOK ON...

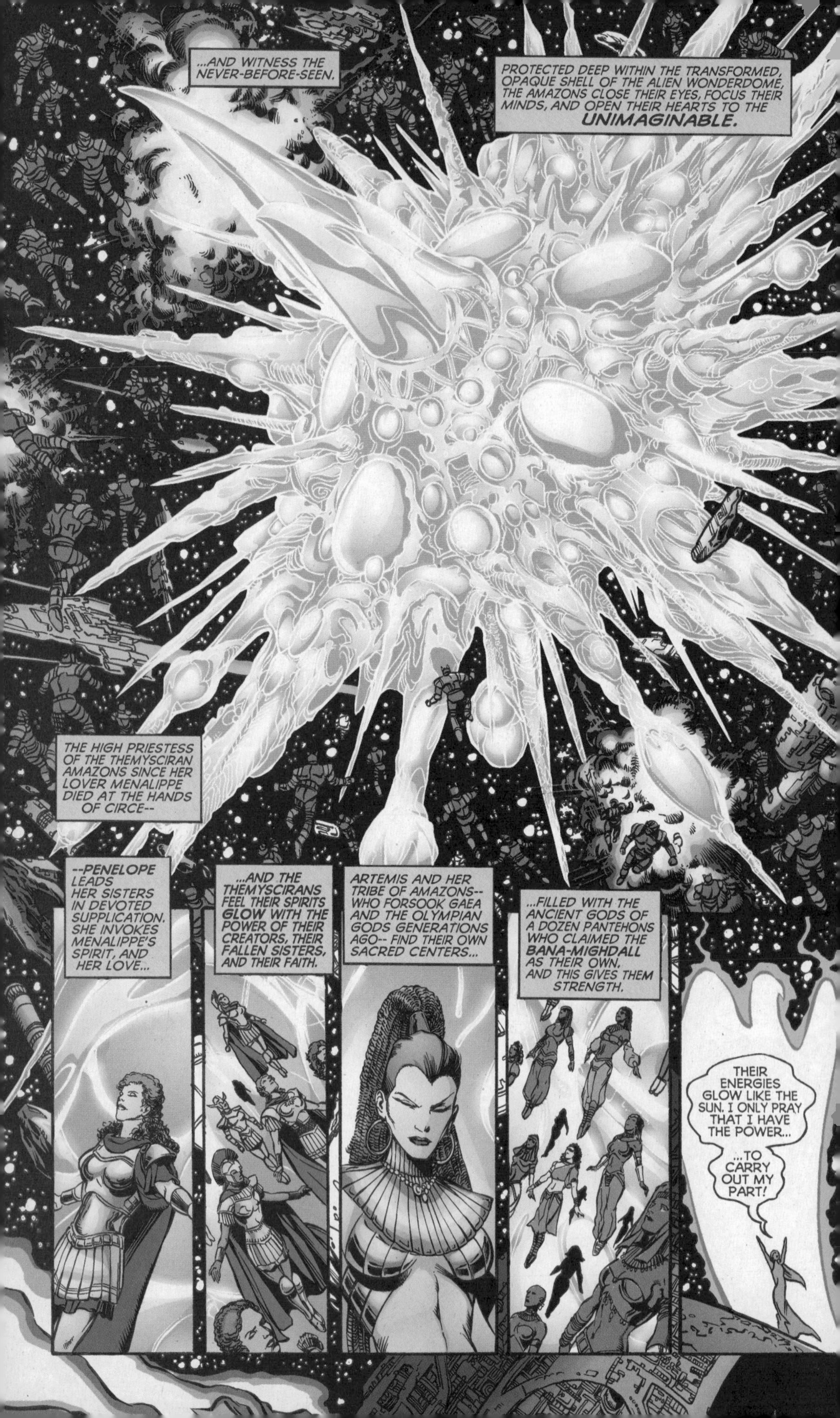
...AND WITNESS THE NEVER-BEFORE-SEEN.
PROTECTED DEEP WITHIN THE TRANSFORMED, OPAQUE SHELL OF THE ALIEN WONDERDOME, THE AMAZONS CLOSE THEIR EYES, FOCUS THEIR MINDS, AND OPEN THEIR HEARTS TO THE UNIMAGINABLE.
THE HIGH PRIESTESS OF THE THEMYSCIRAN AMAZONS SINCE HER LOVER MENALIPPE DIED AT THE HANDS OF CIRCE--
--PENELOPE LEADS HER SISTERS IN DEVOTED SUPPLICATION. SHE INVOKES MENALIPPE'S SPIRIT, AND HER LOVE...
...AND THE THEMYSCIRANS FEEL THEIR SPIRITS GLOW WITH THE POWER OF THEIR CREATORS, THEIR FALLEN SISTERS, AND THEIR FAITH.
ARTEMIS AND HER TRIBE OF AMAZONS-- WHO FORSOOK GAEA AND THE OLYMPIAN GODS GENERATIONS AGO-- FIND THEIR OWN SACRED CENTERS...
...FILLED WITH THE ANCIENT GODS OF A DOZEN PANTEHONS WHO CLAIMED THE BANA-MIGHDALL AS THEIR OWN. AND THIS GIVES THEM STRENGTH.
THEIR ENERGIES GLOW LIKE THE SUN. I ONLY PRAY THAT I HAVE THE POWER...
...TO CARRY OUT MY PART!

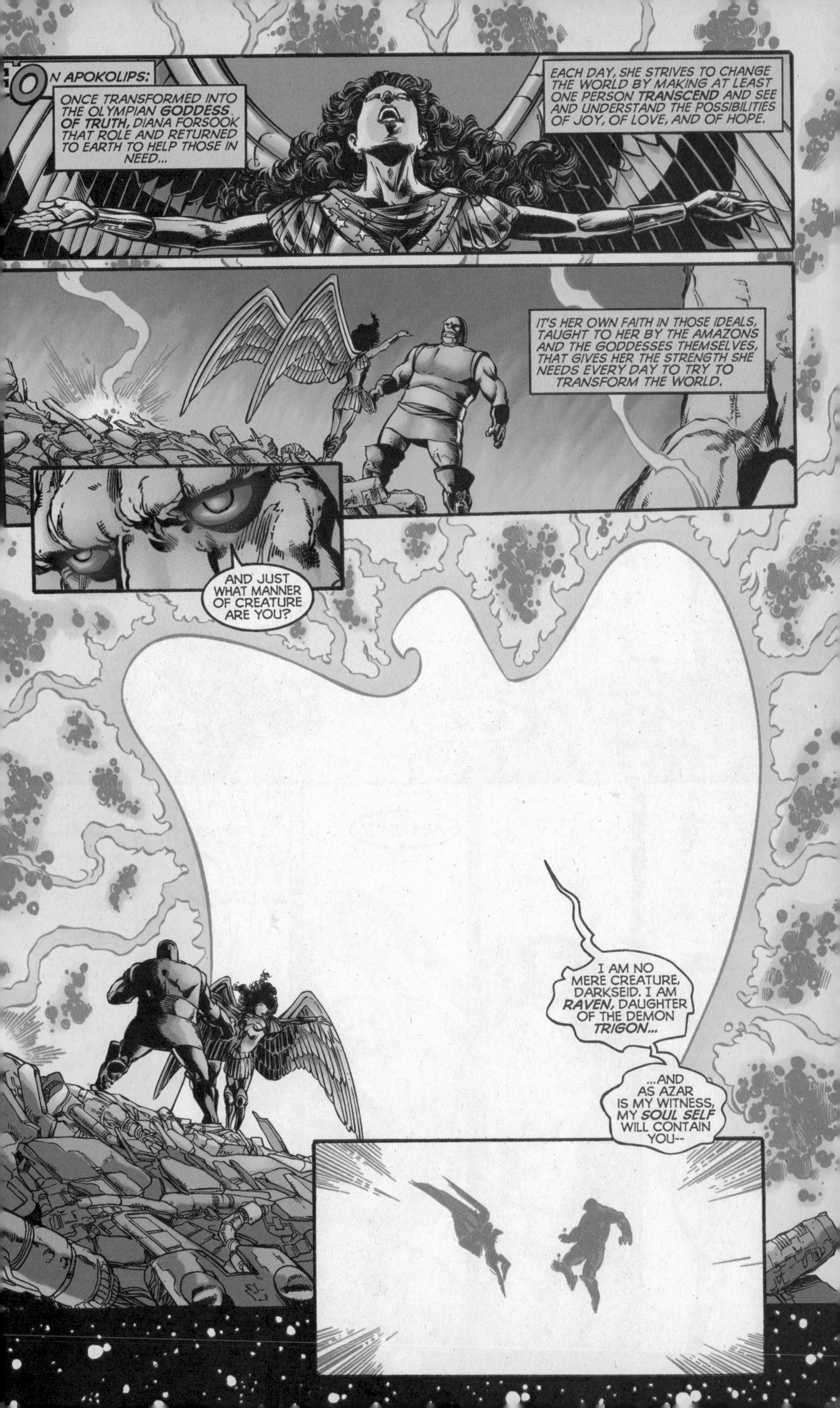
ON APOKOLIPS:
ONCE TRANSFORMED INTO THE OLYMPIAN GODDESS OF TRUTH, DIANA FORSOOK THAT ROLE AND RETURNED TO EARTH TO HELP THOSE IN NEED...
EACH DAY, SHE STRIVES TO CHANGE THE WORLD BY MAKING AT LEAST ONE PERSON TRANSCEND AND SEE AND UNDERSTAND THE POSSIBILITIES OF JOY, OF LOVE, AND OF HOPE.
IT'S HER OWN FAITH IN THOSE IDEALS, TAUGHT TO HER BY THE AMAZONS AND THE GODDESSES THEMSELVES, THAT GIVES HER THE STRENGTH SHE NEEDS EVERY DAY TO TRY TO TRANSFORM THE WORLD.
AND JUST WHAT MANNER OF CREATURE ARE YOU?
I AM NO MERE CREATURE, DARKSEID. I AM RAVEN, DAUGHTER OF THE DEMON TRIGON...
...AND AS AZAR IS MY WITNESS, MY SOUL SELF WILL CONTAIN YOU--

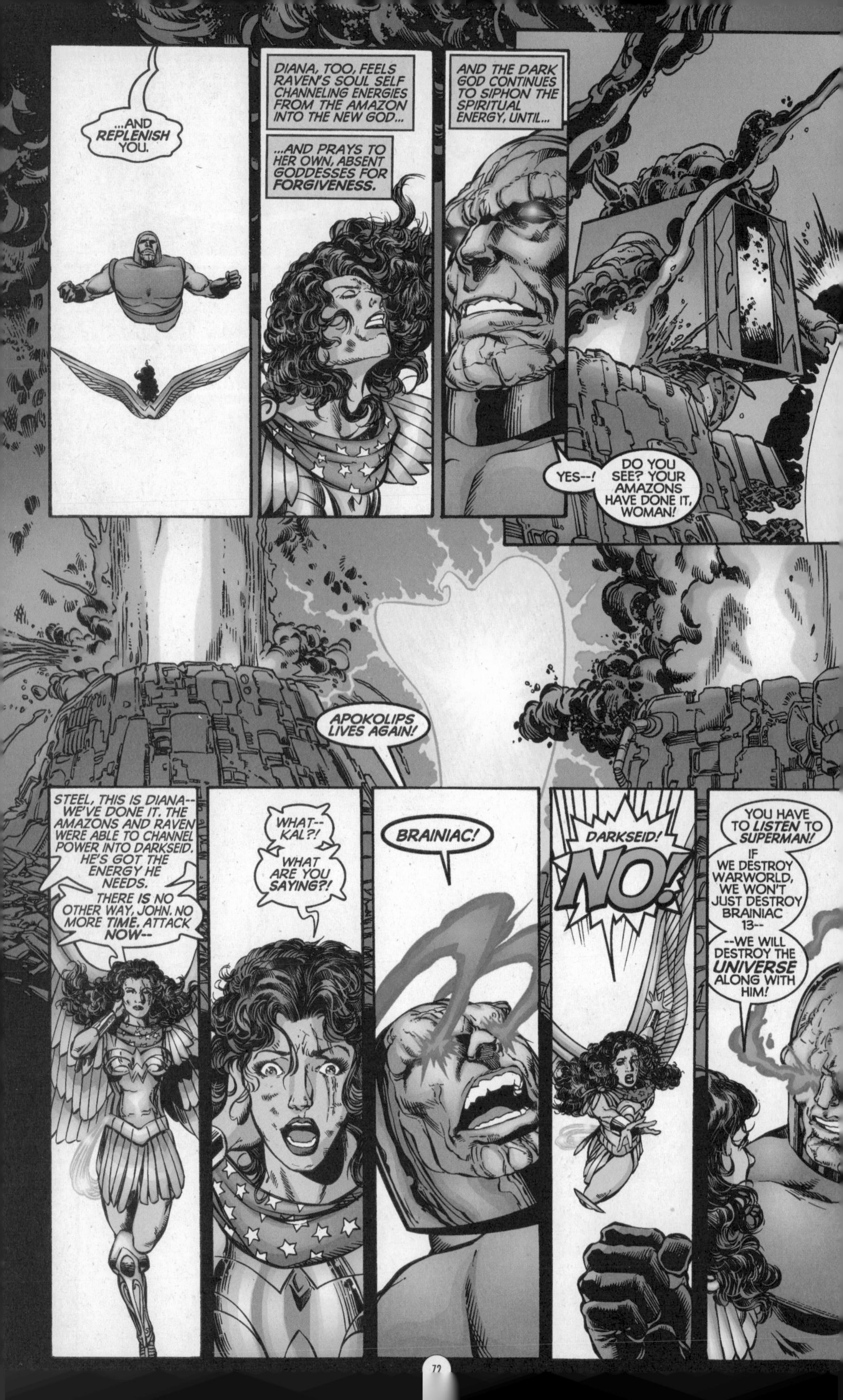

...AND REPLENISH YOU.
DIANA, TOO, FEELS RAVEN'S SOUL SELF CHANNELING ENERGIES FROM THE AMAZON INTO THE NEW GOD...
...AND PRAYS TO HER OWN, ABSENT GODDESSES FOR FORGIVENESS.
AND THE DARK GOD CONTINUES TO SIPHON THE SPIRITUAL ENERGY, UNTIL...
YES--!
DO YOU SEE? YOUR AMAZONS HAVE DONE IT, WOMAN!
APOKOLIPS LIVES AGAIN!
STEEL, THIS IS DIANA-- WE'VE DONE IT. THE AMAZONS AND RAVEN WERE ABLE TO CHANNEL POWER INTO DARKSEID. HE'S GOT THE ENERGY HE NEEDS.
THERE IS NO OTHER WAY, JOHN. NO MORE TIME. ATTACK NOW--
WHAT-- KAL?!
WHAT ARE YOU SAYING?!
BRAINIAC!
DARKSEID!
NO!
YOU HAVE TO LISTEN TO SUPERMAN!
IF WE DESTROY WARWORLD, WE WON'T JUST DESTROY BRAINIAC 13--
--WE WILL DESTROY THE UNIVERSE ALONG WITH HIM!

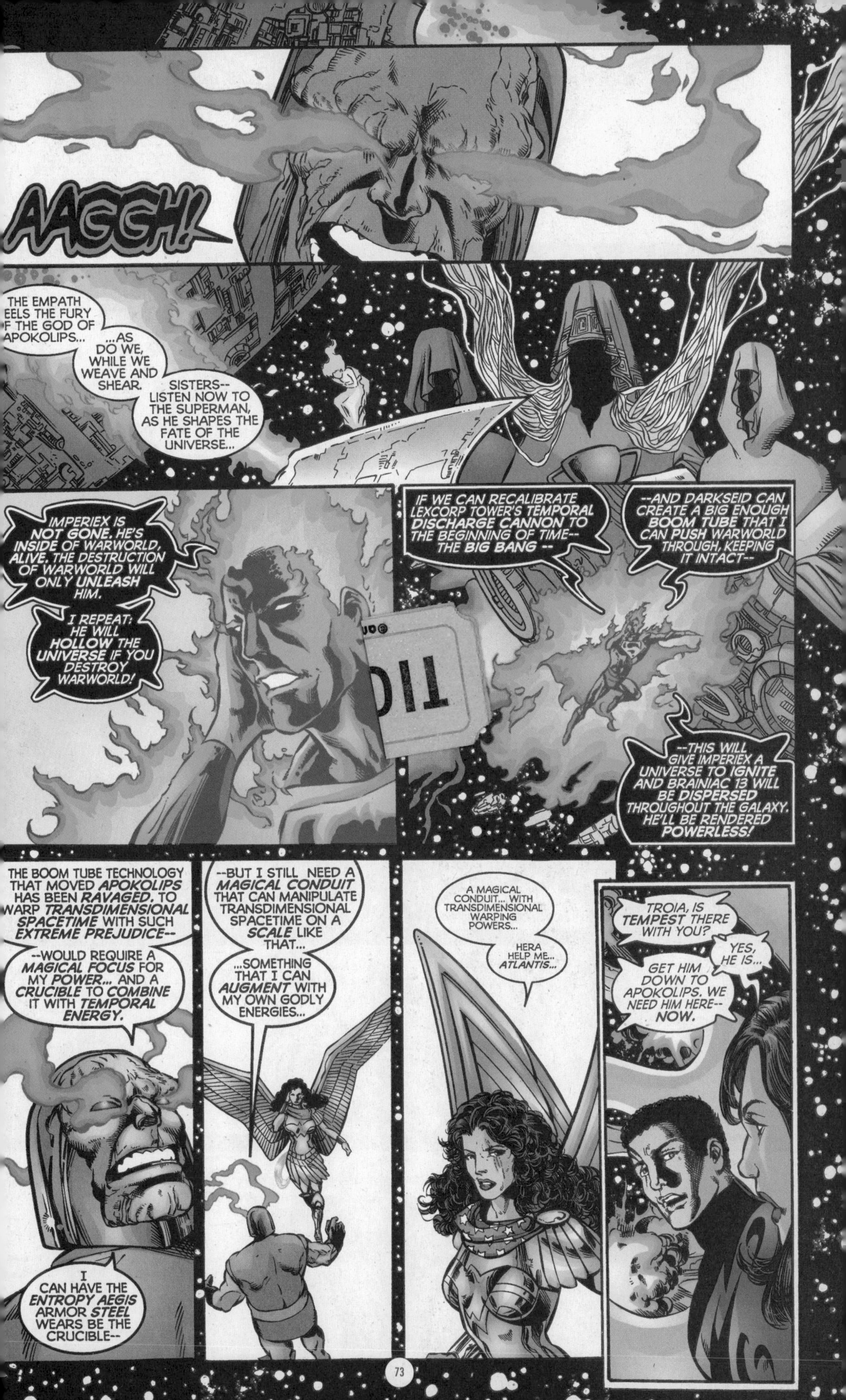
AAGGH!
THE EMPATH EELS THE FURY F THE GOD OF APOKOLIPS...
...AS DO WE, WHILE WE WEAVE AND SHEAR.
SISTERS-- LISTEN NOW TO THE SUPERMAN, AS HE SHAPES THE FATE OF THE UNIVERSE...
IMPERIEX IS NOT GONE. HE'S INSIDE OF WARWORLD, ALIVE. THE DESTRUCTION OF WARWORLD WILL ONLY UNLEASH HIM.
I REPEAT: HE WILL HOLLOW THE UNIVERSE IF YOU DESTROY WARWORLD!
IF WE CAN RECALIBRATE LEXCORP TOWER'S TEMPORAL DISCHARGE CANNON TO THE BEGINNING OF TIME-- THE BIG BANG --
--AND DARKSEID CAN CREATE A BIG ENOUGH BOOM TUBE THAT I CAN PUSH WARWORLD THROUGH, KEEPING IT INTACT--
--THIS WILL GIVE IMPERIEX A UNIVERSE TO IGNITE AND BRAINIAC 13 WILL BE DISPERSED THROUGHOUT THE GALAXY. HE'LL BE RENDERED POWERLESS!
THE BOOM TUBE TECHNOLOGY THAT MOVED APOKOLIPS HAS BEEN RAVAGED. TO WARP TRANSDIMENSIONAL SPACETIME WITH SUCH EXTREME PREJUDICE--
--WOULD REQUIRE A MAGICAL FOCUS FOR MY POWER... AND A CRUCIBLE TO COMBINE IT WITH TEMPORAL ENERGY.
I CAN HAVE THE ENTROPY AEGIS ARMOR STEEL WEARS BE THE CRUCIBLE--
--BUT I STILL NEED A MAGICAL CONDUIT THAT CAN MANIPULATE TRANSDIMENSIONAL SPACETIME ON A SCALE LIKE THAT...
...SOMETHING THAT I CAN AUGMENT WITH MY OWN GODLY ENERGIES...
A MAGICAL CONDUIT... WITH TRANSDIMENSIONAL WARPING POWERS...
HERA HELP ME... ATLANTIS...
TROIA, IS TEMPEST THERE WITH YOU?
YES, HE IS...
GET HIM DOWN TO APOKOLIPS. WE NEED HIM HERE-- NOW.

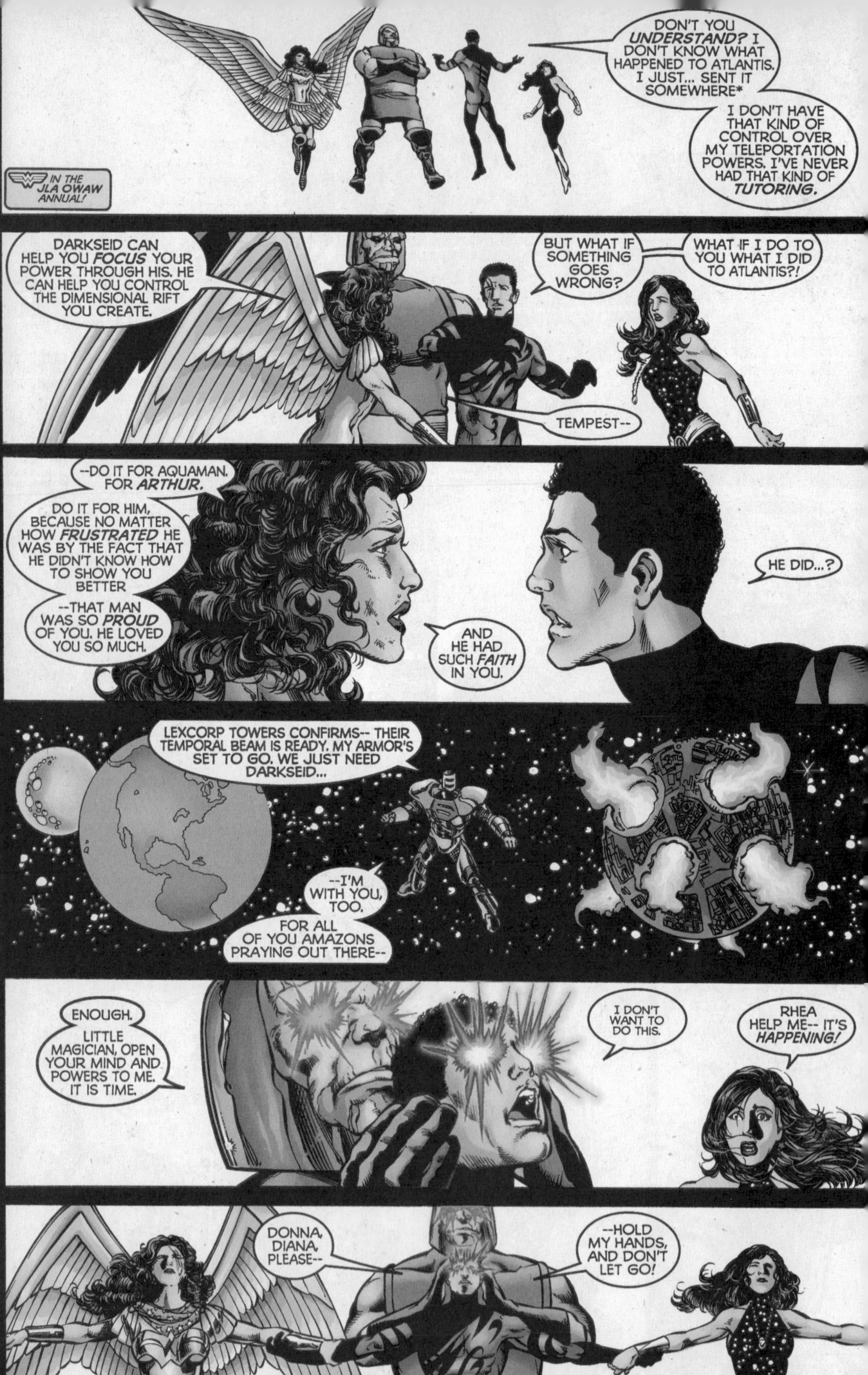

DON'T YOU UNDERSTAND? I DON'T KNOW WHAT HAPPENED TO ATLANTIS. I JUST... SENT IT SOMEWHERE*
I DON'T HAVE THAT KIND OF CONTROL OVER MY TELEPORTATION POWERS. I'VE NEVER HAD THAT KIND OF TUTORING.
*IN THE JLA OWAW ANNUAL!
DARKSEID CAN HELP YOU FOCUS YOUR POWER THROUGH HIS. HE CAN HELP YOU CONTROL THE DIMENSIONAL RIFT YOU CREATE.
BUT WHAT IF SOMETHING GOES WRONG?
WHAT IF I DO TO YOU WHAT I DID TO ATLANTIS?!
TEMPEST--
--DO IT FOR AQUAMAN. FOR ARTHUR.
DO IT FOR HIM, BECAUSE NO MATTER HOW FRUSTRATED HE WAS BY THE FACT THAT HE DIDN'T KNOW HOW TO SHOW YOU BETTER
--THAT MAN WAS SO PROUD OF YOU. HE LOVED YOU SO MUCH.
HE DID...?
AND HE HAD SUCH FAITH IN YOU.
LEXCORP TOWERS CONFIRMS-- THEIR TEMPORAL BEAM IS READY. MY ARMOR'S SET TO GO. WE JUST NEED DARKSEID...
--I'M WITH YOU, TOO.
FOR ALL OF YOU AMAZONS PRAYING OUT THERE--
ENOUGH.
LITTLE MAGICIAN, OPEN YOUR MIND AND POWERS TO ME. IT IS TIME.
I DON'T WANT TO DO THIS.
RHEA HELP ME-- IT'S HAPPENING!
DONNA, DIANA, PLEASE--
--HOLD MY HANDS, AND DON'T LET GO!

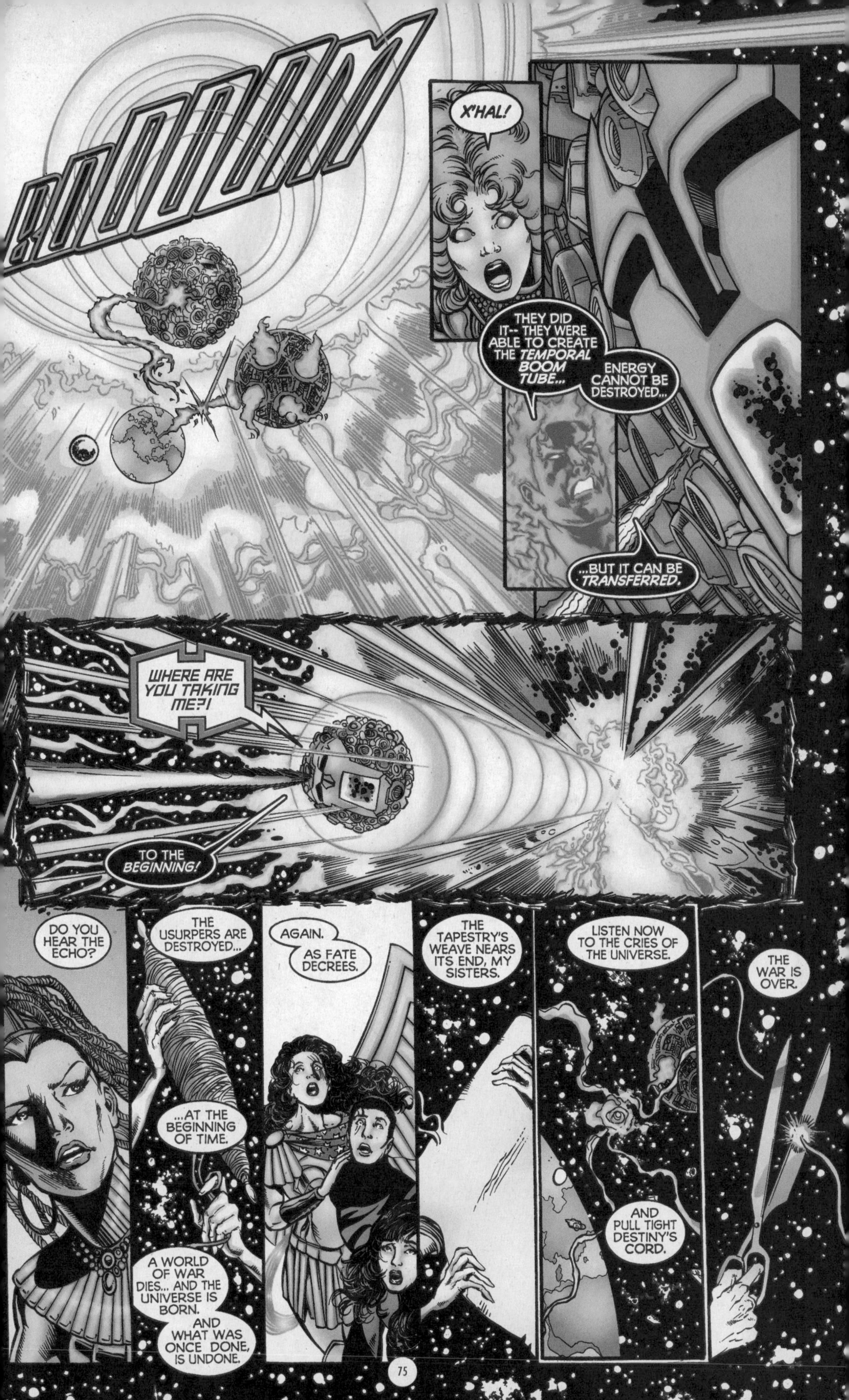

BRAAAAM
X'HAL!
THEY DID IT-- THEY WERE ABLE TO CREATE THE TEMPORAL BOOM TUBE...
ENERGY CANNOT BE DESTROYED...
...BUT IT CAN BE TRANSFERRED.
WHERE ARE YOU TAKING ME?!
TO THE BEGINNING!
DO YOU HEAR THE ECHO?
THE USURPERS ARE DESTROYED...
...AT THE BEGINNING OF TIME.
A WORLD OF WAR DIES... AND THE UNIVERSE IS BORN.
AND WHAT WAS ONCE DONE, IS UNDONE.
AGAIN.
AS FATE DECREES.
THE TAPESTRY'S WEAVE NEARS ITS END, MY SISTERS.
LISTEN NOW TO THE CRIES OF THE UNIVERSE.
AND PULL TIGHT DESTINY'S CORD.
THE WAR IS OVER.

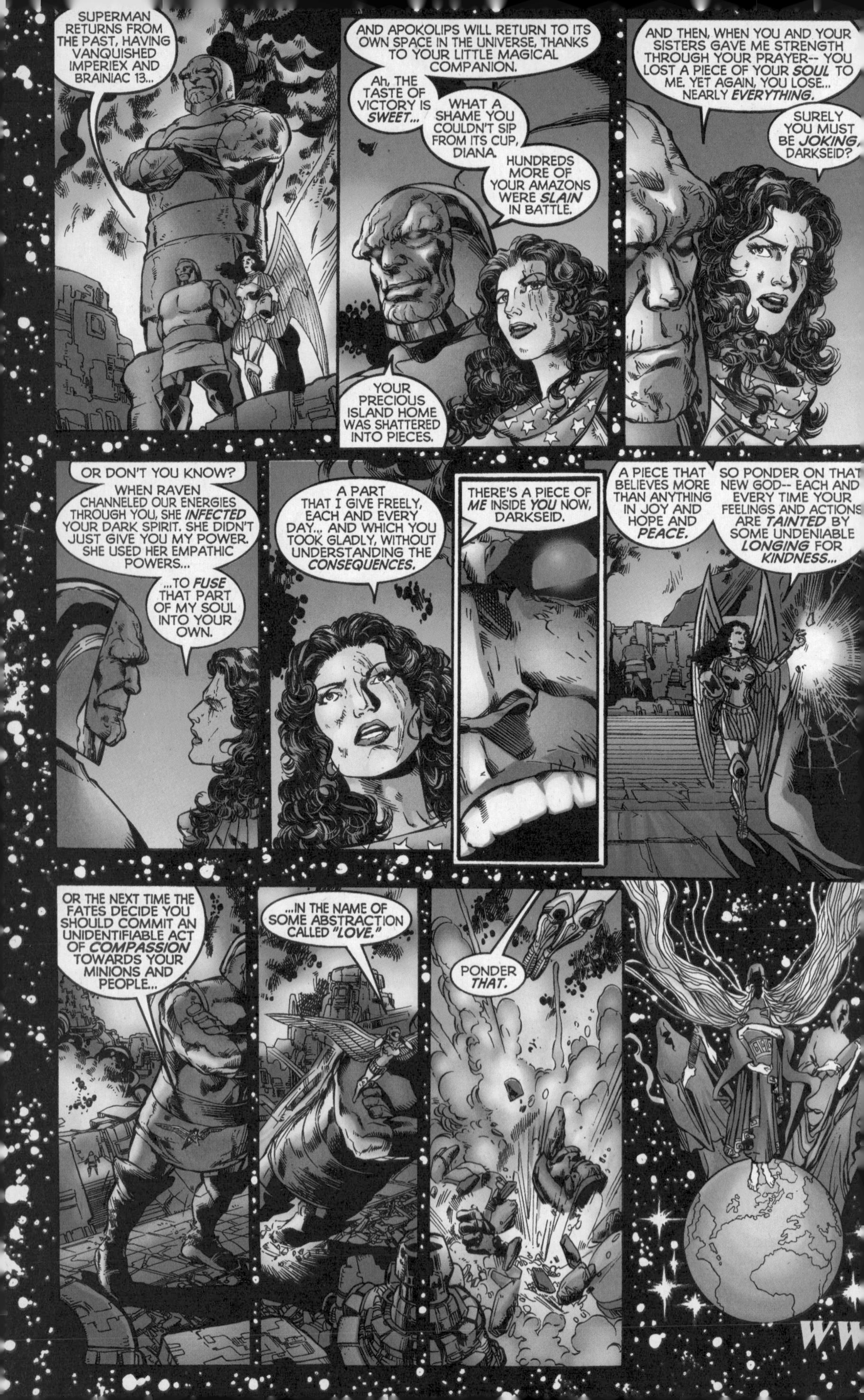

SUPERMAN RETURNS FROM THE PAST, HAVING VANQUISHED IMPERIEX AND BRAINIAC 13...
AND APOKOLIPS WILL RETURN TO ITS OWN SPACE IN THE UNIVERSE, THANKS TO YOUR LITTLE MAGICAL COMPANION.
Ah, THE TASTE OF VICTORY IS SWEET...
WHAT A SHAME YOU COULDN'T SIP FROM ITS CUP, DIANA.
HUNDREDS MORE OF YOUR AMAZONS WERE SLAIN IN BATTLE.
YOUR PRECIOUS ISLAND HOME WAS SHATTERED INTO PIECES.
AND THEN, WHEN YOU AND YOUR SISTERS GAVE ME STRENGTH THROUGH YOUR PRAYER-- YOU LOST A PIECE OF YOUR SOUL TO ME. YET AGAIN, YOU LOSE... NEARLY EVERYTHING.
SURELY YOU MUST BE JOKING, DARKSEID?
OR DON'T YOU KNOW?
WHEN RAVEN CHANNELED OUR ENERGIES THROUGH YOU, SHE INFECTED YOUR DARK SPIRIT. SHE DIDN'T JUST GIVE YOU MY POWER. SHE USED HER EMPATHIC POWERS...
...TO FUSE THAT PART OF MY SOUL INTO YOUR OWN.
A PART THAT I GIVE FREELY, EACH AND EVERY DAY... AND WHICH YOU TOOK GLADLY, WITHOUT UNDERSTANDING THE CONSEQUENCES.
THERE'S A PIECE OF ME INSIDE YOU NOW, DARKSEID.
A PIECE THAT BELIEVES MORE THAN ANYTHING IN JOY AND HOPE AND PEACE.
SO PONDER ON THAT NEW GOD-- EACH AND EVERY TIME YOUR FEELINGS AND ACTIONS ARE TAINTED BY SOME UNDENIABLE LONGING FOR KINDNESS...
OR THE NEXT TIME THE FATES DECIDE YOU SHOULD COMMIT AN UNIDENTIFIABLE ACT OF COMPASSION TOWARDS YOUR MINIONS AND PEOPLE...
...IN THE NAME OF SOME ABSTRACTION CALLED "LOVE."
PONDER THAT.

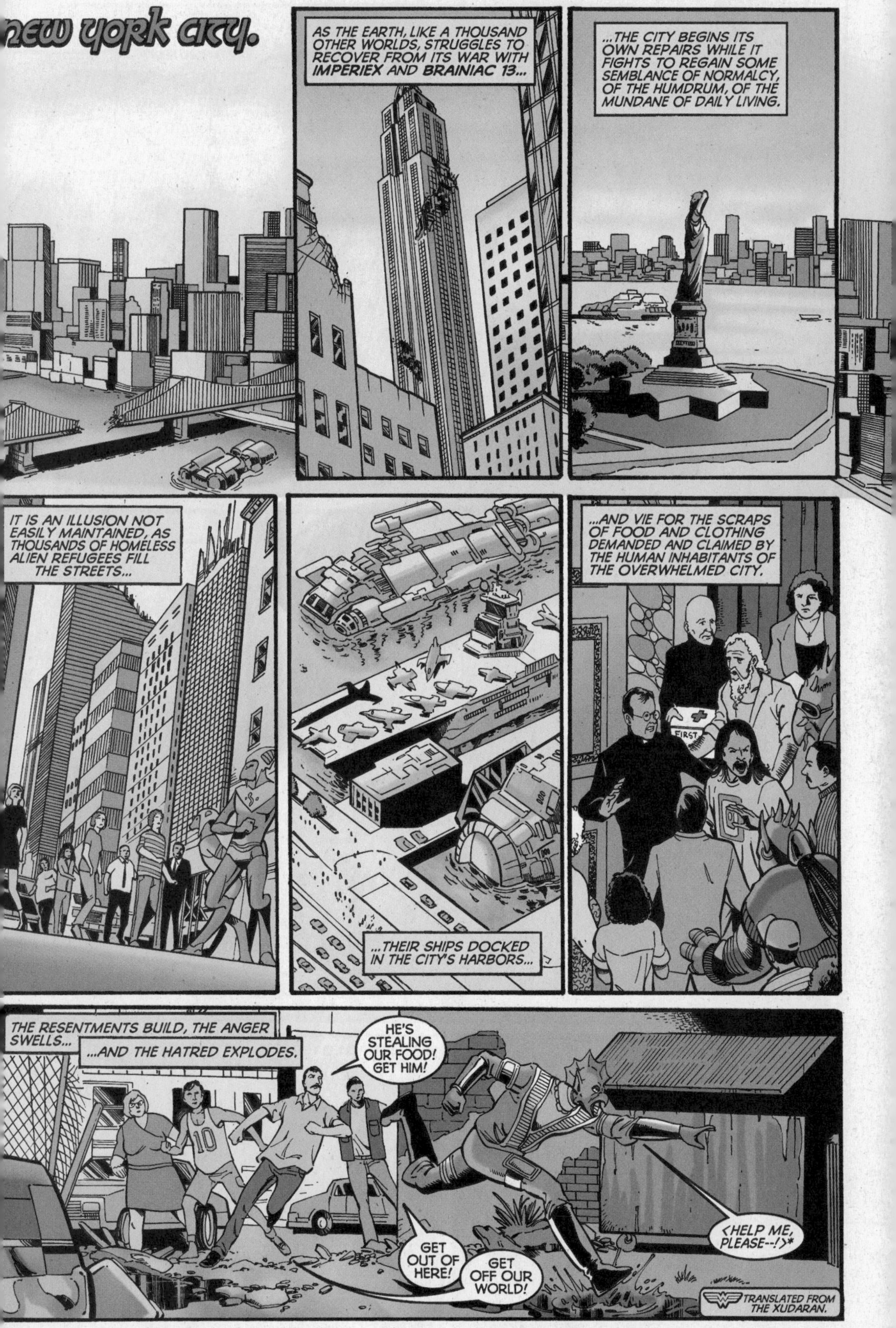
NEW YORK CITY.
AS THE EARTH, LIKE A THOUSAND OTHER WORLDS, STRUGGLES TO RECOVER FROM ITS WAR WITH IMPERIEX AND BRAINIAC 13...
...THE CITY BEGINS ITS OWN REPAIRS WHILE IT FIGHTS TO REGAIN SOME SEMBLANCE OF NORMALCY, OF THE HUMDRUM, OF THE MUNDANE OF DAILY LIVING.
IT IS AN ILLUSION NOT EASILY MAINTAINED, AS THOUSANDS OF HOMELESS ALIEN REFUGEES FILL THE STREETS...
...THEIR SHIPS DOCKED IN THE CITY'S HARBORS...
...AND VIE FOR THE SCRAPS OF FOOD AND CLOTHING DEMANDED AND CLAIMED BY THE HUMAN INHABITANTS OF THE OVERWHELMED CITY.
FIRST
THE RESENTMENTS BUILD, THE ANGER SWELLS...
...AND THE HATRED EXPLODES.
HE'S STEALING OUR FOOD! GET HIM!
GET OUT OF HERE!
GET OFF OUR WORLD!
<HELP ME, PLEASE--!>*
*TRANSLATED FROM THE XUDARAN.

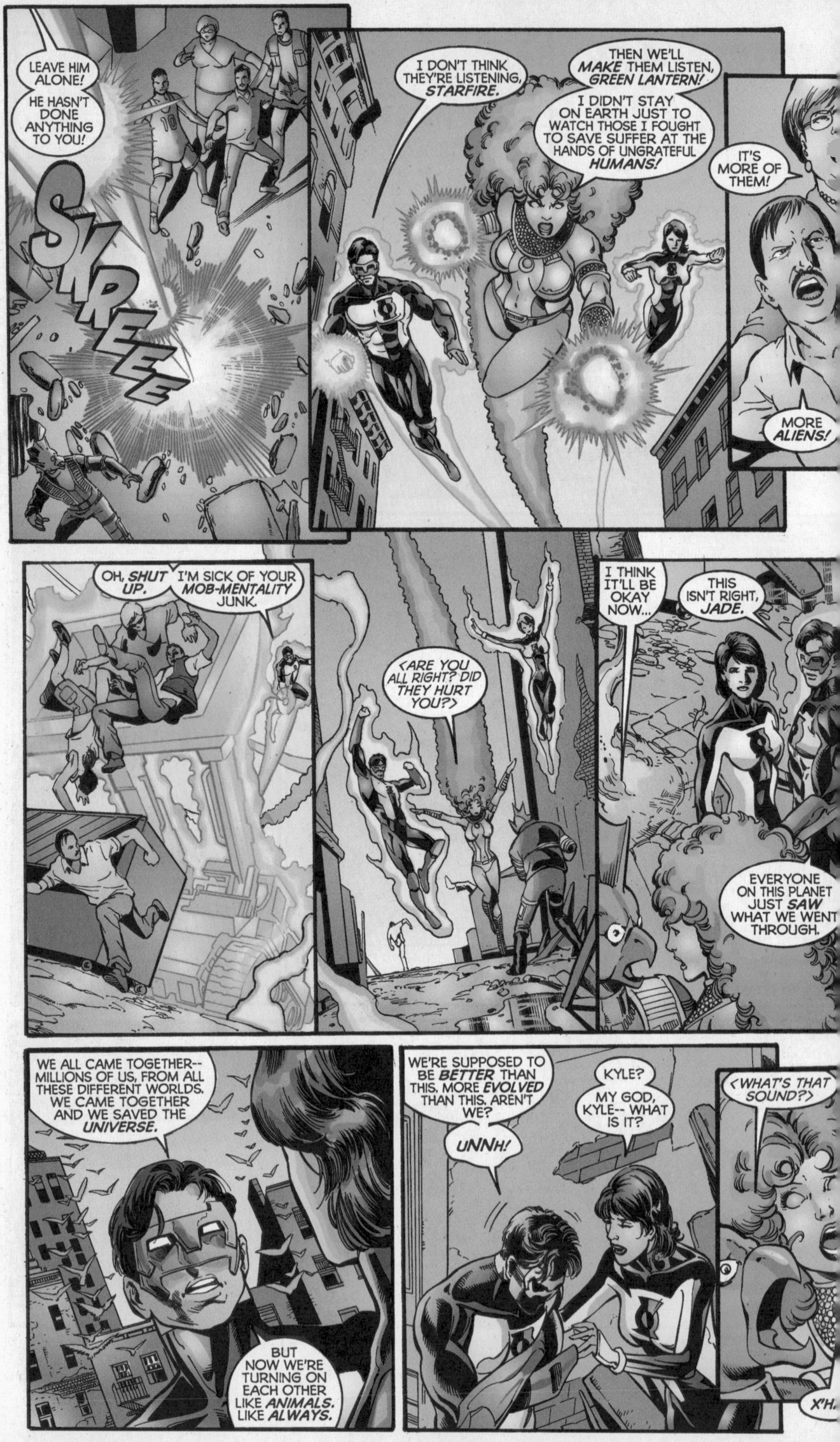
LEAVE HIM ALONE!
HE HASN'T DONE ANYTHING TO YOU!
SKREEEE
I DON'T THINK THEY'RE LISTENING, STARFIRE.
THEN WE'LL MAKE THEM LISTEN, GREEN LANTERN!
I DIDN'T STAY ON EARTH JUST TO WATCH THOSE I FOUGHT TO SAVE SUFFER AT THE HANDS OF UNGRATEFUL HUMANS!
IT'S MORE OF THEM!
MORE ALIENS!
OH, SHUT UP.
I'M SICK OF YOUR MOB-MENTALITY JUNK.
<ARE YOU ALL RIGHT? DID THEY HURT YOU?>
I THINK IT'LL BE OKAY NOW...
THIS ISN'T RIGHT, JADE.
EVERYONE ON THIS PLANET JUST SAW WHAT WE WENT THROUGH.
WE ALL CAME TOGETHER-- MILLIONS OF US, FROM ALL THESE DIFFERENT WORLDS. WE CAME TOGETHER AND WE SAVED THE UNIVERSE.
BUT NOW WE'RE TURNING ON EACH OTHER LIKE ANIMALS. LIKE ALWAYS.
WE'RE SUPPOSED TO BE BETTER THAN THIS. MORE EVOLVED THAN THIS. AREN'T WE?
UNNH!
KYLE?
MY GOD, KYLE-- WHAT IS IT?
<WHAT'S THAT SOUND?>

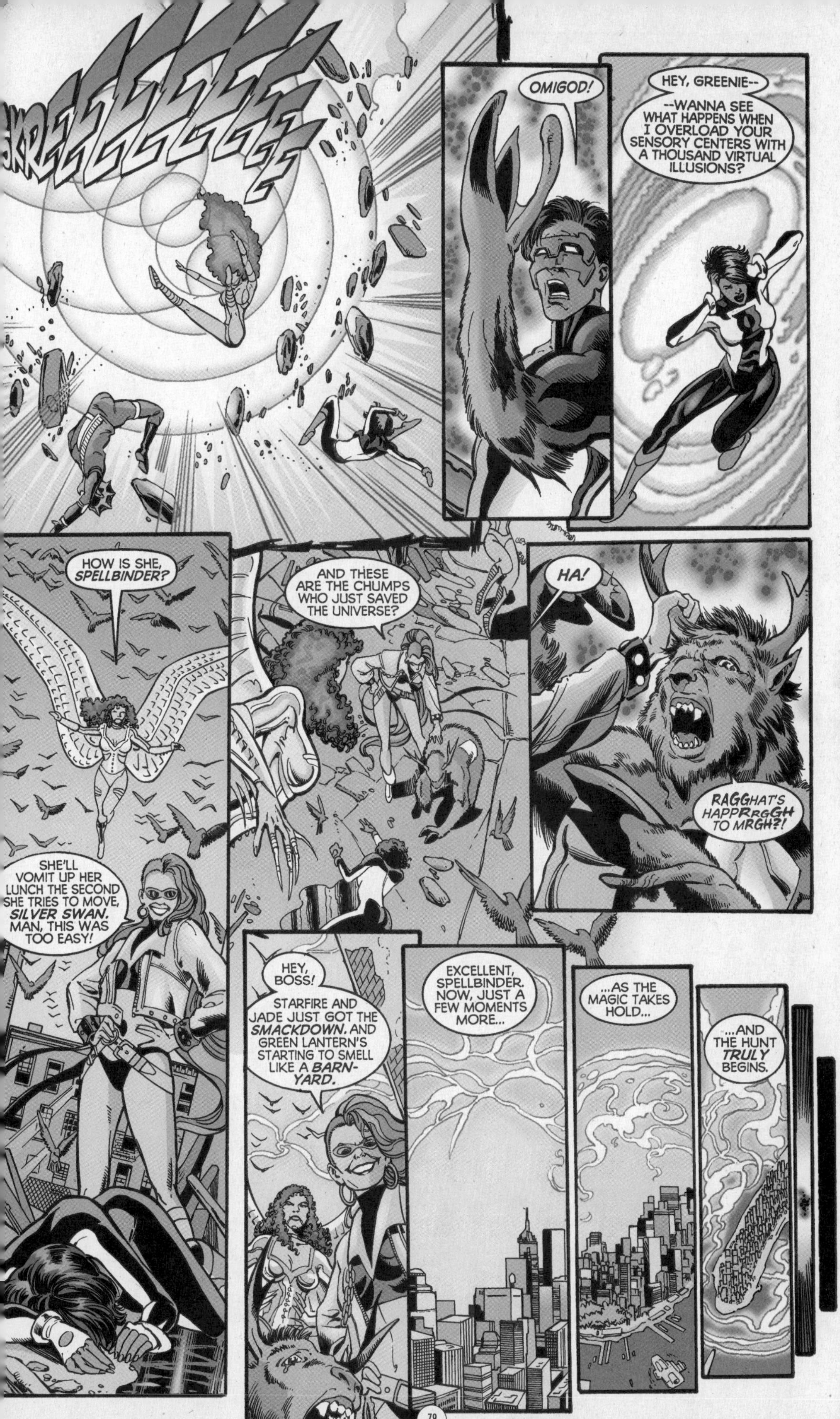
SKREEEEEEEE
OMIGOD!
HEY, GREENIE--
--WANNA SEE WHAT HAPPENS WHEN I OVERLOAD YOUR SENSORY CENTERS WITH A THOUSAND VIRTUAL ILLUSIONS?
HOW IS SHE, SPELLBINDER?
AND THESE ARE THE CHUMPS WHO JUST SAVED THE UNIVERSE?
HA!
RAGGHAT'S HAPPRRGGH TO MRGH?!
SHE'LL VOMIT UP HER LUNCH THE SECOND SHE TRIES TO MOVE, SILVER SWAN. MAN, THIS WAS TOO EASY!
HEY, BOSS!
STARFIRE AND JADE JUST GOT THE SMACKDOWN. AND GREEN LANTERN'S STARTING TO SMELL LIKE A BARN-YARD.
EXCELLENT, SPELLBINDER. NOW, JUST A FEW MOMENTS MORE...
...AS THE MAGIC TAKES HOLD...
...AND THE HUNT TRULY BEGINS.

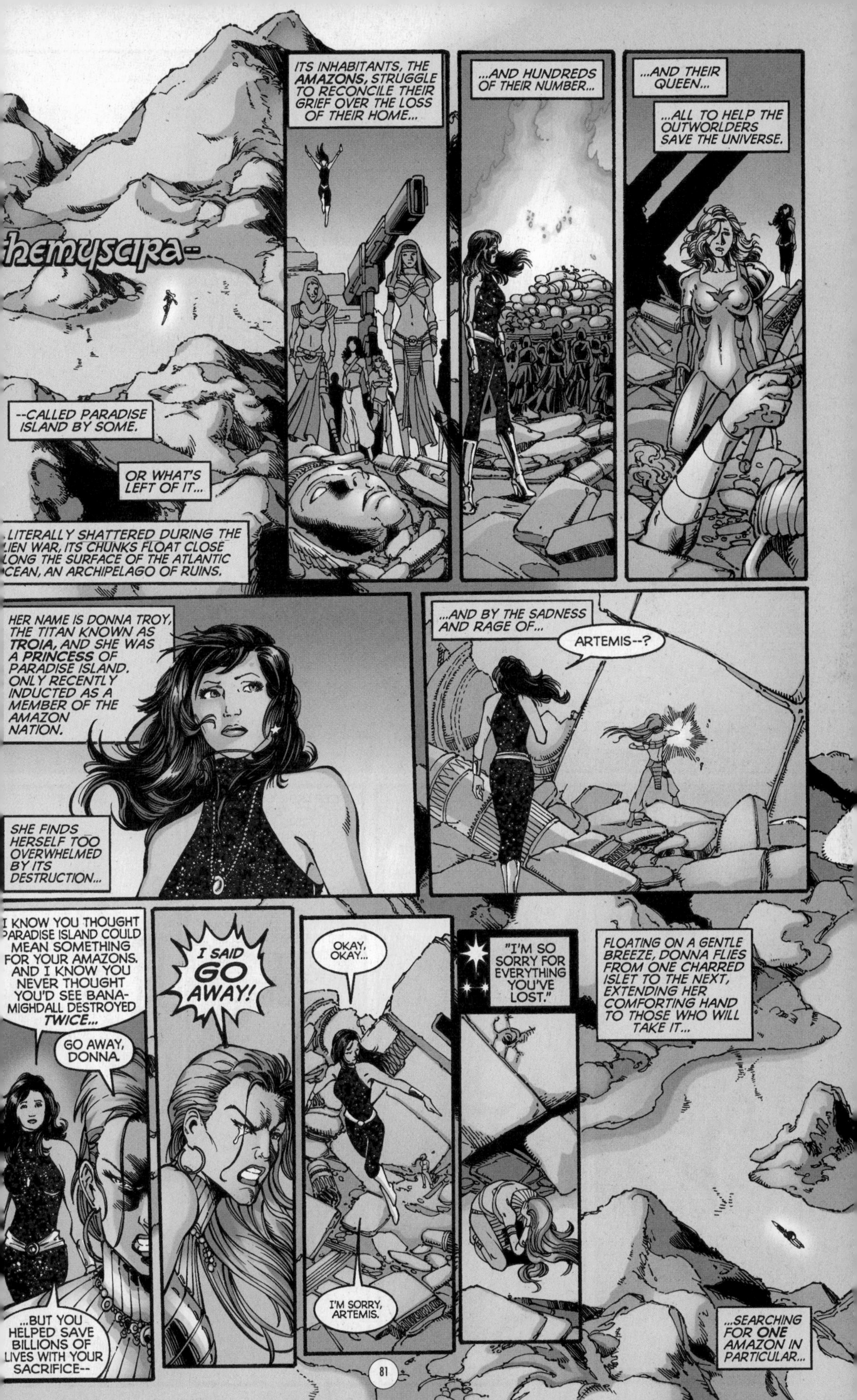

hemyscira-
--CALLED PARADISE ISLAND BY SOME.
OR WHAT'S LEFT OF IT...
LITERALLY SHATTERED DURING THE LIEN WAR, ITS CHUNKS FLOAT CLOSE LONG THE SURFACE OF THE ATLANTIC CEAN, AN ARCHIPELAGO OF RUINS.
ITS INHABITANTS, THE AMAZONS, STRUGGLE TO RECONCILE THEIR GRIEF OVER THE LOSS OF THEIR HOME...
...AND HUNDREDS OF THEIR NUMBER...
...AND THEIR QUEEN...
...ALL TO HELP THE OUTWORLDERS SAVE THE UNIVERSE.
HER NAME IS DONNA TROY, THE TITAN KNOWN AS TROIA, AND SHE WAS A PRINCESS OF PARADISE ISLAND. ONLY RECENTLY INDUCTED AS A MEMBER OF THE AMAZON NATION.
SHE FINDS HERSELF TOO OVERWHELMED BY ITS DESTRUCTION...
...AND BY THE SADNESS AND RAGE OF...
ARTEMIS--?
I KNOW YOU THOUGHT PARADISE ISLAND COULD MEAN SOMETHING FOR YOUR AMAZONS. AND I KNOW YOU NEVER THOUGHT YOU'D SEE BANA-MIGHDALL DESTROYED TWICE...
GO AWAY, DONNA.
...BUT YOU HELPED SAVE BILLIONS OF LIVES WITH YOUR SACRIFICE--
I SAID GO AWAY!
OKAY, OKAY...
I'M SORRY, ARTEMIS.
"I'M SO SORRY FOR EVERYTHING YOU'VE LOST."
FLOATING ON A GENTLE BREEZE, DONNA FLIES FROM ONE CHARRED ISLET TO THE NEXT, EXTENDING HER COMFORTING HAND TO THOSE WHO WILL TAKE IT...
...SEARCHING FOR ONE AMAZON IN PARTICULAR...

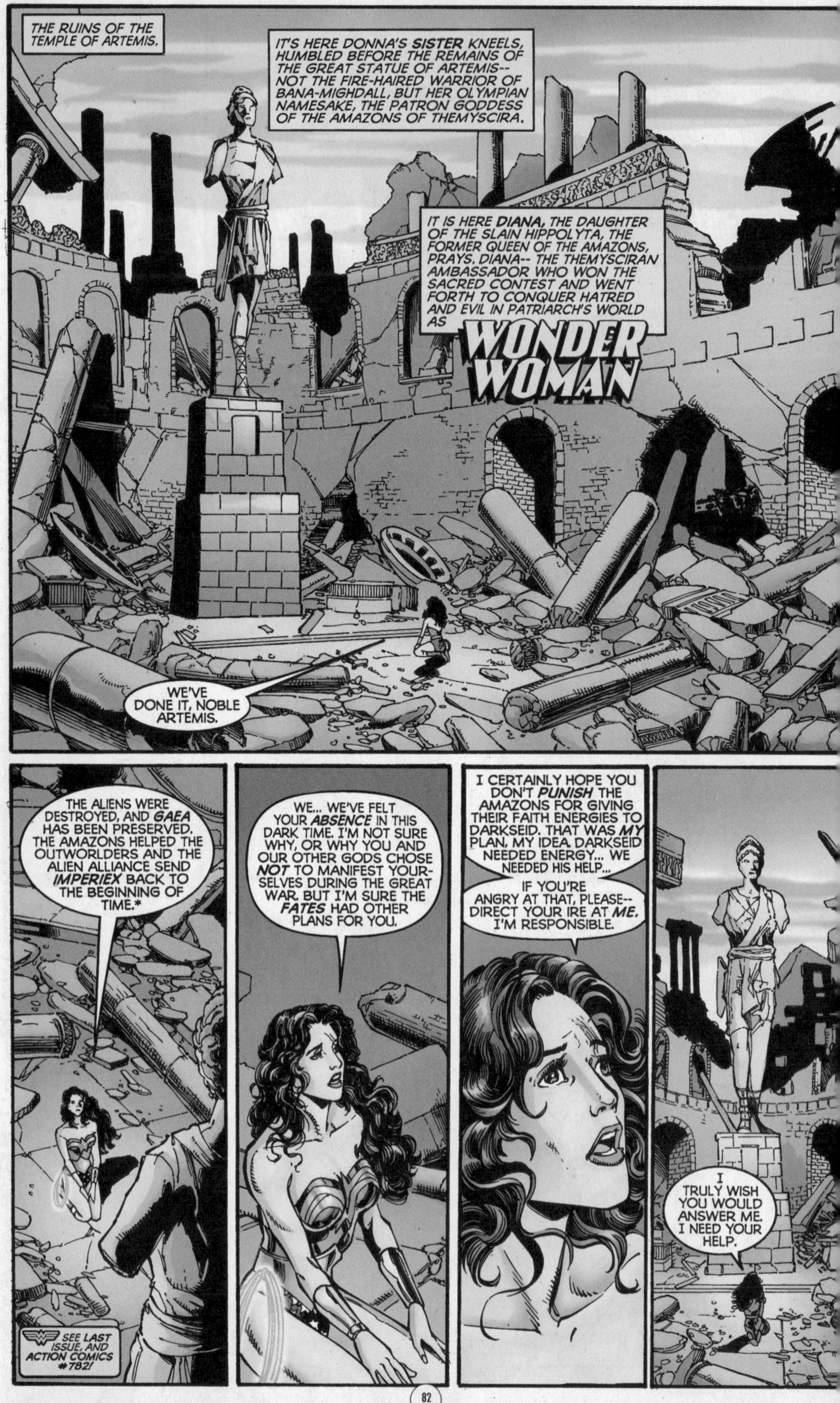
THE RUINS OF THE TEMPLE OF ARTEMIS.
IT'S HERE DONNA'S SISTER KNEELS, HUMBLED BEFORE THE REMAINS OF THE GREAT STATUE OF ARTEMIS-- NOT THE FIRE-HAIRED WARRIOR OF BANA-MIGHDALL, BUT HER OLYMPIAN NAMESAKE, THE PATRON GODDESS OF THE AMAZONS OF THEMYSCIRA.
IT IS HERE DIANA, THE DAUGHTER OF THE SLAIN HIPPOLYTA, THE FORMER QUEEN OF THE AMAZONS, PRAYS. DIANA-- THE THEMYSCIRAN AMBASSADOR WHO WON THE SACRED CONTEST AND WENT FORTH TO CONQUER HATRED AND EVIL IN PATRIARCH'S WORLD AS
WONDER WOMAN
WE'VE DONE IT, NOBLE ARTEMIS.
THE ALIENS WERE DESTROYED, AND GAEA HAS BEEN PRESERVED. THE AMAZONS HELPED THE OUTWORLDERS AND THE ALIEN ALLIANCE SEND IMPERIEX BACK TO THE BEGINNING OF TIME.*
SEE LAST ISSUE, AND ACTION COMICS #782!
WE... WE'VE FELT YOUR ABSENCE IN THIS DARK TIME. I'M NOT SURE WHY, OR WHY YOU AND OUR OTHER GODS CHOSE NOT TO MANIFEST YOURSELVES DURING THE GREAT WAR. BUT I'M SURE THE FATES HAD OTHER PLANS FOR YOU.
I CERTAINLY HOPE YOU DON'T PUNISH THE AMAZONS FOR GIVING THEIR FAITH ENERGIES TO DARKSEID. THAT WAS MY PLAN, MY IDEA. DARKSEID NEEDED ENERGY... WE NEEDED HIS HELP...
IF YOU'RE ANGRY AT THAT, PLEASE-- DIRECT YOUR IRE AT ME. I'M RESPONSIBLE.
I TRULY WISH YOU WOULD ANSWER ME. I NEED YOUR HELP.

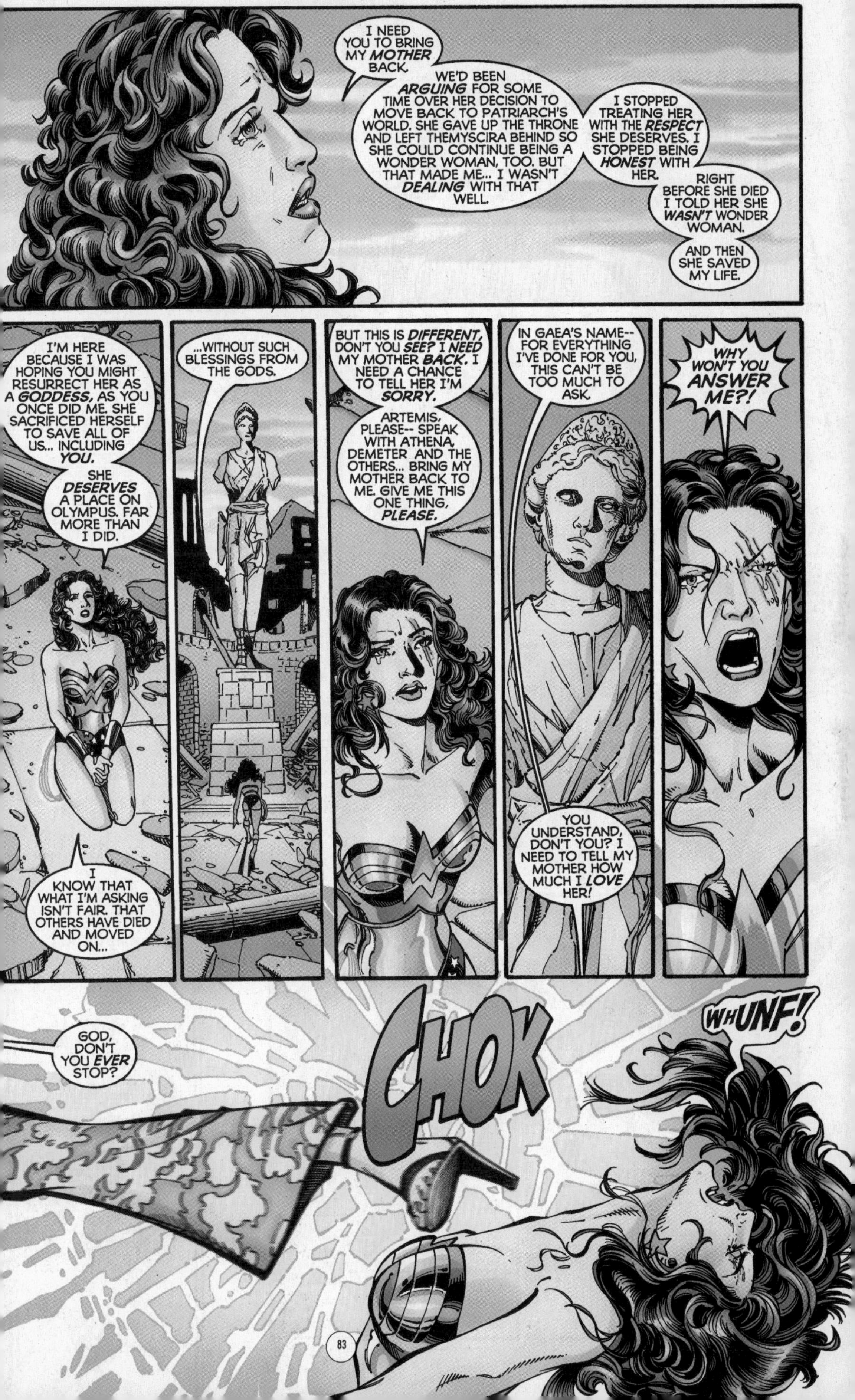

I NEED YOU TO BRING MY *MOTHER* BACK.
WE'D BEEN *ARGUING* FOR SOME TIME OVER HER DECISION TO MOVE BACK TO PATRIARCH'S WORLD. SHE GAVE UP THE THRONE AND LEFT THEMYSCIRA BEHIND SO SHE COULD CONTINUE BEING A WONDER WOMAN, TOO. BUT THAT MADE ME... I WASN'T *DEALING* WITH THAT WELL.
I STOPPED TREATING HER WITH THE *RESPECT* SHE DESERVES. I STOPPED BEING *HONEST* WITH HER.
RIGHT BEFORE SHE DIED I TOLD HER SHE *WASN'T* WONDER WOMAN.
AND THEN SHE SAVED MY LIFE.
I'M HERE BECAUSE I WAS HOPING YOU MIGHT RESURRECT HER AS A *GODDESS,* AS YOU ONCE DID ME. SHE SACRIFICED HERSELF TO SAVE ALL OF US... INCLUDING *YOU.*
SHE *DESERVES* A PLACE ON OLYMPUS. FAR MORE THAN I DID.
I KNOW THAT WHAT I'M ASKING ISN'T FAIR. THAT OTHERS HAVE DIED AND MOVED ON...
...WITHOUT SUCH BLESSINGS FROM THE GODS.
BUT THIS IS *DIFFERENT,* DON'T YOU *SEE?* I *NEED* MY MOTHER *BACK.* I NEED A CHANCE TO TELL HER I'M *SORRY.*
ARTEMIS, PLEASE-- SPEAK WITH ATHENA, DEMETER AND THE OTHERS... BRING MY MOTHER BACK TO ME. GIVE ME THIS ONE THING, *PLEASE.*
IN GAEA'S NAME-- FOR EVERYTHING I'VE DONE FOR YOU, THIS CAN'T BE TOO MUCH TO ASK.
YOU UNDERSTAND, DON'T YOU? I NEED TO TELL MY MOTHER HOW MUCH I *LOVE* HER!
WHY WON'T YOU ANSWER ME?!
GOD, DON'T YOU *EVER* STOP?
CHOK
WHUNF!

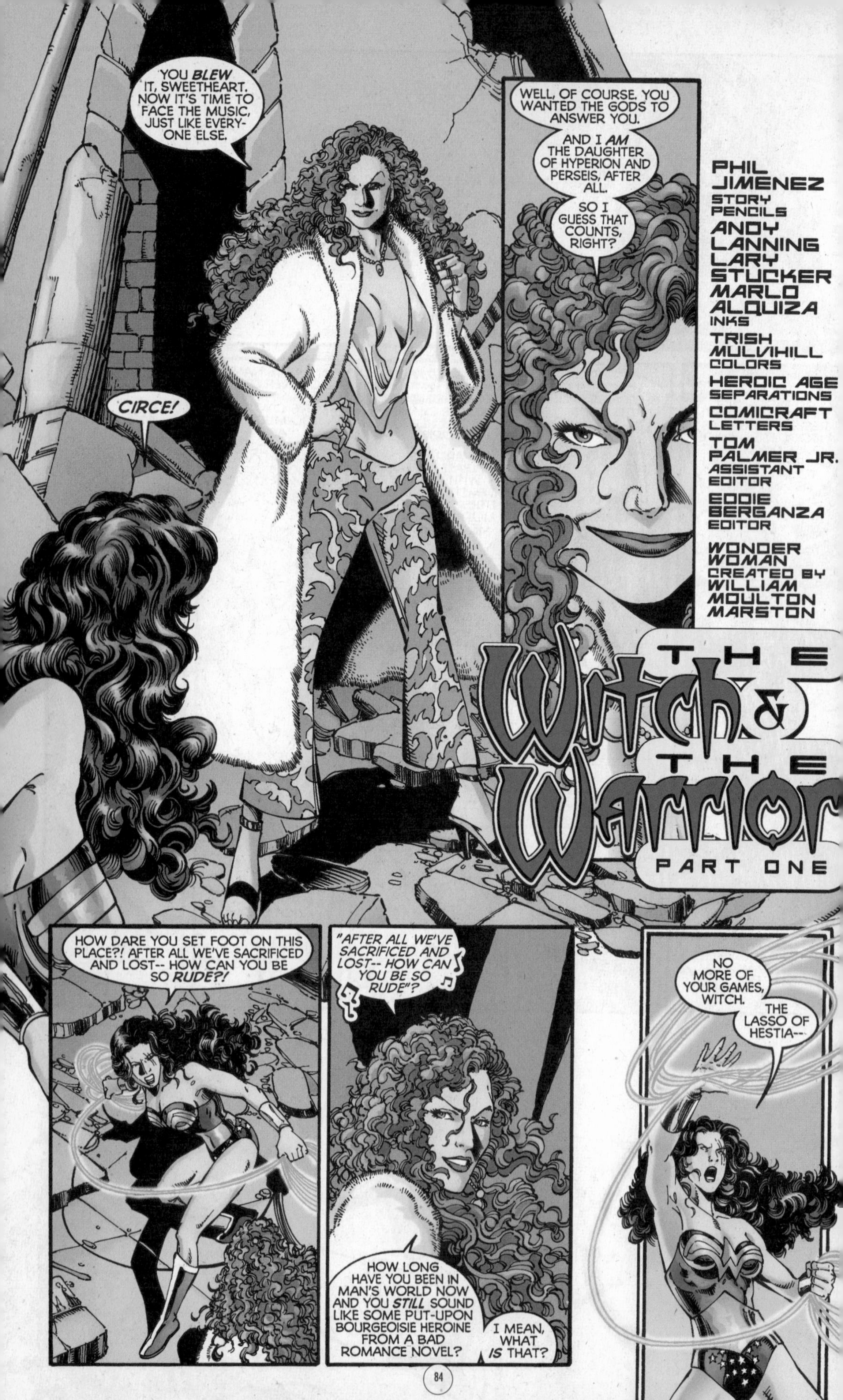

YOU BLEW IT, SWEETHEART. NOW IT'S TIME TO FACE THE MUSIC, JUST LIKE EVERY-ONE ELSE.
CIRCE!
WELL, OF COURSE. YOU WANTED THE GODS TO ANSWER YOU.
AND I AM THE DAUGHTER OF HYPERION AND PERSEIS, AFTER ALL.
SO I GUESS THAT COUNTS, RIGHT?
PHIL JIMENEZ STORY PENCILS
ANDY LANNING LARY STUCKER MARLO ALQUIZA INKS
TRISH MULVIHILL COLORS
HEROIC AGE SEPARATIONS
COMICRAFT LETTERS
TOM PALMER JR. ASSISTANT EDITOR
EDDIE BERGANZA EDITOR
WONDER WOMAN CREATED BY WILLIAM MOULTON MARSTON
THE WITCH & THE WARRIOR
PART ONE
HOW DARE YOU SET FOOT ON THIS PLACE?! AFTER ALL WE'VE SACRIFICED AND LOST-- HOW CAN YOU BE SO RUDE?!
"AFTER ALL WE'VE SACRIFICED AND LOST-- HOW CAN YOU BE SO RUDE"?
HOW LONG HAVE YOU BEEN IN MAN'S WORLD NOW AND YOU STILL SOUND LIKE SOME PUT-UPON BOURGEOISIE HEROINE FROM A BAD ROMANCE NOVEL?
I MEAN, WHAT IS THAT?
NO MORE OF YOUR GAMES, WITCH.
THE LASSO OF HESTIA--

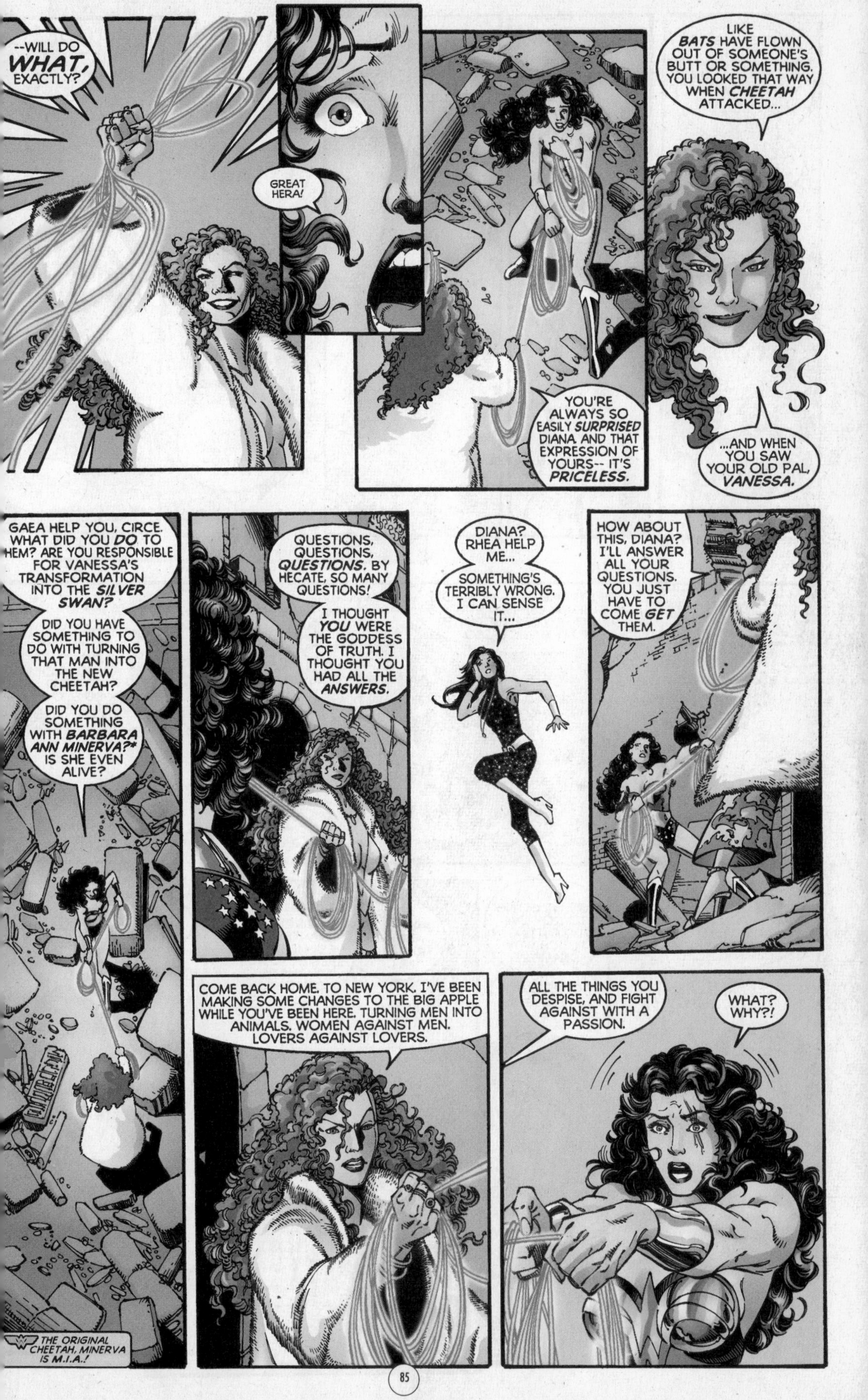
--WILL DO WHAT, EXACTLY?
GREAT HERA!
LIKE BATS HAVE FLOWN OUT OF SOMEONE'S BUTT OR SOMETHING. YOU LOOKED THAT WAY WHEN CHEETAH ATTACKED...
YOU'RE ALWAYS SO EASILY SURPRISED DIANA AND THAT EXPRESSION OF YOURS-- IT'S PRICELESS.
...AND WHEN YOU SAW YOUR OLD PAL, VANESSA.
GAEA HELP YOU, CIRCE. WHAT DID YOU DO TO HEM? ARE YOU RESPONSIBLE FOR VANESSA'S TRANSFORMATION INTO THE SILVER SWAN?
DID YOU HAVE SOMETHING TO DO WITH TURNING THAT MAN INTO THE NEW CHEETAH?
DID YOU DO SOMETHING WITH BARBARA ANN MINERVA?* IS SHE EVEN ALIVE?
*THE ORIGINAL CHEETAH, MINERVA IS M.I.A.!
QUESTIONS, QUESTIONS, QUESTIONS. BY HECATE, SO MANY QUESTIONS!
I THOUGHT YOU WERE THE GODDESS OF TRUTH. I THOUGHT YOU HAD ALL THE ANSWERS.
DIANA? RHEA HELP ME...
SOMETHING'S TERRIBLY WRONG. I CAN SENSE IT...
HOW ABOUT THIS, DIANA? I'LL ANSWER ALL YOUR QUESTIONS. YOU JUST HAVE TO COME GET THEM.
COME BACK HOME. TO NEW YORK. I'VE BEEN MAKING SOME CHANGES TO THE BIG APPLE WHILE YOU'VE BEEN HERE. TURNING MEN INTO ANIMALS. WOMEN AGAINST MEN. LOVERS AGAINST LOVERS.
ALL THE THINGS YOU DESPISE, AND FIGHT AGAINST WITH A PASSION.
WHAT? WHY?!

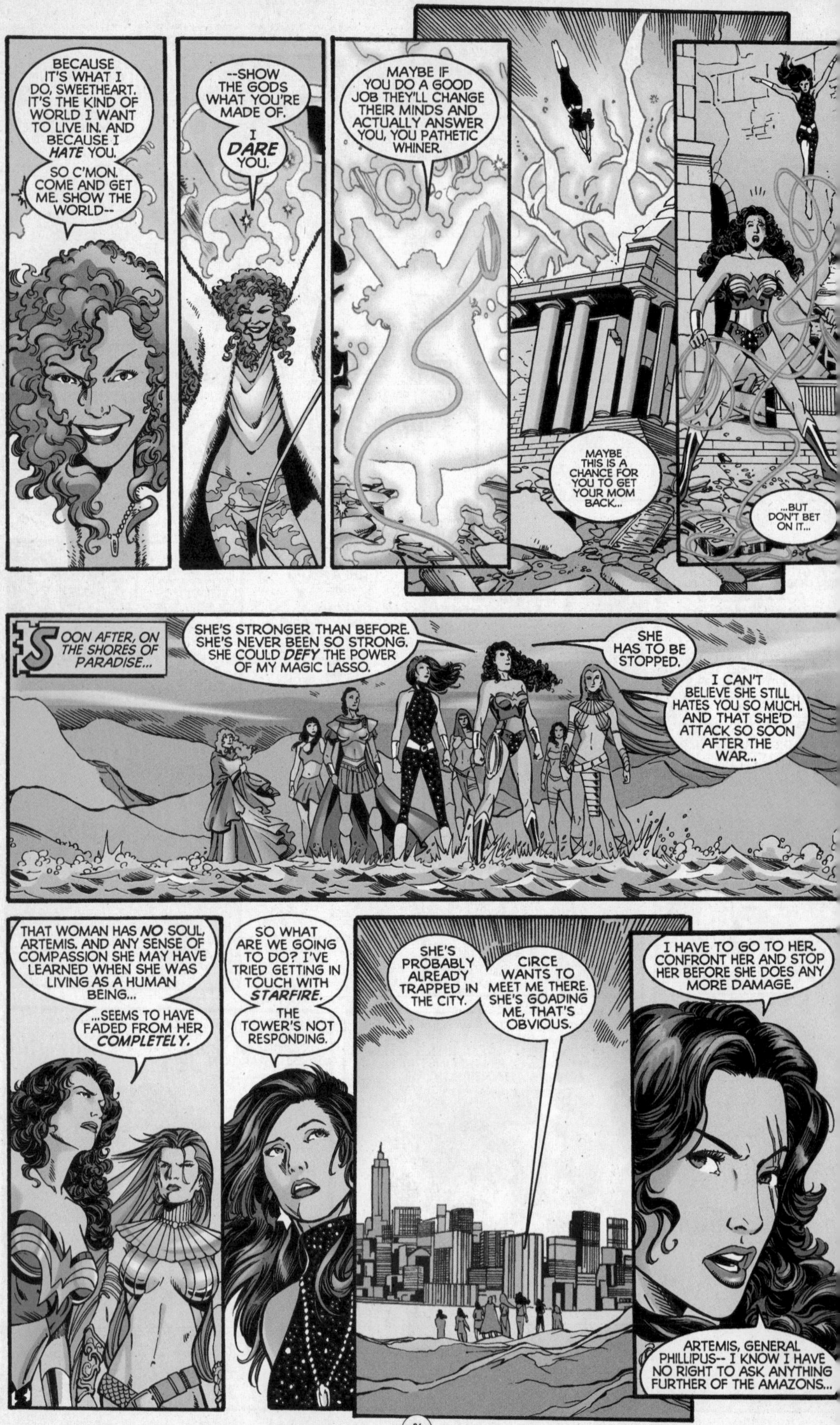
BECAUSE IT'S WHAT I DO, SWEETHEART. IT'S THE KIND OF WORLD I WANT TO LIVE IN. AND BECAUSE I HATE YOU.
SO C'MON. COME AND GET ME. SHOW THE WORLD--
--SHOW THE GODS WHAT YOU'RE MADE OF.
I DARE YOU.
MAYBE IF YOU DO A GOOD JOB THEY'LL CHANGE THEIR MINDS AND ACTUALLY ANSWER YOU, YOU PATHETIC WHINER.
MAYBE THIS IS A CHANCE FOR YOU TO GET YOUR MOM BACK...
...BUT DON'T BET ON IT...
SOON AFTER, ON THE SHORES OF PARADISE...
SHE'S STRONGER THAN BEFORE. SHE'S NEVER BEEN SO STRONG. SHE COULD DEFY THE POWER OF MY MAGIC LASSO.
SHE HAS TO BE STOPPED.
I CAN'T BELIEVE SHE STILL HATES YOU SO MUCH. AND THAT SHE'D ATTACK SO SOON AFTER THE WAR...
THAT WOMAN HAS NO SOUL, ARTEMIS. AND ANY SENSE OF COMPASSION SHE MAY HAVE LEARNED WHEN SHE WAS LIVING AS A HUMAN BEING...
...SEEMS TO HAVE FADED FROM HER COMPLETELY.
SO WHAT ARE WE GOING TO DO? I'VE TRIED GETTING IN TOUCH WITH STARFIRE.
THE TOWER'S NOT RESPONDING.
SHE'S PROBABLY ALREADY TRAPPED IN THE CITY.
CIRCE WANTS TO MEET ME THERE. SHE'S GOADING ME, THAT'S OBVIOUS.
I HAVE TO GO TO HER. CONFRONT HER AND STOP HER BEFORE SHE DOES ANY MORE DAMAGE.
ARTEMIS, GENERAL PHILLIPUS-- I KNOW I HAVE NO RIGHT TO ASK ANYTHING FURTHER OF THE AMAZONS...

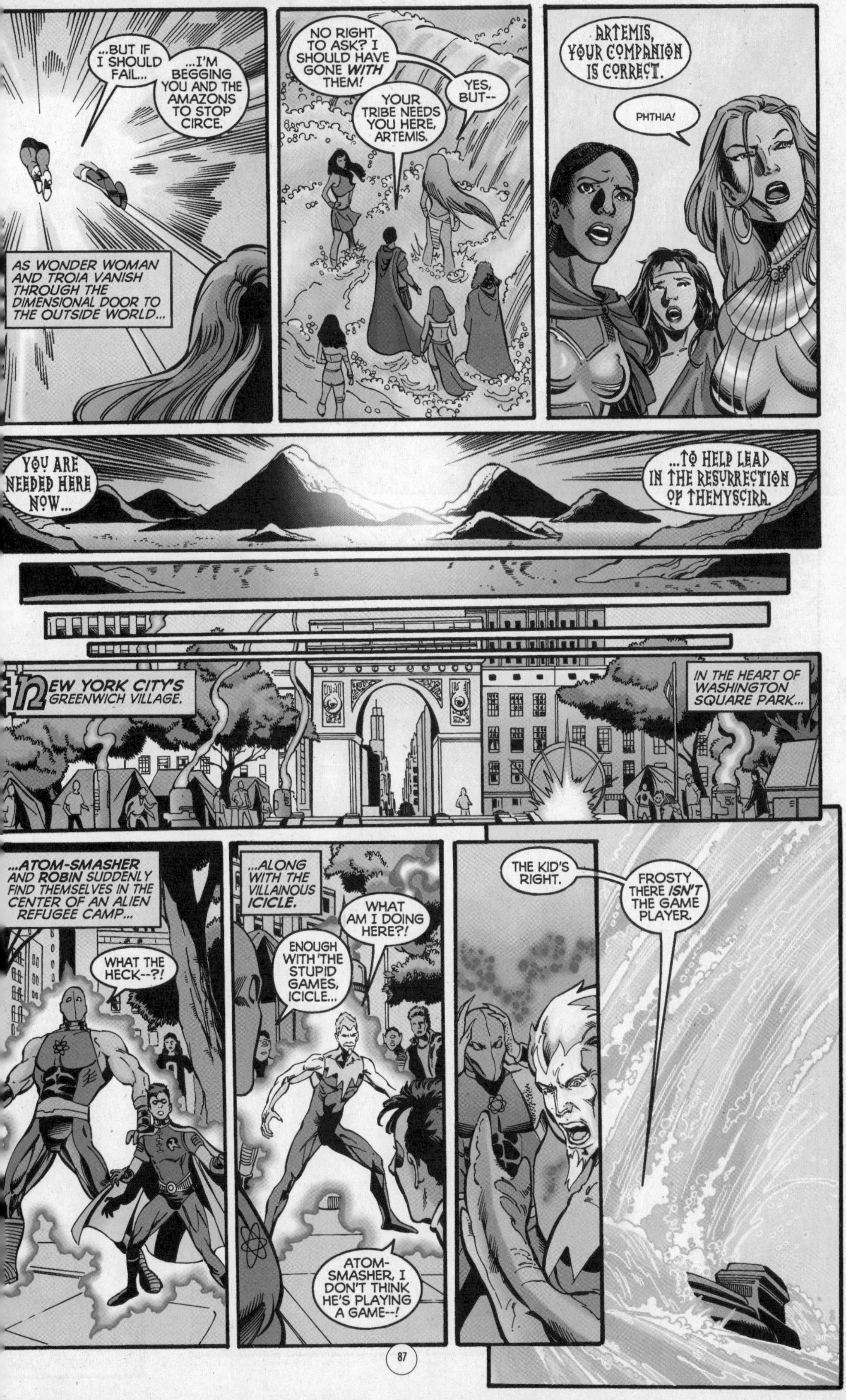
...BUT IF I SHOULD FAIL...
...I'M BEGGING YOU AND THE AMAZONS TO STOP CIRCE.
AS WONDER WOMAN AND TROIA VANISH THROUGH THE DIMENSIONAL DOOR TO THE OUTSIDE WORLD...
NO RIGHT TO ASK? I SHOULD HAVE GONE WITH THEM!
YES, BUT--
YOUR TRIBE NEEDS YOU HERE, ARTEMIS.
ARTEMIS, YOUR COMPANION IS CORRECT.
PHTHIA!
YOU ARE NEEDED HERE NOW...
...TO HELP LEAD IN THE RESURRECTION OF THEMYSCIRA.
NEW YORK CITY'S GREENWICH VILLAGE.
IN THE HEART OF WASHINGTON SQUARE PARK...
...ATOM-SMASHER AND ROBIN SUDDENLY FIND THEMSELVES IN THE CENTER OF AN ALIEN REFUGEE CAMP...
WHAT THE HECK--?!
...ALONG WITH THE VILLAINOUS ICICLE.
WHAT AM I DOING HERE?!
ENOUGH WITH THE STUPID GAMES, ICICLE...
ATOM-SMASHER, I DON'T THINK HE'S PLAYING A GAME--!
THE KID'S RIGHT.
FROSTY THERE ISN'T THE GAME PLAYER.

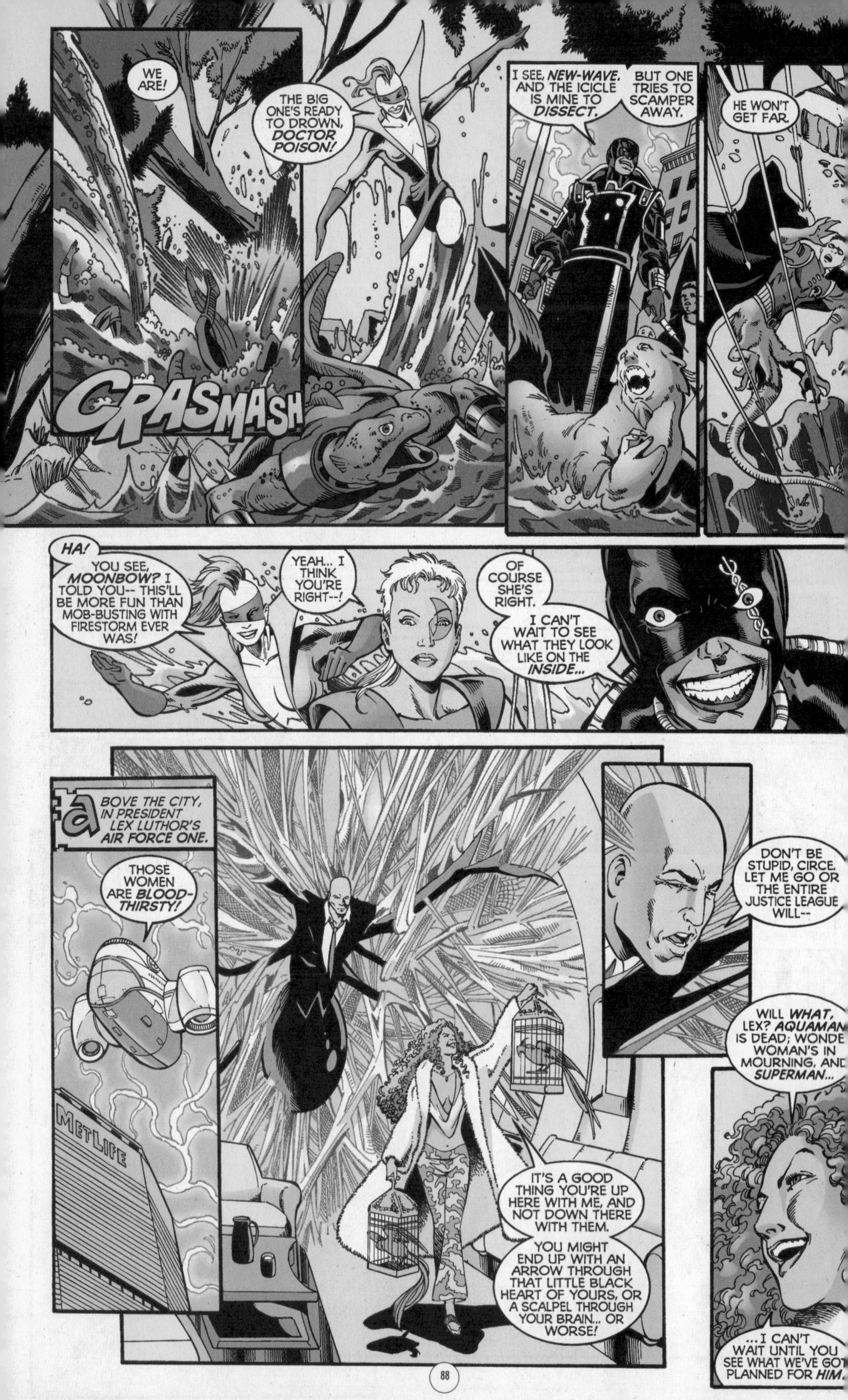
WE ARE!
THE BIG ONE'S READY TO DROWN, DOCTOR POISON!
CRASMASH
I SEE, NEW-WAVE. AND THE ICICLE IS MINE TO DISSECT.
BUT ONE TRIES TO SCAMPER AWAY.
HE WON'T GET FAR.
HA!
YOU SEE, MOONBOW? I TOLD YOU-- THIS'LL BE MORE FUN THAN MOB-BUSTING WITH FIRESTORM EVER WAS!
YEAH... I THINK YOU'RE RIGHT--!
OF COURSE SHE'S RIGHT.
I CAN'T WAIT TO SEE WHAT THEY LOOK LIKE ON THE INSIDE...
ABOVE THE CITY, IN PRESIDENT LEX LUTHOR'S AIR FORCE ONE.
THOSE WOMEN ARE BLOOD-THIRSTY!
METLIFE
IT'S A GOOD THING YOU'RE UP HERE WITH ME, AND NOT DOWN THERE WITH THEM.
YOU MIGHT END UP WITH AN ARROW THROUGH THAT LITTLE BLACK HEART OF YOURS, OR A SCALPEL THROUGH YOUR BRAIN... OR WORSE!
DON'T BE STUPID, CIRCE. LET ME GO OR THE ENTIRE JUSTICE LEAGUE WILL--
WILL WHAT, LEX? AQUAMAN IS DEAD; WONDE WOMAN'S IN MOURNING, AND SUPERMAN...
...I CAN'T WAIT UNTIL YOU SEE WHAT WE'VE GOT PLANNED FOR HIM.

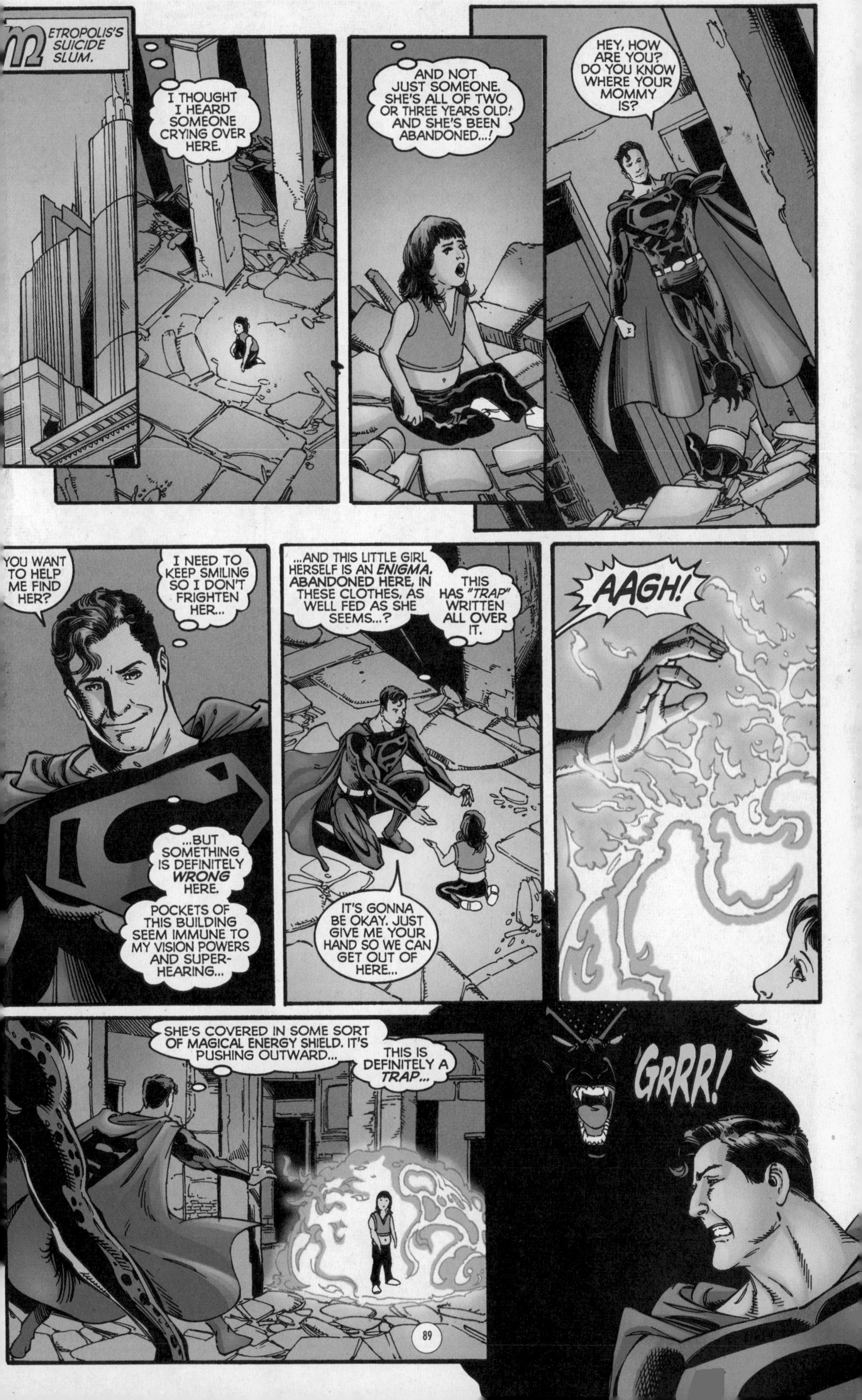
METROPOLIS'S SUICIDE SLUM.
I THOUGHT I HEARD SOMEONE CRYING OVER HERE.
AND NOT JUST SOMEONE. SHE'S ALL OF TWO OR THREE YEARS OLD! AND SHE'S BEEN ABANDONED...!
HEY, HOW ARE YOU? DO YOU KNOW WHERE YOUR MOMMY IS?
YOU WANT TO HELP ME FIND HER?
I NEED TO KEEP SMILING SO I DON'T FRIGHTEN HER...
...BUT SOMETHING IS DEFINITELY WRONG HERE.
POCKETS OF THIS BUILDING SEEM IMMUNE TO MY VISION POWERS AND SUPER-HEARING...
...AND THIS LITTLE GIRL HERSELF IS AN ENIGMA. ABANDONED HERE, IN THESE CLOTHES, AS WELL FED AS SHE SEEMS...?
THIS HAS "TRAP" WRITTEN ALL OVER IT.
IT'S GONNA BE OKAY. JUST GIVE ME YOUR HAND SO WE CAN GET OUT OF HERE...
AAGH!
SHE'S COVERED IN SOME SORT OF MAGICAL ENERGY SHIELD. IT'S PUSHING OUTWARD...
THIS IS DEFINITELY A TRAP...
GRRR!

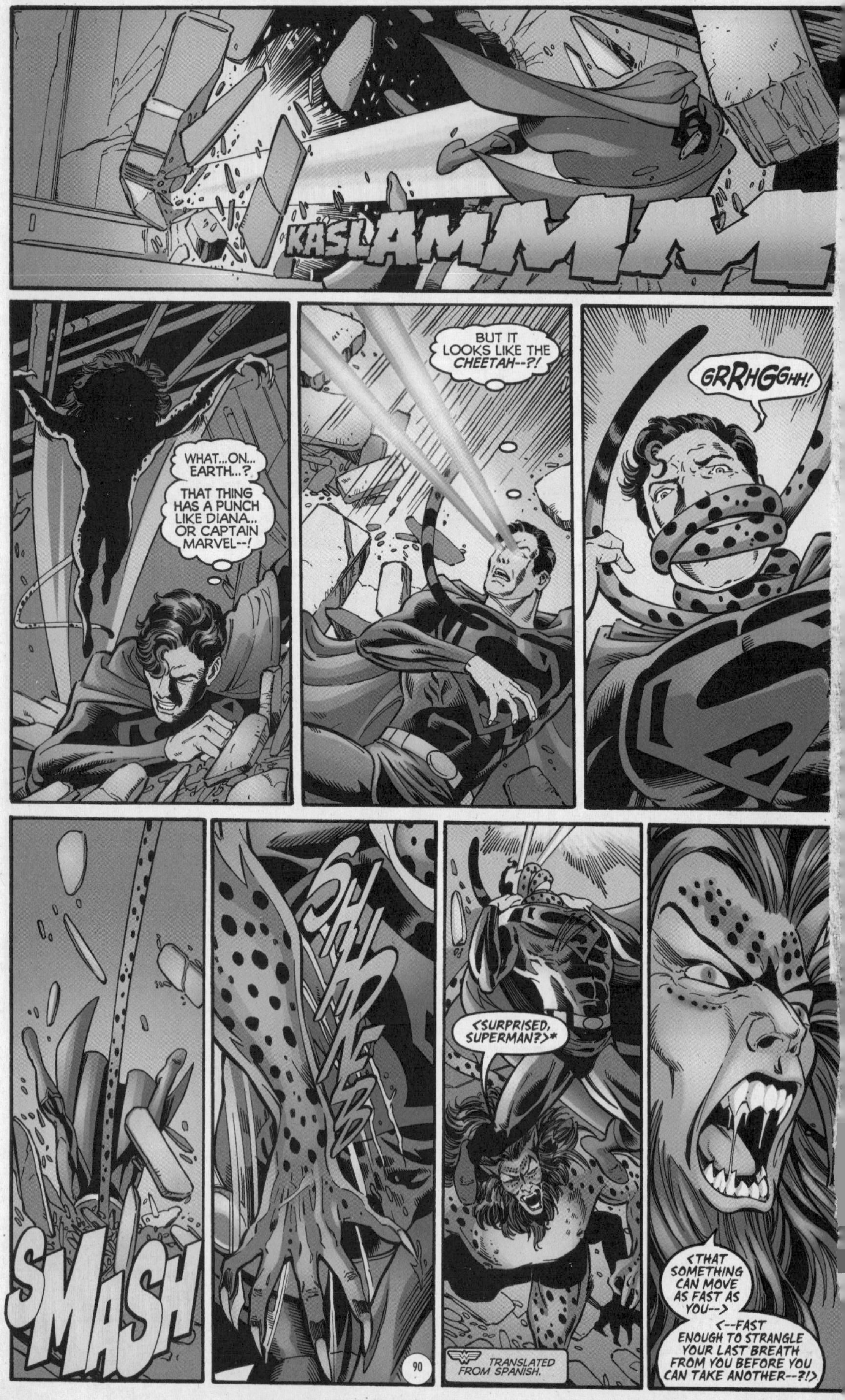
KASLAMMMM
WHAT...ON... EARTH...? THAT THING HAS A PUNCH LIKE DIANA... OR CAPTAIN MARVEL--!
BUT IT LOOKS LIKE THE CHEETAH--?!
GRRHGGHH!
SMASH
<SURPRISED, SUPERMAN?>*
<THAT SOMETHING CAN MOVE AS FAST AS YOU-->
<--FAST ENOUGH TO STRANGLE YOUR LAST BREATH FROM YOU BEFORE YOU CAN TAKE ANOTHER--?!>
*TRANSLATED FROM SPANISH.

‹WHAT'S THE MATTER, SUPERMAN?› ‹CAT GOT YOUR TONGUE?›

GGLLHH!

ABOVE NEW YORK CITY.

SURELY A SETUP AS WELL EQUIPPED AS THIS HAS A KITCHEN.

OPE AND MERCY MAY NOT HAVE BEEN TERRIBLY IMPRESSIVE AS BODYGUARDS...

...BUT I BET THEY'D TASTE FABULOUS WITH SOME BROCCOLI AND A NICE BROWN SAUCE.

HUNGRY, LEX?

CIRCE, LISTEN TO ME. WITH OUR COMBINED TALENTS, WE CAN STILL TAKE THIS PLANET OVER--

I GAVE YOU YOUR CHANCE, LEX.* AND YOU ONLY GET ONE WITH ME.

*PRESIDENT LUTHOR SECRET FILES #1.

NOW, I THINK I HEAR MY DAUGHTER. LYTA!

MOMMY!

AND HOW'S MY LITTLE GIRL? DID YOU WATCH AS MOMMY'S FRIEND TOOK CARE OF THE BIG MAN IN BLUE?

MOMMY, IT WAS SO MUCH FUN!

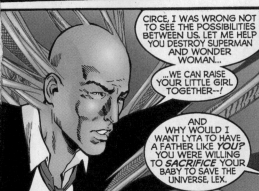

CIRCE, I WAS WRONG NOT TO SEE THE POSSIBILITIES BETWEEN US. LET ME HELP YOU DESTROY SUPERMAN AND WONDER WOMAN...

...WE CAN RAISE YOUR LITTLE GIRL TOGETHER--!

AND WHY WOULD I WANT LYTA TO HAVE A FATHER LIKE YOU? YOU WERE WILLING TO SACRIFICE YOUR BABY TO SAVE THE UNIVERSE, LEX.

AND I'M WILLING TO SACRIFICE THE UNIVERSE FOR MY BABY.

I THINK THAT ABOUT SAYS IT ALL, DON'T YOU?

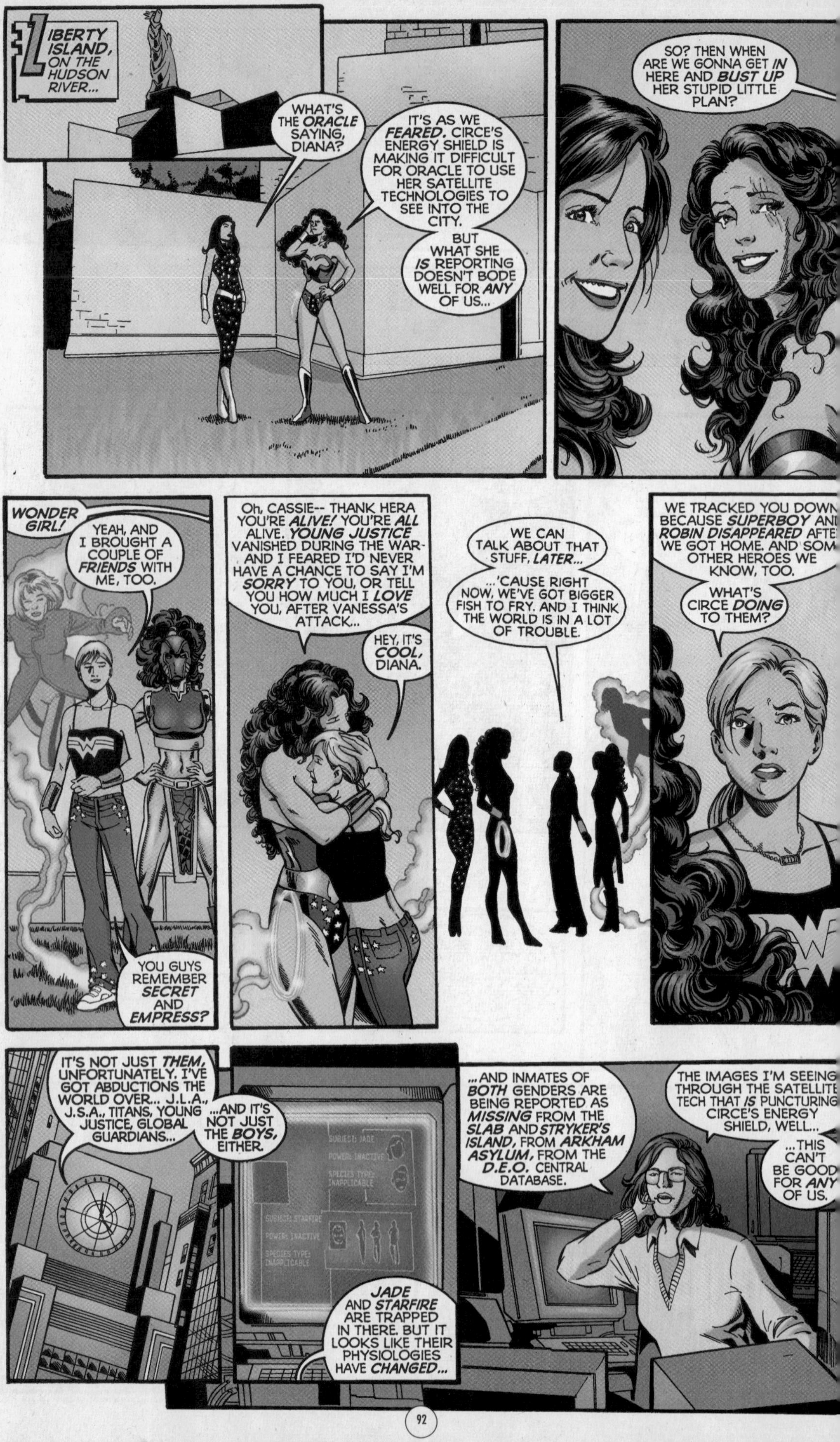
LIBERTY ISLAND, ON THE HUDSON RIVER...
WHAT'S THE ORACLE SAYING, DIANA?
IT'S AS WE FEARED. CIRCE'S ENERGY SHIELD IS MAKING IT DIFFICULT FOR ORACLE TO USE HER SATELLITE TECHNOLOGIES TO SEE INTO THE CITY.
BUT WHAT SHE IS REPORTING DOESN'T BODE WELL FOR ANY OF US...
SO? THEN WHEN ARE WE GONNA GET IN HERE AND BUST UP HER STUPID LITTLE PLAN?
WONDER GIRL!
YEAH, AND I BROUGHT A COUPLE OF FRIENDS WITH ME, TOO.
YOU GUYS REMEMBER SECRET AND EMPRESS?
Oh, CASSIE-- THANK HERA YOU'RE ALIVE! YOU'RE ALL ALIVE. YOUNG JUSTICE VANISHED DURING THE WAR-- AND I FEARED I'D NEVER HAVE A CHANCE TO SAY I'M SORRY TO YOU, OR TELL YOU HOW MUCH I LOVE YOU, AFTER VANESSA'S ATTACK...
HEY, IT'S COOL, DIANA.
WE CAN TALK ABOUT THAT STUFF, LATER...
...'CAUSE RIGHT NOW, WE'VE GOT BIGGER FISH TO FRY. AND I THINK THE WORLD IS IN A LOT OF TROUBLE.
WE TRACKED YOU DOWN BECAUSE SUPERBOY AND ROBIN DISAPPEARED AFTER WE GOT HOME. AND SOME OTHER HEROES WE KNOW, TOO.
WHAT'S CIRCE DOING TO THEM?
IT'S NOT JUST THEM, UNFORTUNATELY. I'VE GOT ABDUCTIONS THE WORLD OVER... J.L.A., J.S.A., TITANS, YOUNG JUSTICE, GLOBAL GUARDIANS...
...AND IT'S NOT JUST THE BOYS, EITHER.
SUBJECT: JADE
POWER: INACTIVE
SPECIES TYPE: INAPPLICABLE
SUBJECT: STARFIRE
POWER: INACTIVE
SPECIES TYPE: INAPPLICABLE
JADE AND STARFIRE ARE TRAPPED IN THERE. BUT IT LOOKS LIKE THEIR PHYSIOLOGIES HAVE CHANGED...
...AND INMATES OF BOTH GENDERS ARE BEING REPORTED AS MISSING FROM THE SLAB AND STRYKER'S ISLAND, FROM ARKHAM ASYLUM, FROM THE D.E.O. CENTRAL DATABASE.
THE IMAGES I'M SEEING THROUGH THE SATELLITE TECH THAT IS PUNCTURING CIRCE'S ENERGY SHIELD, WELL...
...THIS CAN'T BE GOOD FOR ANY OF US.

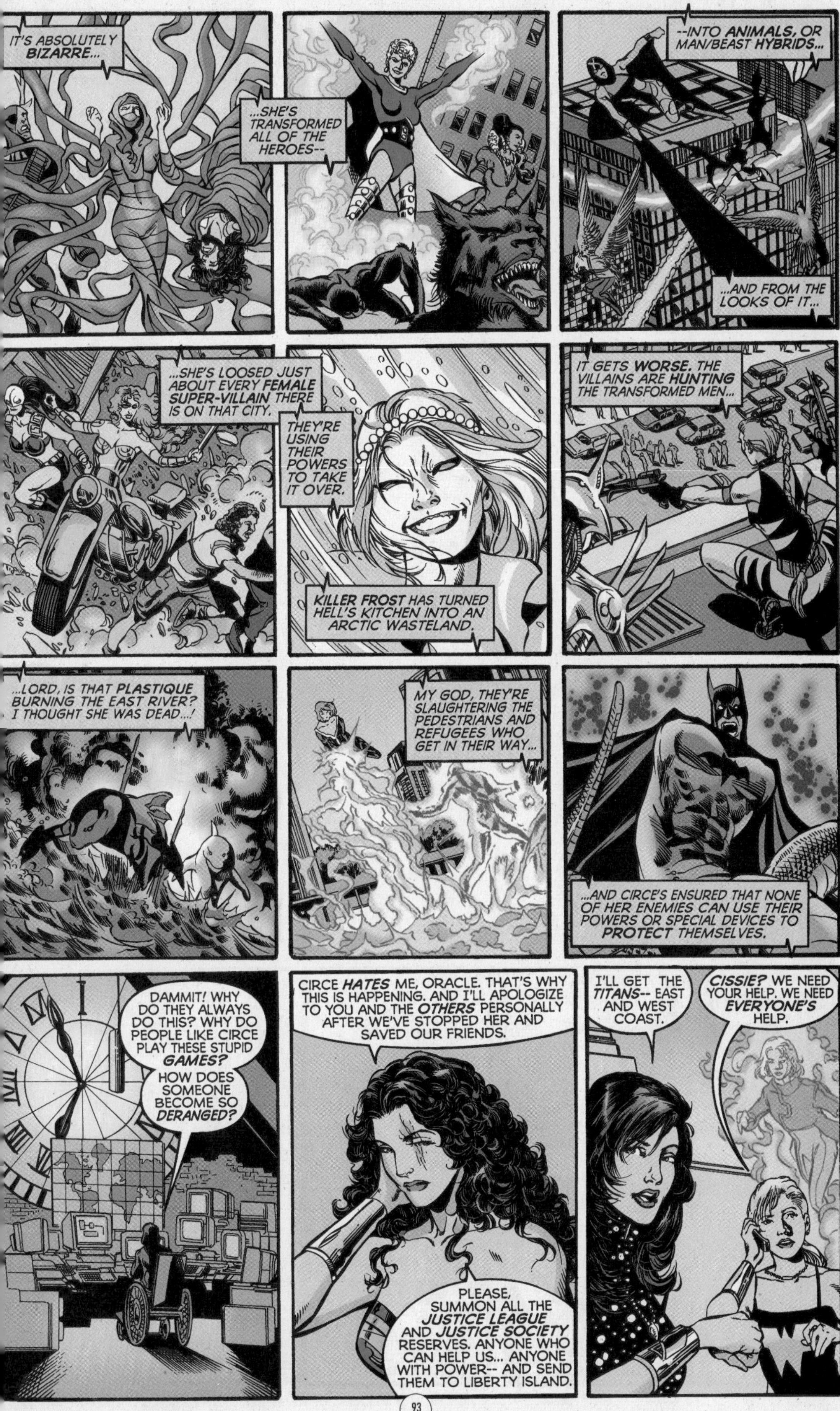

IT'S ABSOLUTELY BIZARRE...
...SHE'S TRANSFORMED ALL OF THE HEROES--
--INTO ANIMALS, OR MAN/BEAST HYBRIDS...
...AND FROM THE LOOKS OF IT...
...SHE'S LOOSED JUST ABOUT EVERY FEMALE SUPER-VILLAIN THERE IS ON THAT CITY.
THEY'RE USING THEIR POWERS TO TAKE IT OVER.
KILLER FROST HAS TURNED HELL'S KITCHEN INTO AN ARCTIC WASTELAND.
IT GETS WORSE. THE VILLAINS ARE HUNTING THE TRANSFORMED MEN...
...LORD, IS THAT PLASTIQUE BURNING THE EAST RIVER? I THOUGHT SHE WAS DEAD...!
MY GOD, THEY'RE SLAUGHTERING THE PEDESTRIANS AND REFUGEES WHO GET IN THEIR WAY...
...AND CIRCE'S ENSURED THAT NONE OF HER ENEMIES CAN USE THEIR POWERS OR SPECIAL DEVICES TO PROTECT THEMSELVES.
DAMMIT! WHY DO THEY ALWAYS DO THIS? WHY DO PEOPLE LIKE CIRCE PLAY THESE STUPID GAMES?
HOW DOES SOMEONE BECOME SO DERANGED?
CIRCE HATES ME, ORACLE. THAT'S WHY THIS IS HAPPENING. AND I'LL APOLOGIZE TO YOU AND THE OTHERS PERSONALLY AFTER WE'VE STOPPED HER AND SAVED OUR FRIENDS.
PLEASE, SUMMON ALL THE JUSTICE LEAGUE AND JUSTICE SOCIETY RESERVES. ANYONE WHO CAN HELP US... ANYONE WITH POWER-- AND SEND THEM TO LIBERTY ISLAND.
I'LL GET THE TITANS-- EAST AND WEST COAST.
CISSIE? WE NEED YOUR HELP. WE NEED EVERYONE'S HELP.

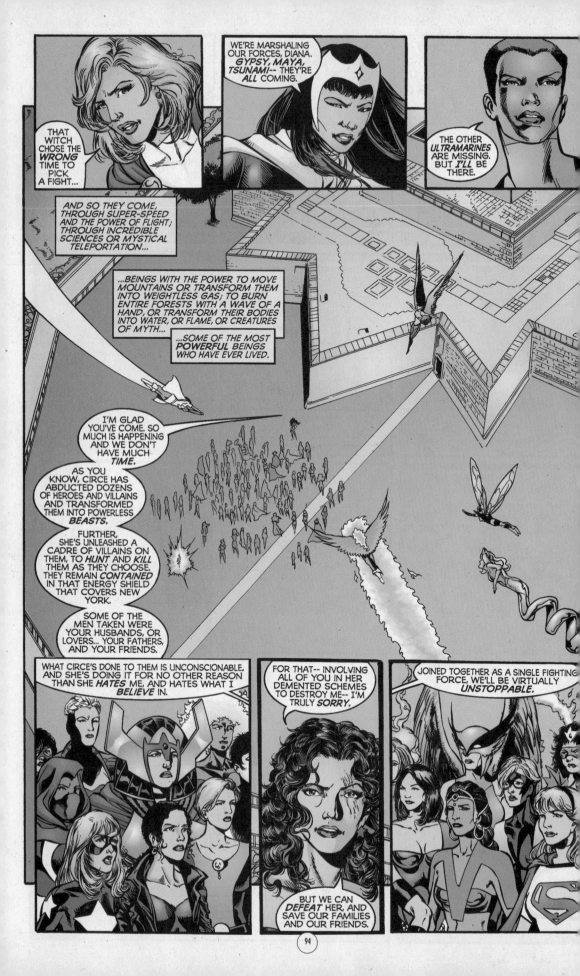

THAT WITCH CHOSE THE **WRONG** TIME TO PICK A FIGHT...

WE'RE MARSHALING OUR FORCES, DIANA. *GYPSY, MAYA, TSUNAMI*-- THEY'RE **ALL** COMING.

THE OTHER *ULTRAMARINES* ARE MISSING. BUT *I'LL* BE THERE.

AND SO THEY COME, THROUGH SUPER-SPEED AND THE POWER OF FLIGHT; THROUGH INCREDIBLE SCIENCES OR MYSTICAL TELEPORTATION...

...BEINGS WITH THE POWER TO MOVE MOUNTAINS OR TRANSFORM THEM INTO WEIGHTLESS GAS; TO BURN ENTIRE FORESTS WITH A WAVE OF A HAND, OR TRANSFORM THEIR BODIES INTO WATER, OR FLAME, OR CREATURES OF MYTH...

...SOME OF THE MOST **POWERFUL** BEINGS WHO HAVE EVER LIVED.

I'M GLAD YOU'VE COME. SO MUCH IS HAPPENING AND WE DON'T HAVE MUCH *TIME.*

AS YOU KNOW, CIRCE HAS ABDUCTED DOZENS OF HEROES AND VILLAINS AND TRANSFORMED THEM INTO POWERLESS **BEASTS.**

FURTHER, SHE'S UNLEASHED A CADRE OF VILLAINS ON THEM, TO *HUNT* AND *KILL* THEM AS THEY CHOOSE. THEY REMAIN *CONTAINED* IN THAT ENERGY SHIELD THAT COVERS NEW YORK.

SOME OF THE MEN TAKEN WERE YOUR HUSBANDS, OR LOVERS... YOUR FATHERS, AND YOUR FRIENDS.

WHAT CIRCE'S DONE TO THEM IS UNCONSCIONABLE. AND SHE'S DOING IT FOR NO OTHER REASON THAN SHE *HATES* ME, AND HATES WHAT I *BELIEVE* IN.

FOR THAT-- INVOLVING ALL OF YOU IN HER DEMENTED SCHEMES TO DESTROY ME-- I'M TRULY *SORRY.*

JOINED TOGETHER AS A SINGLE FIGHTING FORCE, WE'LL BE VIRTUALLY *UNSTOPPABLE.*

BUT WE CAN *DEFEAT* HER, AND SAVE OUR FAMILIES AND OUR FRIENDS.

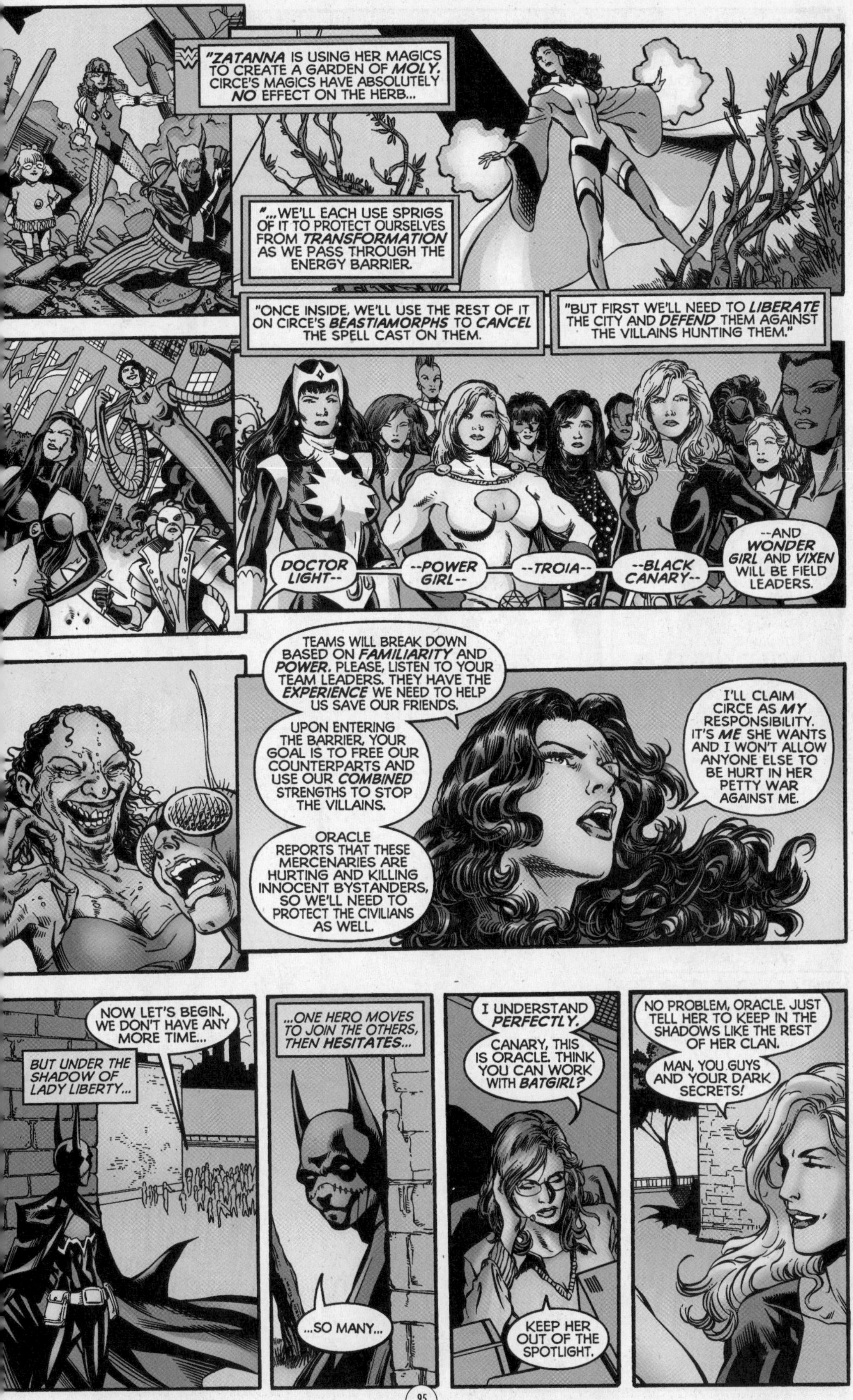

"ZATANNA IS USING HER MAGICS TO CREATE A GARDEN OF MOLY. CIRCE'S MAGICS HAVE ABSOLUTELY NO EFFECT ON THE HERB...
"...WE'LL EACH USE SPRIGS OF IT TO PROTECT OURSELVES FROM TRANSFORMATION AS WE PASS THROUGH THE ENERGY BARRIER.
"ONCE INSIDE, WE'LL USE THE REST OF IT ON CIRCE'S BEASTIAMORPHS TO CANCEL THE SPELL CAST ON THEM.
"BUT FIRST WE'LL NEED TO LIBERATE THE CITY AND DEFEND THEM AGAINST THE VILLAINS HUNTING THEM."
DOCTOR LIGHT--
--POWER GIRL--
--TROIA--
--BLACK CANARY--
--AND WONDER GIRL AND VIXEN WILL BE FIELD LEADERS.
TEAMS WILL BREAK DOWN BASED ON FAMILIARITY AND POWER. PLEASE, LISTEN TO YOUR TEAM LEADERS. THEY HAVE THE EXPERIENCE WE NEED TO HELP US SAVE OUR FRIENDS.
UPON ENTERING THE BARRIER, YOUR GOAL IS TO FREE OUR COUNTERPARTS AND USE OUR COMBINED STRENGTHS TO STOP THE VILLAINS.
ORACLE REPORTS THAT THESE MERCENARIES ARE HURTING AND KILLING INNOCENT BYSTANDERS, SO WE'LL NEED TO PROTECT THE CIVILIANS AS WELL.
I'LL CLAIM CIRCE AS MY RESPONSIBILITY. IT'S ME SHE WANTS AND I WON'T ALLOW ANYONE ELSE TO BE HURT IN HER PETTY WAR AGAINST ME.
NOW LET'S BEGIN. WE DON'T HAVE ANY MORE TIME...
BUT UNDER THE SHADOW OF LADY LIBERTY...
...ONE HERO MOVES TO JOIN THE OTHERS, THEN HESITATES...
...SO MANY...
I UNDERSTAND PERFECTLY.
CANARY, THIS IS ORACLE. THINK YOU CAN WORK WITH BATGIRL?
KEEP HER OUT OF THE SPOTLIGHT.
NO PROBLEM, ORACLE. JUST TELL HER TO KEEP IN THE SHADOWS LIKE THE REST OF HER CLAN.
MAN, YOU GUYS AND YOUR DARK SECRETS!

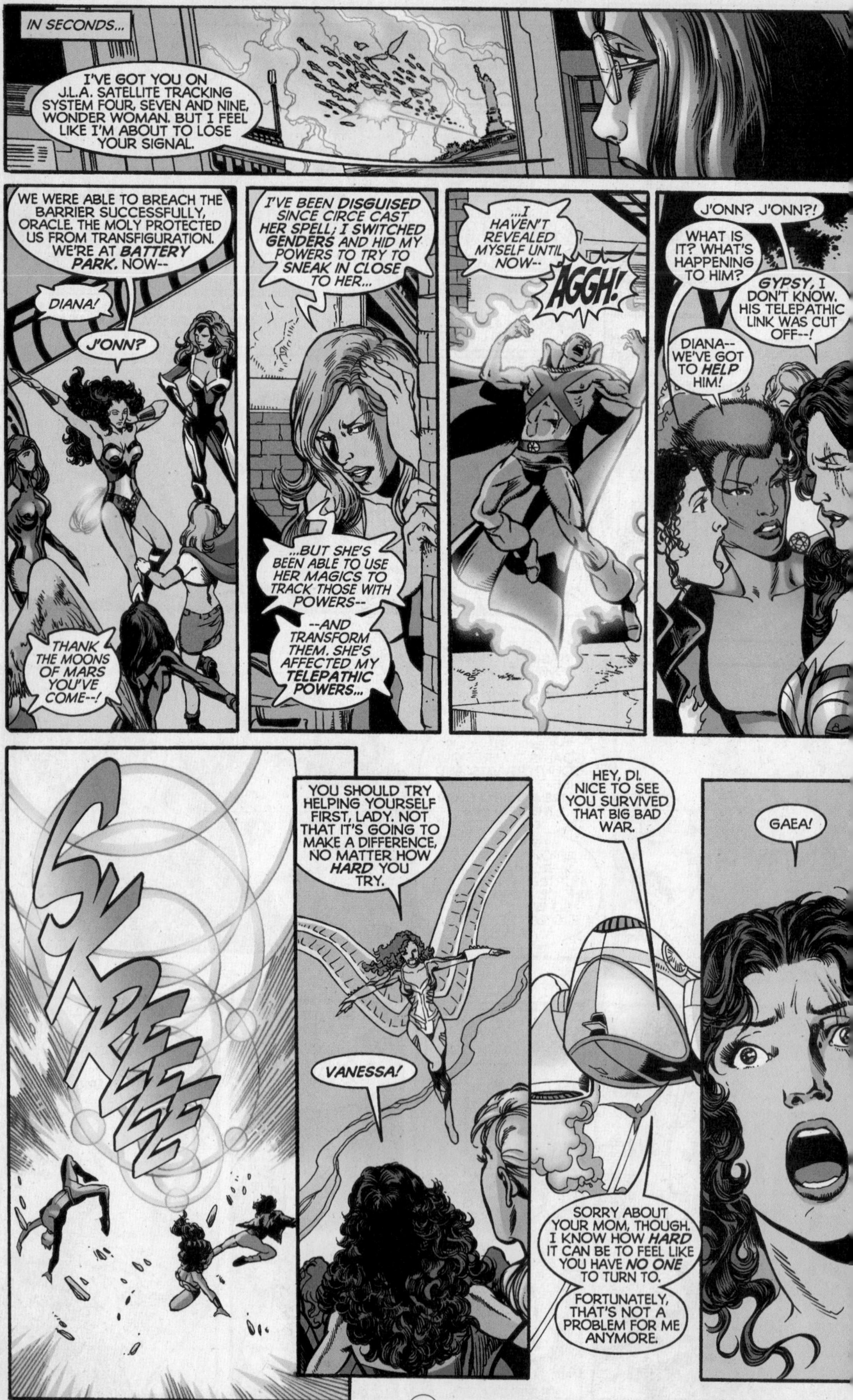
IN SECONDS...
I'VE GOT YOU ON J.L.A. SATELLITE TRACKING SYSTEM FOUR, SEVEN AND NINE, WONDER WOMAN. BUT I FEEL LIKE I'M ABOUT TO LOSE YOUR SIGNAL.
WE WERE ABLE TO BREACH THE BARRIER SUCCESSFULLY, ORACLE. THE MOLY PROTECTED US FROM TRANSFIGURATION. WE'RE AT BATTERY PARK. NOW--
DIANA!
J'ONN?
THANK THE MOONS OF MARS YOU'VE COME--!
I'VE BEEN DISGUISED SINCE CIRCE CAST HER SPELL; I SWITCHED GENDERS AND HID MY POWERS TO TRY TO SNEAK IN CLOSE TO HER...
...BUT SHE'S BEEN ABLE TO USE HER MAGICS TO TRACK THOSE WITH POWERS--
--AND TRANSFORM THEM. SHE'S AFFECTED MY TELEPATHIC POWERS...
...I HAVEN'T REVEALED MYSELF UNTIL NOW--
AGGH!
J'ONN? J'ONN?!
WHAT IS IT? WHAT'S HAPPENING TO HIM?
GYPSY, I DON'T KNOW. HIS TELEPATHIC LINK WAS CUT OFF--!
DIANA-- WE'VE GOT TO HELP HIM!
SKREEEEN
YOU SHOULD TRY HELPING YOURSELF FIRST, LADY. NOT THAT IT'S GOING TO MAKE A DIFFERENCE, NO MATTER HOW HARD YOU TRY.
VANESSA!
HEY, DI. NICE TO SEE YOU SURVIVED THAT BIG BAD WAR.
SORRY ABOUT YOUR MOM, THOUGH. I KNOW HOW HARD IT CAN BE TO FEEL LIKE YOU HAVE NO ONE TO TURN TO.
FORTUNATELY, THAT'S NOT A PROBLEM FOR ME ANYMORE.
GAEA!

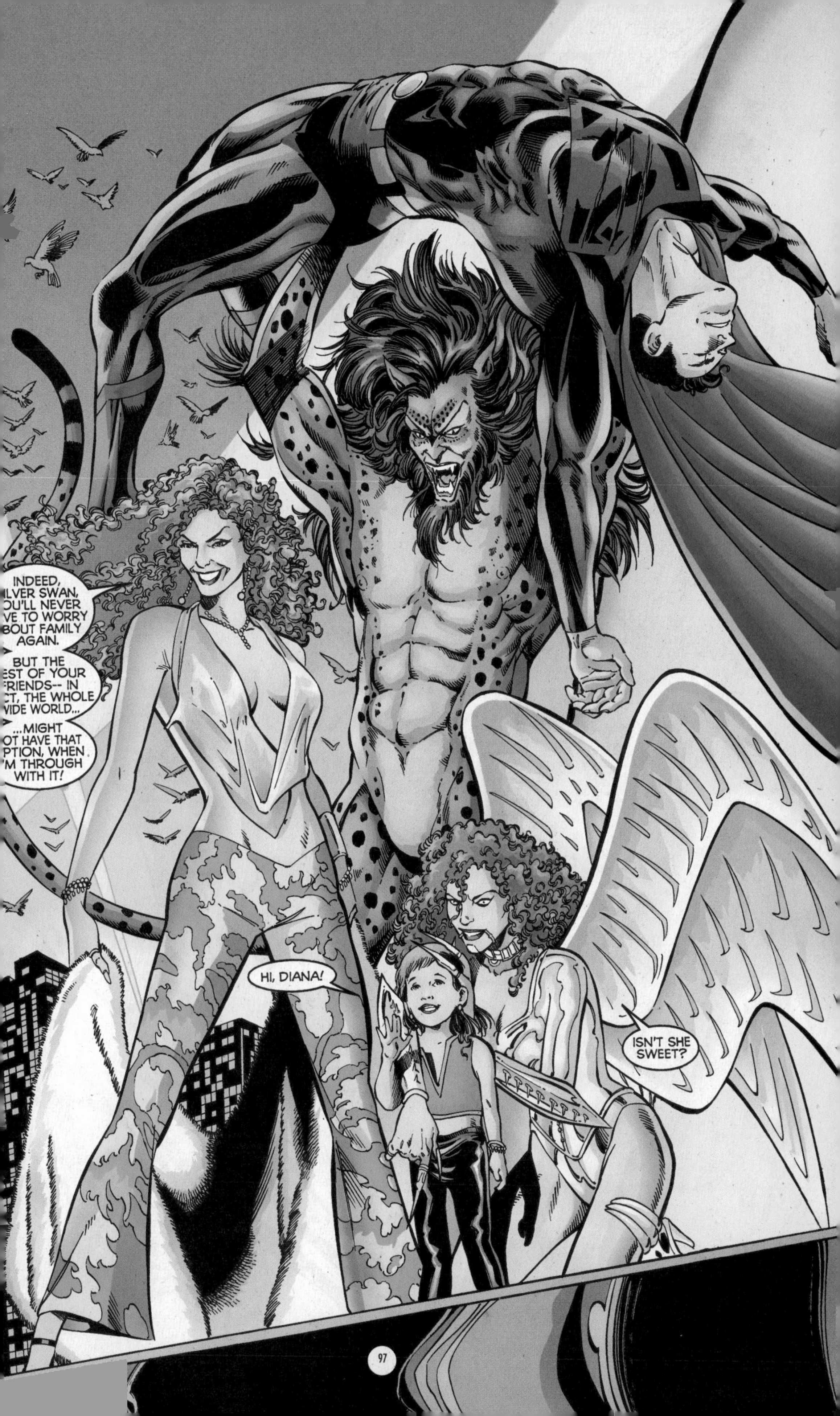
INDEED, ILVER SWAN, OU'LL NEVER VE TO WORRY BOUT FAMILY AGAIN.
BUT THE EST OF YOUR FRIENDS-- IN CT, THE WHOLE VIDE WORLD...
...MIGHT OT HAVE THAT PTION, WHEN 'M THROUGH WITH IT!
HI, DIANA!
ISN'T SHE SWEET?

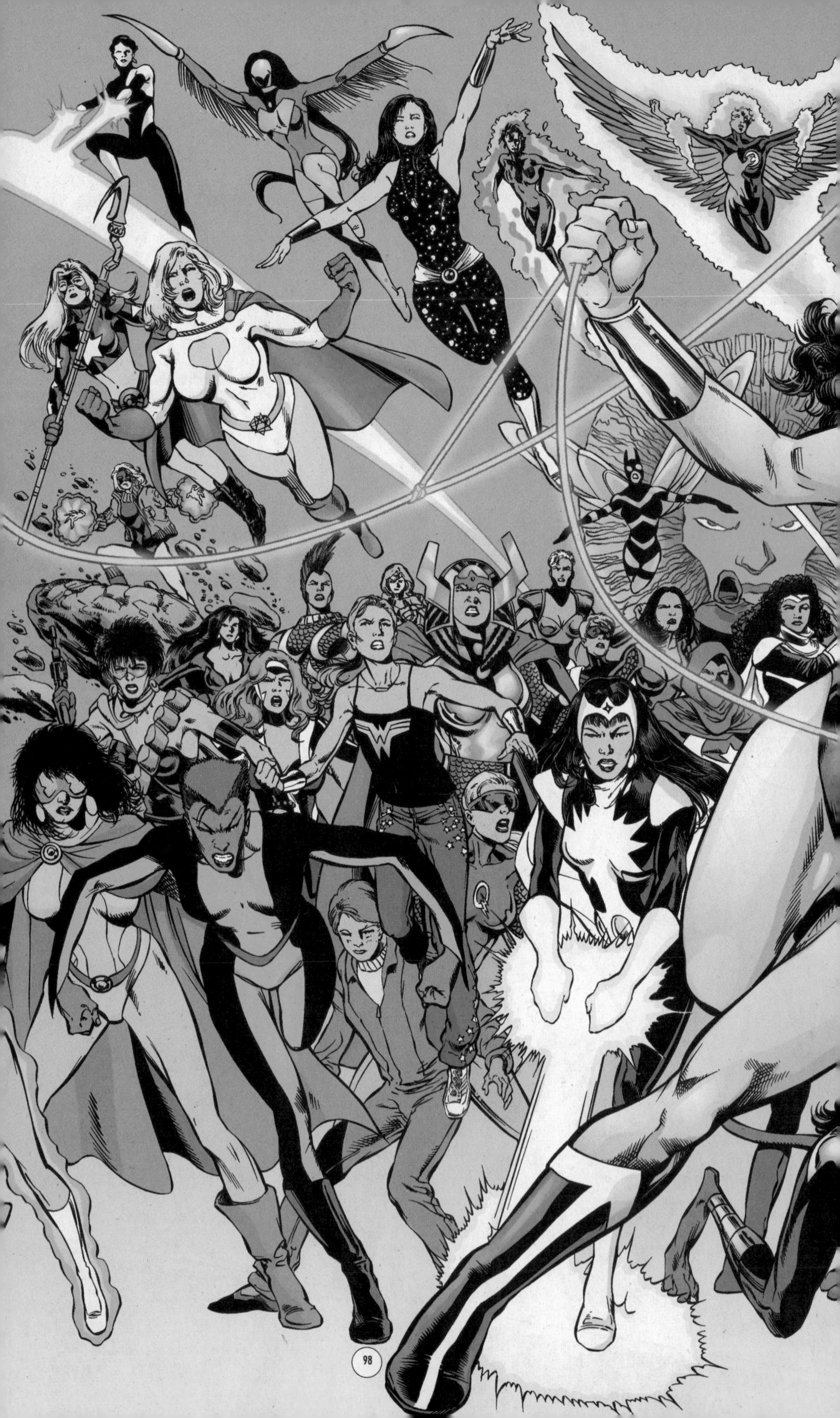

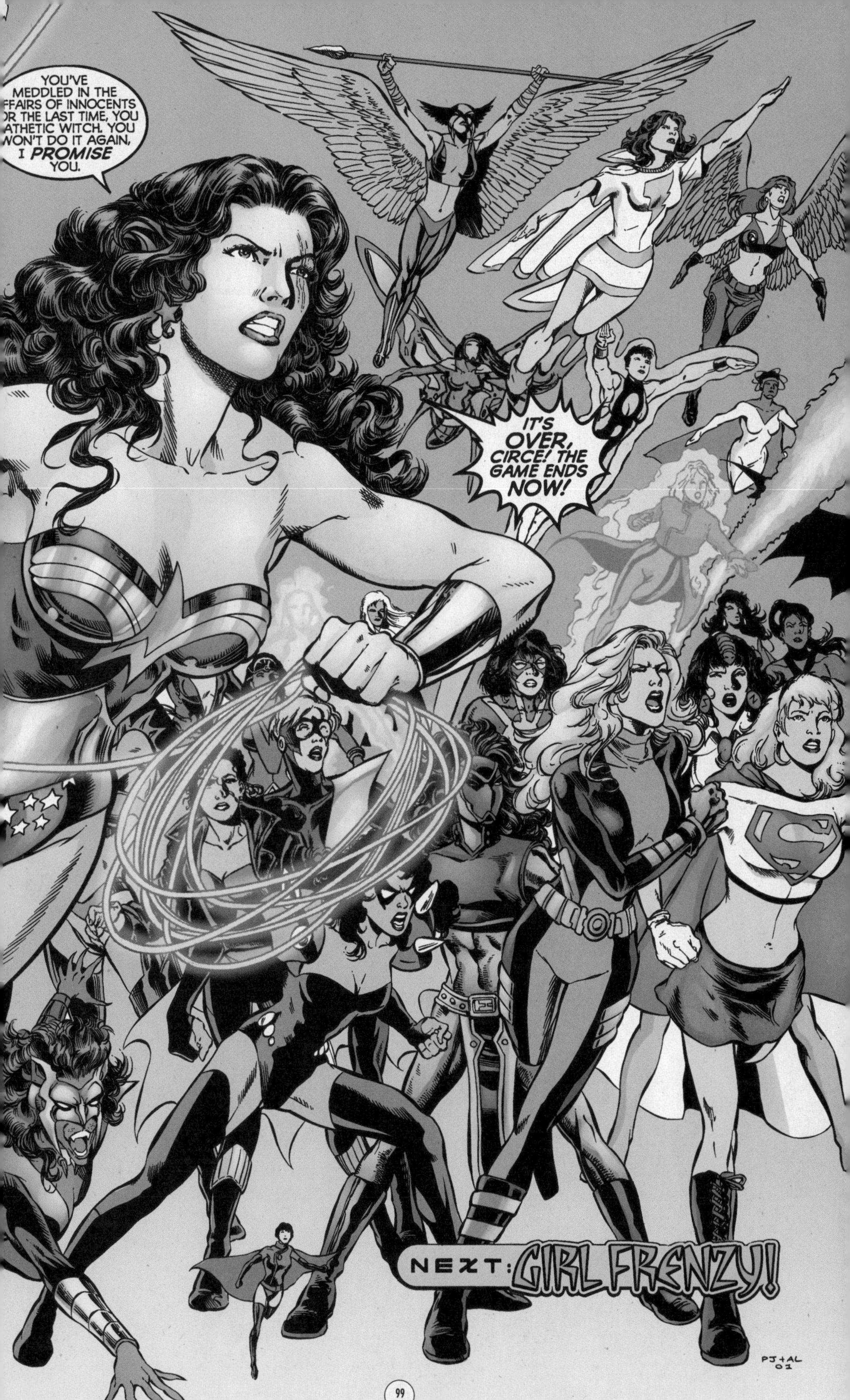
YOU'VE MEDDLED IN THE AFFAIRS OF INNOCENTS FOR THE LAST TIME, YOU PATHETIC WITCH. YOU WON'T DO IT AGAIN, I PROMISE YOU.
IT'S OVER, CIRCE! THE GAME ENDS NOW!
NEXT: GIRL FRENZY!
PJ+AL 01

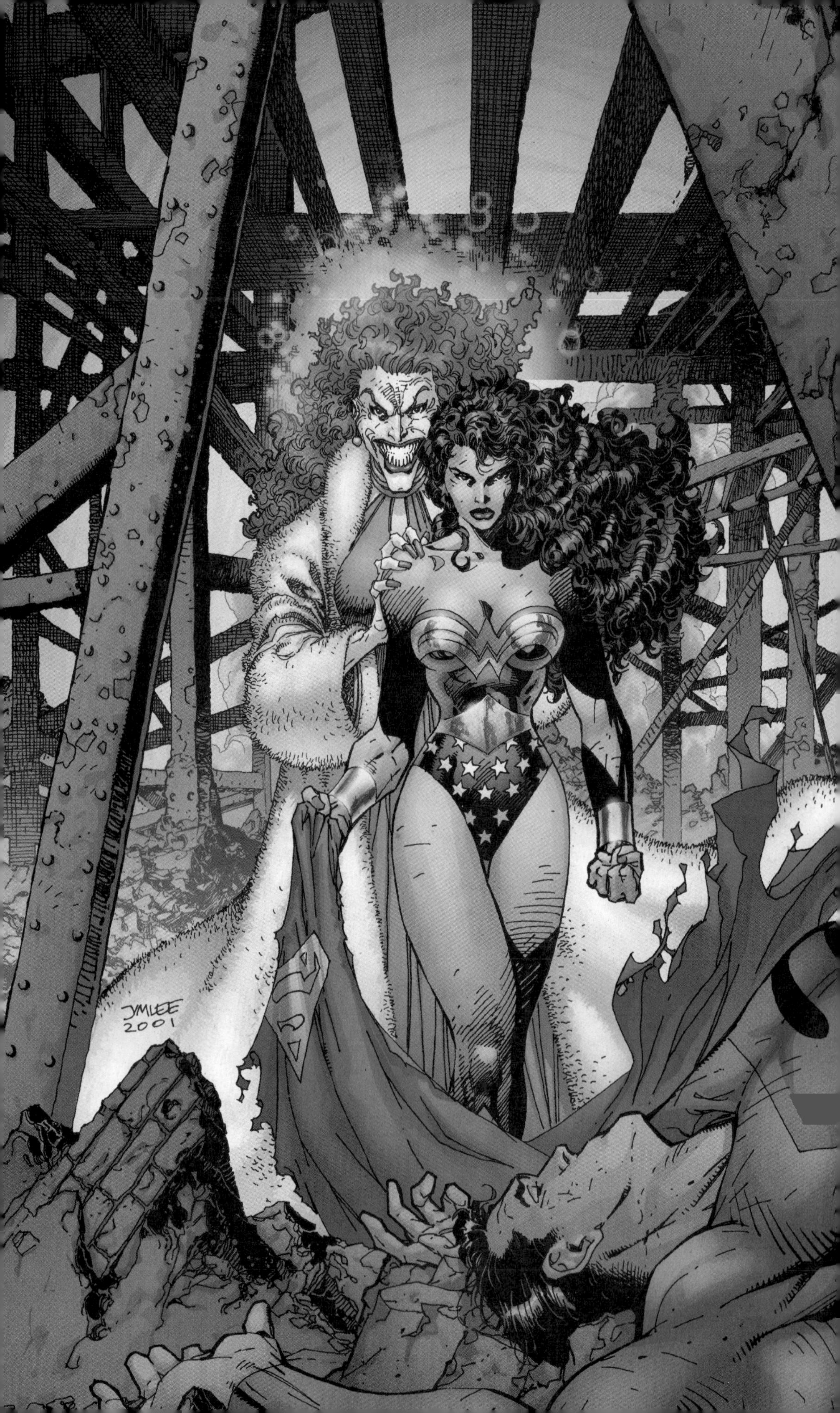
JYMLEE
2001

BEFORE THE RAIN OF THE JOKER, BEFORE HIS LAST LAUGH:

ACTIVATE: J.L.A. WATCHOWER EMERGENCY OVERRIDE SIGNAL OMEGA DELTA. SATELLITE NETWORK 3467L THROUGH 89 M. UPLOAD ON ALL FREQUENCIES AND TARGET:

THEY'RE COMING AFTER US AGAIN --!

AND I STILL CAN'T USE MY POWERS!

SUBLOCATE: ROCKEFELLER CENTER:

TERRA! PULL BACK ON THE SANDSTORM -- I CAN'T SEE A THING --!

TERRA!?

ARGENT.

IT'S NOT TERRA'S POWER THAT'S BLINDING YOU, TITAN --

-- IT'S MINE!

SCIROCCO.

TERRA.

BUMBLEBEE.

SHE'S BURNING, TAO --

-- AS WE USE HER OWN ELECTRICAL POWERS AGAINST HER!

TAO JONES AND PENNY DREADFUL.

CAN YOU HEAR THAT? CAN YOU HEAR YOUR FRIEND SCREAM, MIRAGE?

DEATH-DOLL.

ROSIE.

MIRAGE.

KAREN --?!

EVERYONE, REMEMBER DIANA'S PLAN! WE NEED TO USE THE MOLY AND FREE FLASH, SAND AND THE OTHERS.

USE OUR COMBINED FORCES TO --

-AGGHH!

IT WILL TAKE A FAR GREATER LEADER THAN YOU TO GUIDE THESE FOOLS TO VICTORY, WOMAN.

THE FACE OF WAR WILL SEE TO THAT.

DEMOLITIA.

TROIA.

TRINITY.

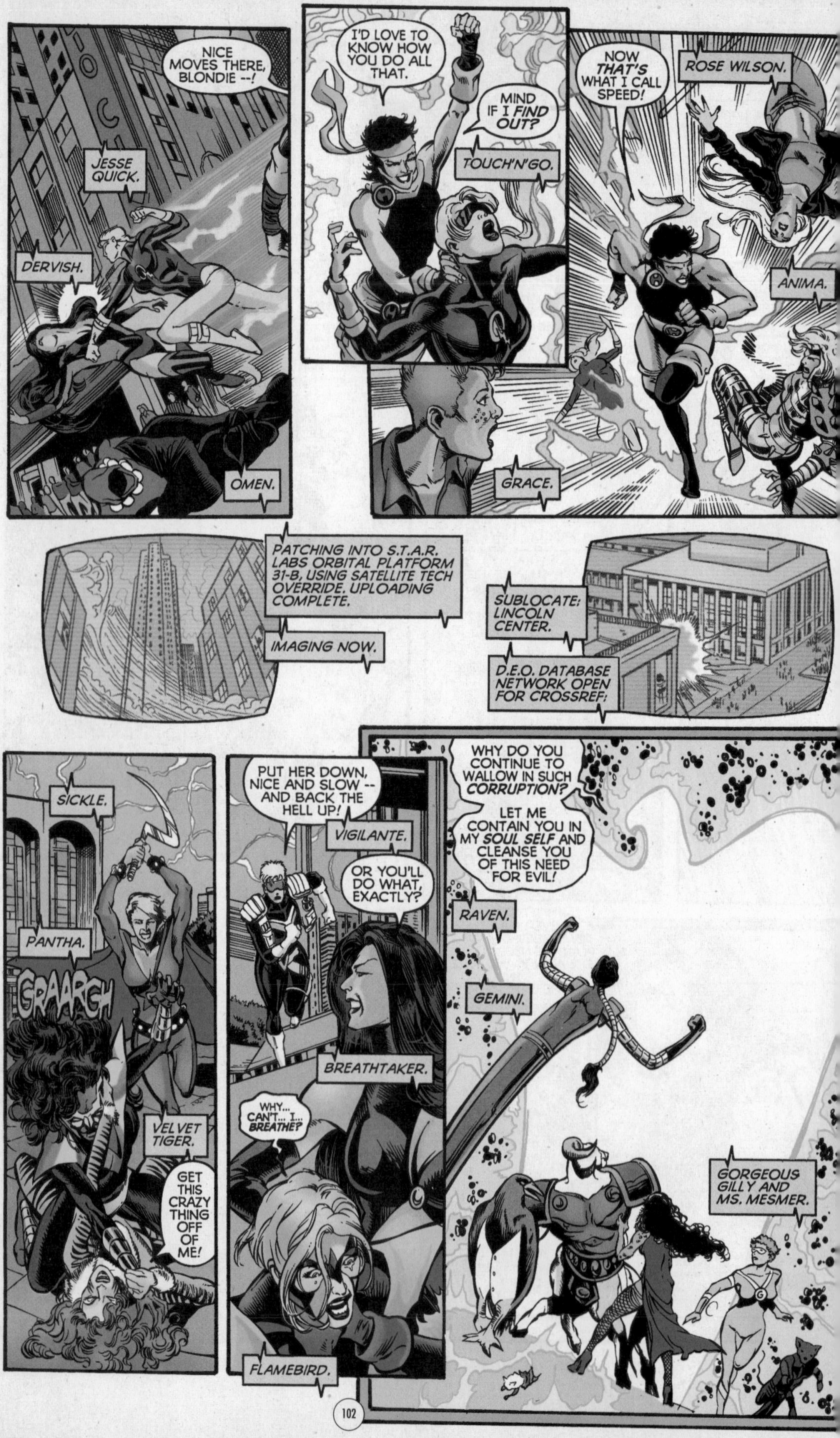
NICE MOVES THERE, BLONDIE --!
JESSE QUICK.
DERVISH.
OMEN.
I'D LOVE TO KNOW HOW YOU DO ALL THAT.
MIND IF I FIND OUT?
TOUCH'N'GO.
GRACE.
NOW THAT'S WHAT I CALL SPEED!
ROSE WILSON.
ANIMA.
PATCHING INTO S.T.A.R. LABS ORBITAL PLATFORM 31-B, USING SATELLITE TECH OVERRIDE. UPLOADING COMPLETE.
IMAGING NOW.
SUBLOCATE: LINCOLN CENTER.
D.E.O. DATABASE NETWORK OPEN FOR CROSSREF:
SICKLE.
PANTHA.
GRAARCH
VELVET TIGER.
GET THIS CRAZY THING OFF OF ME!
PUT HER DOWN, NICE AND SLOW -- AND BACK THE HELL UP!
VIGILANTE.
OR YOU'LL DO WHAT, EXACTLY?
BREATHTAKER.
WHY... CAN'T... I... BREATHE?
FLAMEBIRD.
WHY DO YOU CONTINUE TO WALLOW IN SUCH CORRUPTION?
LET ME CONTAIN YOU IN MY SOUL SELF AND CLEANSE YOU OF THIS NEED FOR EVIL!
RAVEN.
GEMINI.
GORGEOUS GILLY AND MS. MESMER.

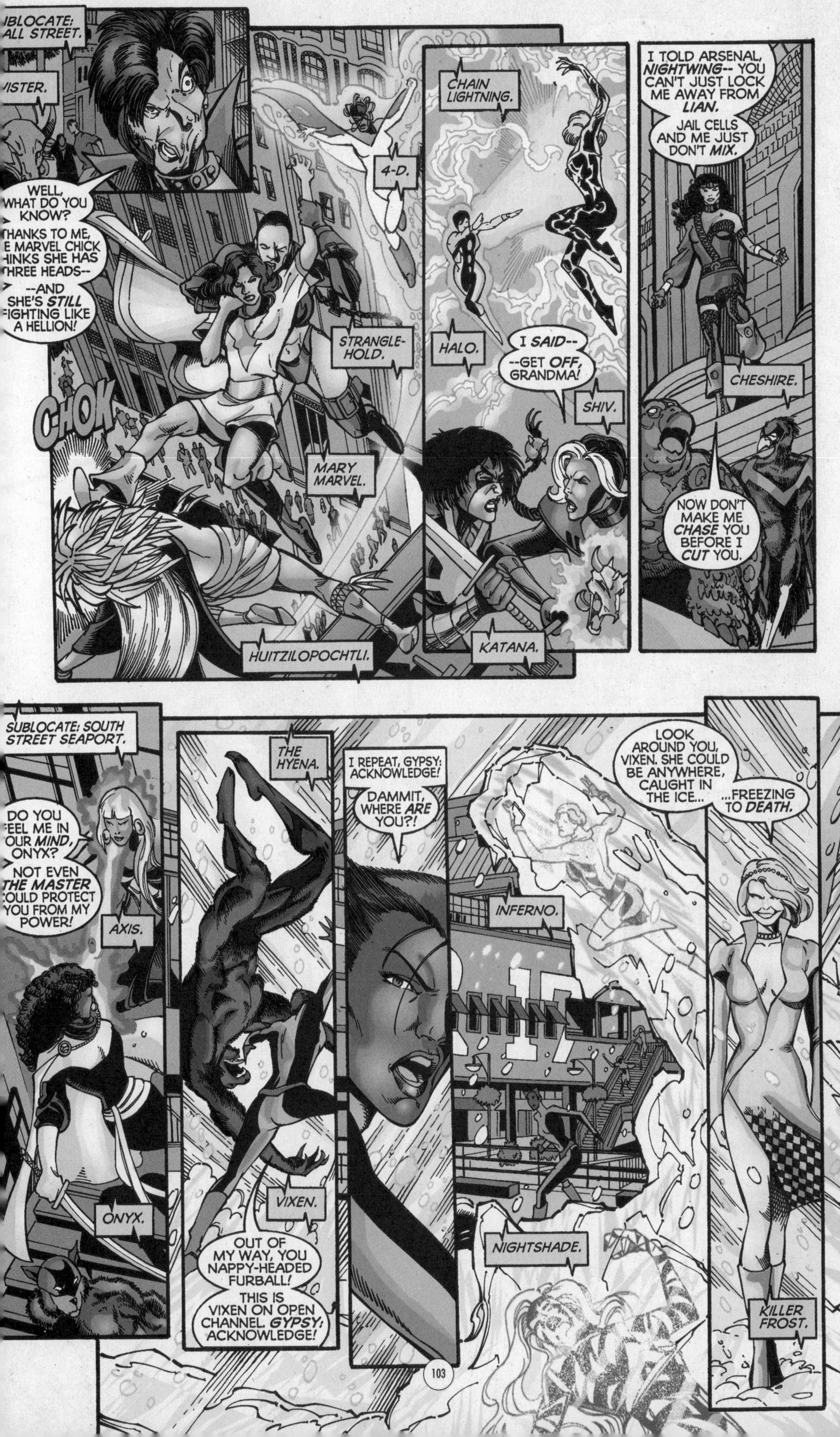

SUBLOCATE: WALL STREET.
TWISTER.
WELL, WHAT DO YOU KNOW?
THANKS TO ME, THE MARVEL CHICK THINKS SHE HAS THREE HEADS--
--AND SHE'S STILL FIGHTING LIKE A HELLION!
4-D.
STRANGLE-HOLD.
CHOK
MARY MARVEL.
HUITZILOPOCHTLI.
CHAIN LIGHTNING.
HALO.
I SAID--
--GET OFF, GRANDMA!
SHIV.
KATANA.
I TOLD ARSENAL, NIGHTWING-- YOU CAN'T JUST LOCK ME AWAY FROM LIAN.
JAIL CELLS AND ME JUST DON'T MIX.
CHESHIRE.
NOW DON'T MAKE ME CHASE YOU BEFORE I CUT YOU.
SUBLOCATE: SOUTH STREET SEAPORT.
DO YOU FEEL ME IN YOUR MIND, ONYX?
NOT EVEN THE MASTER COULD PROTECT YOU FROM MY POWER!
AXIS.
ONYX.
THE HYENA.
VIXEN.
OUT OF MY WAY, YOU NAPPY-HEADED FURBALL!
THIS IS VIXEN ON OPEN CHANNEL GYPSY: ACKNOWLEDGE!
I REPEAT, GYPSY: ACKNOWLEDGE!
DAMMIT, WHERE ARE YOU?!
INFERNO.
NIGHTSHADE.
LOOK AROUND YOU, VIXEN. SHE COULD BE ANYWHERE, CAUGHT IN THE ICE...
...FREEZING TO DEATH.
KILLER FROST.

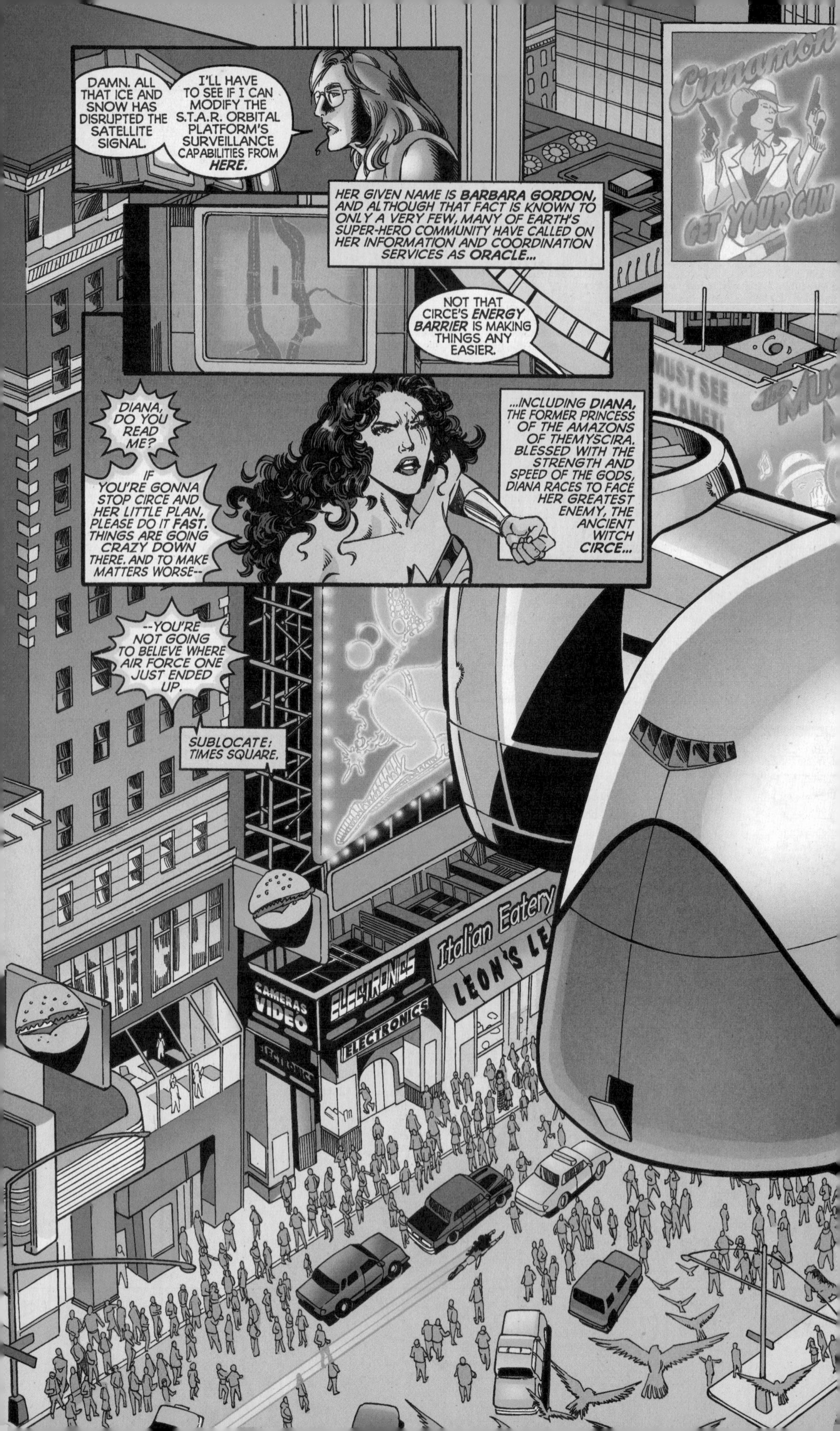
DAMN. ALL THAT ICE AND SNOW HAS DISRUPTED THE SATELLITE SIGNAL.
I'LL HAVE TO SEE IF I CAN MODIFY THE S.T.A.R. ORBITAL PLATFORM'S SURVEILLANCE CAPABILITIES FROM HERE.
Cinnamon
GET YOUR GUN
HER GIVEN NAME IS BARBARA GORDON, AND ALTHOUGH THAT FACT IS KNOWN TO ONLY A VERY FEW, MANY OF EARTH'S SUPER-HERO COMMUNITY HAVE CALLED ON HER INFORMATION AND COORDINATION SERVICES AS ORACLE...
NOT THAT CIRCE'S ENERGY BARRIER IS MAKING THINGS ANY EASIER.
MUST SEE PLANET!
DIANA, DO YOU READ ME?
IF YOU'RE GONNA STOP CIRCE AND HER LITTLE PLAN, PLEASE DO IT FAST. THINGS ARE GOING CRAZY DOWN THERE. AND TO MAKE MATTERS WORSE--
...INCLUDING DIANA, THE FORMER PRINCESS OF THE AMAZONS OF THEMYSCIRA. BLESSED WITH THE STRENGTH AND SPEED OF THE GODS, DIANA RACES TO FACE HER GREATEST ENEMY, THE ANCIENT WITCH CIRCE...
--YOU'RE NOT GOING TO BELIEVE WHERE AIR FORCE ONE JUST ENDED UP.
SUBLOCATE: TIMES SQUARE.
Italian Eatery
LEON'S
CAMERAS VIDEO
ELECTRONICS
ELECTRONICS
ELECTRONICS

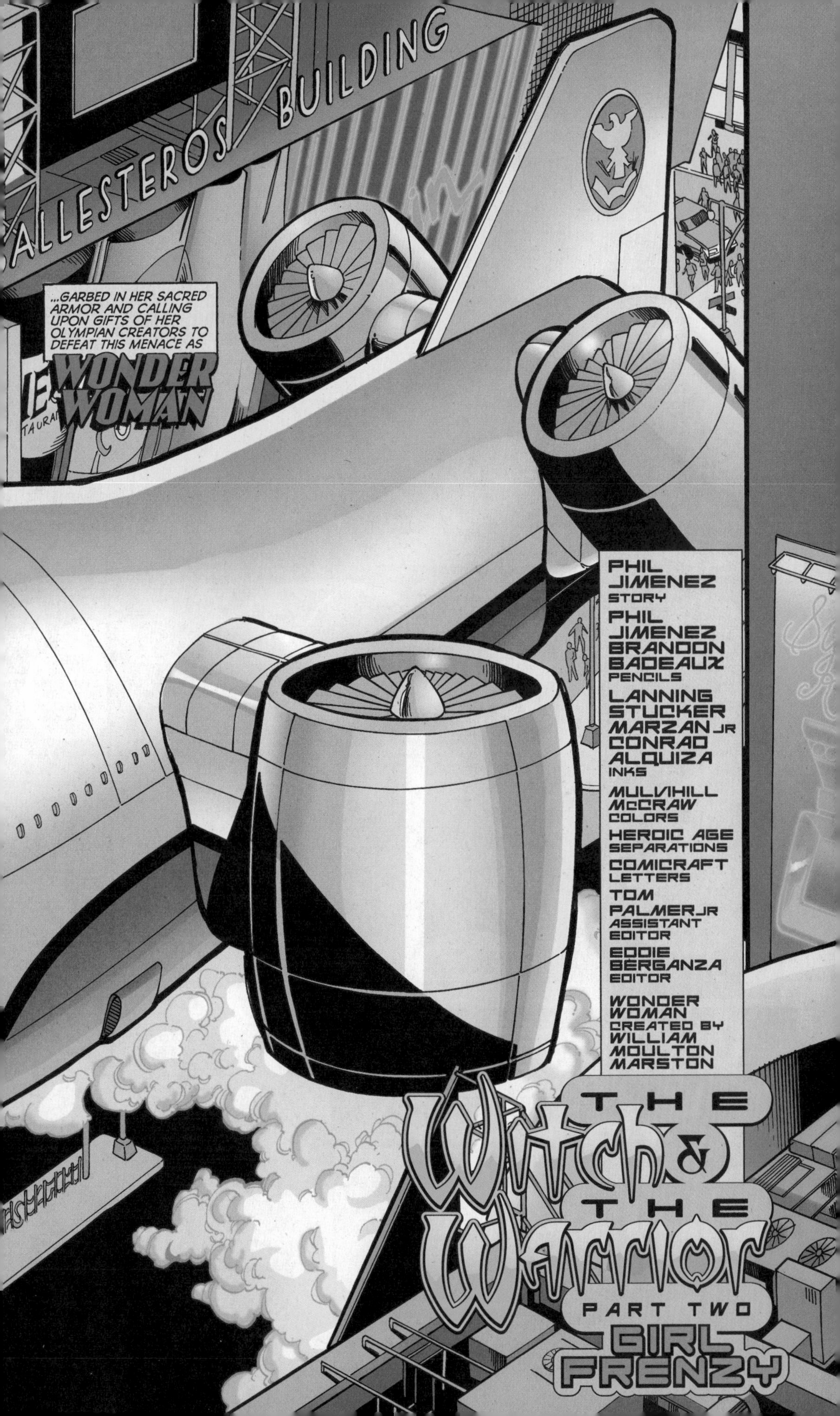

BALLESTEROS BUILDING
...GARBED IN HER SACRED ARMOR AND CALLING UPON GIFTS OF HER OLYMPIAN CREATORS TO DEFEAT THIS MENACE AS
WONDER WOMAN
PHIL JIMENEZ STORY
PHIL JIMENEZ BRANDON BADEAUX PENCILS
LANNING STUCKER MARZAN JR CONRAD ALQUIZA INKS
MULVIHILL McCRAW COLORS
HEROIC AGE SEPARATIONS
COMICRAFT LETTERS
TOM PALMER JR ASSISTANT EDITOR
EDDIE BERGANZA EDITOR
WONDER WOMAN CREATED BY WILLIAM MOULTON MARSTON
THE Witch & THE Warrior
PART TWO
GIRL FRENZY

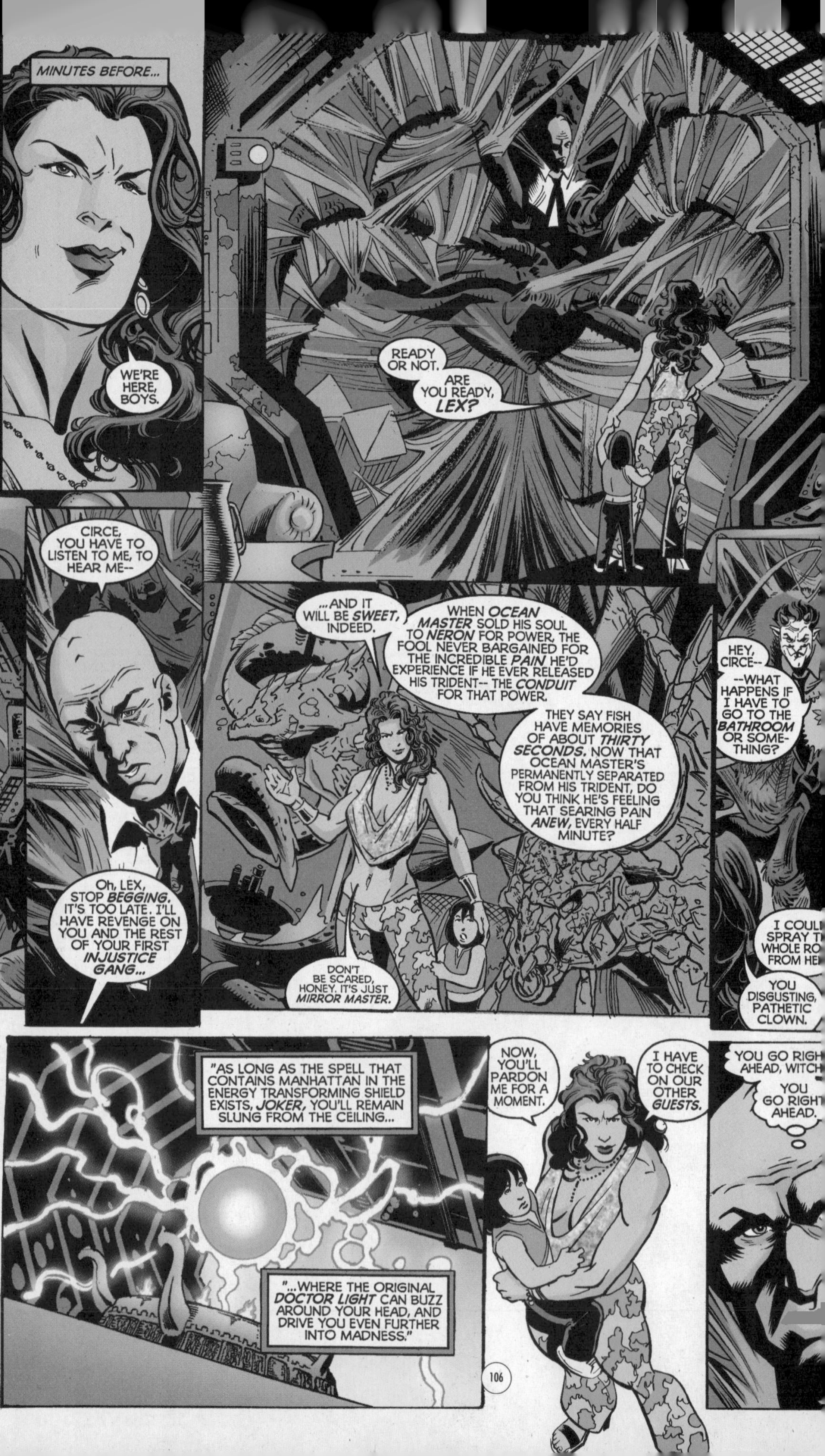
MINUTES BEFORE...
WE'RE HERE, BOYS.
READY OR NOT.
ARE YOU READY, LEX?
CIRCE, YOU HAVE TO LISTEN TO ME, TO HEAR ME--
Oh, LEX, STOP BEGGING. IT'S TOO LATE. I'LL HAVE REVENGE ON YOU AND THE REST OF YOUR FIRST INJUSTICE GANG...
...AND IT WILL BE SWEET, INDEED.
WHEN OCEAN MASTER SOLD HIS SOUL TO NERON FOR POWER, THE FOOL NEVER BARGAINED FOR THE INCREDIBLE PAIN HE'D EXPERIENCE IF HE EVER RELEASED HIS TRIDENT-- THE CONDUIT FOR THAT POWER.
THEY SAY FISH HAVE MEMORIES OF ABOUT THIRTY SECONDS. NOW THAT OCEAN MASTER'S PERMANENTLY SEPARATED FROM HIS TRIDENT, DO YOU THINK HE'S FEELING THAT SEARING PAIN ANEW, EVERY HALF MINUTE?
DON'T BE SCARED, HONEY. IT'S JUST MIRROR MASTER.
HEY, CIRCE--
--WHAT HAPPENS IF I HAVE TO GO TO THE BATHROOM OR SOME-THING?
YOU DISGUSTING, PATHETIC CLOWN.
"AS LONG AS THE SPELL THAT CONTAINS MANHATTAN IN THE ENERGY TRANSFORMING SHIELD EXISTS, JOKER, YOU'LL REMAIN SLUNG FROM THE CEILING...
"...WHERE THE ORIGINAL DOCTOR LIGHT CAN BUZZ AROUND YOUR HEAD, AND DRIVE YOU EVEN FURTHER INTO MADNESS."
NOW, YOU'LL PARDON ME FOR A MOMENT.
I HAVE TO CHECK ON OUR OTHER GUESTS.

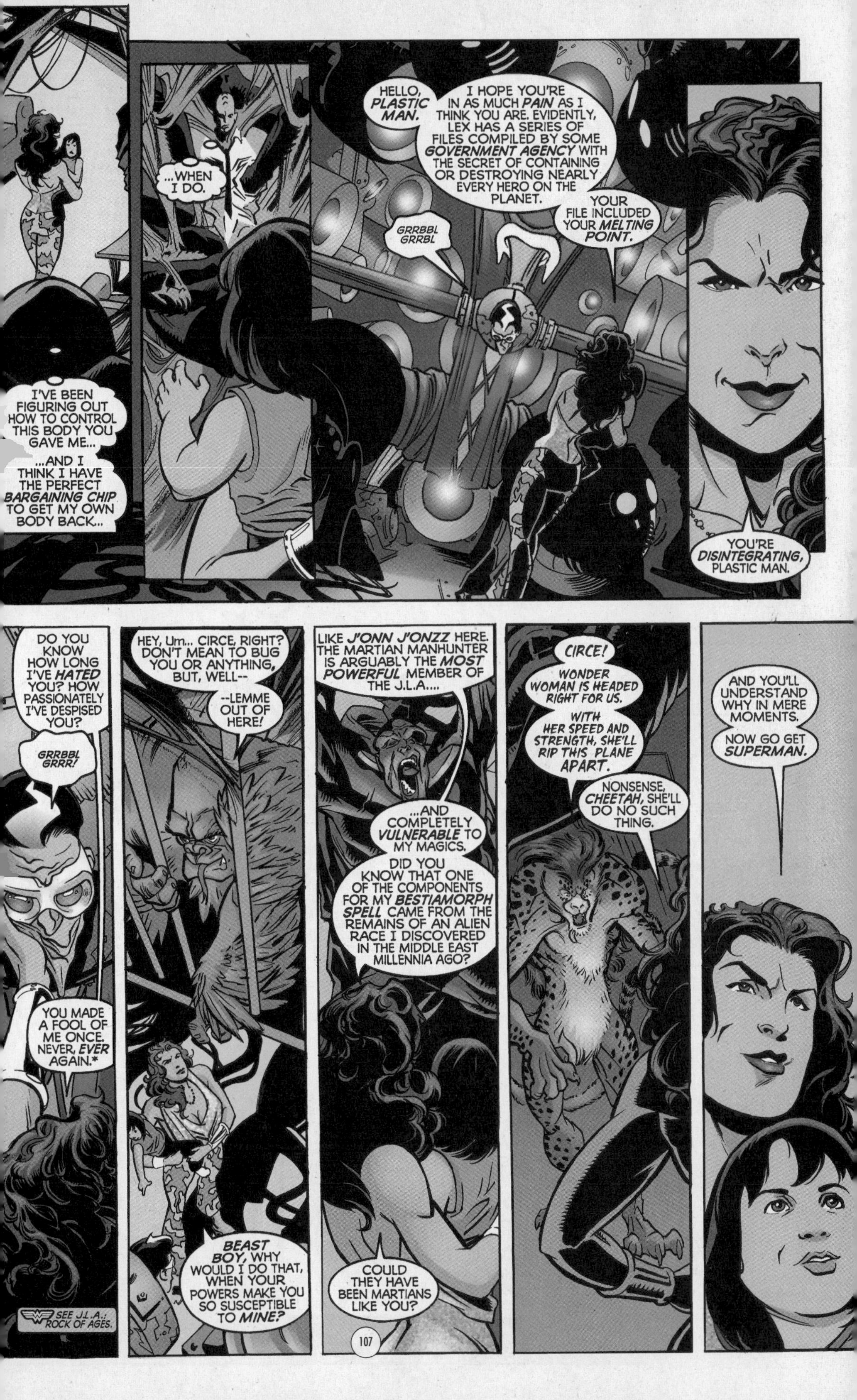
...WHEN I DO.
I'VE BEEN FIGURING OUT HOW TO CONTROL THIS BODY YOU GAVE ME...
...AND I THINK I HAVE THE PERFECT BARGAINING CHIP TO GET MY OWN BODY BACK...
HELLO, PLASTIC MAN.
I HOPE YOU'RE IN AS MUCH PAIN AS I THINK YOU ARE. EVIDENTLY, LEX HAS A SERIES OF FILES COMPILED BY SOME GOVERNMENT AGENCY WITH THE SECRET OF CONTAINING OR DESTROYING NEARLY EVERY HERO ON THE PLANET.
GRRBBL GRRBL
YOUR FILE INCLUDED YOUR MELTING POINT.
YOU'RE DISINTEGRATING, PLASTIC MAN.
DO YOU KNOW HOW LONG I'VE HATED YOU? HOW PASSIONATELY I'VE DESPISED YOU?
GRRBBL GRRR!
YOU MADE A FOOL OF ME ONCE. NEVER, EVER AGAIN.*
*SEE J.L.A.: ROCK OF AGES.
HEY, Um... CIRCE, RIGHT? DON'T MEAN TO BUG YOU OR ANYTHING, BUT, WELL--
--LEMME OUT OF HERE!
BEAST BOY, WHY WOULD I DO THAT, WHEN YOUR POWERS MAKE YOU SO SUSCEPTIBLE TO MINE?
LIKE J'ONN J'ONZZ HERE. THE MARTIAN MANHUNTER IS ARGUABLY THE MOST POWERFUL MEMBER OF THE J.L.A....
...AND COMPLETELY VULNERABLE TO MY MAGICS.
DID YOU KNOW THAT ONE OF THE COMPONENTS FOR MY BESTIAMORPH SPELL CAME FROM THE REMAINS OF AN ALIEN RACE I DISCOVERED IN THE MIDDLE EAST MILLENNIA AGO?
COULD THEY HAVE BEEN MARTIANS LIKE YOU?
CIRCE!
WONDER WOMAN IS HEADED RIGHT FOR US.
WITH HER SPEED AND STRENGTH, SHE'LL RIP THIS PLANE APART.
NONSENSE, CHEETAH, SHE'LL DO NO SUCH THING.
AND YOU'LL UNDERSTAND WHY IN MERE MOMENTS.
NOW GO GET SUPERMAN.

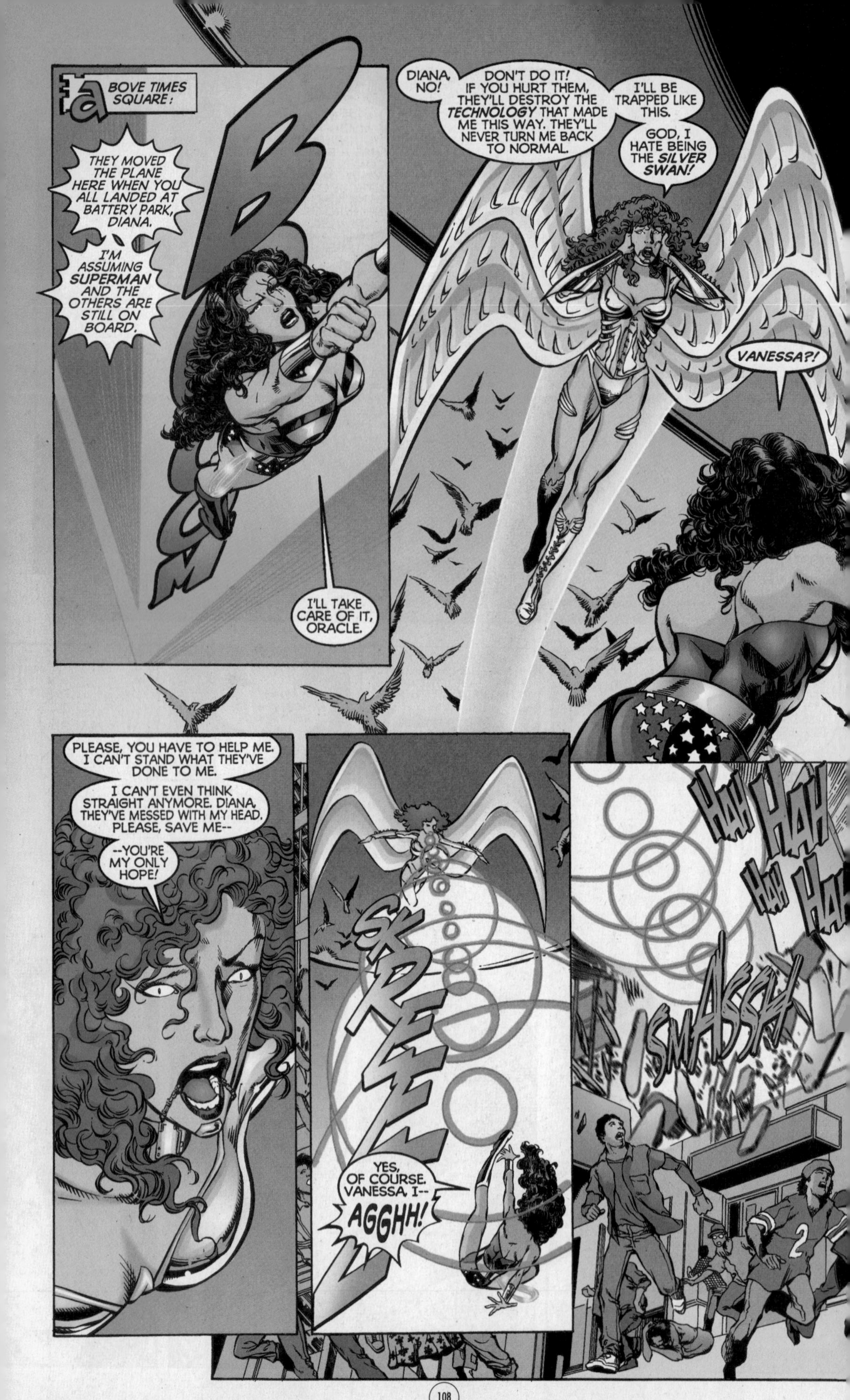
ABOVE TIMES SQUARE:
THEY MOVED THE PLANE HERE WHEN YOU ALL LANDED AT BATTERY PARK, DIANA.
I'M ASSUMING SUPERMAN AND THE OTHERS ARE STILL ON BOARD.
BOOM
I'LL TAKE CARE OF IT, ORACLE.
DIANA, NO!
DON'T DO IT! IF YOU HURT THEM, THEY'LL DESTROY THE TECHNOLOGY THAT MADE ME THIS WAY. THEY'LL NEVER TURN ME BACK TO NORMAL.
I'LL BE TRAPPED LIKE THIS.
GOD, I HATE BEING THE SILVER SWAN!
VANESSA?!
PLEASE, YOU HAVE TO HELP ME. I CAN'T STAND WHAT THEY'VE DONE TO ME.
I CAN'T EVEN THINK STRAIGHT ANYMORE. DIANA, THEY'VE MESSED WITH MY HEAD. PLEASE, SAVE ME--
--YOU'RE MY ONLY HOPE!
SKREEEE
YES, OF COURSE. VANESSA, I--
AGGHH!
HAH HAH HAH HAH
SMASH

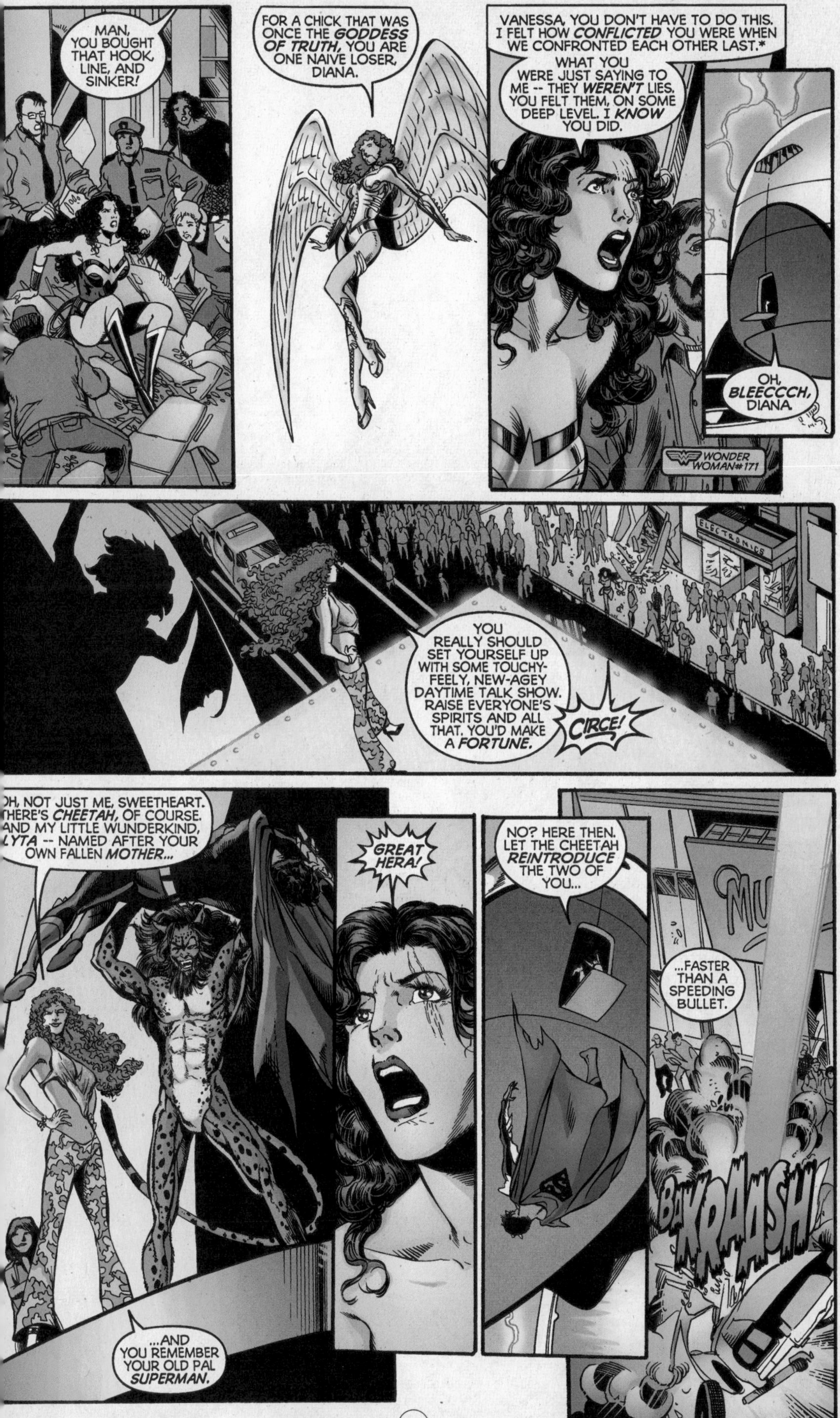
MAN, YOU BOUGHT THAT HOOK, LINE, AND SINKER!
FOR A CHICK THAT WAS ONCE THE GODDESS OF TRUTH, YOU ARE ONE NAIVE LOSER, DIANA.
VANESSA, YOU DON'T HAVE TO DO THIS. I FELT HOW CONFLICTED YOU WERE WHEN WE CONFRONTED EACH OTHER LAST.*
WHAT YOU WERE JUST SAYING TO ME -- THEY WEREN'T LIES. YOU FELT THEM, ON SOME DEEP LEVEL. I KNOW YOU DID.
OH, BLEECCCH, DIANA.
*WONDER WOMAN #171
YOU REALLY SHOULD SET YOURSELF UP WITH SOME TOUCHY-FEELY, NEW-AGEY DAYTIME TALK SHOW. RAISE EVERYONE'S SPIRITS AND ALL THAT. YOU'D MAKE A FORTUNE.
CIRCE!
ELECTRONICS
OH, NOT JUST ME, SWEETHEART. THERE'S CHEETAH, OF COURSE. AND MY LITTLE WUNDERKIND, LYTA -- NAMED AFTER YOUR OWN FALLEN MOTHER...
...AND YOU REMEMBER YOUR OLD PAL SUPERMAN.
GREAT HERA!
NO? HERE THEN. LET THE CHEETAH REINTRODUCE THE TWO OF YOU...
...FASTER THAN A SPEEDING BULLET.
BKRAASH

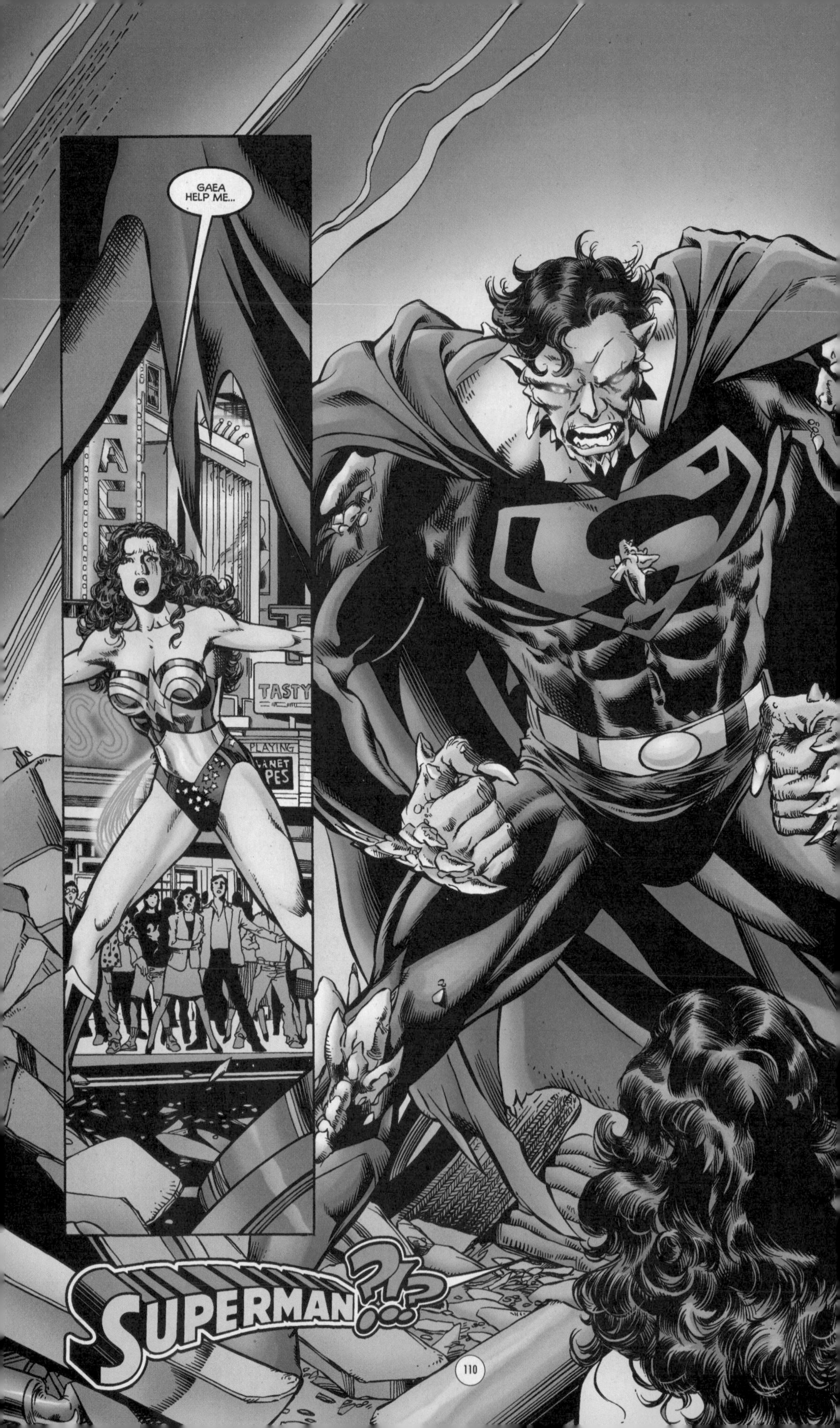
GAEA HELP ME...
TASTY
PLAYING
SUPERMAN?!?...

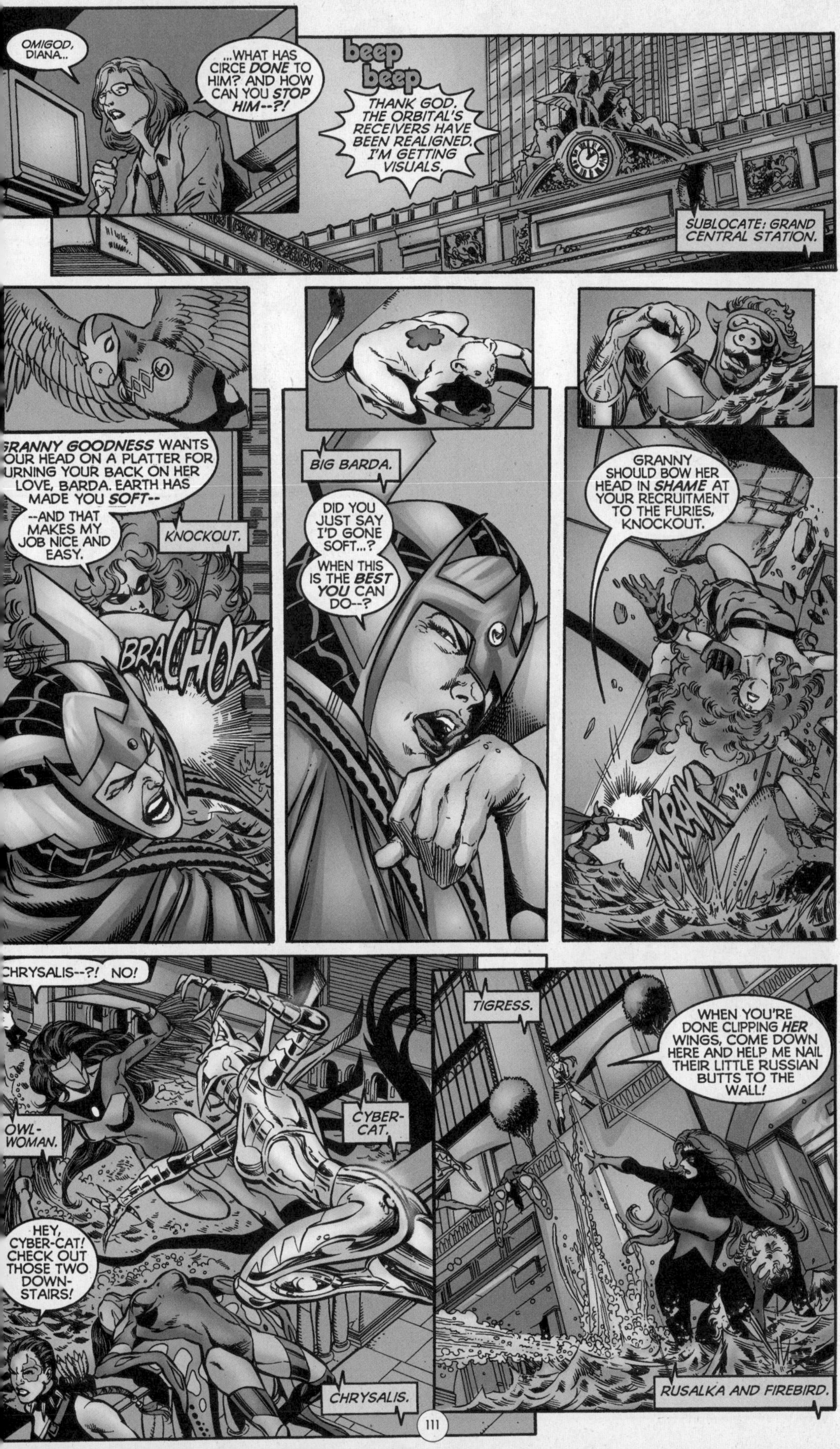

OMIGOD, DIANA...
...WHAT HAS CIRCE DONE TO HIM? AND HOW CAN YOU STOP HIM--?!
beep beep
THANK GOD. THE ORBITAL'S RECEIVERS HAVE BEEN REALIGNED. I'M GETTING VISUALS.
SUBLOCATE: GRAND CENTRAL STATION.
GRANNY GOODNESS WANTS OUR HEAD ON A PLATTER FOR URNING YOUR BACK ON HER LOVE, BARDA. EARTH HAS MADE YOU SOFT--
--AND THAT MAKES MY JOB NICE AND EASY.
KNOCKOUT.
BRACHOK
BIG BARDA.
DID YOU JUST SAY I'D GONE SOFT...?
WHEN THIS IS THE BEST YOU CAN DO--?
GRANNY SHOULD BOW HER HEAD IN SHAME AT YOUR RECRUITMENT TO THE FURIES, KNOCKOUT.
KRAK
CHRYSALIS--?! NO!
OWL-WOMAN.
CYBER-CAT.
HEY, CYBER-CAT! CHECK OUT THOSE TWO DOWN-STAIRS!
CHRYSALIS.
TIGRESS.
WHEN YOU'RE DONE CLIPPING HER WINGS, COME DOWN HERE AND HELP ME NAIL THEIR LITTLE RUSSIAN BUTTS TO THE WALL!
RUSALKA AND FIREBIRD.

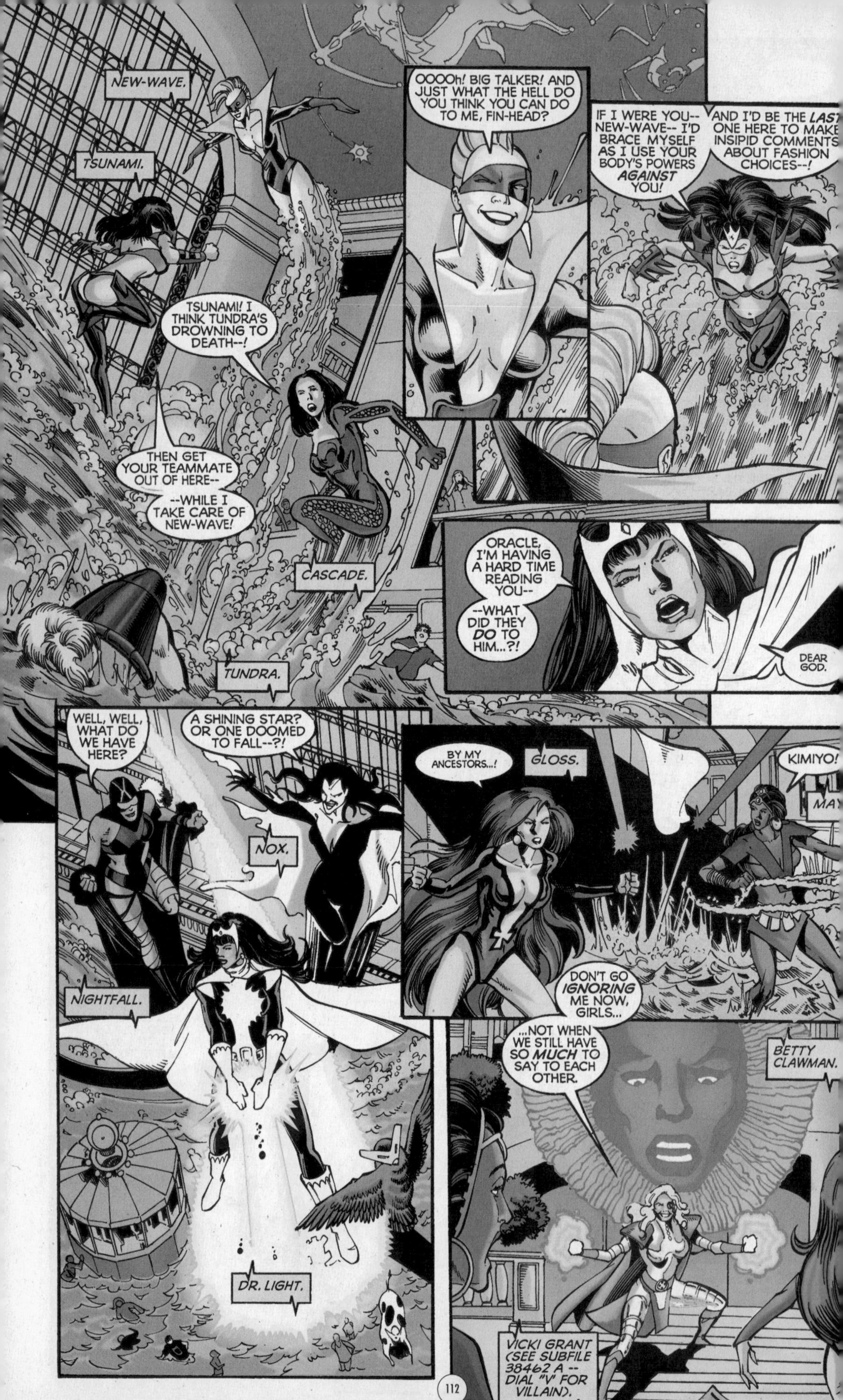
NEW-WAVE.
TSUNAMI.
OOOOh! BIG TALKER! AND JUST WHAT THE HELL DO YOU THINK YOU CAN DO TO ME, FIN-HEAD?
IF I WERE YOU-- NEW-WAVE-- I'D BRACE MYSELF AS I USE YOUR BODY'S POWERS AGAINST YOU!
AND I'D BE THE LAST ONE HERE TO MAKE INSIPID COMMENTS ABOUT FASHION CHOICES--!
TSUNAMI! I THINK TUNDRA'S DROWNING TO DEATH--!
THEN GET YOUR TEAMMATE OUT OF HERE--
--WHILE I TAKE CARE OF NEW-WAVE!
CASCADE.
TUNDRA.
ORACLE, I'M HAVING A HARD TIME READING YOU--
--WHAT DID THEY DO TO HIM...?!
DEAR GOD.
WELL, WELL, WHAT DO WE HAVE HERE?
A SHINING STAR? OR ONE DOOMED TO FALL--?!
NOX.
NIGHTFALL.
DR. LIGHT.
BY MY ANCESTORS...!
GLOSS.
KIMIYO!
DON'T GO IGNORING ME NOW, GIRLS...
...NOT WHEN WE STILL HAVE SO MUCH TO SAY TO EACH OTHER.
BETTY CLAWMAN.
VICKI GRANT (SEE SUBFILE 38462 A -- DIAL "V" FOR VILLAIN).

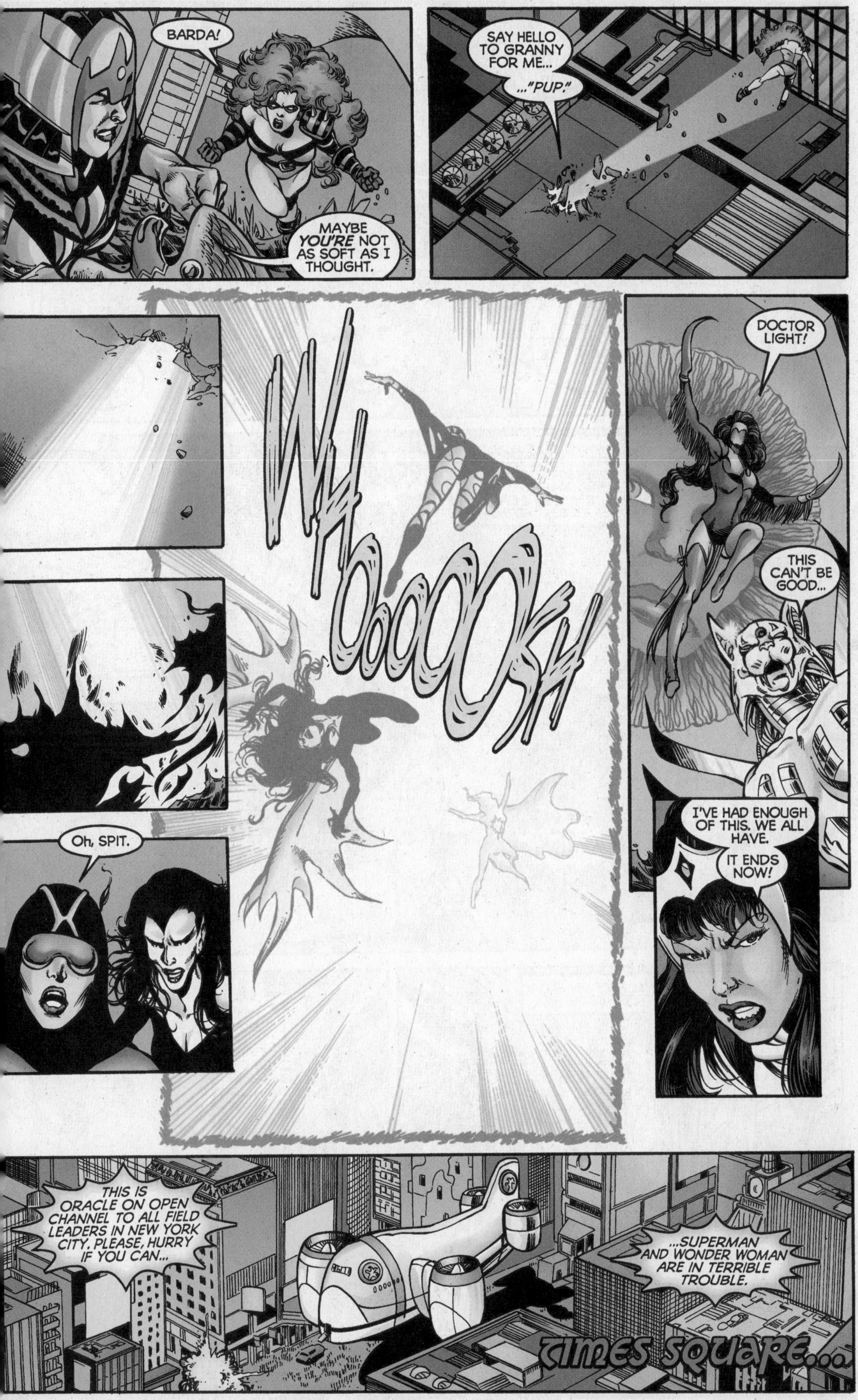
BARDA!
MAYBE *YOU'RE* NOT AS SOFT AS I THOUGHT.
SAY HELLO TO GRANNY FOR ME...
..."PUP."
WHOOOOOKH
DOCTOR LIGHT!
THIS CAN'T BE GOOD...
Oh, SPIT.
I'VE HAD ENOUGH OF THIS. WE ALL HAVE.
IT ENDS NOW!
THIS IS ORACLE ON OPEN CHANNEL TO ALL FIELD LEADERS IN NEW YORK CITY. PLEASE, HURRY IF YOU CAN...
...SUPERMAN AND WONDER WOMAN ARE IN TERRIBLE TROUBLE.
TIMES SQUARE...

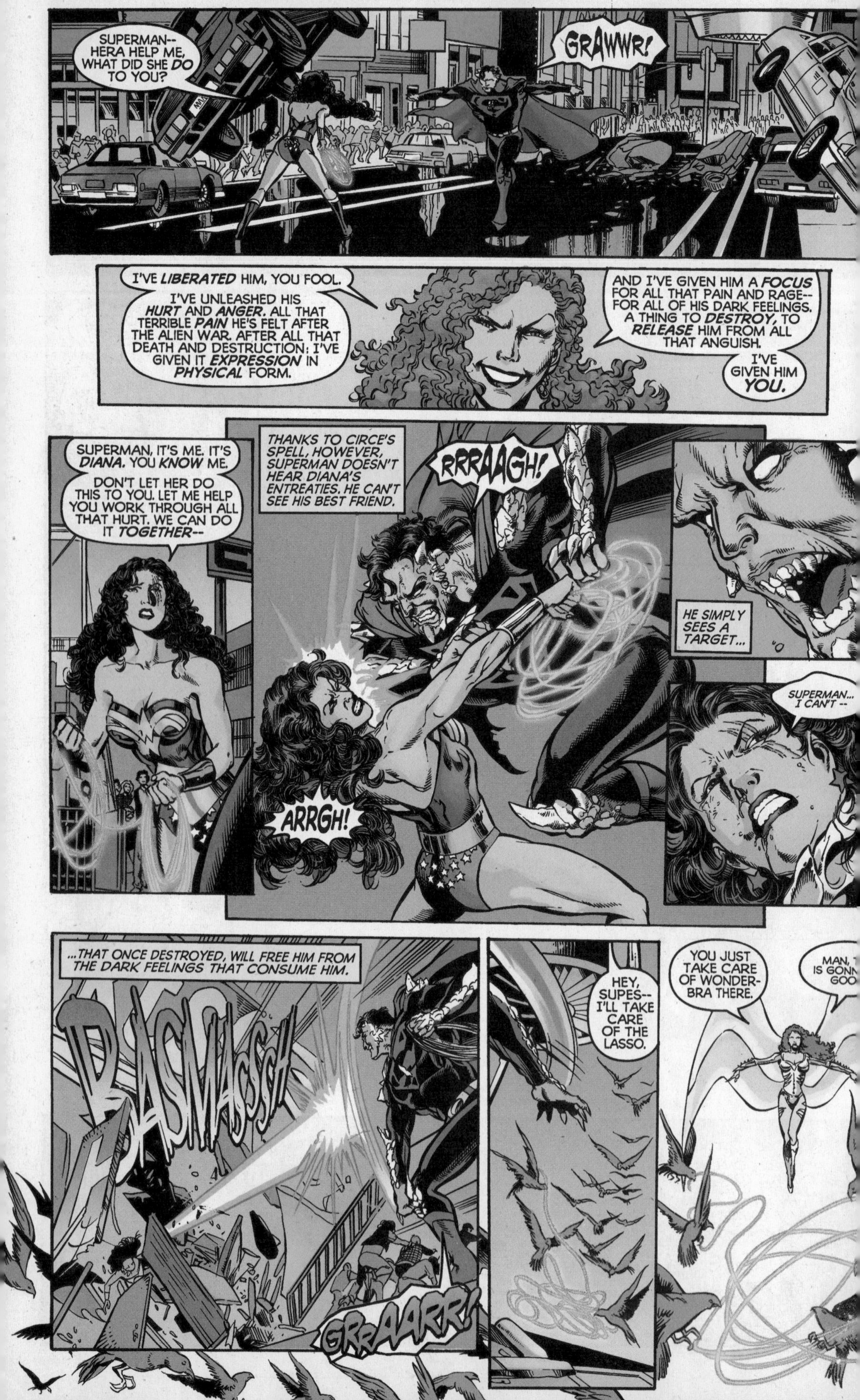
SUPERMAN-- HERA HELP ME, WHAT DID SHE DO TO YOU?
GRAWWR!
I'VE LIBERATED HIM, YOU FOOL.
I'VE UNLEASHED HIS HURT AND ANGER. ALL THAT TERRIBLE PAIN HE'S FELT AFTER THE ALIEN WAR. AFTER ALL THAT DEATH AND DESTRUCTION: I'VE GIVEN IT EXPRESSION IN PHYSICAL FORM.
AND I'VE GIVEN HIM A FOCUS FOR ALL THAT PAIN AND RAGE-- FOR ALL OF HIS DARK FEELINGS. A THING TO DESTROY, TO RELEASE HIM FROM ALL THAT ANGUISH.
I'VE GIVEN HIM YOU.
SUPERMAN, IT'S ME. IT'S DIANA. YOU KNOW ME.
DON'T LET HER DO THIS TO YOU. LET ME HELP YOU WORK THROUGH ALL THAT HURT. WE CAN DO IT TOGETHER--
THANKS TO CIRCE'S SPELL, HOWEVER, SUPERMAN DOESN'T HEAR DIANA'S ENTREATIES. HE CAN'T SEE HIS BEST FRIEND.
RRRAAGH!
ARRGH!
HE SIMPLY SEES A TARGET...
SUPERMAN... I CAN'T --
...THAT ONCE DESTROYED, WILL FREE HIM FROM THE DARK FEELINGS THAT CONSUME HIM.
BASMASSH!
GRRAARR!
HEY, SUPES-- I'LL TAKE CARE OF THE LASSO.
YOU JUST TAKE CARE OF WONDER-BRA THERE.
MAN, T
IS GONN
GOO

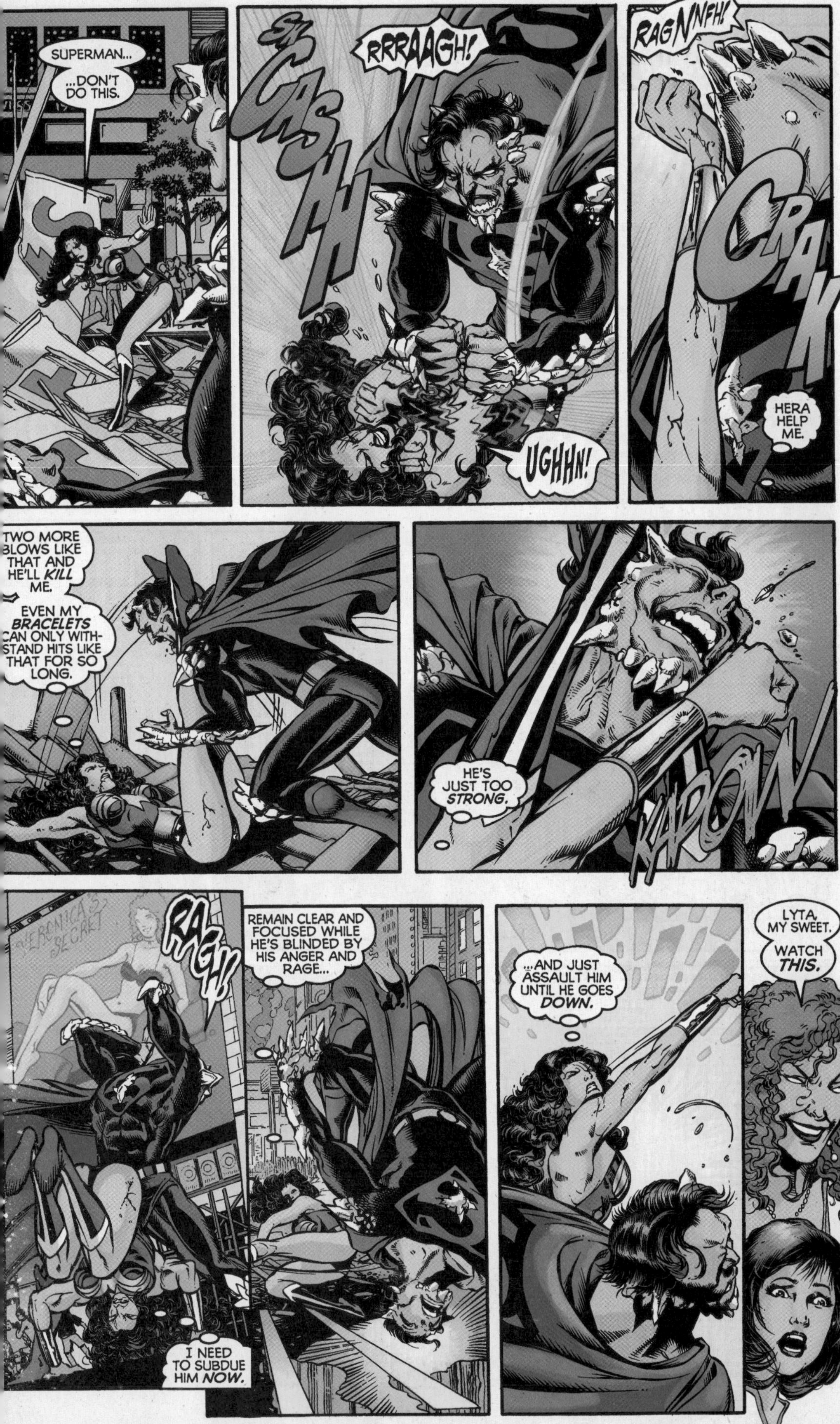

SUPERMAN...
...DON'T DO THIS.
SHK
CASHH
RRRAAGH!
UGHHN!
RAGNNFH!
CRAK
HERA HELP ME.
TWO MORE BLOWS LIKE THAT AND HE'LL KILL ME.
EVEN MY BRACELETS CAN ONLY WITHSTAND HITS LIKE THAT FOR SO LONG.
HE'S JUST TOO STRONG.
KADOW
VERONICA'S SECRET
RAGH!
I NEED TO SUBDUE HIM NOW.
REMAIN CLEAR AND FOCUSED WHILE HE'S BLINDED BY HIS ANGER AND RAGE...
...AND JUST ASSAULT HIM UNTIL HE GOES DOWN.
LYTA, MY SWEET.
WATCH THIS.

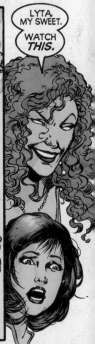

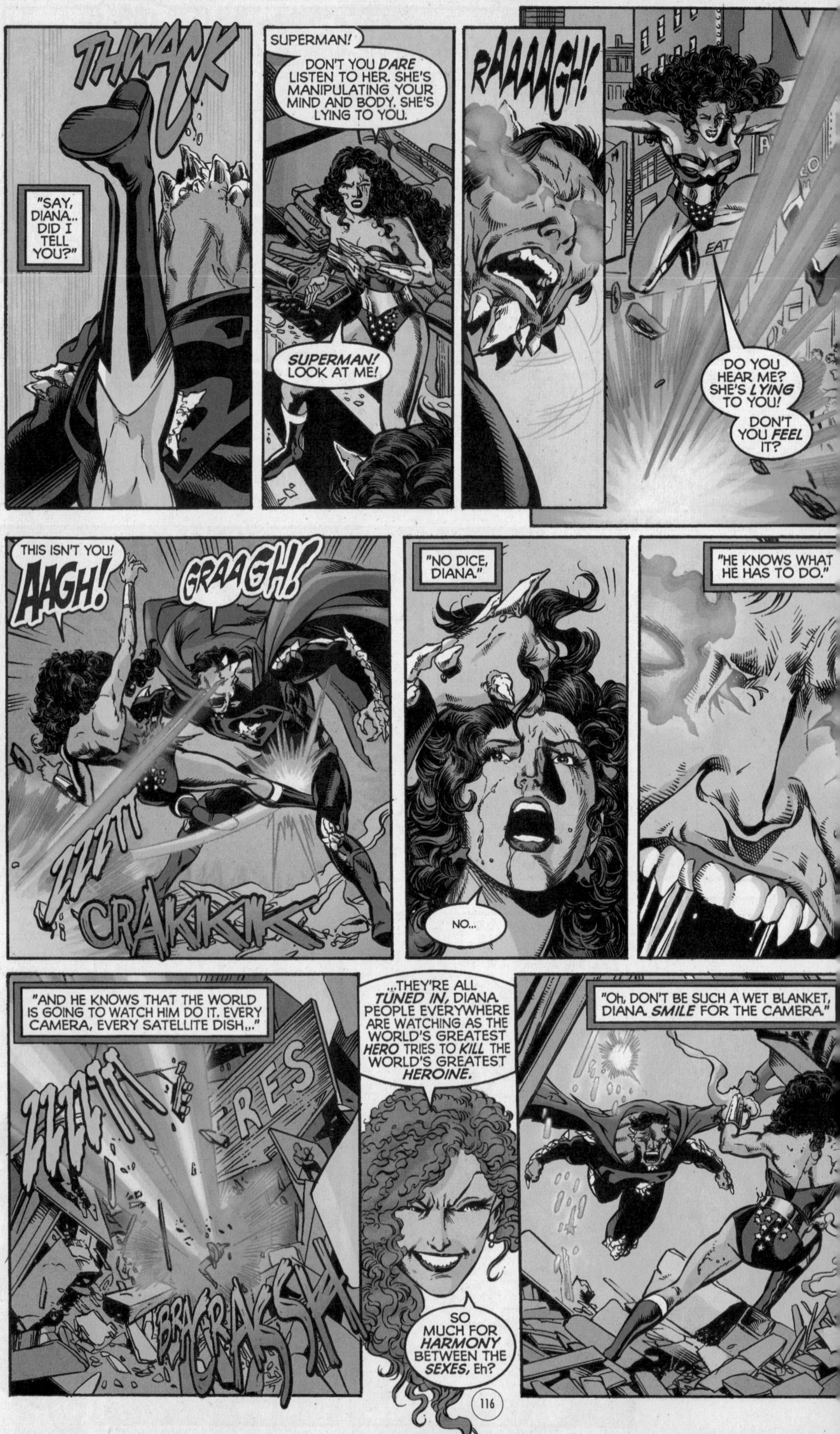
THWACK
"SAY, DIANA... DID I TELL YOU?"
SUPERMAN!
DON'T YOU DARE LISTEN TO HER. SHE'S MANIPULATING YOUR MIND AND BODY. SHE'S LYING TO YOU.
SUPERMAN! LOOK AT ME!
RAAAAGH!
DO YOU HEAR ME? SHE'S LYING TO YOU!
DON'T YOU FEEL IT?
THIS ISN'T YOU!
AAGH!
GRAAGH!
ZZZTT
CRAKKKK
"NO DICE, DIANA."
NO...
"HE KNOWS WHAT HE HAS TO DO."
"AND HE KNOWS THAT THE WORLD IS GOING TO WATCH HIM DO IT. EVERY CAMERA, EVERY SATELLITE DISH..."
ZZZTT
BRAKRAKSH
...THEY'RE ALL TUNED IN, DIANA. PEOPLE EVERYWHERE ARE WATCHING AS THE WORLD'S GREATEST HERO TRIES TO KILL THE WORLD'S GREATEST HEROINE.
SO MUCH FOR HARMONY BETWEEN THE SEXES, Eh?
"Oh, DON'T BE SUCH A WET BLANKET, DIANA. SMILE FOR THE CAMERA."

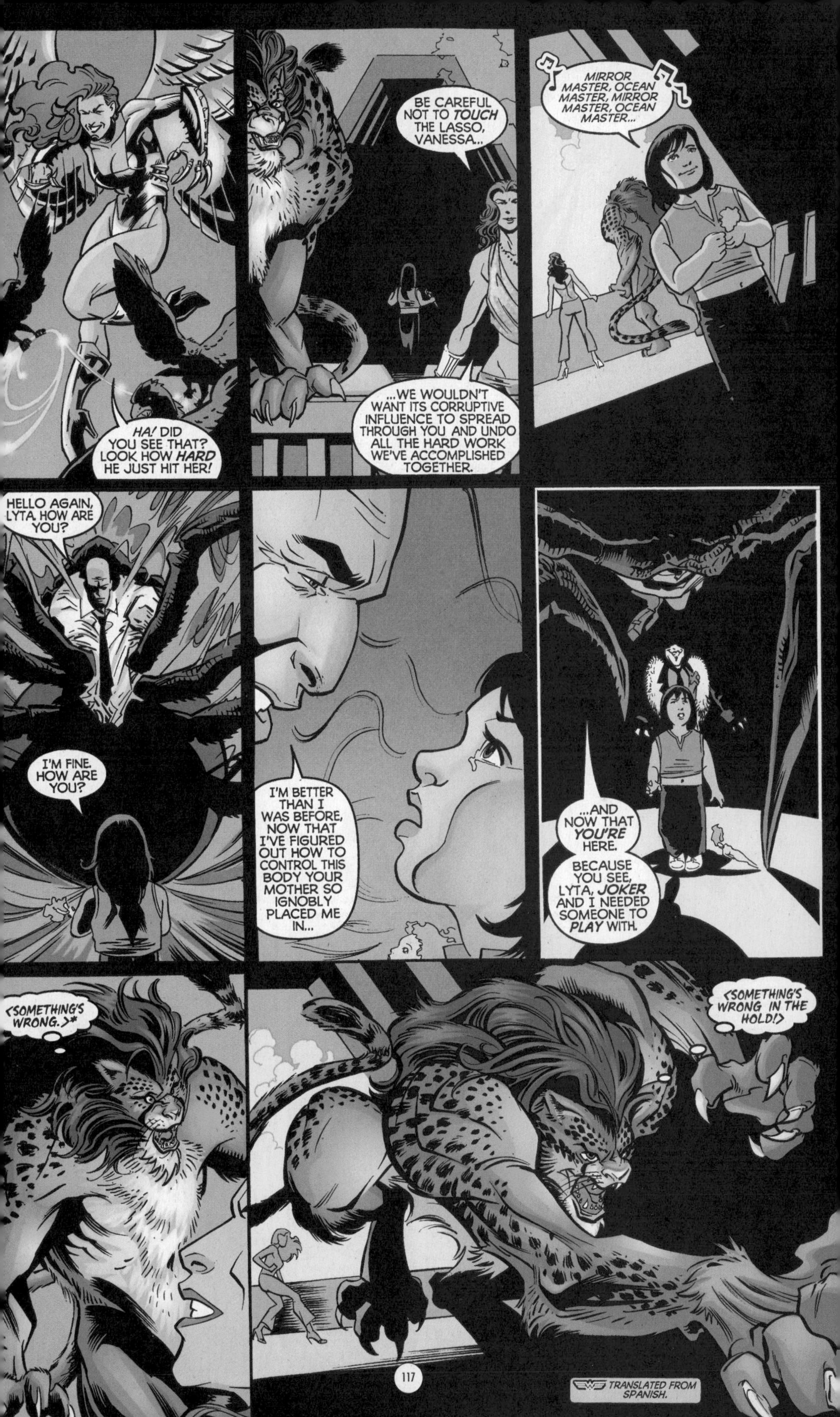
HA! DID YOU SEE THAT? LOOK HOW HARD HE JUST HIT HER!
BE CAREFUL NOT TO TOUCH THE LASSO, VANESSA...
...WE WOULDN'T WANT ITS CORRUPTIVE INFLUENCE TO SPREAD THROUGH YOU AND UNDO ALL THE HARD WORK WE'VE ACCOMPLISHED TOGETHER.
MIRROR MASTER, OCEAN MASTER, MIRROR MASTER, OCEAN MASTER...
HELLO AGAIN, LYTA. HOW ARE YOU?
I'M FINE. HOW ARE YOU?
I'M BETTER THAN I WAS BEFORE, NOW THAT I'VE FIGURED OUT HOW TO CONTROL THIS BODY YOUR MOTHER SO IGNOBLY PLACED ME IN...
...AND NOW THAT YOU'RE HERE.
BECAUSE YOU SEE, LYTA, JOKER AND I NEEDED SOMEONE TO PLAY WITH.
<SOMETHING'S WRONG.>*
<SOMETHING'S WRONG IN THE HOLD!>
*TRANSLATED FROM SPANISH.

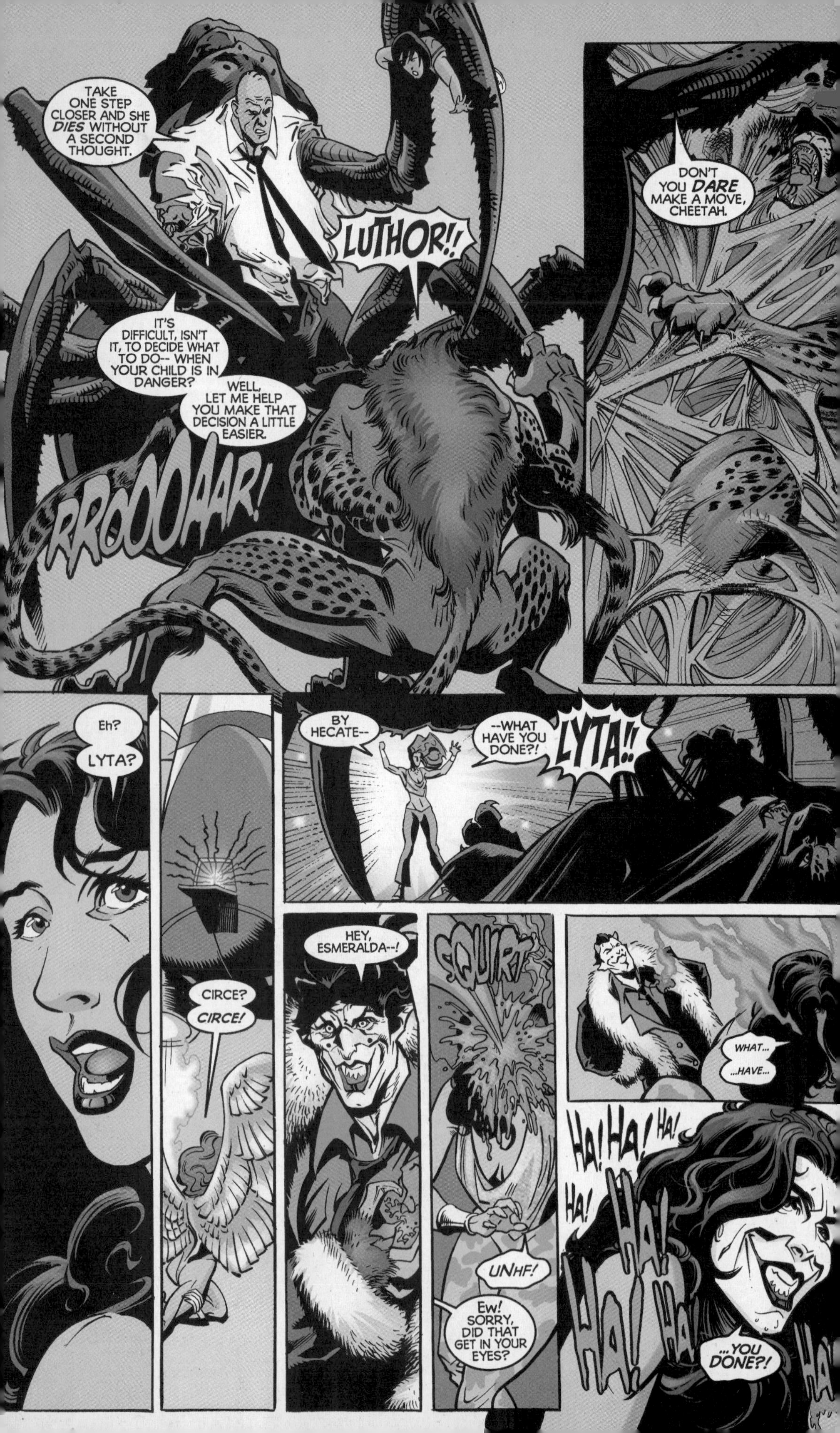
TAKE ONE STEP CLOSER AND SHE *DIES* WITHOUT A SECOND THOUGHT.
LUTHOR!!
IT'S DIFFICULT, ISN'T IT, TO DECIDE WHAT TO DO-- WHEN YOUR CHILD IS IN DANGER?
WELL, LET ME HELP YOU MAKE THAT DECISION A LITTLE EASIER.
RROOOAAR!
DON'T YOU *DARE* MAKE A MOVE, CHEETAH.
Eh?
LYTA?
CIRCE? *CIRCE!*
BY HECATE--
--WHAT HAVE YOU DONE?!
LYTA!!
HEY, ESMERALDA--!
SQUIRT
UNHF!
Ew! SORRY, DID THAT GET IN YOUR EYES?
WHAT...
...HAVE...
HA! HA! HA! HA! HA! HA! HA! HA! HA!
...YOU DONE?!

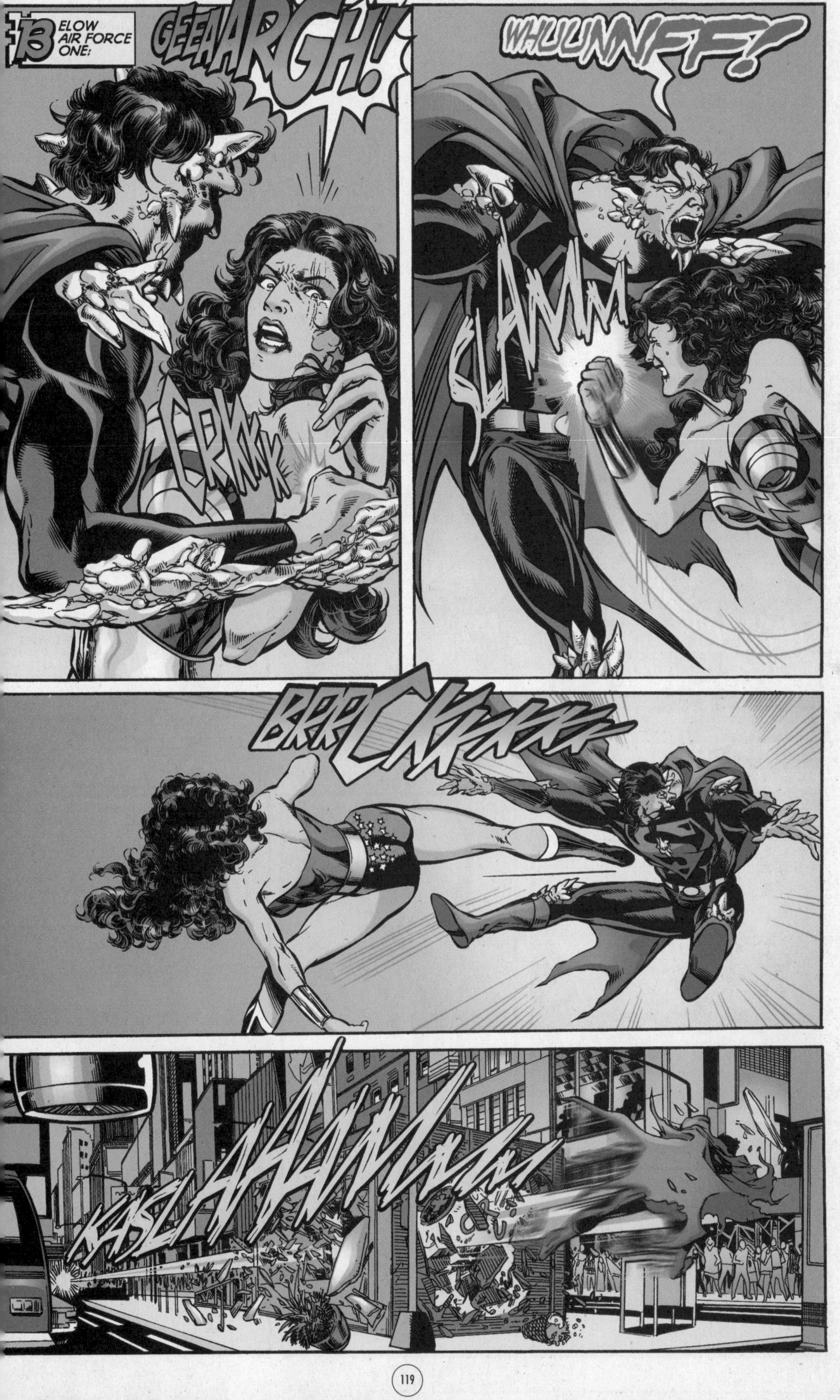
BELOW AIR FORCE ONE:
GEEAARGH!
CRKKKK
WHUUNNFF!
SLAMM
BRRRCKKKKKK
KASLAHHMMM

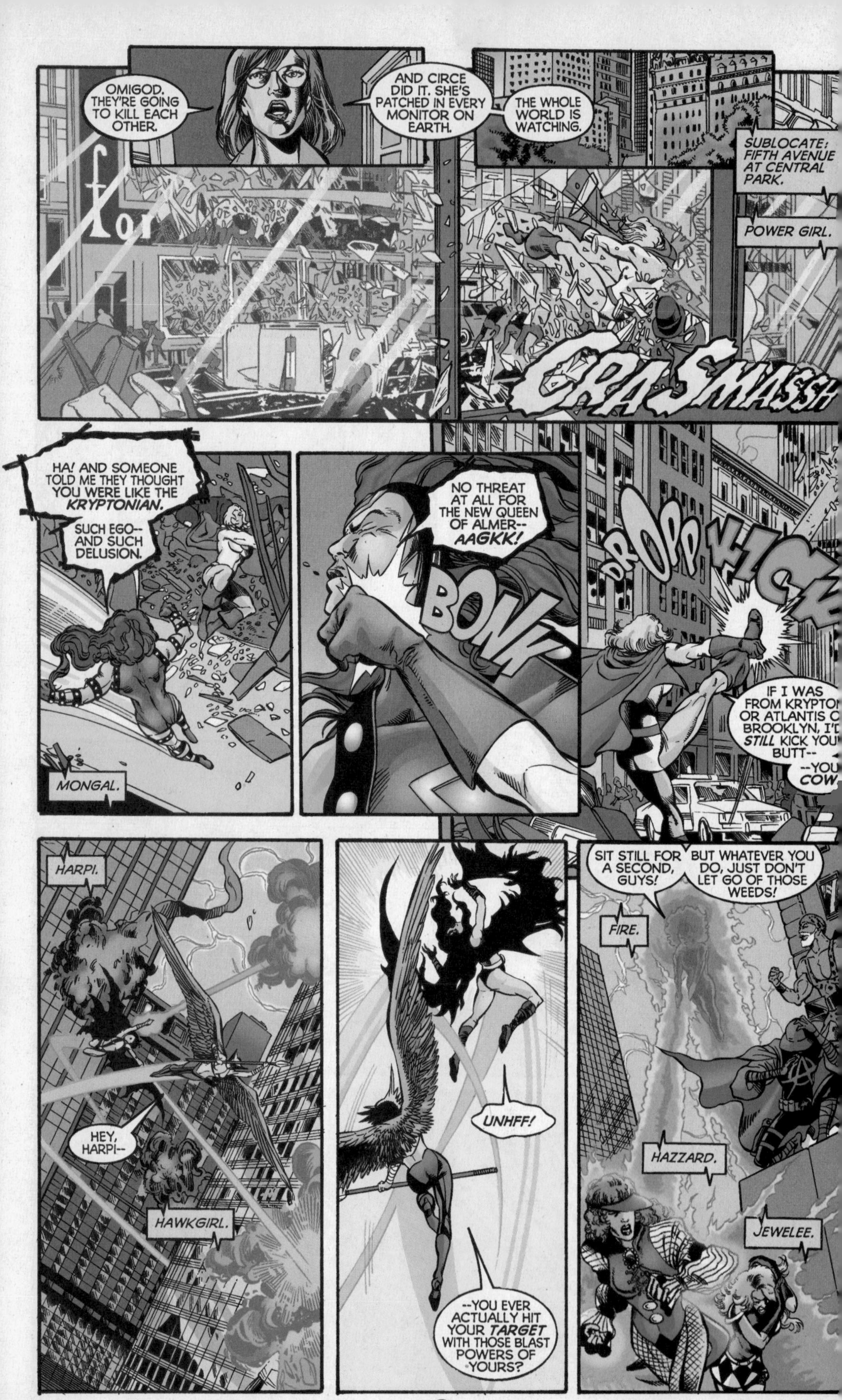

OMIGOD. THEY'RE GOING TO KILL EACH OTHER.
AND CIRCE DID IT. SHE'S PATCHED IN EVERY MONITOR ON EARTH.
THE WHOLE WORLD IS WATCHING.
SUBLOCATE: FIFTH AVENUE AT CENTRAL PARK.
POWER GIRL.
CRASMASSH
HA! AND SOMEONE TOLD ME THEY THOUGHT YOU WERE LIKE THE KRYPTONIAN.
SUCH EGO--AND SUCH DELUSION.
MONGAL.
NO THREAT AT ALL FOR THE NEW QUEEN OF ALMER--AAGKK!
BONK
IF I WAS FROM KRYPTO OR ATLANTIS O BROOKLYN, I'D STILL KICK YOU BUTT--
--YOU COW
HARPI.
HEY, HARPI--
HAWKGIRL.
UNHFF!
--YOU EVER ACTUALLY HIT YOUR TARGET WITH THOSE BLAST POWERS OF YOURS?
SIT STILL FOR A SECOND, GUYS!
BUT WHATEVER YOU DO, JUST DON'T LET GO OF THOSE WEEDS!
FIRE.
HAZZARD.
JEWELEE.

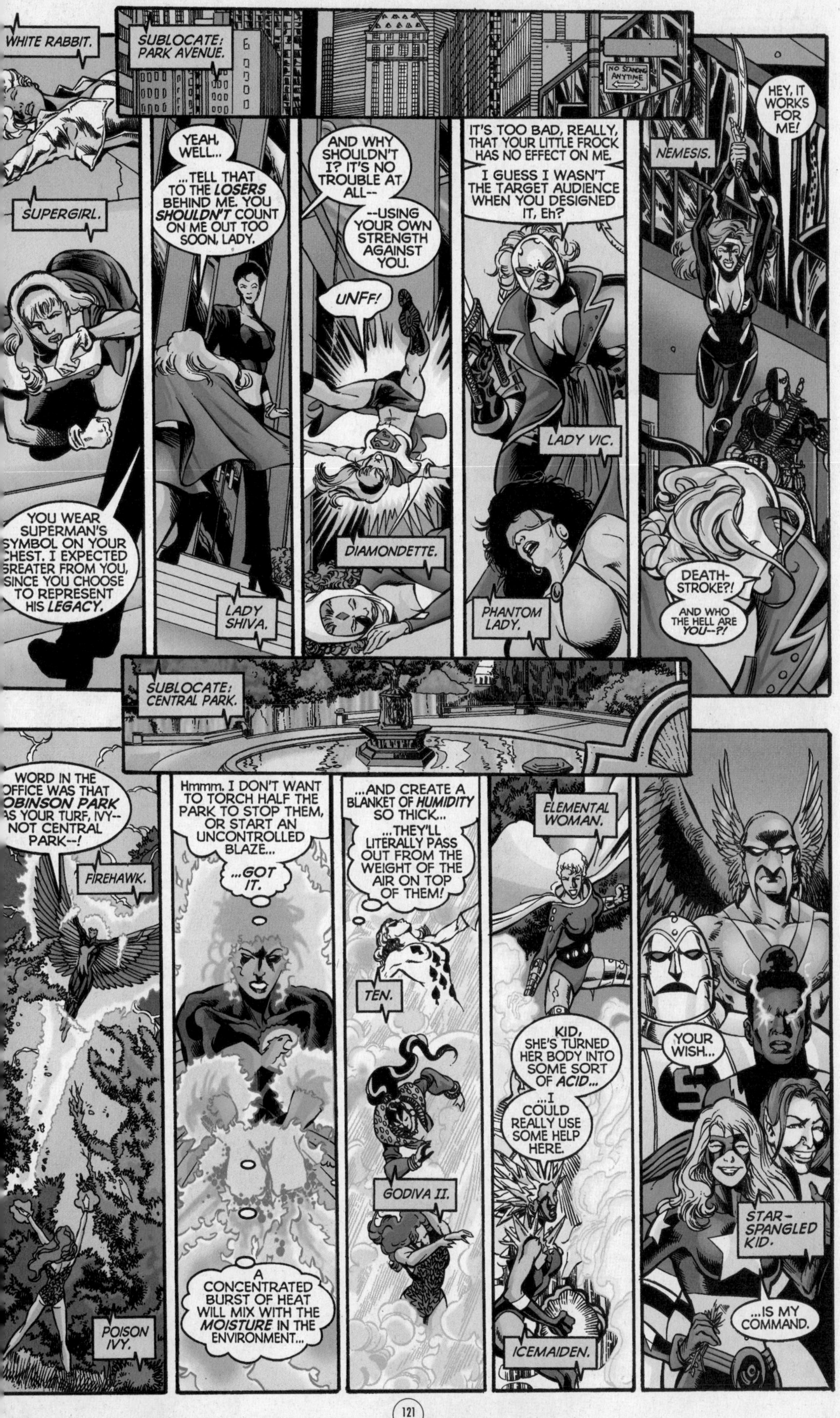
WHITE RABBIT.
SUBLOCATE: PARK AVENUE.
NO STANDING ANYTIME
SUPERGIRL.
YOU WEAR SUPERMAN'S SYMBOL ON YOUR CHEST. I EXPECTED GREATER FROM YOU, SINCE YOU CHOOSE TO REPRESENT HIS LEGACY.
YEAH, WELL...
...TELL THAT TO THE LOSERS BEHIND ME. YOU SHOULDN'T COUNT ON ME OUT TOO SOON, LADY.
LADY SHIVA.
AND WHY SHOULDN'T I? IT'S NO TROUBLE AT ALL--
--USING YOUR OWN STRENGTH AGAINST YOU.
UNFF!
DIAMONDETTE.
IT'S TOO BAD, REALLY, THAT YOUR LITTLE FROCK HAS NO EFFECT ON ME.
I GUESS I WASN'T THE TARGET AUDIENCE WHEN YOU DESIGNED IT, Eh?
LADY VIC.
PHANTOM LADY.
HEY, IT WORKS FOR ME!
NEMESIS.
DEATH-STROKE?!
AND WHO THE HELL ARE YOU--?!
SUBLOCATE: CENTRAL PARK.
WORD IN THE OFFICE WAS THAT ROBINSON PARK WAS YOUR TURF, IVY-- NOT CENTRAL PARK--!
FIREHAWK.
POISON IVY.
Hmmm. I DON'T WANT TO TORCH HALF THE PARK TO STOP THEM, OR START AN UNCONTROLLED BLAZE...
...GOT IT.
A CONCENTRATED BURST OF HEAT WILL MIX WITH THE MOISTURE IN THE ENVIRONMENT...
...AND CREATE A BLANKET OF HUMIDITY SO THICK...
...THEY'LL LITERALLY PASS OUT FROM THE WEIGHT OF THE AIR ON TOP OF THEM!
TEN.
GODIVA II.
ELEMENTAL WOMAN.
KID, SHE'S TURNED HER BODY INTO SOME SORT OF ACID...
...I COULD REALLY USE SOME HELP HERE.
ICEMAIDEN.
YOUR WISH...
...IS MY COMMAND.
STAR-SPANGLED KID.

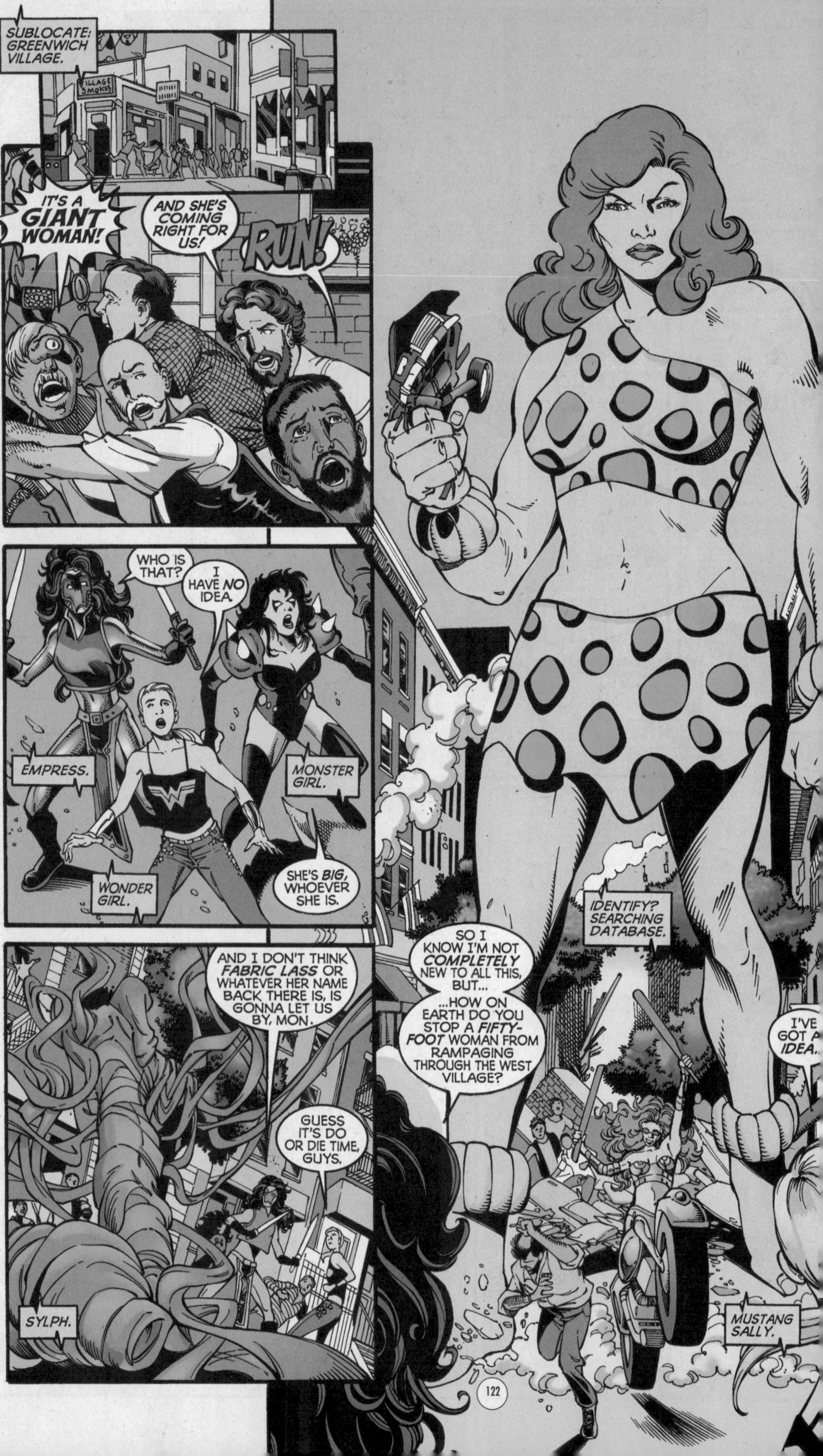

SUBLOCATE: GREENWICH VILLAGE.
VILLAGE SMOKES
COMING
IT'S A GIANT WOMAN!
AND SHE'S COMING RIGHT FOR US!
RUN!
WHO IS THAT?
I HAVE NO IDEA.
EMPRESS.
MONSTER GIRL.
WONDER GIRL.
SHE'S BIG, WHOEVER SHE IS.
AND I DON'T THINK FABRIC LASS OR WHATEVER HER NAME BACK THERE IS, IS GONNA LET US BY, MON.
GUESS IT'S DO OR DIE TIME, GUYS.
SYLPH.
IDENTIFY? SEARCHING DATABASE.
SO I KNOW I'M NOT COMPLETELY NEW TO ALL THIS, BUT...
...HOW ON EARTH DO YOU STOP A FIFTY-FOOT WOMAN FROM RAMPAGING THROUGH THE WEST VILLAGE?
I'VE GOT A IDEA...
MUSTANG SALLY.

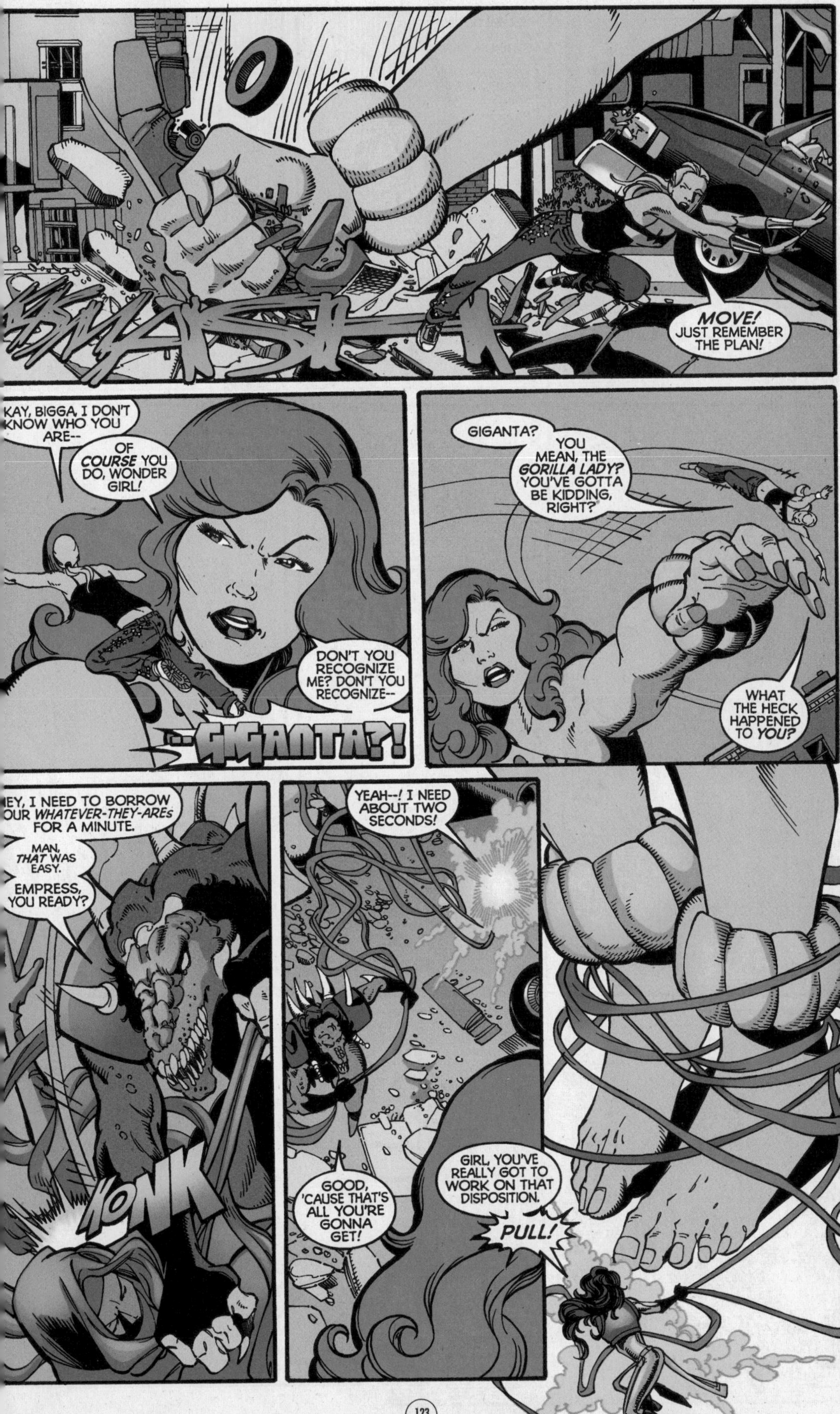

KASNAK
MOVE! JUST REMEMBER THE PLAN!
KAY, BIGGA, I DON'T KNOW WHO YOU ARE--
OF COURSE YOU DO, WONDER GIRL!
DON'T YOU RECOGNIZE ME? DON'T YOU RECOGNIZE--
--GIGANTA?!
GIGANTA?
YOU MEAN, THE GORILLA LADY? YOU'VE GOTTA BE KIDDING, RIGHT?
WHAT THE HECK HAPPENED TO YOU?
EY, I NEED TO BORROW OUR WHATEVER-THEY-AREs FOR A MINUTE.
MAN, THAT WAS EASY.
EMPRESS, YOU READY?
KONK
YEAH--! I NEED ABOUT TWO SECONDS!
GOOD, 'CAUSE THAT'S ALL YOU'RE GONNA GET!
GIRL, YOU'VE REALLY GOT TO WORK ON THAT DISPOSITION.
PULL!

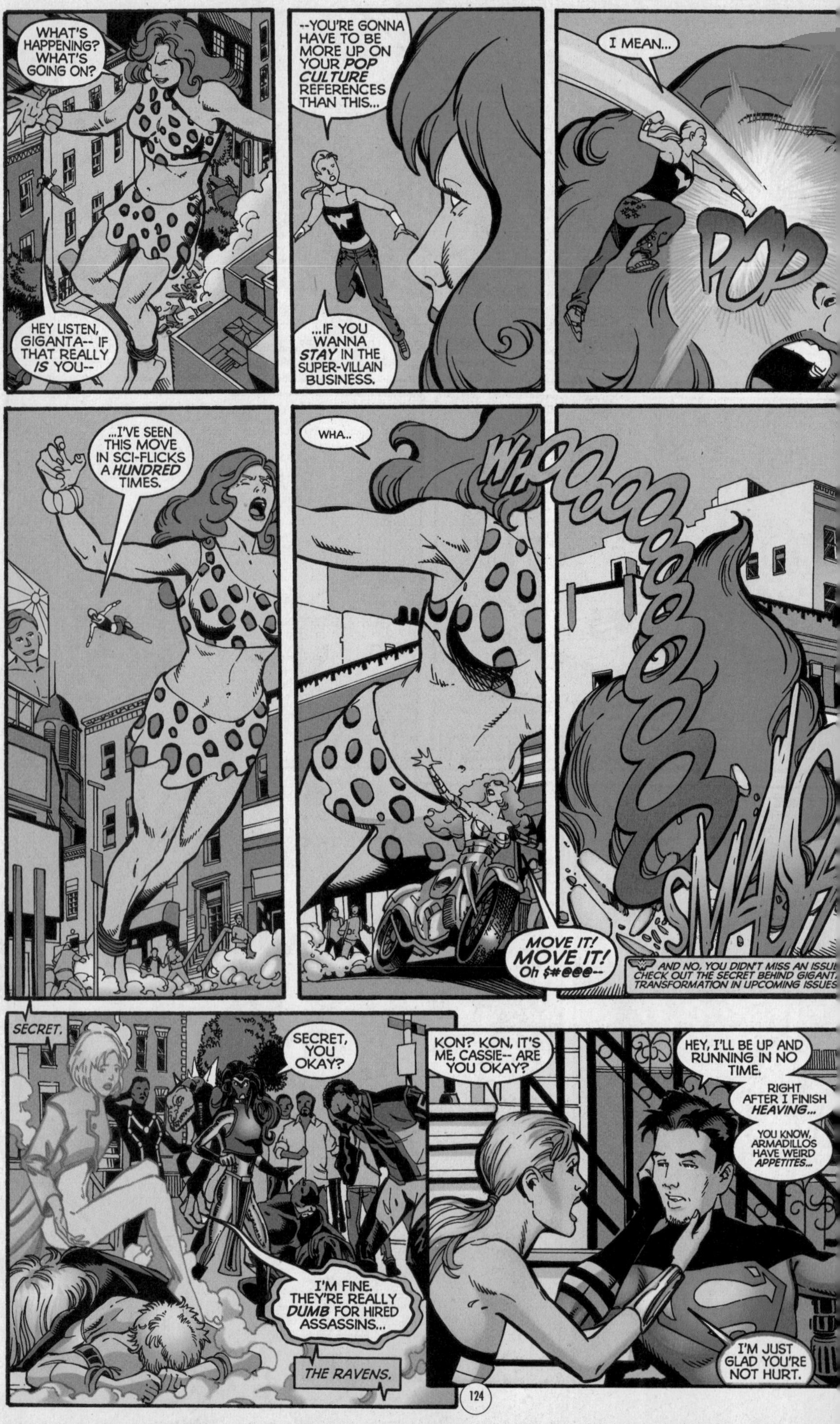

WHAT'S HAPPENING? WHAT'S GOING ON?
HEY LISTEN, GIGANTA-- IF THAT REALLY IS YOU--
--YOU'RE GONNA HAVE TO BE MORE UP ON YOUR POP CULTURE REFERENCES THAN THIS...
...IF YOU WANNA STAY IN THE SUPER-VILLAIN BUSINESS.
I MEAN...
POP
...I'VE SEEN THIS MOVE IN SCI-FLICKS A HUNDRED TIMES.
WHA..
WHOOOOOOOOOOOOM
MOVE IT! MOVE IT! Oh $#@@@--
SMASH
AND NO, YOU DIDN'T MISS AN ISSUE. CHECK OUT THE SECRET BEHIND GIGANTA'S TRANSFORMATION IN UPCOMING ISSUES.
SECRET.
SECRET, YOU OKAY?
I'M FINE. THEY'RE REALLY DUMB FOR HIRED ASSASSINS...
THE RAVENS.
KON? KON, IT'S ME, CASSIE-- ARE YOU OKAY?
HEY, I'LL BE UP AND RUNNING IN NO TIME.
RIGHT AFTER I FINISH HEAVING...
YOU KNOW, ARMADILLOS HAVE WEIRD APPETITES...
I'M JUST GLAD YOU'RE NOT HURT.

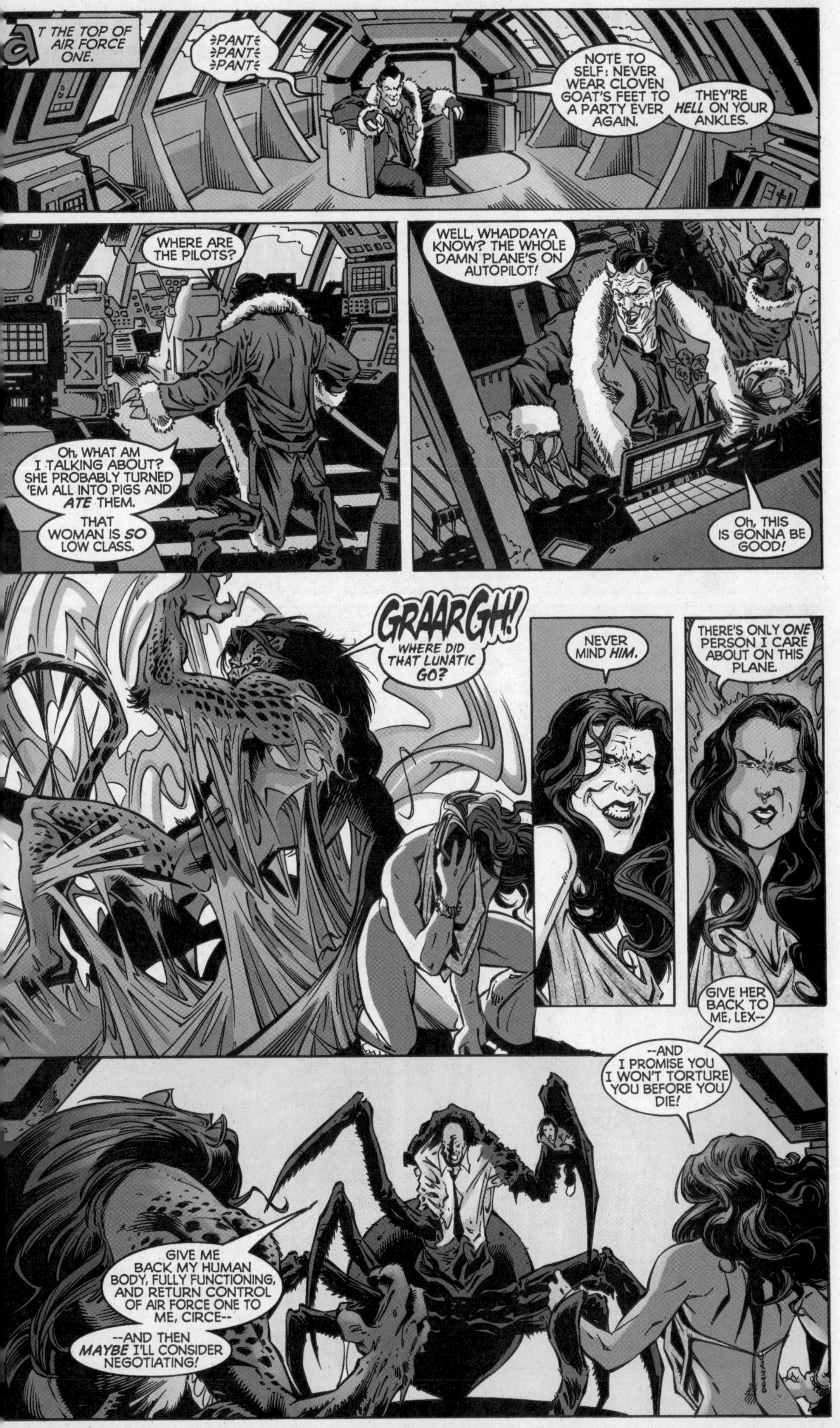
AT THE TOP OF AIR FORCE ONE.
PANT PANT PANT
NOTE TO SELF: NEVER WEAR CLOVEN GOAT'S FEET TO A PARTY EVER AGAIN.
THEY'RE HELL ON YOUR ANKLES.
WHERE ARE THE PILOTS?
Oh, WHAT AM I TALKING ABOUT? SHE PROBABLY TURNED 'EM ALL INTO PIGS AND ATE THEM.
THAT WOMAN IS SO LOW CLASS.
WELL, WHADDAYA KNOW? THE WHOLE DAMN PLANE'S ON AUTOPILOT!
Oh, THIS IS GONNA BE GOOD!
GRAARGH!
WHERE DID THAT LUNATIC GO?
NEVER MIND HIM.
THERE'S ONLY ONE PERSON I CARE ABOUT ON THIS PLANE.
GIVE HER BACK TO ME, LEX--
--AND I PROMISE YOU I WON'T TORTURE YOU BEFORE YOU DIE!
GIVE ME BACK MY HUMAN BODY, FULLY FUNCTIONING, AND RETURN CONTROL OF AIR FORCE ONE TO ME, CIRCE--
--AND THEN MAYBE I'LL CONSIDER NEGOTIATING!

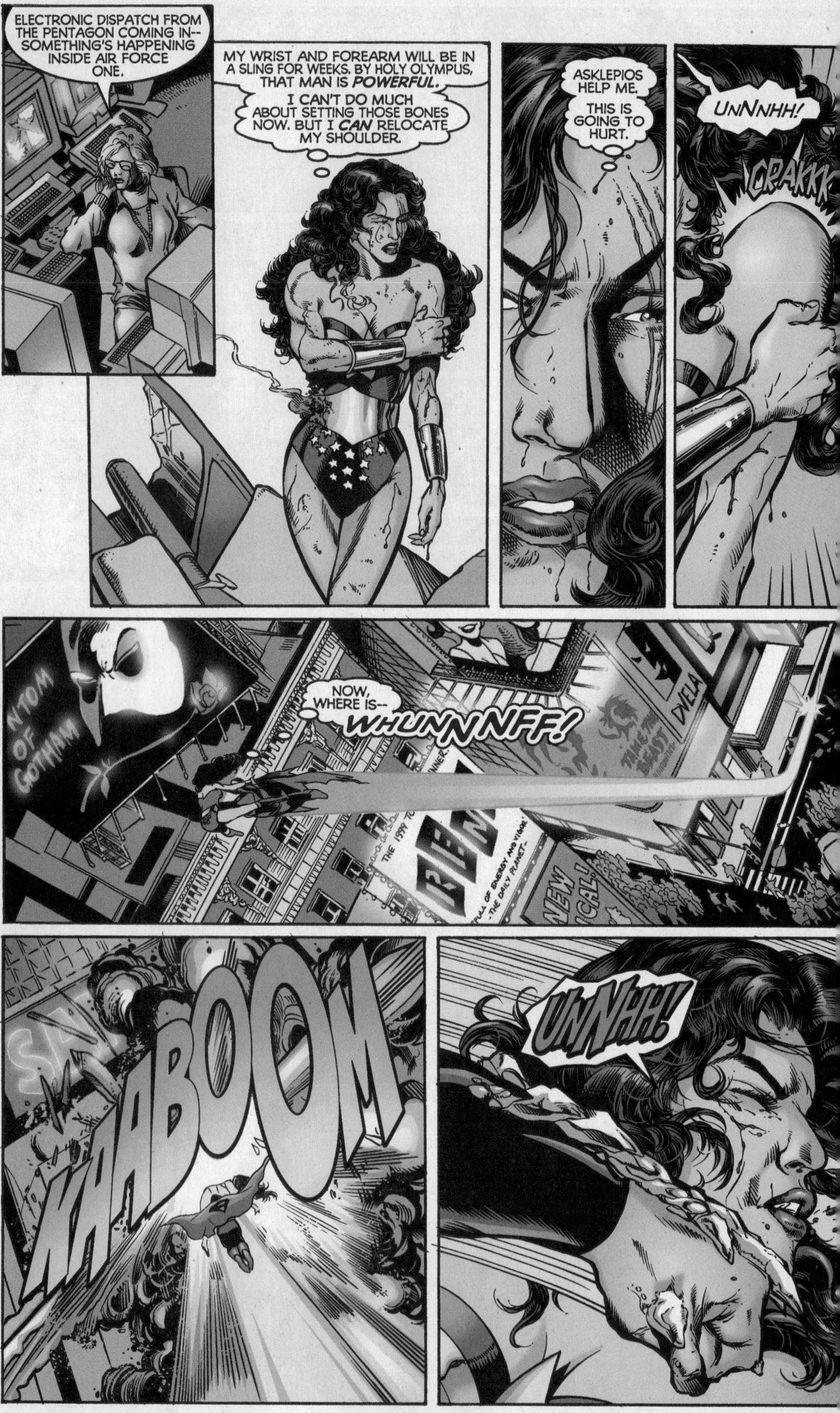

ELECTRONIC DISPATCH FROM THE PENTAGON COMING IN-- SOMETHING'S HAPPENING INSIDE AIR FORCE ONE.
MY WRIST AND FOREARM WILL BE IN A SLING FOR WEEKS. BY HOLY OLYMPUS, THAT MAN IS *POWERFUL.*
I CAN'T DO MUCH ABOUT SETTING THOSE BONES NOW. BUT I *CAN* RELOCATE MY SHOULDER.
ASKLEPIOS HELP ME.
THIS IS GOING TO HURT.
UNNNHH!
CRAKKK
NTOM OF GOTHAM
NOW, WHERE IS--
WHUNNNFF!
TAME THE BEAST
FULL OF ENERGY AND VIGOR! -THE DAILY PLANET-
NEW ...ICAL!
KABOOM
UNNHH!

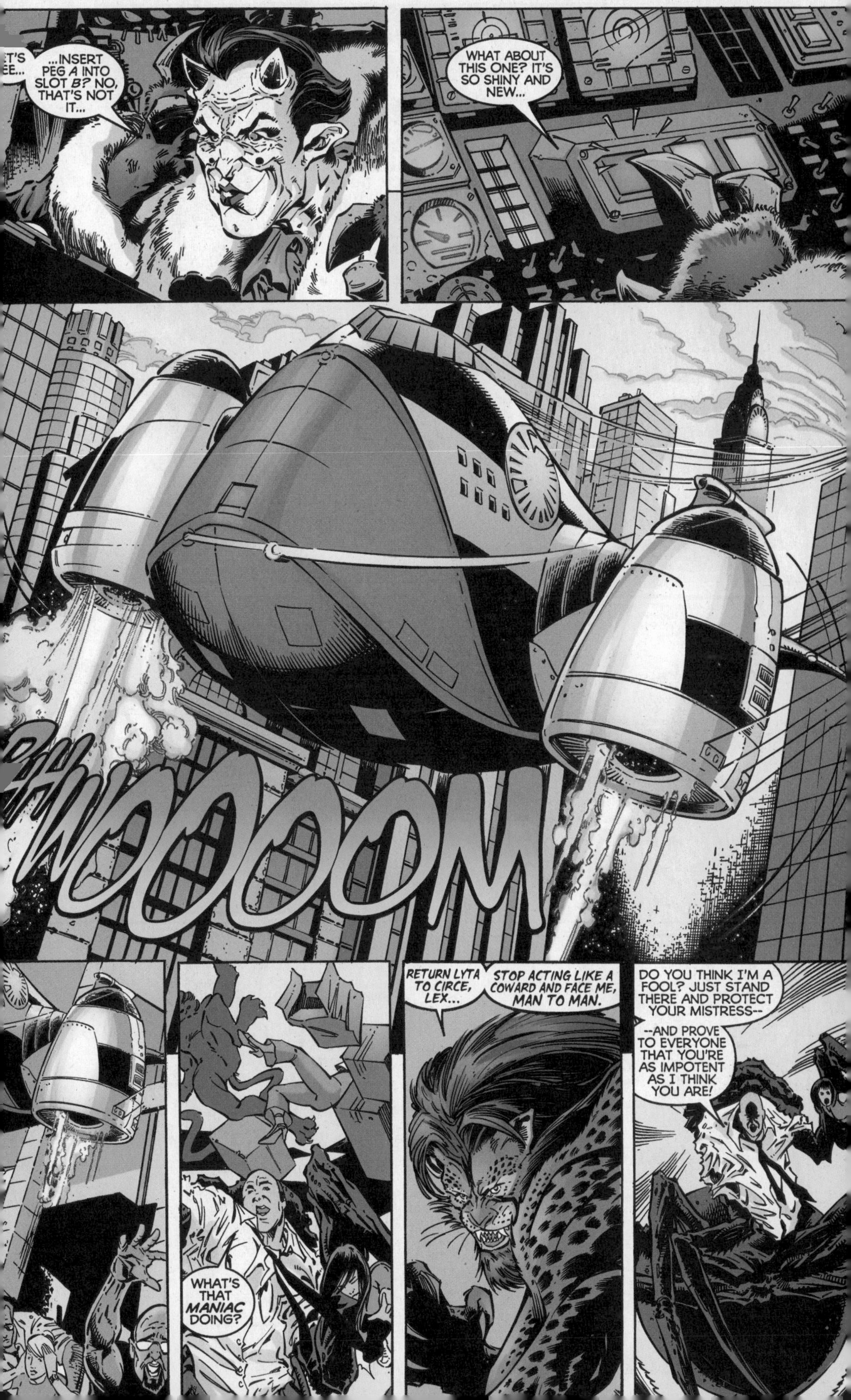
...INSERT PEG *A* INTO SLOT *B?* NO, THAT'S NOT IT...
WHAT ABOUT THIS ONE? IT'S SO SHINY AND NEW...
WHOOOOM
WHAT'S THAT *MANIAC* DOING?
RETURN LYTA TO CIRCE, LEX...
STOP ACTING LIKE A COWARD AND FACE ME, MAN TO MAN.
DO YOU THINK I'M A FOOL? JUST STAND THERE AND PROTECT YOUR MISTRESS--
--AND PROVE TO EVERYONE THAT YOU'RE AS IMPOTENT AS I THINK YOU ARE!

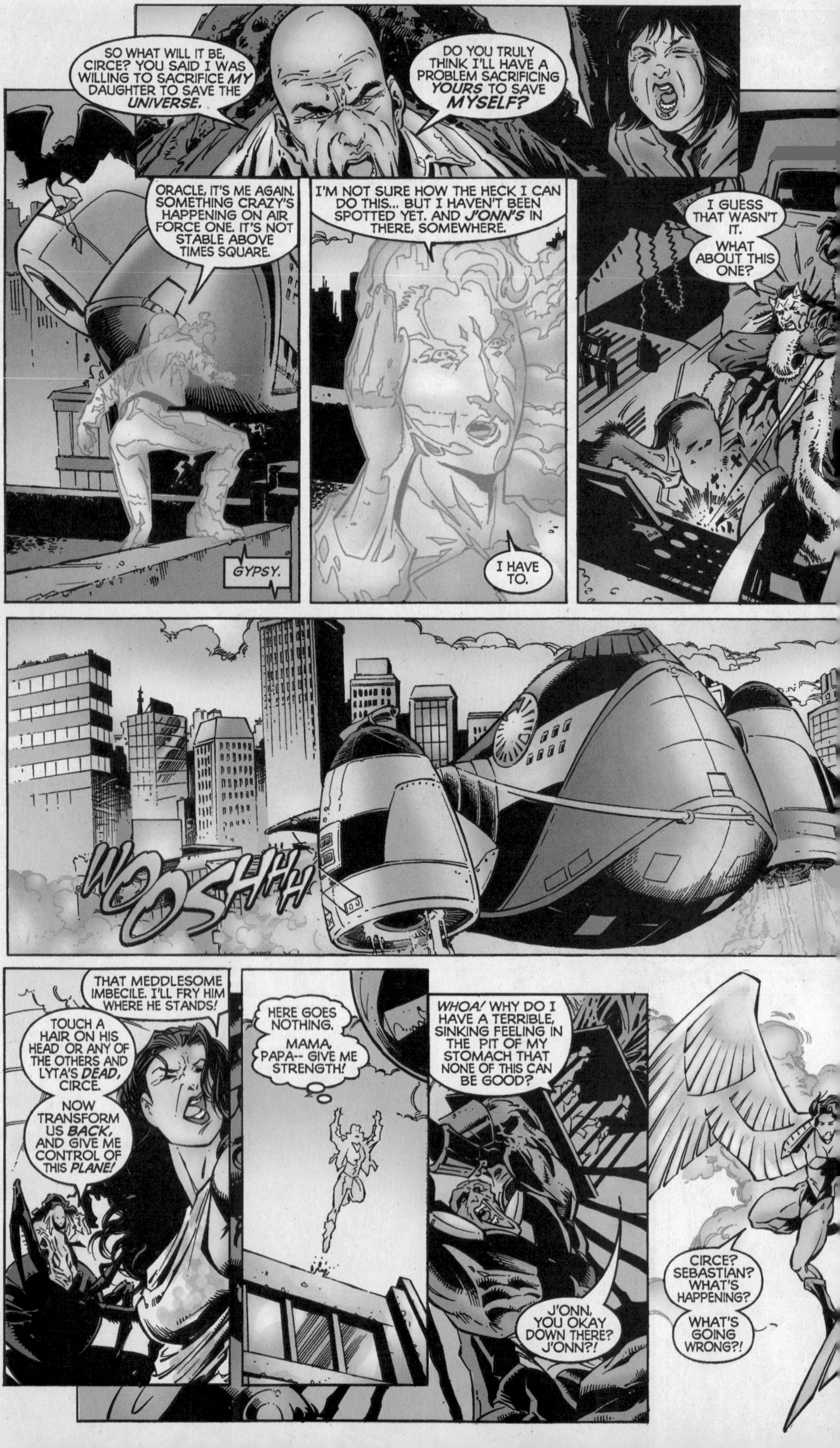
SO WHAT WILL IT BE, CIRCE? YOU SAID I WAS WILLING TO SACRIFICE MY DAUGHTER TO SAVE THE UNIVERSE.
DO YOU TRULY THINK I'LL HAVE A PROBLEM SACRIFICING YOURS TO SAVE MYSELF?
ORACLE, IT'S ME AGAIN. SOMETHING CRAZY'S HAPPENING ON AIR FORCE ONE. IT'S NOT STABLE ABOVE TIMES SQUARE.
GYPSY.
I'M NOT SURE HOW THE HECK I CAN DO THIS... BUT I HAVEN'T BEEN SPOTTED YET. AND J'ONN'S IN THERE, SOMEWHERE.
I HAVE TO.
I GUESS THAT WASN'T IT.
WHAT ABOUT THIS ONE?
WOOSHHH
THAT MEDDLESOME IMBECILE. I'LL FRY HIM WHERE HE STANDS!
TOUCH A HAIR ON HIS HEAD OR ANY OF THE OTHERS AND LYTA'S DEAD, CIRCE.
NOW TRANSFORM US BACK, AND GIVE ME CONTROL OF THIS PLANE!
HERE GOES NOTHING.
MAMA, PAPA-- GIVE ME STRENGTH!
WHOA! WHY DO I HAVE A TERRIBLE, SINKING FEELING IN THE PIT OF MY STOMACH THAT NONE OF THIS CAN BE GOOD?
J'ONN, YOU OKAY DOWN THERE? J'ONN?!
CIRCE? SEBASTIAN? WHAT'S HAPPENING?
WHAT'S GOING WRONG?!

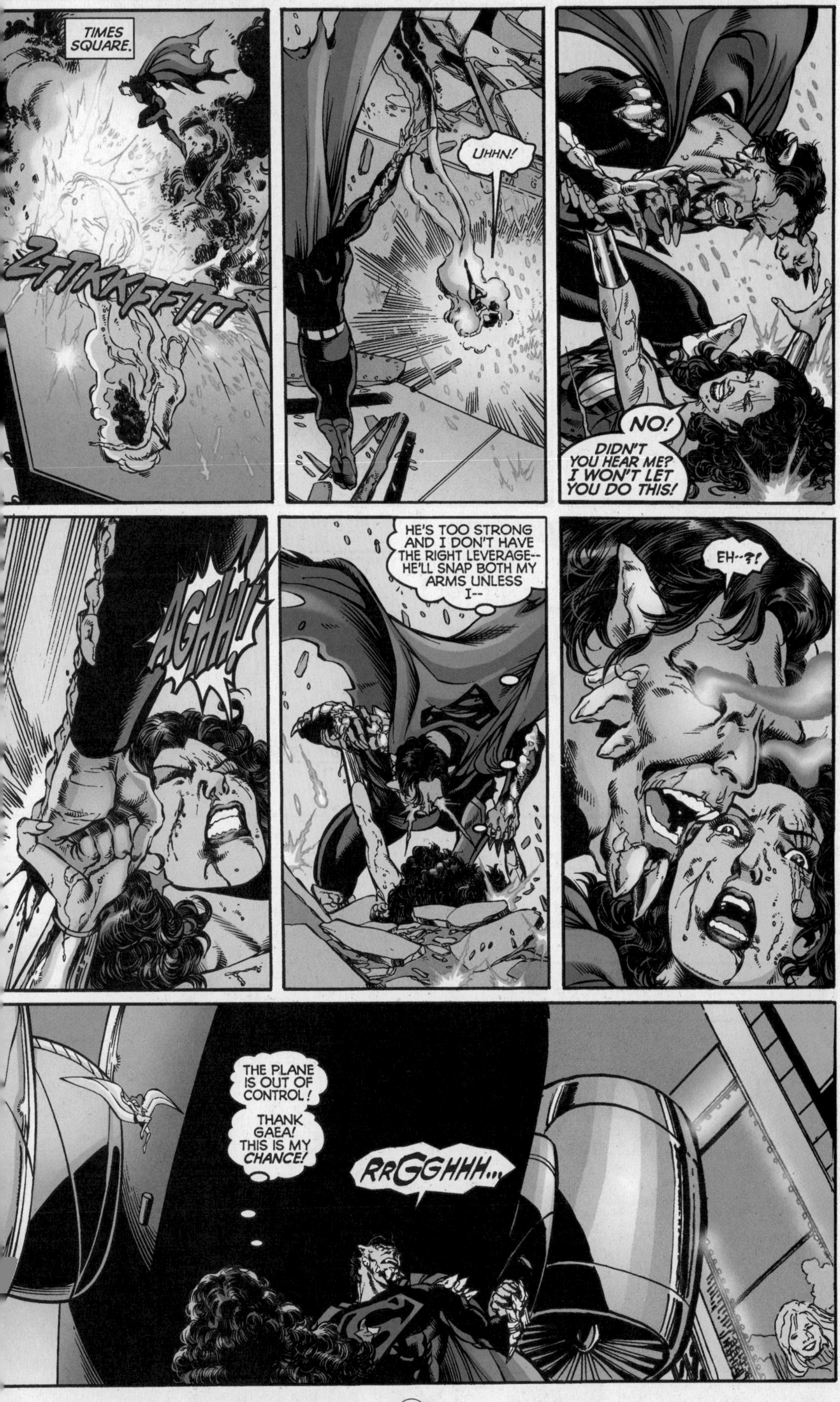
TIMES SQUARE.
ZTIKKEFTTT
UHHN!
NO!
DIDN'T YOU HEAR ME? I WON'T LET YOU DO THIS!
AGHH!
HE'S TOO STRONG AND I DON'T HAVE THE RIGHT LEVERAGE-- HE'LL SNAP BOTH MY ARMS UNLESS I--
EH--?!
THE PLANE IS OUT OF CONTROL!
THANK GAEA! THIS IS MY CHANCE!
RRGGHHH...

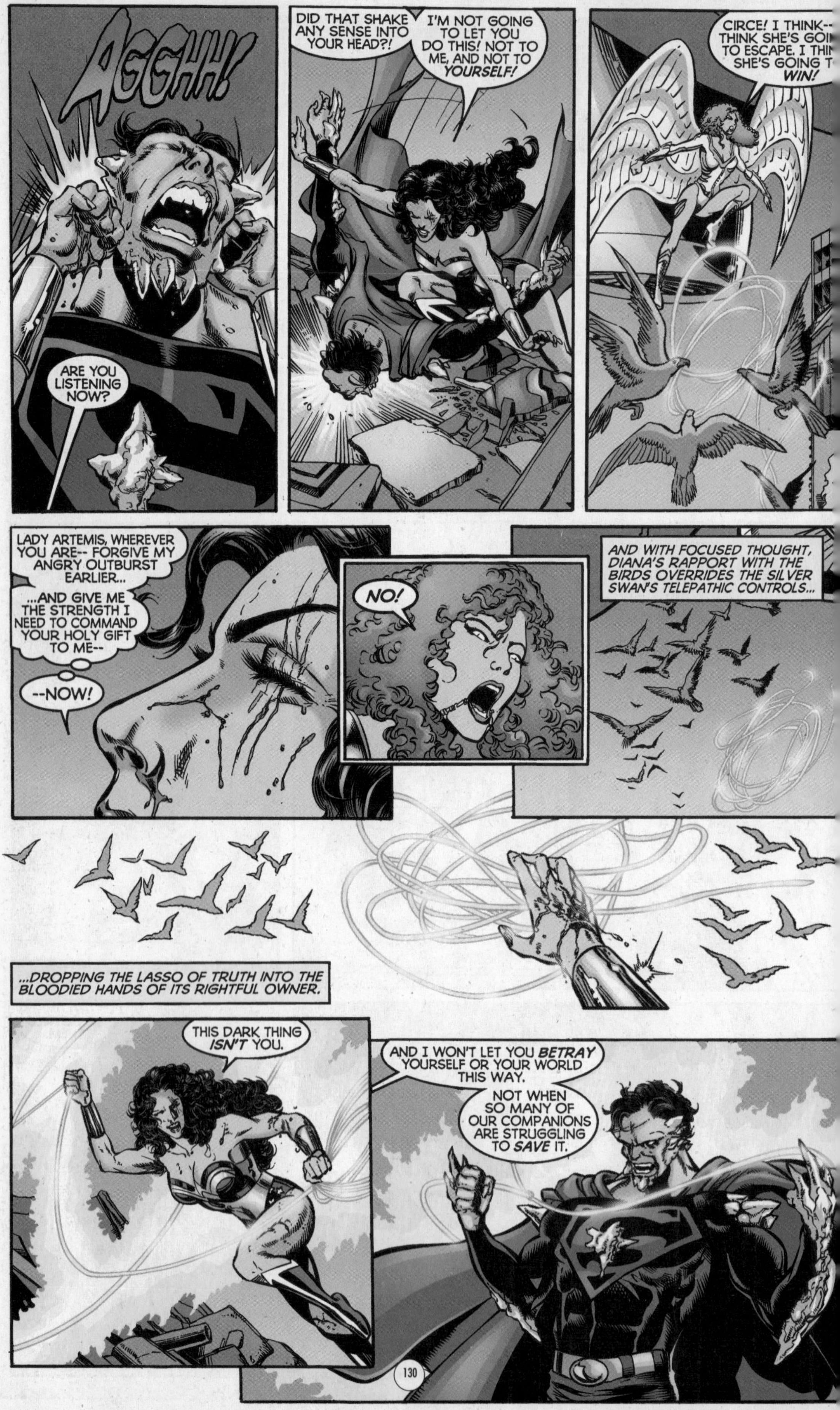

AGGHH!
ARE YOU LISTENING NOW?
DID THAT SHAKE ANY SENSE INTO YOUR HEAD?!
I'M NOT GOING TO LET YOU DO THIS! NOT TO ME, AND NOT TO YOURSELF!
CIRCE! I THINK-- THINK SHE'S GOI TO ESCAPE. I THIN SHE'S GOING T WIN!
LADY ARTEMIS, WHEREVER YOU ARE-- FORGIVE MY ANGRY OUTBURST EARLIER...
...AND GIVE ME THE STRENGTH I NEED TO COMMAND YOUR HOLY GIFT TO ME--
--NOW!
NO!
AND WITH FOCUSED THOUGHT, DIANA'S RAPPORT WITH THE BIRDS OVERRIDES THE SILVER SWAN'S TELEPATHIC CONTROLS...
...DROPPING THE LASSO OF TRUTH INTO THE BLOODIED HANDS OF ITS RIGHTFUL OWNER.
THIS DARK THING ISN'T YOU.
AND I WON'T LET YOU BETRAY YOURSELF OR YOUR WORLD THIS WAY.
NOT WHEN SO MANY OF OUR COMPANIONS ARE STRUGGLING TO SAVE IT.

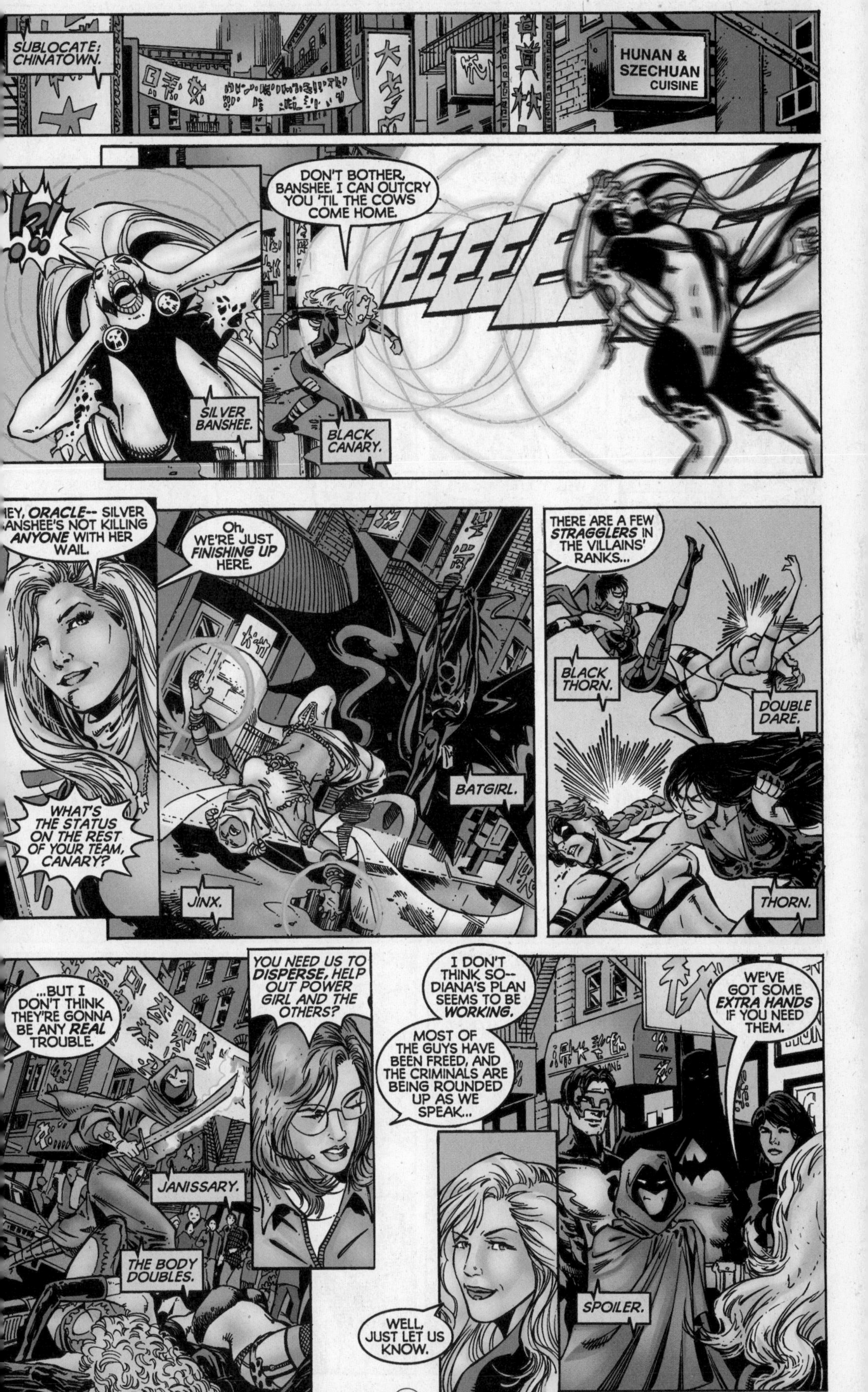
SUBLOCATE: CHINATOWN.
HUNAN & SZECHUAN CUISINE
DON'T BOTHER, BANSHEE. I CAN OUTCRY YOU 'TIL THE COWS COME HOME.
!?!
EEEEE
SILVER BANSHEE.
BLACK CANARY.
HEY, ORACLE-- SILVER BANSHEE'S NOT KILLING ANYONE WITH HER WAIL.
Oh, WE'RE JUST FINISHING UP HERE.
WHAT'S THE STATUS ON THE REST OF YOUR TEAM, CANARY?
JINX.
BATGIRL.
THERE ARE A FEW STRAGGLERS IN THE VILLAINS' RANKS...
BLACK THORN.
DOUBLE DARE.
THORN.
...BUT I DON'T THINK THEY'RE GONNA BE ANY REAL TROUBLE.
JANISSARY.
THE BODY DOUBLES.
YOU NEED US TO DISPERSE, HELP OUT POWER GIRL AND THE OTHERS?
I DON'T THINK SO-- DIANA'S PLAN SEEMS TO BE WORKING.
MOST OF THE GUYS HAVE BEEN FREED, AND THE CRIMINALS ARE BEING ROUNDED UP AS WE SPEAK...
WE'VE GOT SOME EXTRA HANDS IF YOU NEED THEM.
SPOILER.
WELL, JUST LET US KNOW.

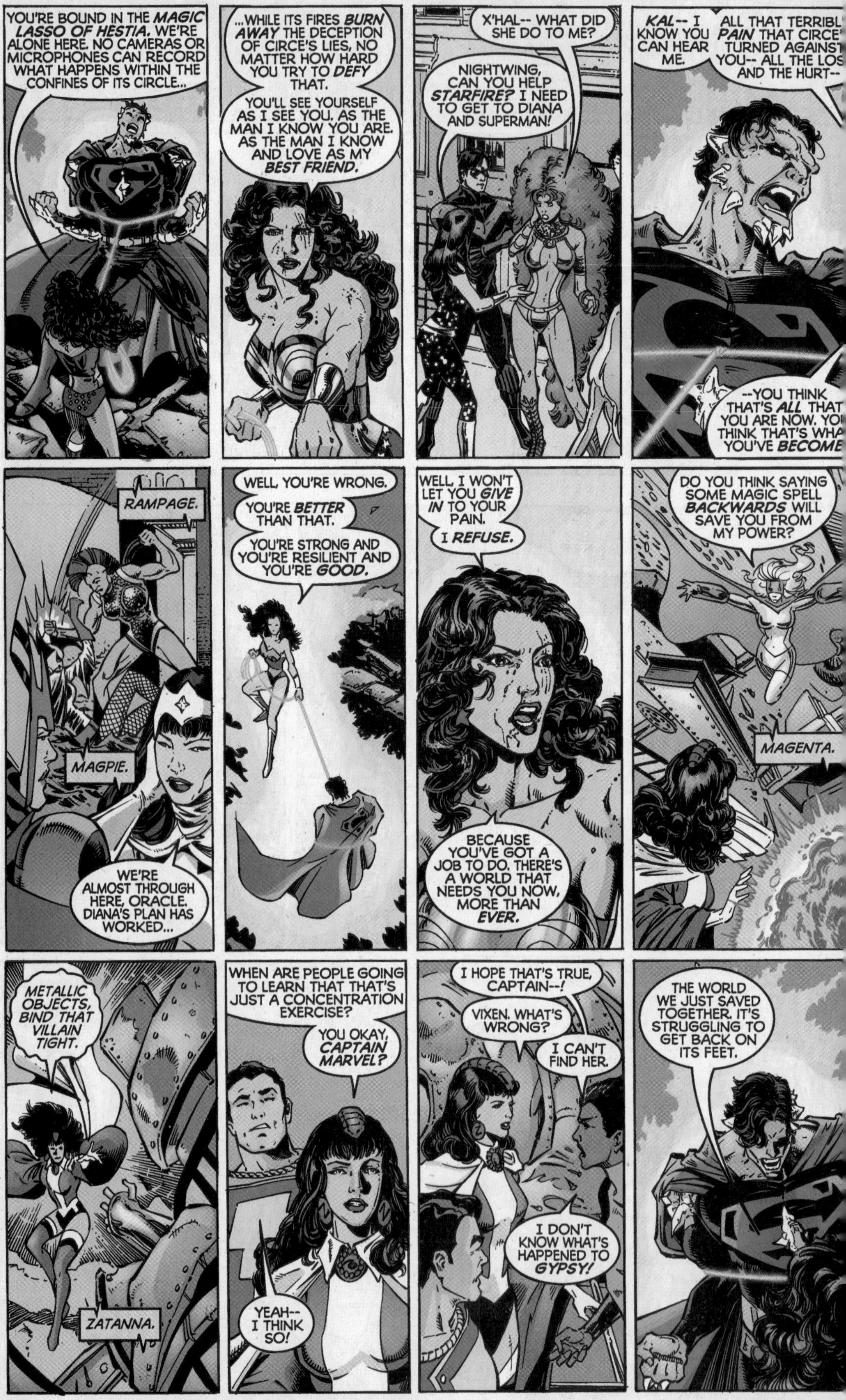

YOU'RE BOUND IN THE MAGIC LASSO OF HESTIA. WE'RE ALONE HERE. NO CAMERAS OR MICROPHONES CAN RECORD WHAT HAPPENS WITHIN THE CONFINES OF ITS CIRCLE...
...WHILE ITS FIRES BURN AWAY THE DECEPTION OF CIRCE'S LIES, NO MATTER HOW HARD YOU TRY TO DEFY THAT.
YOU'LL SEE YOURSELF AS I SEE YOU. AS THE MAN I KNOW YOU ARE. AS THE MAN I KNOW AND LOVE AS MY BEST FRIEND.
X'HAL-- WHAT DID SHE DO TO ME?
NIGHTWING, CAN YOU HELP STARFIRE? I NEED TO GET TO DIANA AND SUPERMAN!
KAL-- I KNOW YOU CAN HEAR ME.
ALL THAT TERRIBL PAIN THAT CIRCE TURNED AGAINST YOU-- ALL THE LOS AND THE HURT--
--YOU THINK THAT'S ALL THAT YOU ARE NOW. YO THINK THAT'S WHA YOU'VE BECOME
RAMPAGE.
MAGPIE.
WE'RE ALMOST THROUGH HERE, ORACLE. DIANA'S PLAN HAS WORKED...
WELL, YOU'RE WRONG.
YOU'RE BETTER THAN THAT.
YOU'RE STRONG AND YOU'RE RESILIENT AND YOU'RE GOOD.
WELL, I WON'T LET YOU GIVE IN TO YOUR PAIN.
I REFUSE.
BECAUSE YOU'VE GOT A JOB TO DO. THERE'S A WORLD THAT NEEDS YOU NOW, MORE THAN EVER.
DO YOU THINK SAYING SOME MAGIC SPELL BACKWARDS WILL SAVE YOU FROM MY POWER?
MAGENTA.
METALLIC OBJECTS, BIND THAT VILLAIN TIGHT.
ZATANNA.
WHEN ARE PEOPLE GOING TO LEARN THAT THAT'S JUST A CONCENTRATION EXERCISE?
YOU OKAY, CAPTAIN MARVEL?
YEAH-- I THINK SO!
I HOPE THAT'S TRUE, CAPTAIN--!
VIXEN. WHAT'S WRONG?
I CAN'T FIND HER.
I DON'T KNOW WHAT'S HAPPENED TO GYPSY!
THE WORLD WE JUST SAVED TOGETHER. IT'S STRUGGLING TO GET BACK ON ITS FEET.

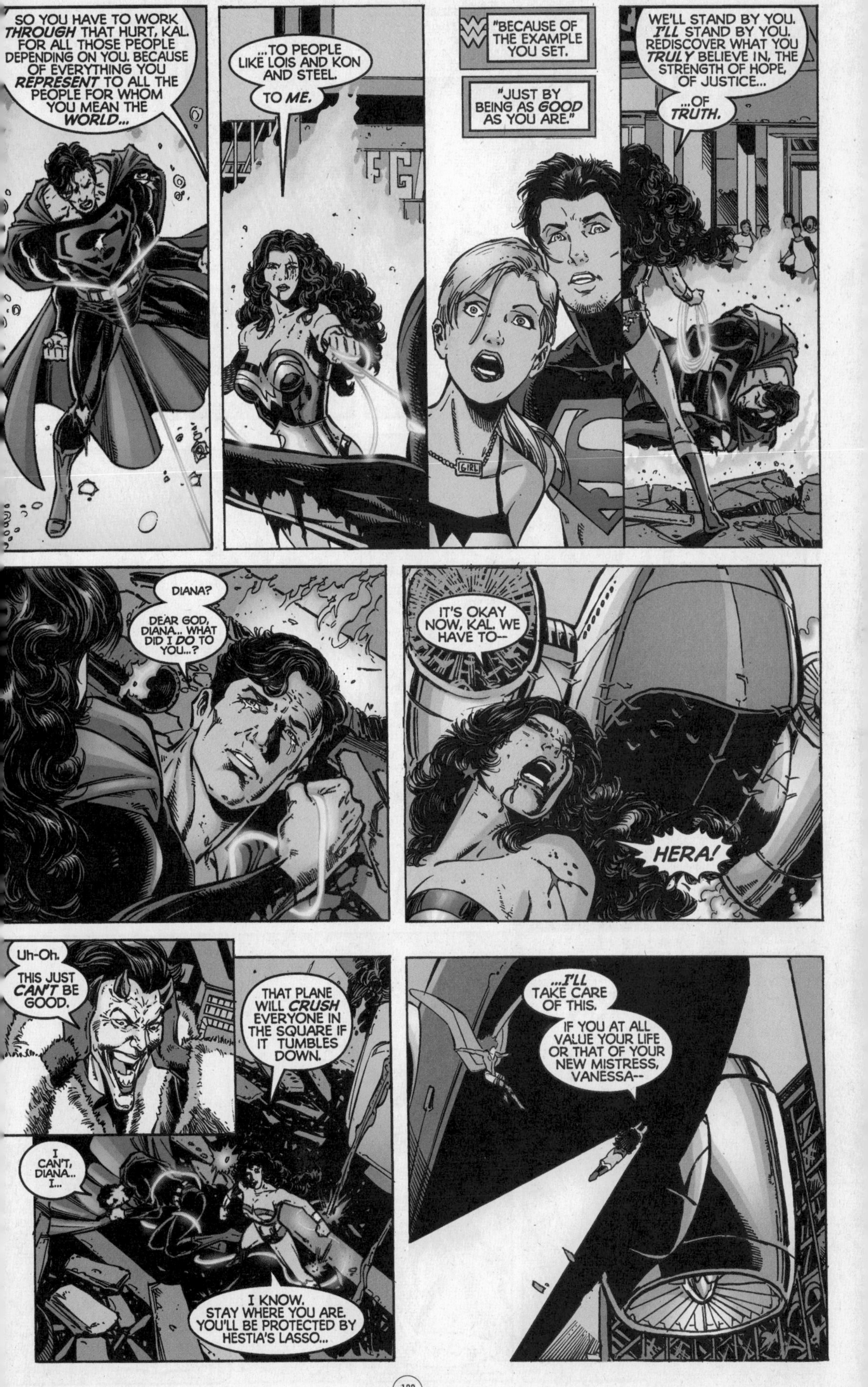
SO YOU HAVE TO WORK THROUGH THAT HURT, KAL. FOR ALL THOSE PEOPLE DEPENDING ON YOU. BECAUSE OF EVERYTHING YOU REPRESENT TO ALL THE PEOPLE FOR WHOM YOU MEAN THE WORLD...
...TO PEOPLE LIKE LOIS AND KON AND STEEL.
TO ME.
"BECAUSE OF THE EXAMPLE YOU SET.
"JUST BY BEING AS GOOD AS YOU ARE."
WE'LL STAND BY YOU. I'LL STAND BY YOU. REDISCOVER WHAT YOU TRULY BELIEVE IN, THE STRENGTH OF HOPE, OF JUSTICE...
...OF TRUTH.
DIANA?
DEAR GOD, DIANA... WHAT DID I DO TO YOU...?
IT'S OKAY NOW, KAL. WE HAVE TO--
HERA!
Uh-Oh.
THIS JUST CAN'T BE GOOD.
THAT PLANE WILL CRUSH EVERYONE IN THE SQUARE IF IT TUMBLES DOWN.
I CAN'T, DIANA... I...
I KNOW. STAY WHERE YOU ARE. YOU'LL BE PROTECTED BY HESTIA'S LASSO...
...I'LL TAKE CARE OF THIS.
IF YOU AT ALL VALUE YOUR LIFE OR THAT OF YOUR NEW MISTRESS, VANESSA--

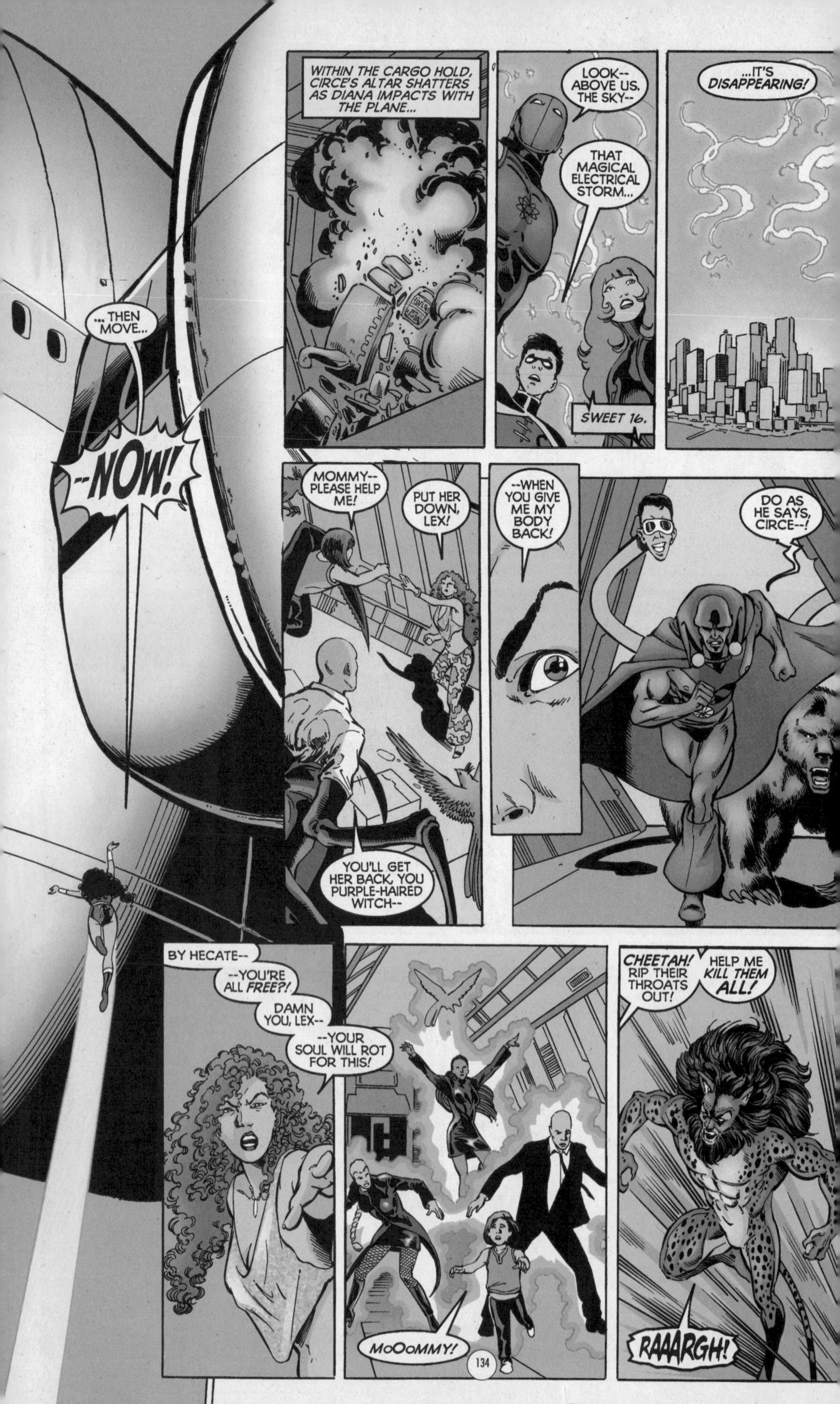
...THEN MOVE...
--NOW!
WITHIN THE CARGO HOLD, CIRCE'S ALTAR SHATTERS AS DIANA IMPACTS WITH THE PLANE...
LOOK-- ABOVE US. THE SKY--
THAT MAGICAL ELECTRICAL STORM...
SWEET 16.
...IT'S DISAPPEARING!
MOMMY-- PLEASE HELP ME!
PUT HER DOWN, LEX!
YOU'LL GET HER BACK, YOU PURPLE-HAIRED WITCH--
--WHEN YOU GIVE ME MY BODY BACK!
DO AS HE SAYS, CIRCE--!
BY HECATE--
--YOU'RE ALL FREE?!
DAMN YOU, LEX--
--YOUR SOUL WILL ROT FOR THIS!
MoOoMMY!
CHEETAH! RIP THEIR THROATS OUT!
HELP ME KILL THEM ALL!
RAAARGH!

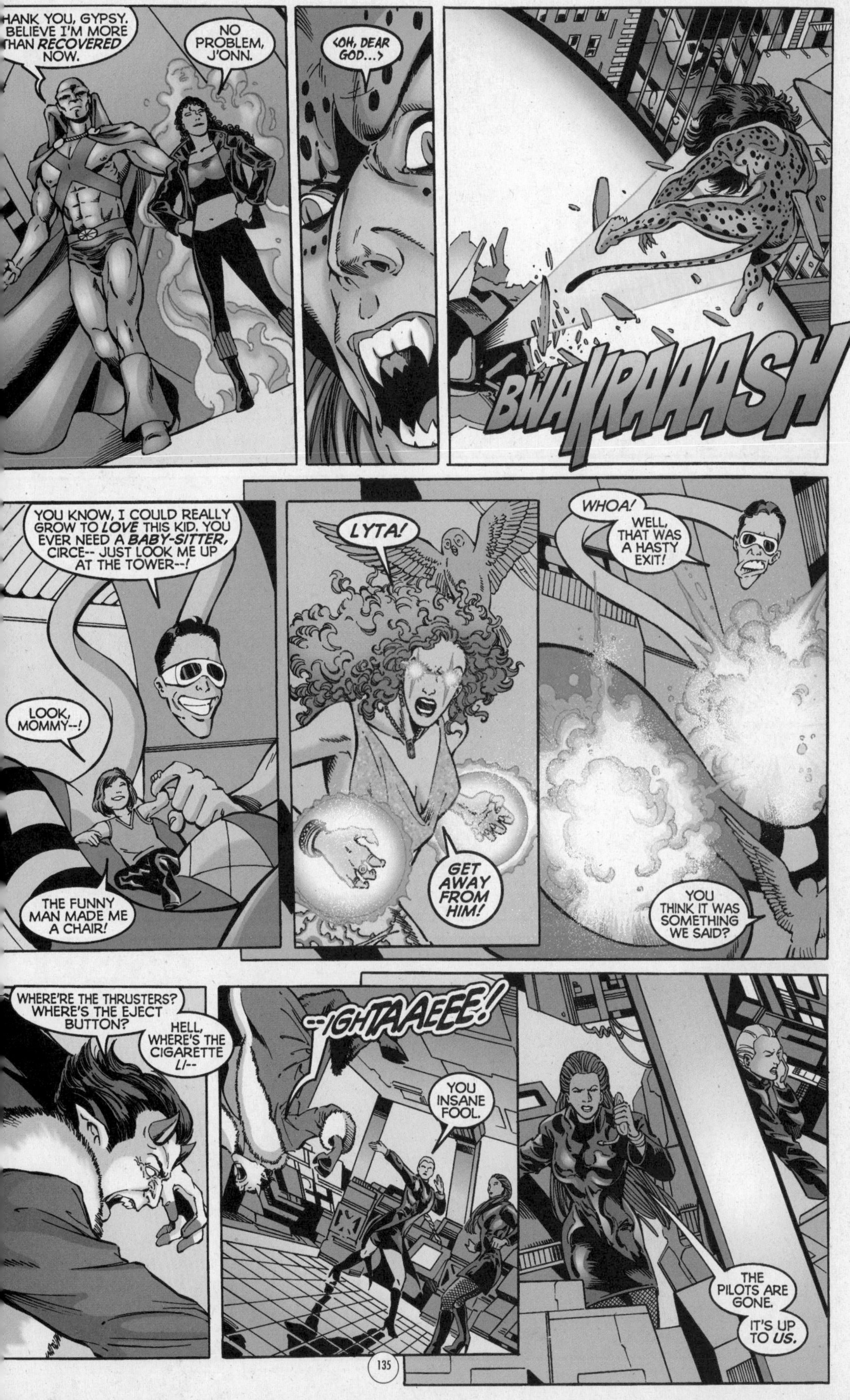
HANK YOU, GYPSY. BELIEVE I'M MORE THAN *RECOVERED* NOW.
NO PROBLEM, J'ONN.
<OH, DEAR GOD...>
BWAKRAAAASH
YOU KNOW, I COULD REALLY GROW TO *LOVE* THIS KID. YOU EVER NEED A *BABY-SITTER,* CIRCE-- JUST LOOK ME UP AT THE TOWER--!
LOOK, MOMMY--!
THE FUNNY MAN MADE ME A CHAIR!
LYTA!
GET AWAY FROM HIM!
WHOA!
WELL, THAT WAS A HASTY EXIT!
YOU THINK IT WAS SOMETHING WE SAID?
WHERE'RE THE THRUSTERS? WHERE'S THE EJECT BUTTON?
HELL, WHERE'S THE CIGARETTE *LI*--
--IGHTAAAEEE!
YOU INSANE FOOL.
THE PILOTS ARE GONE.
IT'S UP TO *US.*

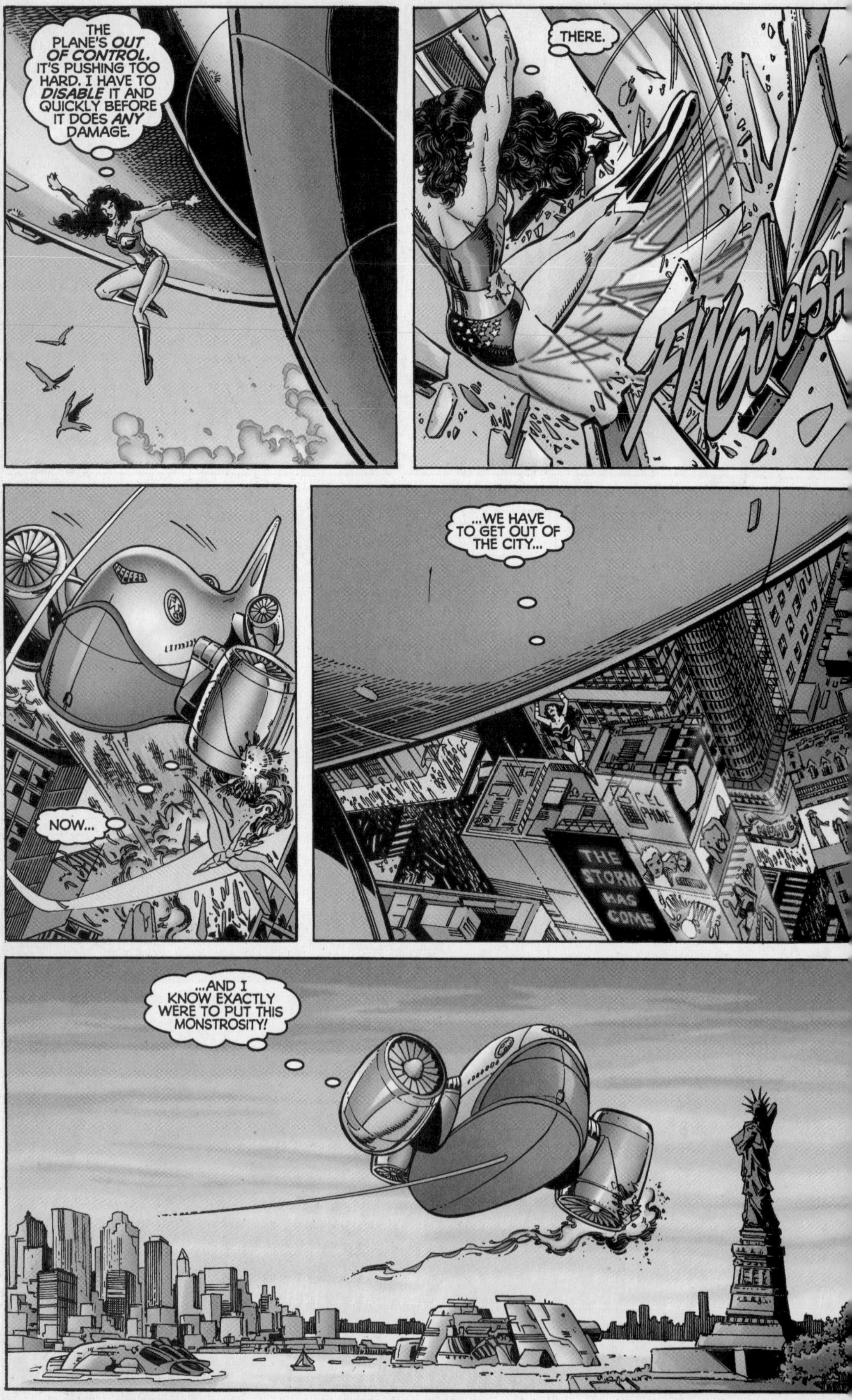
THE PLANE'S *OUT OF CONTROL.* IT'S PUSHING TOO HARD. I HAVE TO *DISABLE* IT AND QUICKLY BEFORE IT DOES *ANY* DAMAGE.
THERE.
FWOOOSH
NOW...
...WE HAVE TO GET OUT OF THE CITY...
THE STORM HAS COME
...AND I KNOW EXACTLY WERE TO PUT THIS MONSTROSITY!

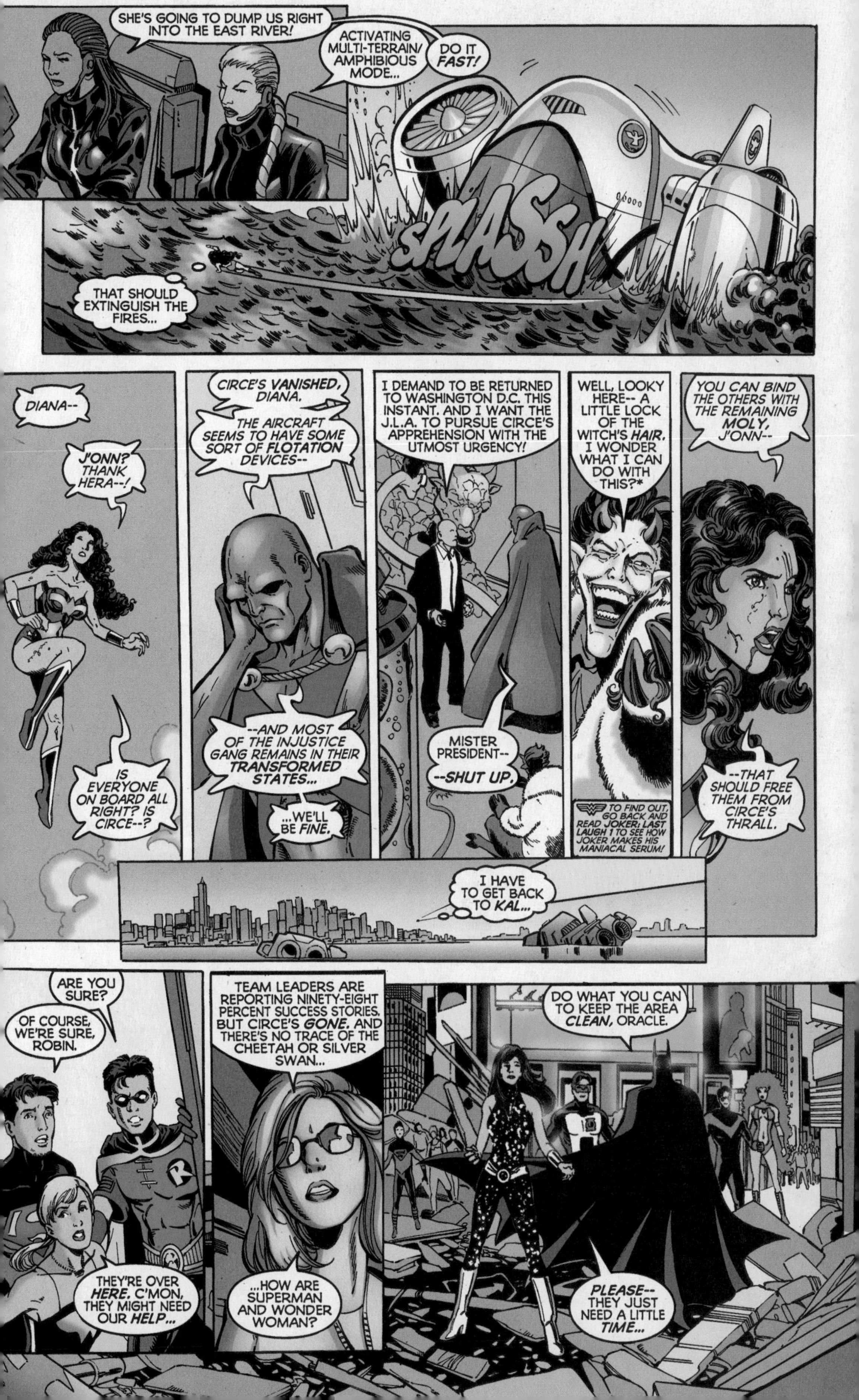
SHE'S GOING TO DUMP US RIGHT INTO THE EAST RIVER!
ACTIVATING MULTI-TERRAIN/ AMPHIBIOUS MODE...
DO IT FAST!
SPLASSH
THAT SHOULD EXTINGUISH THE FIRES...
DIANA--
J'ONN? THANK HERA--!
IS EVERYONE ON BOARD ALL RIGHT? IS CIRCE--?
CIRCE'S VANISHED, DIANA.
THE AIRCRAFT SEEMS TO HAVE SOME SORT OF FLOTATION DEVICES--
--AND MOST OF THE INJUSTICE GANG REMAINS IN THEIR TRANSFORMED STATES...
...WE'LL BE FINE.
I DEMAND TO BE RETURNED TO WASHINGTON D.C. THIS INSTANT. AND I WANT THE J.L.A. TO PURSUE CIRCE'S APPREHENSION WITH THE UTMOST URGENCY!
MISTER PRESIDENT--
--SHUT UP.
WELL, LOOKY HERE-- A LITTLE LOCK OF THE WITCH'S HAIR. I WONDER WHAT I CAN DO WITH THIS?*
*TO FIND OUT, GO BACK AND READ JOKER: LAST LAUGH 1 TO SEE HOW JOKER MAKES HIS MANIACAL SERUM!
YOU CAN BIND THE OTHERS WITH THE REMAINING MOLY, J'ONN--
--THAT SHOULD FREE THEM FROM CIRCE'S THRALL.
I HAVE TO GET BACK TO KAL...
ARE YOU SURE?
OF COURSE, WE'RE SURE, ROBIN.
THEY'RE OVER HERE. C'MON, THEY MIGHT NEED OUR HELP...
TEAM LEADERS ARE REPORTING NINETY-EIGHT PERCENT SUCCESS STORIES. BUT CIRCE'S GONE. AND THERE'S NO TRACE OF THE CHEETAH OR SILVER SWAN...
...HOW ARE SUPERMAN AND WONDER WOMAN?
DO WHAT YOU CAN TO KEEP THE AREA CLEAN, ORACLE.
PLEASE-- THEY JUST NEED A LITTLE TIME...

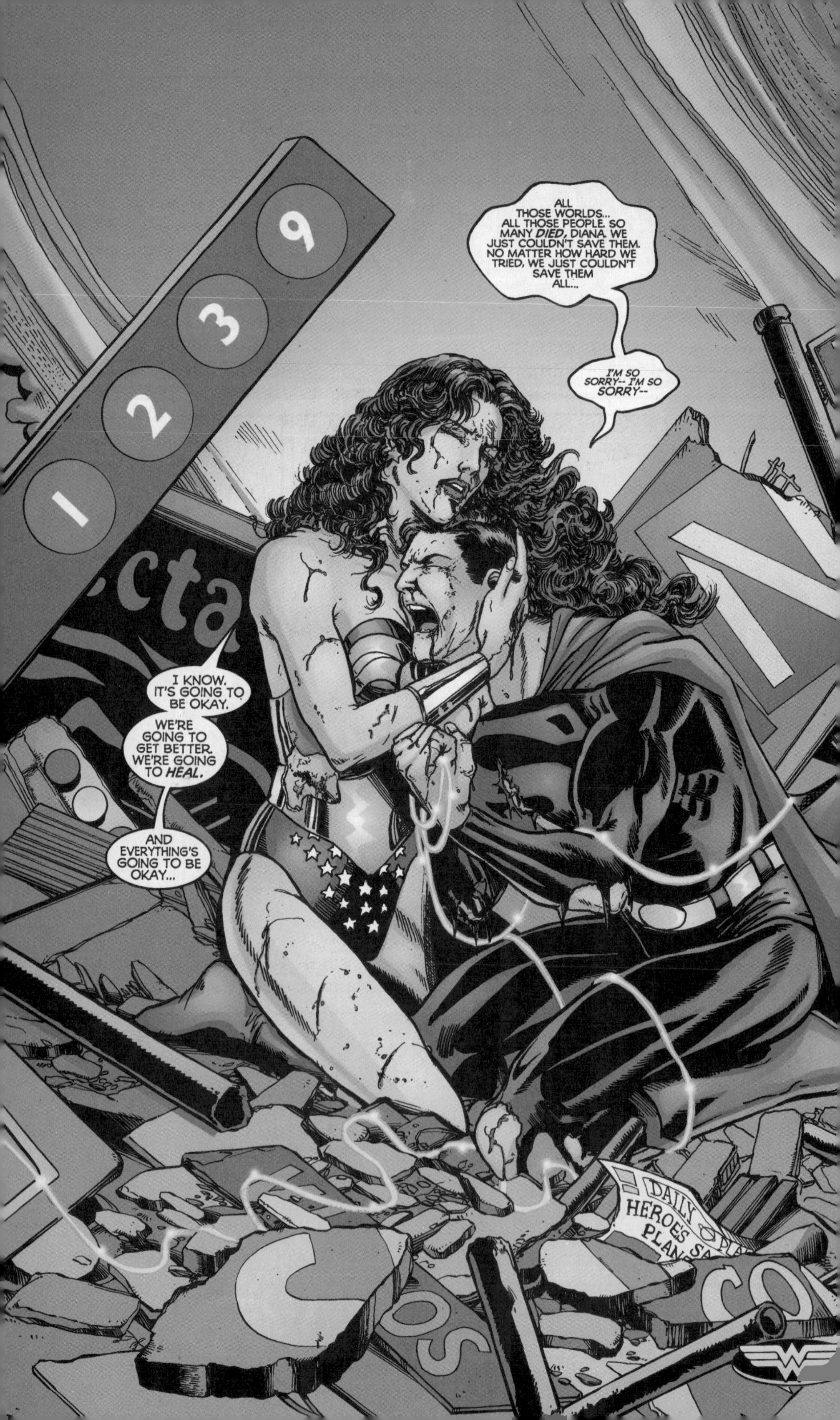
ALL THOSE WORLDS... ALL THOSE PEOPLE. SO MANY DIED, DIANA. WE JUST COULDN'T SAVE THEM. NO MATTER HOW HARD WE TRIED, WE JUST COULDN'T SAVE THEM ALL...
I'M SO SORRY-- I'M SO SORRY--
I KNOW. IT'S GOING TO BE OKAY.
WE'RE GOING TO GET BETTER. WE'RE GOING TO HEAL.
AND EVERYTHING'S GOING TO BE OKAY...
DAILY
HEROE'S SA
PLAN
PLANE

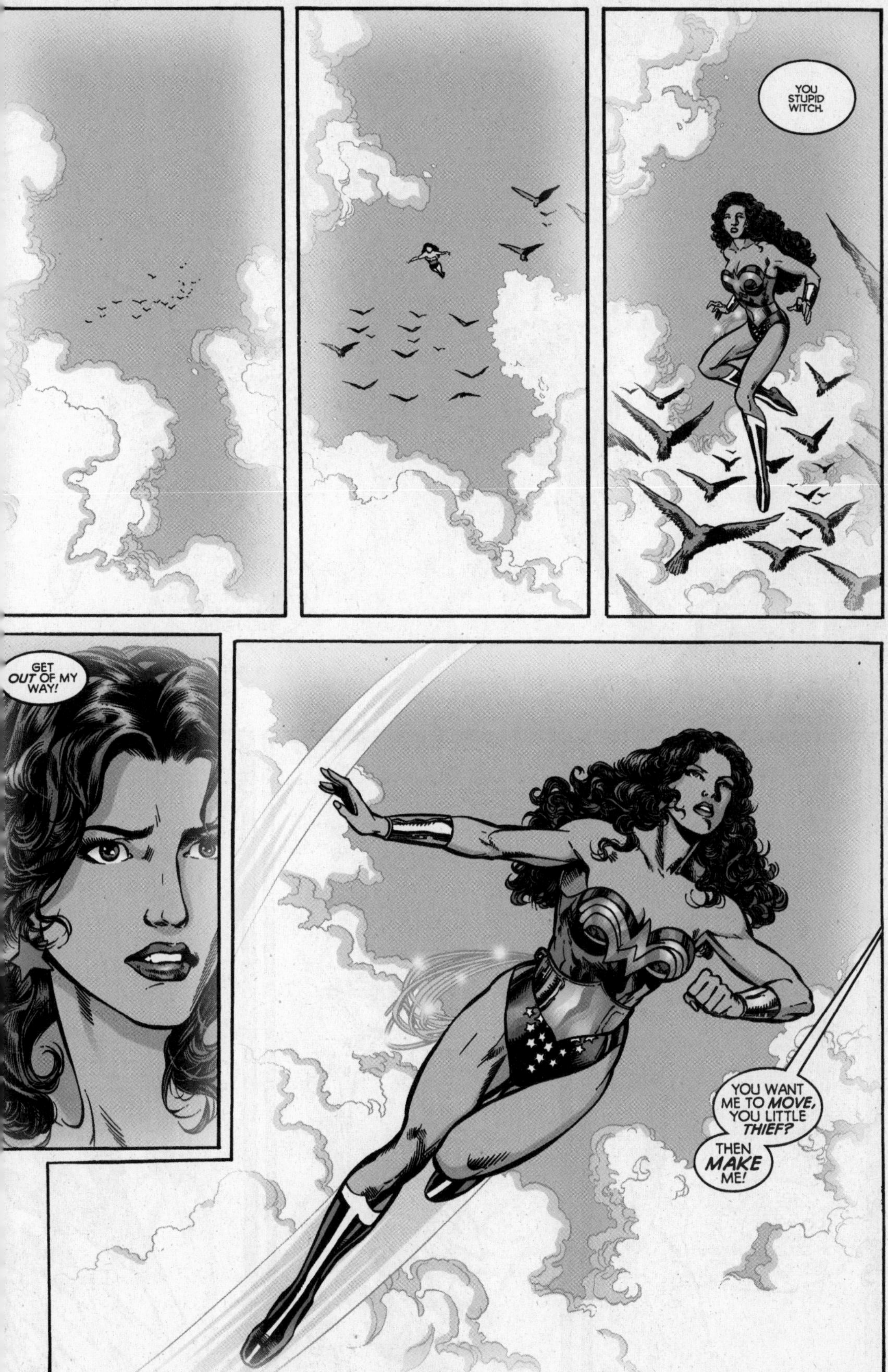
YOU STUPID WITCH.
GET OUT OF MY WAY!
YOU WANT ME TO MOVE, YOU LITTLE THIEF?
THEN MAKE ME!

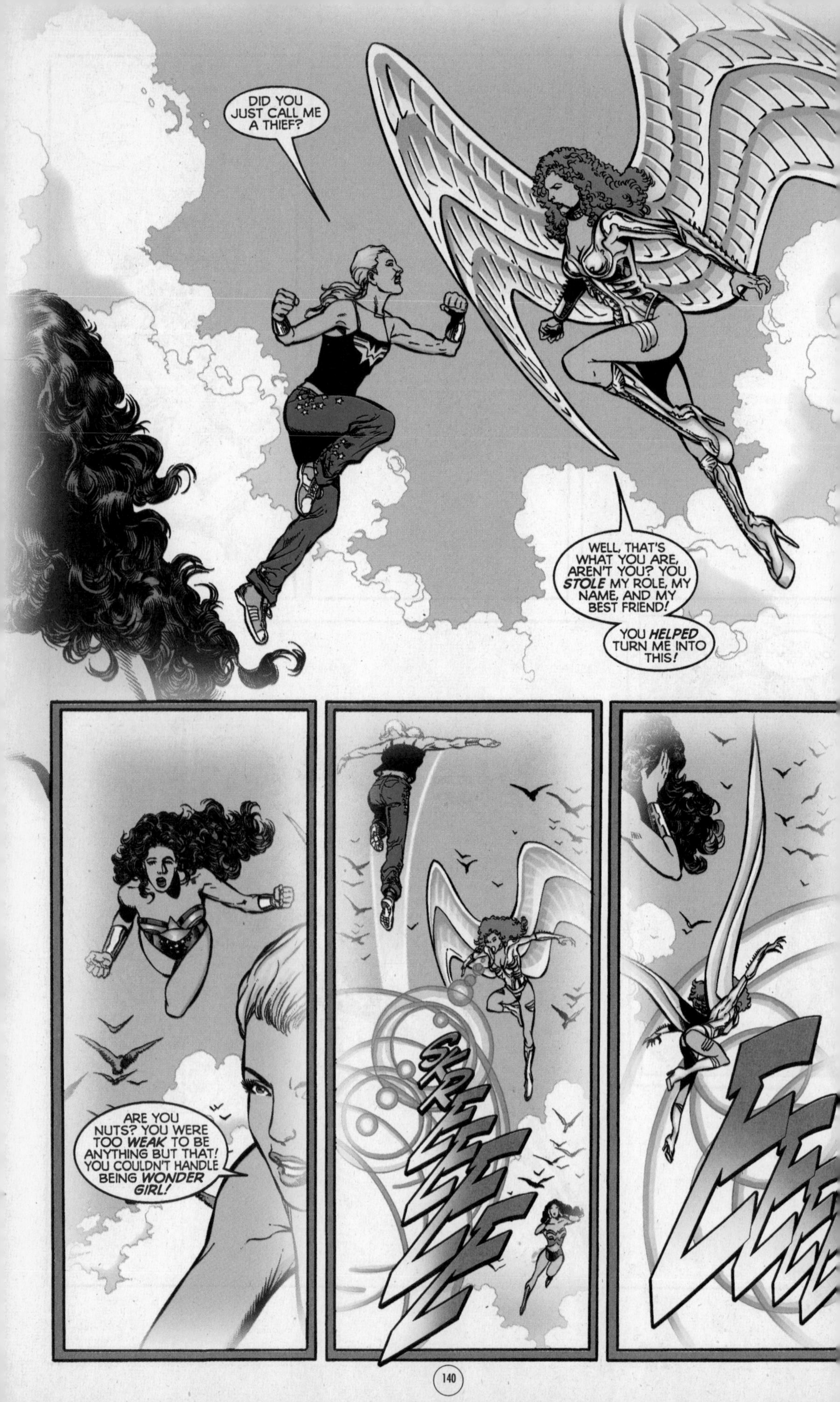
DID YOU JUST CALL ME A THIEF?
WELL, THAT'S WHAT YOU ARE, AREN'T YOU? YOU *STOLE* MY ROLE, MY NAME, AND MY BEST FRIEND!
YOU *HELPED* TURN ME INTO THIS!
ARE YOU NUTS? YOU WERE TOO *WEAK* TO BE ANYTHING BUT THAT! YOU COULDN'T HANDLE BEING *WONDER GIRL!*

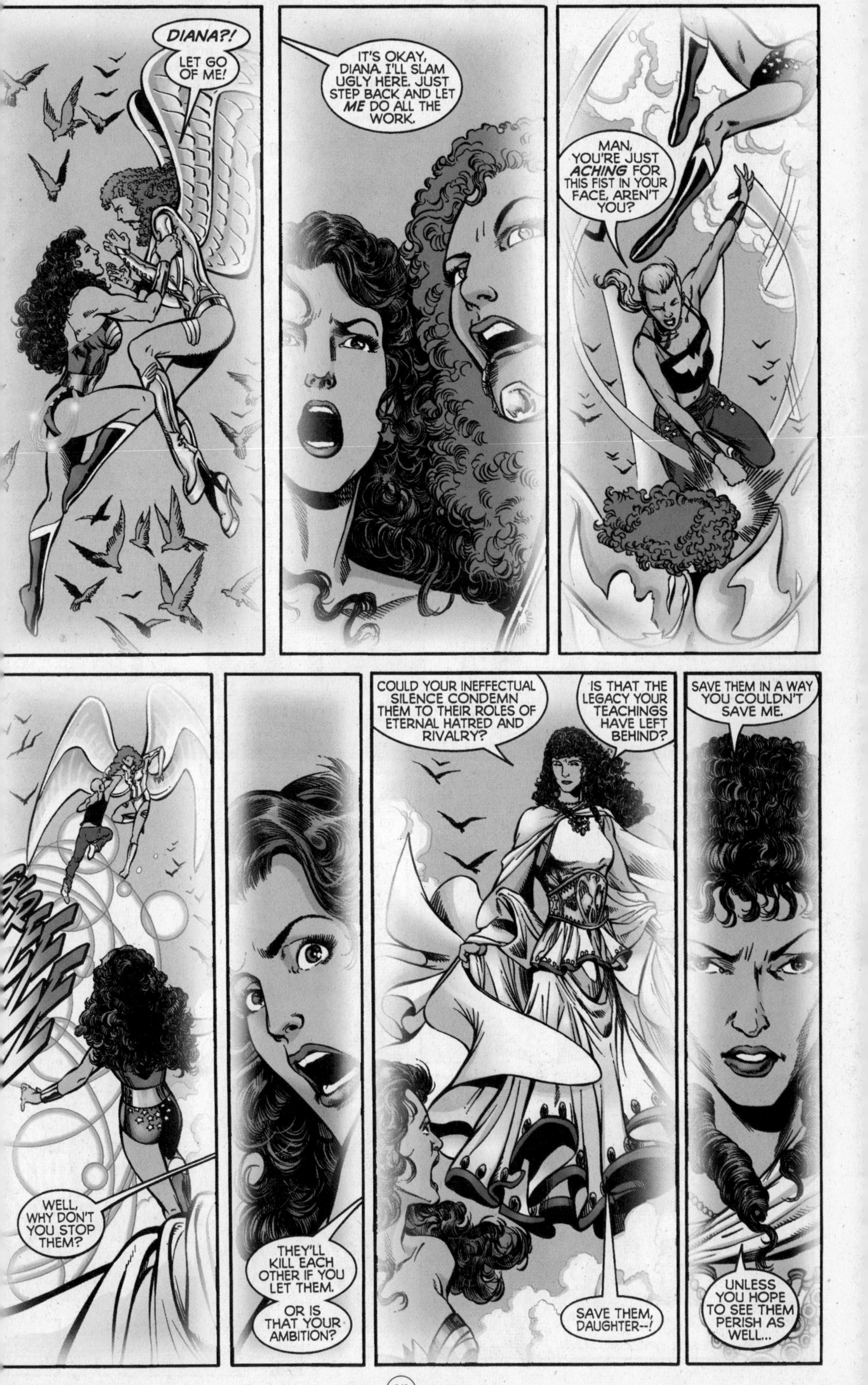
DIANA?!
LET GO OF ME!
IT'S OKAY, DIANA. I'LL SLAM UGLY HERE. JUST STEP BACK AND LET ME DO ALL THE WORK.
MAN, YOU'RE JUST ACHING FOR THIS FIST IN YOUR FACE, AREN'T YOU?
WELL, WHY DON'T YOU STOP THEM?
THEY'LL KILL EACH OTHER IF YOU LET THEM.
OR IS THAT YOUR AMBITION?
COULD YOUR INEFFECTUAL SILENCE CONDEMN THEM TO THEIR ROLES OF ETERNAL HATRED AND RIVALRY?
IS THAT THE LEGACY YOUR TEACHINGS HAVE LEFT BEHIND?
SAVE THEM, DAUGHTER--!
SAVE THEM IN A WAY YOU COULDN'T SAVE ME.
UNLESS YOU HOPE TO SEE THEM PERISH AS WELL...

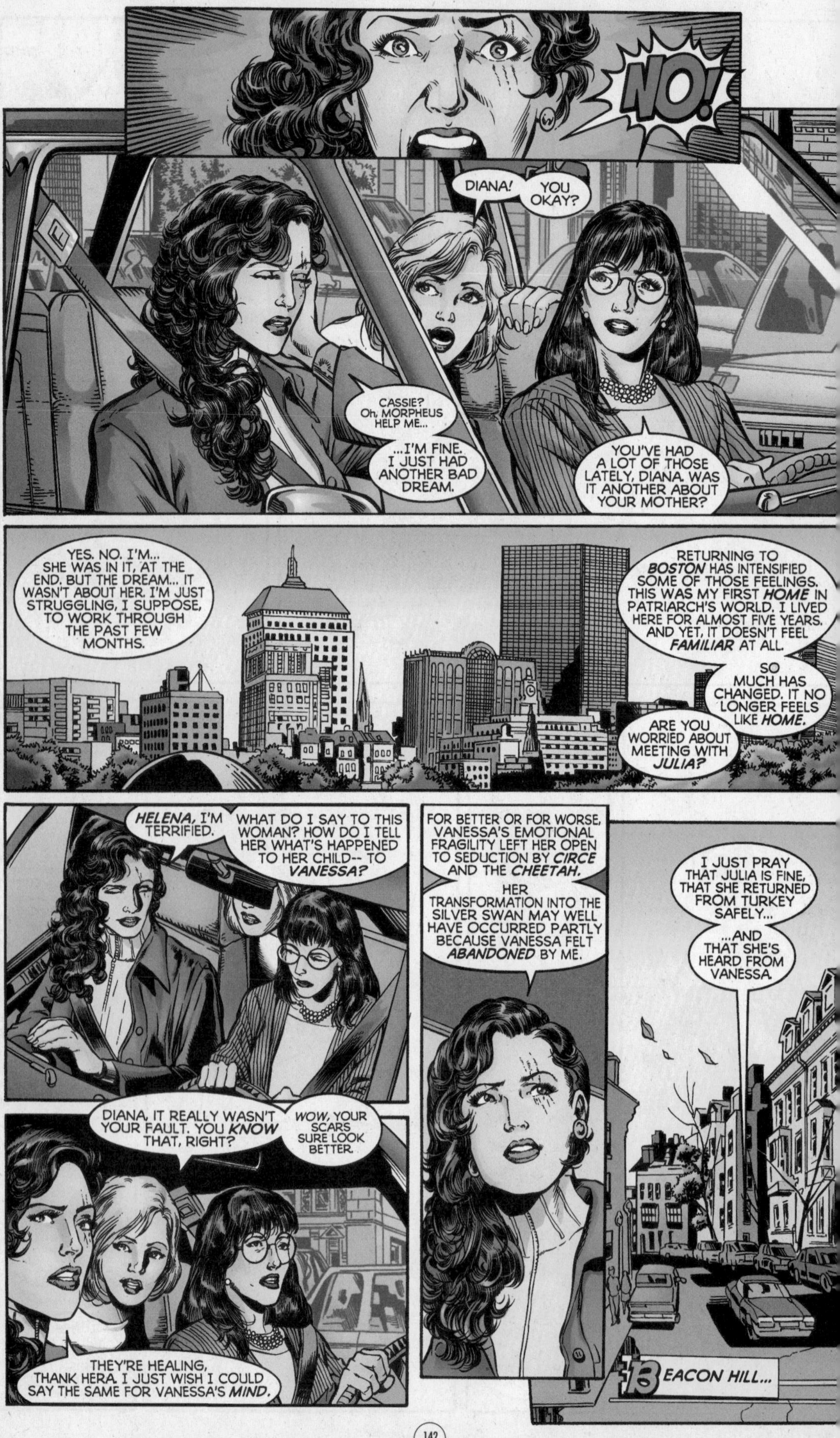
NO!
DIANA!
YOU OKAY?
CASSIE? Oh, MORPHEUS HELP ME...
...I'M FINE. I JUST HAD ANOTHER BAD DREAM.
YOU'VE HAD A LOT OF THOSE LATELY, DIANA. WAS IT ANOTHER ABOUT YOUR MOTHER?
YES. NO. I'M... SHE WAS IN IT, AT THE END. BUT THE DREAM... IT WASN'T ABOUT HER. I'M JUST STRUGGLING, I SUPPOSE, TO WORK THROUGH THE PAST FEW MONTHS.
RETURNING TO BOSTON HAS INTENSIFIED SOME OF THOSE FEELINGS. THIS WAS MY FIRST HOME IN PATRIARCH'S WORLD. I LIVED HERE FOR ALMOST FIVE YEARS. AND YET, IT DOESN'T FEEL FAMILIAR AT ALL.
SO MUCH HAS CHANGED. IT NO LONGER FEELS LIKE HOME.
ARE YOU WORRIED ABOUT MEETING WITH JULIA?
HELENA, I'M TERRIFIED.
WHAT DO I SAY TO THIS WOMAN? HOW DO I TELL HER WHAT'S HAPPENED TO HER CHILD-- TO VANESSA?
DIANA, IT REALLY WASN'T YOUR FAULT. YOU KNOW THAT, RIGHT?
WOW, YOUR SCARS SURE LOOK BETTER.
THEY'RE HEALING, THANK HERA. I JUST WISH I COULD SAY THE SAME FOR VANESSA'S MIND.
FOR BETTER OR FOR WORSE, VANESSA'S EMOTIONAL FRAGILITY LEFT HER OPEN TO SEDUCTION BY CIRCE AND THE CHEETAH.
HER TRANSFORMATION INTO THE SILVER SWAN MAY WELL HAVE OCCURRED PARTLY BECAUSE VANESSA FELT ABANDONED BY ME.
I JUST PRAY THAT JULIA IS FINE, THAT SHE RETURNED FROM TURKEY SAFELY...
...AND THAT SHE'S HEARD FROM VANESSA.
BEACON HILL...

The Witch & The Warrior Part Three

HATEFUL HATE

PHIL JIMENEZ STORY/PENCILS
ANDY LANNING INKS
TRISH MULVIHILL COLORS
HEROIC AGE SEPARATIONS
COMICRAFT LETTERS
TOM PALMER JR ASSISTANT EDITOR
EDDIE BERGANZA EDITOR

WONDER WOMAN CREATED BY WILLIAM MOULTON MARSTON

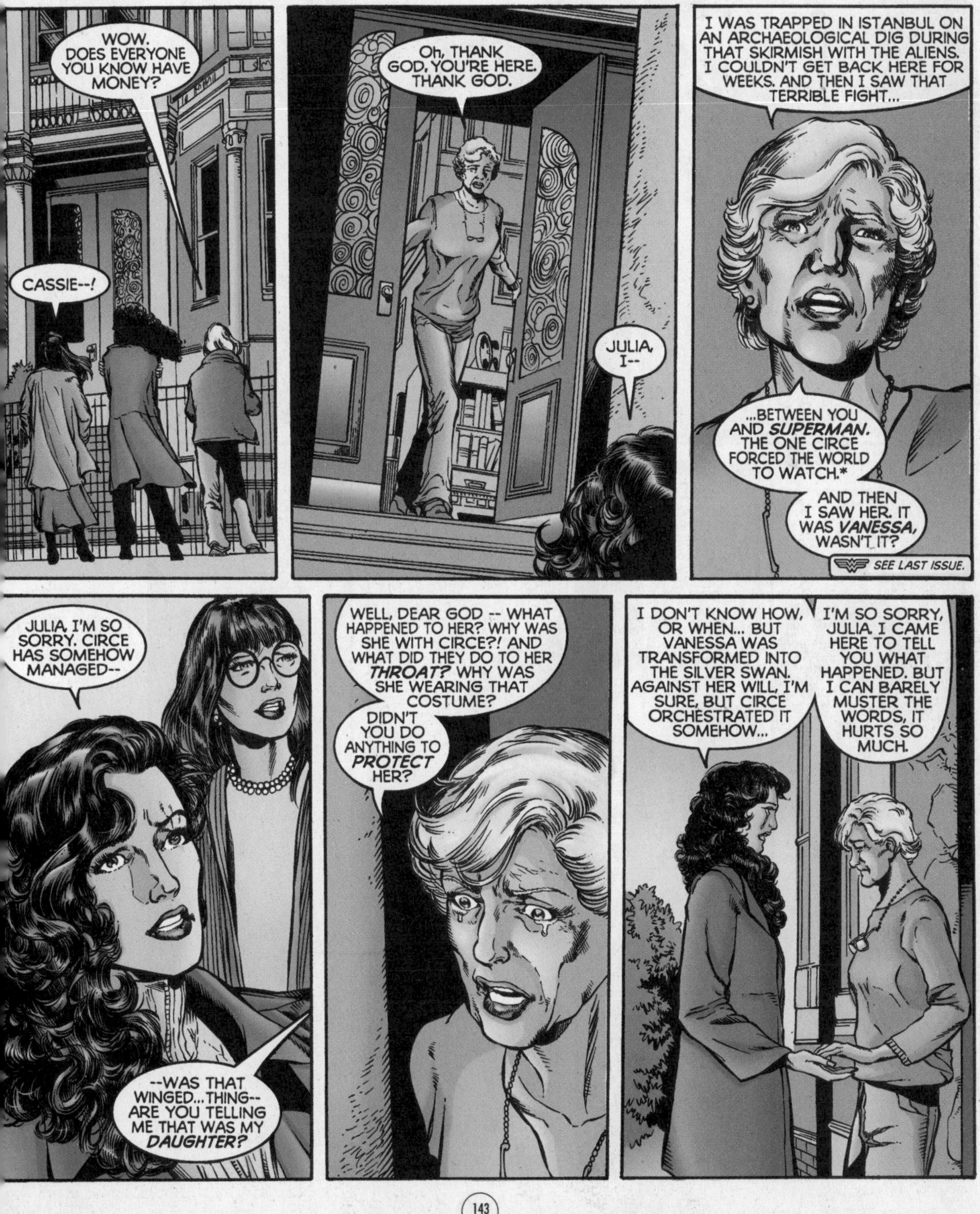

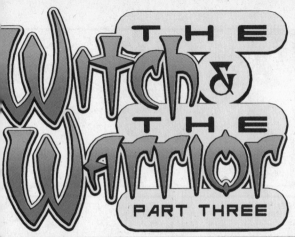

WOW. DOES EVERYONE YOU KNOW HAVE MONEY?
CASSIE--!
Oh, THANK GOD, YOU'RE HERE. THANK GOD.
JULIA, I--
I WAS TRAPPED IN ISTANBUL ON AN ARCHAEOLOGICAL DIG DURING THAT SKIRMISH WITH THE ALIENS. I COULDN'T GET BACK HERE FOR WEEKS. AND THEN I SAW THAT TERRIBLE FIGHT...
...BETWEEN YOU AND SUPERMAN. THE ONE CIRCE FORCED THE WORLD TO WATCH.*
AND THEN I SAW HER. IT WAS VANESSA, WASN'T IT?
*SEE LAST ISSUE.
JULIA, I'M SO SORRY. CIRCE HAS SOMEHOW MANAGED--
--WAS THAT WINGED... THING-- ARE YOU TELLING ME THAT WAS MY DAUGHTER?
WELL, DEAR GOD -- WHAT HAPPENED TO HER? WHY WAS SHE WITH CIRCE?! AND WHAT DID THEY DO TO HER THROAT? WHY WAS SHE WEARING THAT COSTUME?
DIDN'T YOU DO ANYTHING TO PROTECT HER?
I DON'T KNOW HOW, OR WHEN... BUT VANESSA WAS TRANSFORMED INTO THE SILVER SWAN. AGAINST HER WILL, I'M SURE, BUT CIRCE ORCHESTRATED IT SOMEHOW...
I'M SO SORRY, JULIA. I CAME HERE TO TELL YOU WHAT HAPPENED. BUT I CAN BARELY MUSTER THE WORDS, IT HURTS SO MUCH.

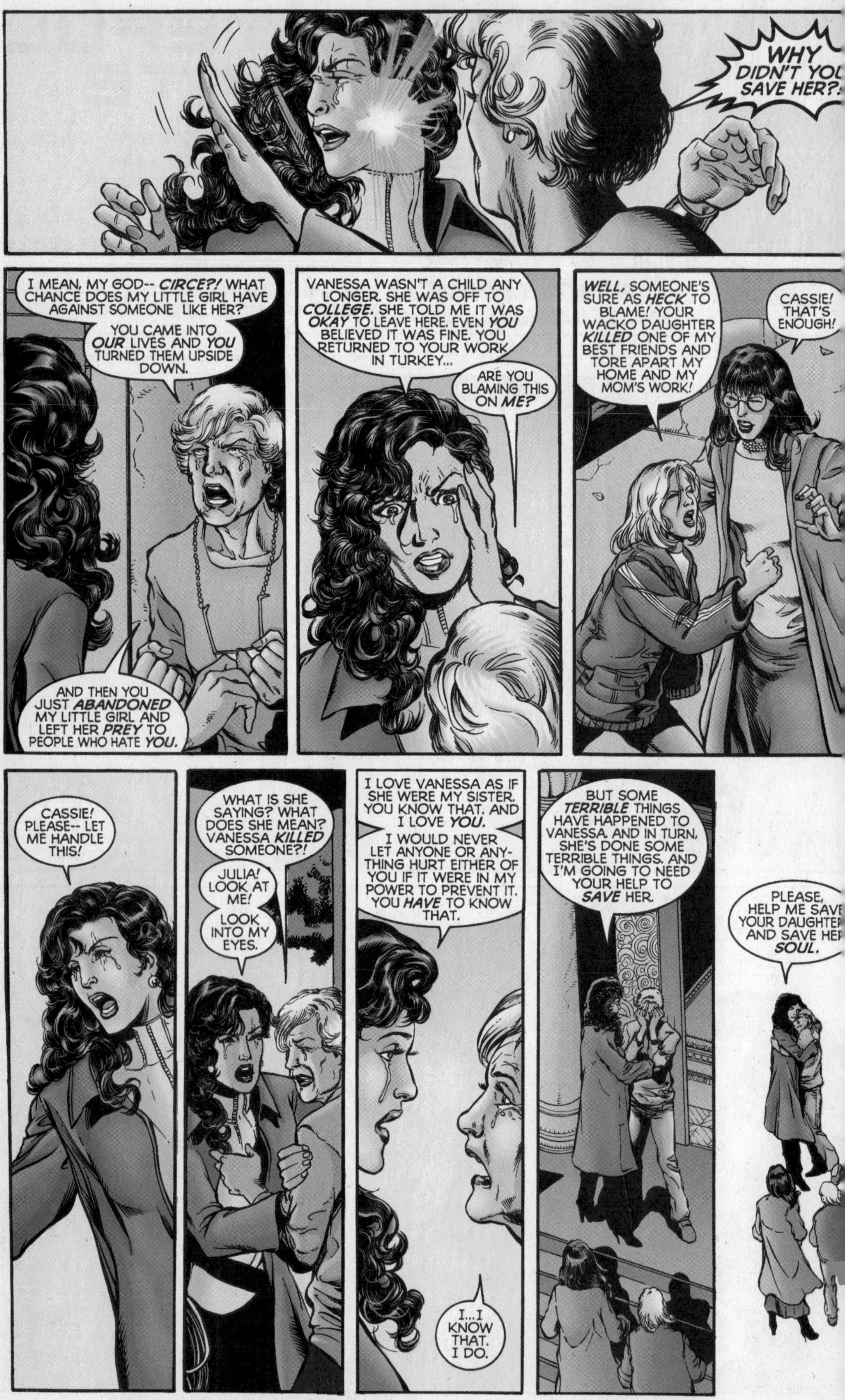
WHY DIDN'T YOU SAVE HER?!
I MEAN, MY GOD-- CIRCE?! WHAT CHANCE DOES MY LITTLE GIRL HAVE AGAINST SOMEONE LIKE HER?
YOU CAME INTO OUR LIVES AND YOU TURNED THEM UPSIDE DOWN.
AND THEN YOU JUST ABANDONED MY LITTLE GIRL AND LEFT HER PREY TO PEOPLE WHO HATE YOU.
VANESSA WASN'T A CHILD ANY LONGER. SHE WAS OFF TO COLLEGE. SHE TOLD ME IT WAS OKAY TO LEAVE HERE. EVEN YOU BELIEVED IT WAS FINE. YOU RETURNED TO YOUR WORK IN TURKEY...
ARE YOU BLAMING THIS ON ME?
WELL, SOMEONE'S SURE AS HECK TO BLAME! YOUR WACKO DAUGHTER KILLED ONE OF MY BEST FRIENDS AND TORE APART MY HOME AND MY MOM'S WORK!
CASSIE! THAT'S ENOUGH!
CASSIE! PLEASE-- LET ME HANDLE THIS!
WHAT IS SHE SAYING? WHAT DOES SHE MEAN? VANESSA KILLED SOMEONE?!
JULIA! LOOK AT ME!
LOOK INTO MY EYES.
I LOVE VANESSA AS IF SHE WERE MY SISTER. YOU KNOW THAT. AND I LOVE YOU.
I WOULD NEVER LET ANYONE OR ANYTHING HURT EITHER OF YOU IF IT WERE IN MY POWER TO PREVENT IT. YOU HAVE TO KNOW THAT.
I...I KNOW THAT. I DO.
BUT SOME TERRIBLE THINGS HAVE HAPPENED TO VANESSA. AND IN TURN, SHE'S DONE SOME TERRIBLE THINGS. AND I'M GOING TO NEED YOUR HELP TO SAVE HER.
PLEASE, HELP ME SAVE YOUR DAUGHTER AND SAVE HER SOUL.

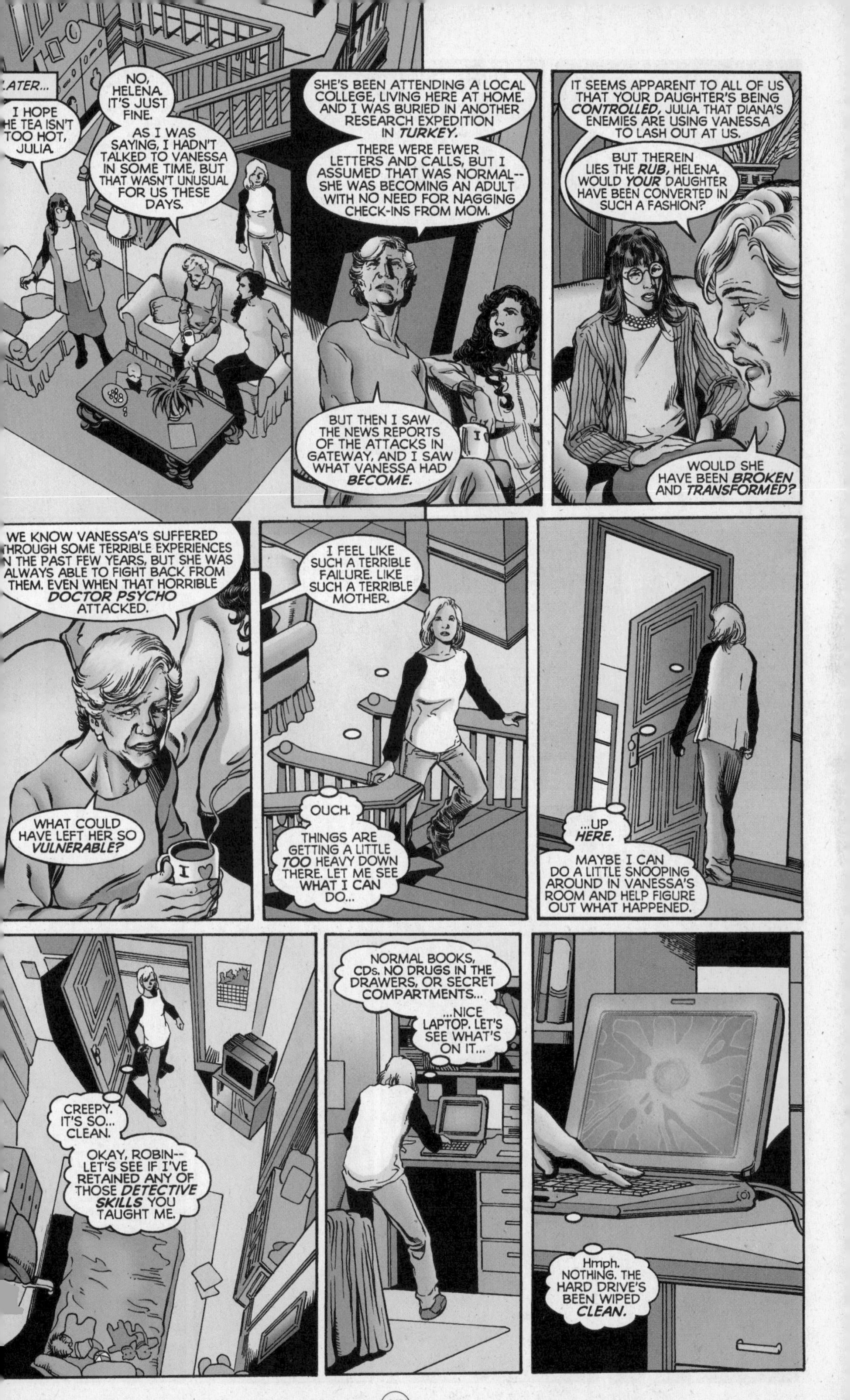
LATER...
I HOPE THE TEA ISN'T TOO HOT, JULIA.
NO, HELENA. IT'S JUST FINE.
AS I WAS SAYING, I HADN'T TALKED TO VANESSA IN SOME TIME, BUT THAT WASN'T UNUSUAL FOR US THESE DAYS.
SHE'S BEEN ATTENDING A LOCAL COLLEGE, LIVING HERE AT HOME. AND I WAS BURIED IN ANOTHER RESEARCH EXPEDITION IN TURKEY.
THERE WERE FEWER LETTERS AND CALLS, BUT I ASSUMED THAT WAS NORMAL-- SHE WAS BECOMING AN ADULT WITH NO NEED FOR NAGGING CHECK-INS FROM MOM.
BUT THEN I SAW THE NEWS REPORTS OF THE ATTACKS IN GATEWAY, AND I SAW WHAT VANESSA HAD BECOME.
IT SEEMS APPARENT TO ALL OF US THAT YOUR DAUGHTER'S BEING CONTROLLED, JULIA. THAT DIANA'S ENEMIES ARE USING VANESSA TO LASH OUT AT US.
BUT THEREIN LIES THE RUB, HELENA. WOULD YOUR DAUGHTER HAVE BEEN CONVERTED IN SUCH A FASHION?
WOULD SHE HAVE BEEN BROKEN AND TRANSFORMED?
WE KNOW VANESSA'S SUFFERED THROUGH SOME TERRIBLE EXPERIENCES IN THE PAST FEW YEARS, BUT SHE WAS ALWAYS ABLE TO FIGHT BACK FROM THEM. EVEN WHEN THAT HORRIBLE DOCTOR PSYCHO ATTACKED.
WHAT COULD HAVE LEFT HER SO VULNERABLE?
I FEEL LIKE SUCH A TERRIBLE FAILURE. LIKE SUCH A TERRIBLE MOTHER.
OUCH.
THINGS ARE GETTING A LITTLE TOO HEAVY DOWN THERE. LET ME SEE WHAT I CAN DO...
...UP HERE.
MAYBE I CAN DO A LITTLE SNOOPING AROUND IN VANESSA'S ROOM AND HELP FIGURE OUT WHAT HAPPENED.
CREEPY. IT'S SO... CLEAN.
OKAY, ROBIN-- LET'S SEE IF I'VE RETAINED ANY OF THOSE DETECTIVE SKILLS YOU TAUGHT ME.
NORMAL BOOKS, CDs. NO DRUGS IN THE DRAWERS, OR SECRET COMPARTMENTS...
...NICE LAPTOP. LET'S SEE WHAT'S ON IT...
Hmph. NOTHING. THE HARD DRIVE'S BEEN WIPED CLEAN.

NOPE.

WONDER WHAT SHE KEEPS UNDER HERE. WHIPS AND CHAINS FOR HER OUTFIT? DIET PILLS TO SQUEEZE INTO IT?

THAT'S A *CRAZY* LOOK, MAN...

Oh, YOU'VE GOTTA BE KIDDING ME. *GENIUS.*

Diary

PROPERTY OF Ms. Vanessa Kapatelis

WOW. SHE'S BEEN WRITING IN THIS THING FOR *YEARS*. THERE'S STUFF ABOUT THE FIRST TIME SHE MET DIANA...

WEIRD. WE WERE ALMOST THE *SAME AGE* WHEN WE EACH MET DIANA. AND LOOK WHAT HAPPENED TO HER, AND LOOK WHAT HAPPENED TO *ME.*

I WONDER WHY SHE NEVER BECAME A *WONDER GIRL?* I GUESS *DONNA* WAS AROUND AT THE TIME, BUT STILL...

Oh, MAN.

VANESSA MUST SERIOUSLY BE NAILED IN THE HEAD.

I THINK I CAN SKIP THE STUFF ABOUT LUCY AND SUMMER CAMP, AND THE EIGHT NERD BOYFRIENDS...

I'VE JUST GOTTA FIND *ANYTHING* THAT MIGHT MENTION WHAT'S HAPPENED RECENTLY. A CLUE TO WHY SHE *CHANGED...*

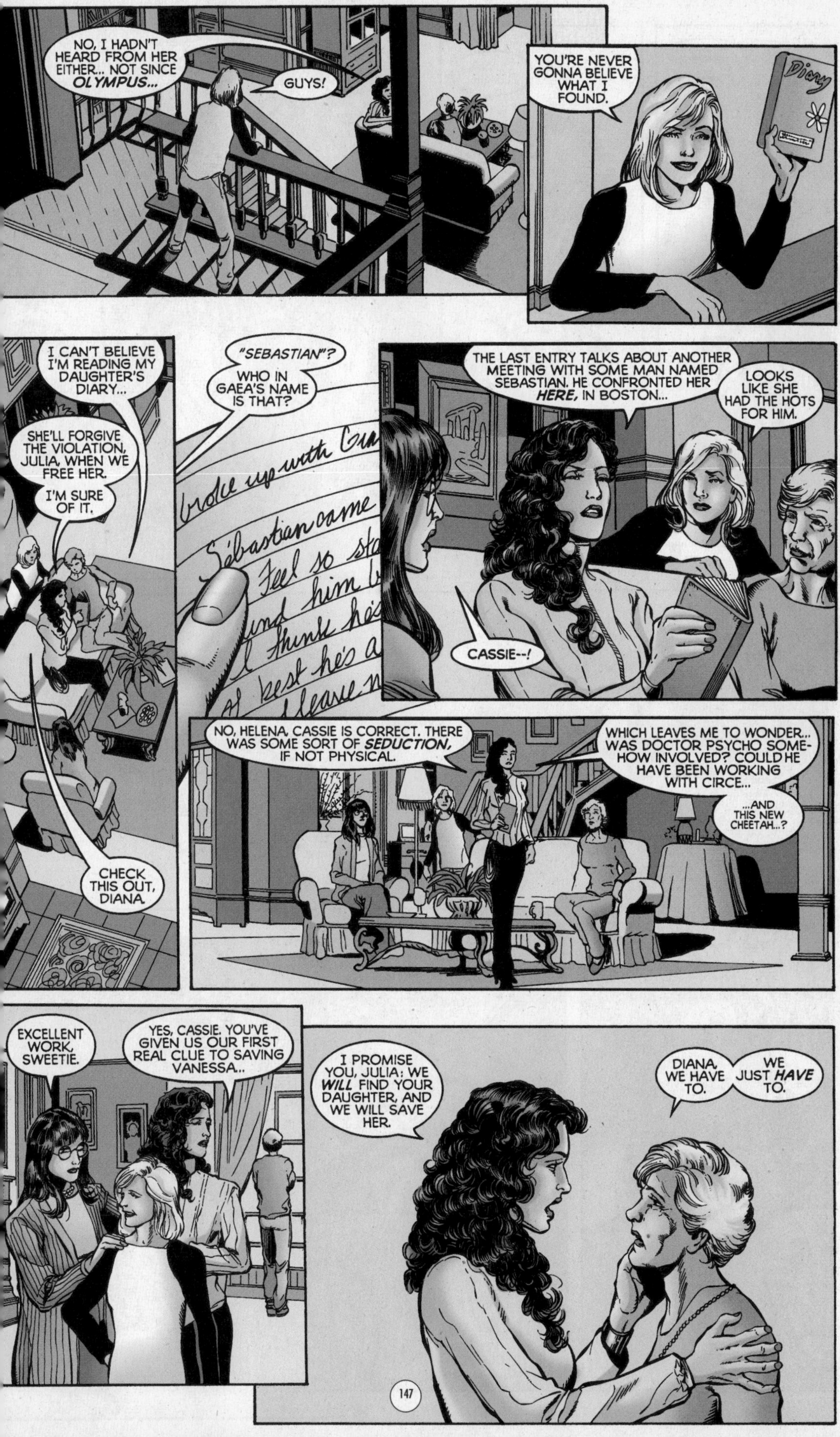
NO, I HADN'T HEARD FROM HER EITHER... NOT SINCE OLYMPUS...
GUYS!
YOU'RE NEVER GONNA BELIEVE WHAT I FOUND.
Diary
I CAN'T BELIEVE I'M READING MY DAUGHTER'S DIARY...
SHE'LL FORGIVE THE VIOLATION, JULIA, WHEN WE FREE HER.
I'M SURE OF IT.
CHECK THIS OUT, DIANA.
"SEBASTIAN"? WHO IN GAEA'S NAME IS THAT?
THE LAST ENTRY TALKS ABOUT ANOTHER MEETING WITH SOME MAN NAMED SEBASTIAN. HE CONFRONTED HER HERE, IN BOSTON...
LOOKS LIKE SHE HAD THE HOTS FOR HIM.
CASSIE--!
NO, HELENA, CASSIE IS CORRECT. THERE WAS SOME SORT OF SEDUCTION, IF NOT PHYSICAL.
WHICH LEAVES ME TO WONDER... WAS DOCTOR PSYCHO SOMEHOW INVOLVED? COULD HE HAVE BEEN WORKING WITH CIRCE...
...AND THIS NEW CHEETAH...?
EXCELLENT WORK, SWEETIE.
YES, CASSIE. YOU'VE GIVEN US OUR FIRST REAL CLUE TO SAVING VANESSA...
I PROMISE YOU, JULIA: WE WILL FIND YOUR DAUGHTER, AND WE WILL SAVE HER.
DIANA, WE HAVE TO.
WE JUST HAVE TO.

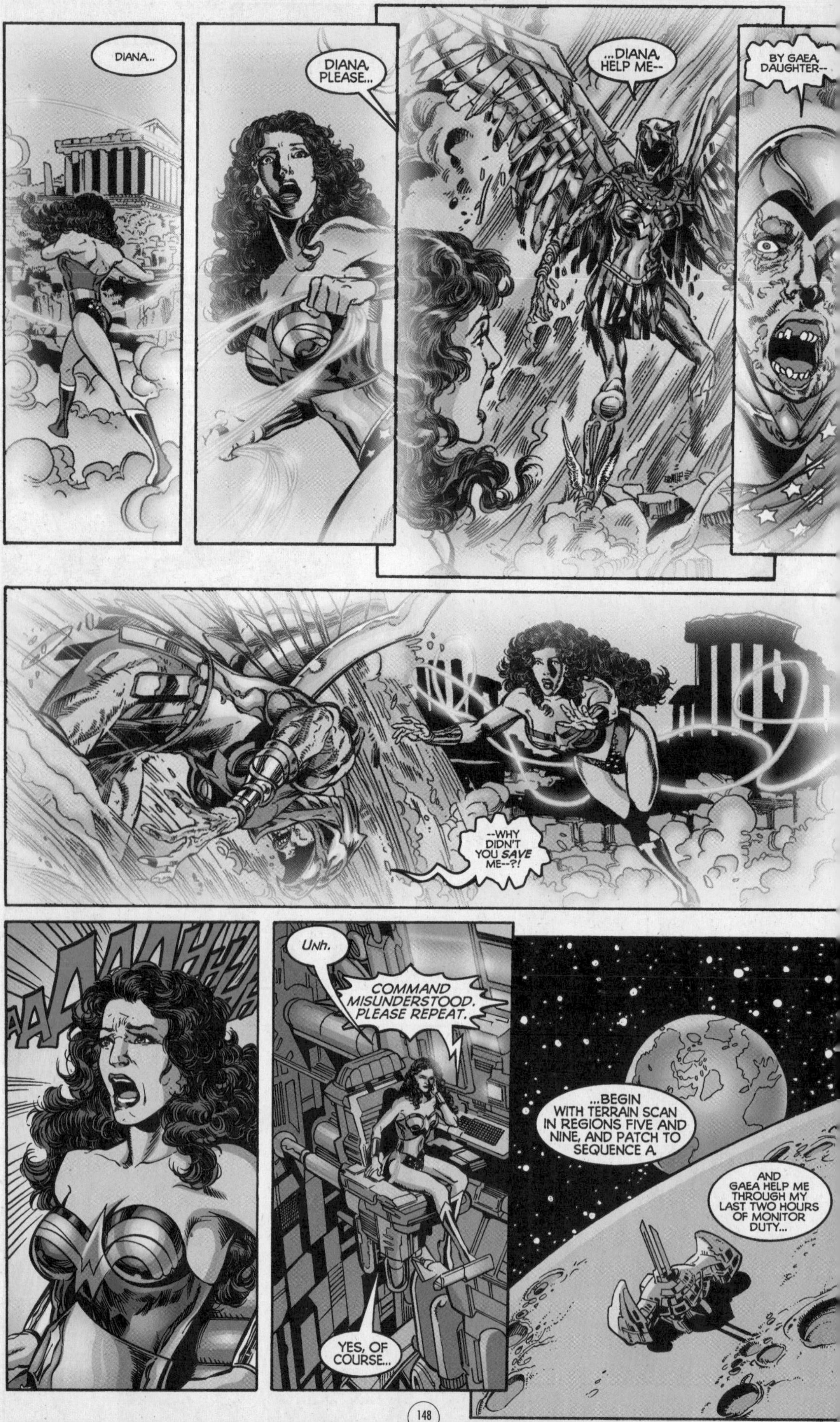
DIANA..
DIANA, PLEASE...
...DIANA, HELP ME--
BY GAEA, DAUGHTER--
--WHY DIDN'T YOU *SAVE* ME--?!
Unh.
COMMAND MISUNDERSTOOD. PLEASE REPEAT.
YES, OF COURSE...
...BEGIN WITH TERRAIN SCAN IN REGIONS FIVE AND NINE, AND PATCH TO SEQUENCE A.
AND GAEA HELP ME THROUGH MY LAST TWO HOURS OF MONITOR DUTY...

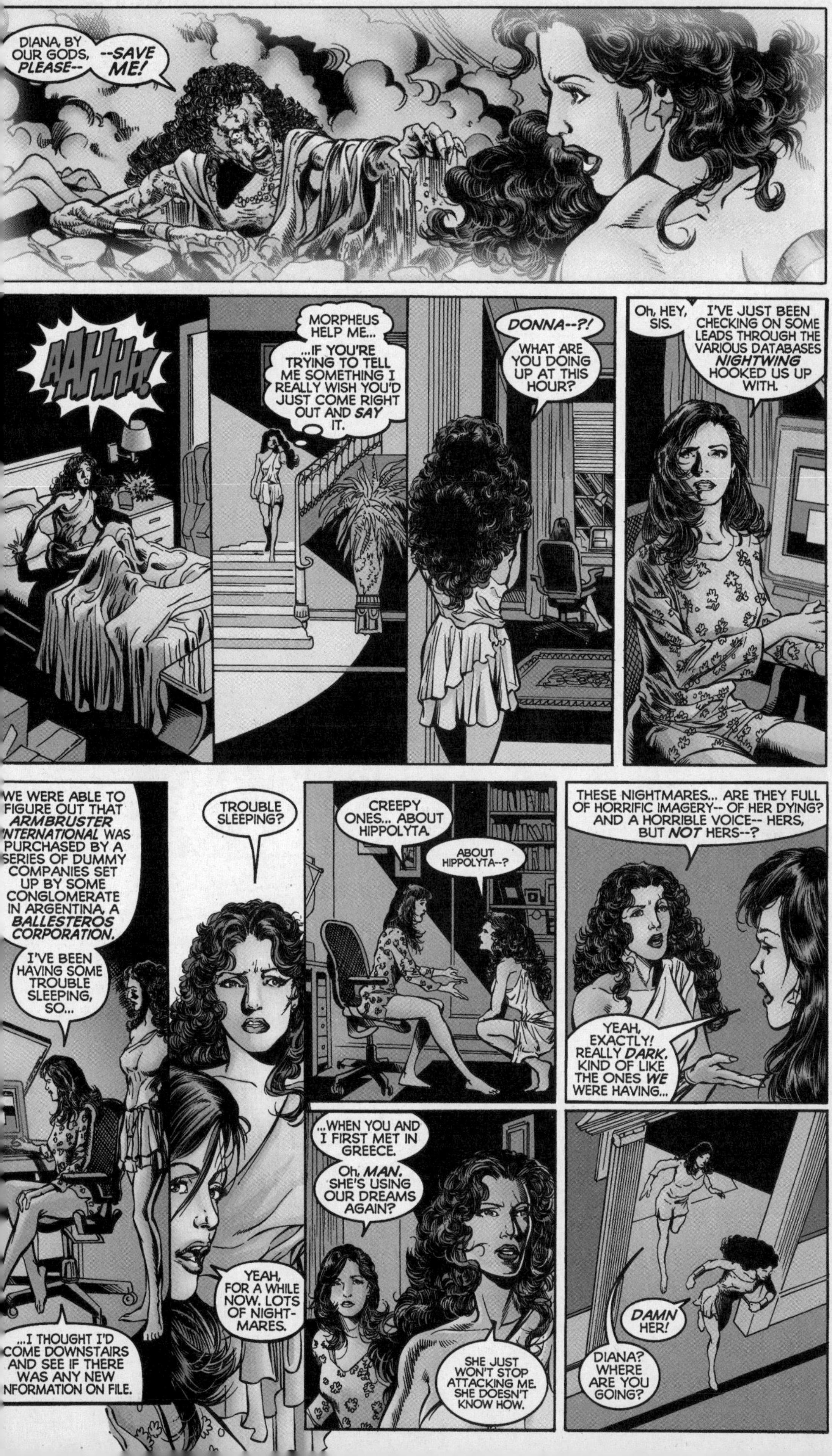
DIANA, BY OUR GODS, PLEASE--
--SAVE ME!
AAHHH!
MORPHEUS HELP ME...
...IF YOU'RE TRYING TO TELL ME SOMETHING I REALLY WISH YOU'D JUST COME RIGHT OUT AND SAY IT.
DONNA--?!
WHAT ARE YOU DOING UP AT THIS HOUR?
Oh, HEY, SIS.
I'VE JUST BEEN CHECKING ON SOME LEADS THROUGH THE VARIOUS DATABASES NIGHTWING HOOKED US UP WITH.
WE WERE ABLE TO FIGURE OUT THAT ARMBRUSTER INTERNATIONAL WAS PURCHASED BY A SERIES OF DUMMY COMPANIES SET UP BY SOME CONGLOMERATE IN ARGENTINA, A BALLESTEROS CORPORATION.
I'VE BEEN HAVING SOME TROUBLE SLEEPING, SO...
...I THOUGHT I'D COME DOWNSTAIRS AND SEE IF THERE WAS ANY NEW INFORMATION ON FILE.
TROUBLE SLEEPING?
YEAH, FOR A WHILE NOW. LOTS OF NIGHT-MARES.
CREEPY ONES... ABOUT HIPPOLYTA.
ABOUT HIPPOLYTA--?
THESE NIGHTMARES... ARE THEY FULL OF HORRIFIC IMAGERY-- OF HER DYING? AND A HORRIBLE VOICE-- HERS, BUT NOT HERS--?
YEAH, EXACTLY! REALLY DARK. KIND OF LIKE THE ONES WE WERE HAVING...
...WHEN YOU AND I FIRST MET IN GREECE.
Oh, MAN. SHE'S USING OUR DREAMS AGAIN?
SHE JUST WON'T STOP ATTACKING ME. SHE DOESN'T KNOW HOW.
DAMN HER!
DIANA? WHERE ARE YOU GOING?

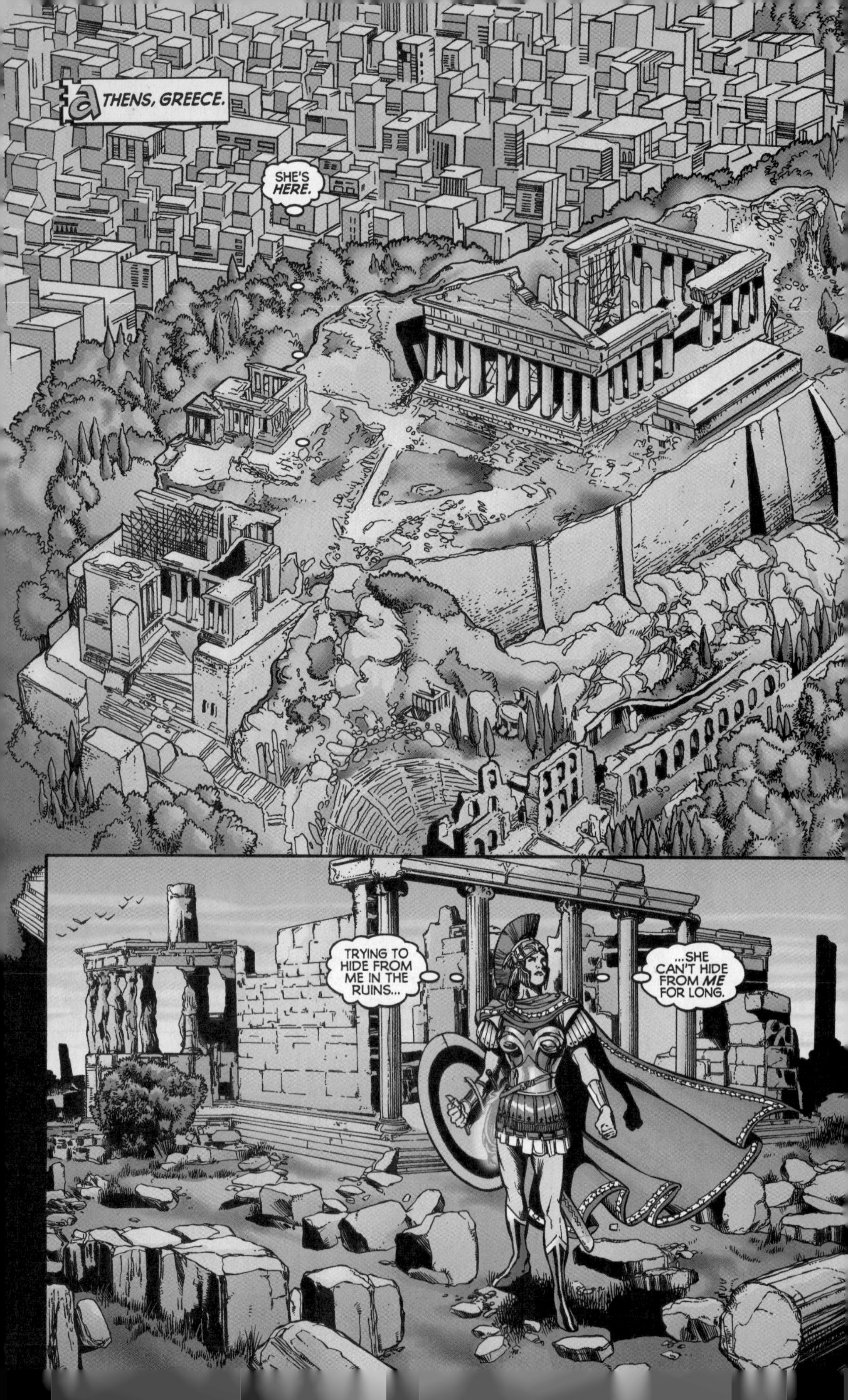
ATHENS, GREECE.
SHE'S *HERE.*
TRYING TO HIDE FROM ME IN THE RUINS...
...SHE CAN'T HIDE FROM *ME* FOR LONG.

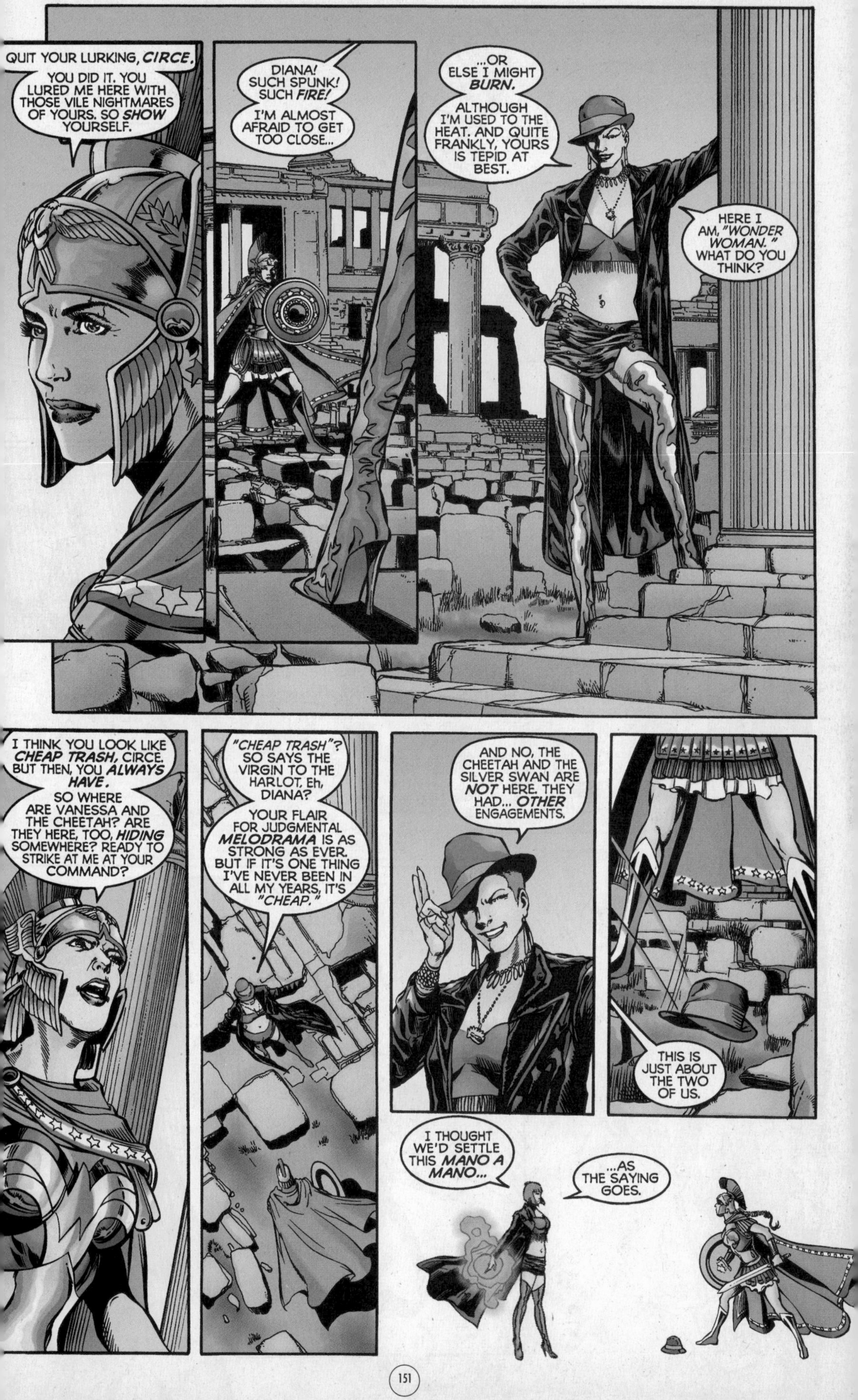
QUIT YOUR LURKING, *CIRCE*.
YOU DID IT. YOU LURED ME HERE WITH THOSE VILE NIGHTMARES OF YOURS. SO *SHOW* YOURSELF.
DIANA! SUCH SPUNK! SUCH *FIRE!*
I'M ALMOST AFRAID TO GET TOO CLOSE...
...OR ELSE I MIGHT *BURN.*
ALTHOUGH I'M USED TO THE HEAT. AND QUITE FRANKLY, YOURS IS TEPID AT BEST.
HERE I AM, *"WONDER WOMAN."* WHAT DO YOU THINK?
I THINK YOU LOOK LIKE *CHEAP TRASH*, CIRCE. BUT THEN, YOU *ALWAYS HAVE*.
SO WHERE ARE VANESSA AND THE CHEETAH? ARE THEY HERE, TOO, *HIDING* SOMEWHERE? READY TO STRIKE AT ME AT YOUR COMMAND?
"CHEAP TRASH"? SO SAYS THE VIRGIN TO THE HARLOT, Eh, DIANA?
YOUR FLAIR FOR JUDGMENTAL *MELODRAMA* IS AS STRONG AS EVER. BUT IF IT'S ONE THING I'VE NEVER BEEN IN ALL MY YEARS, IT'S *"CHEAP."*
AND NO, THE CHEETAH AND THE SILVER SWAN ARE *NOT* HERE. THEY HAD... *OTHER* ENGAGEMENTS.
THIS IS JUST ABOUT THE TWO OF US.
I THOUGHT WE'D SETTLE THIS *MANO A MANO...*
...AS THE SAYING GOES.

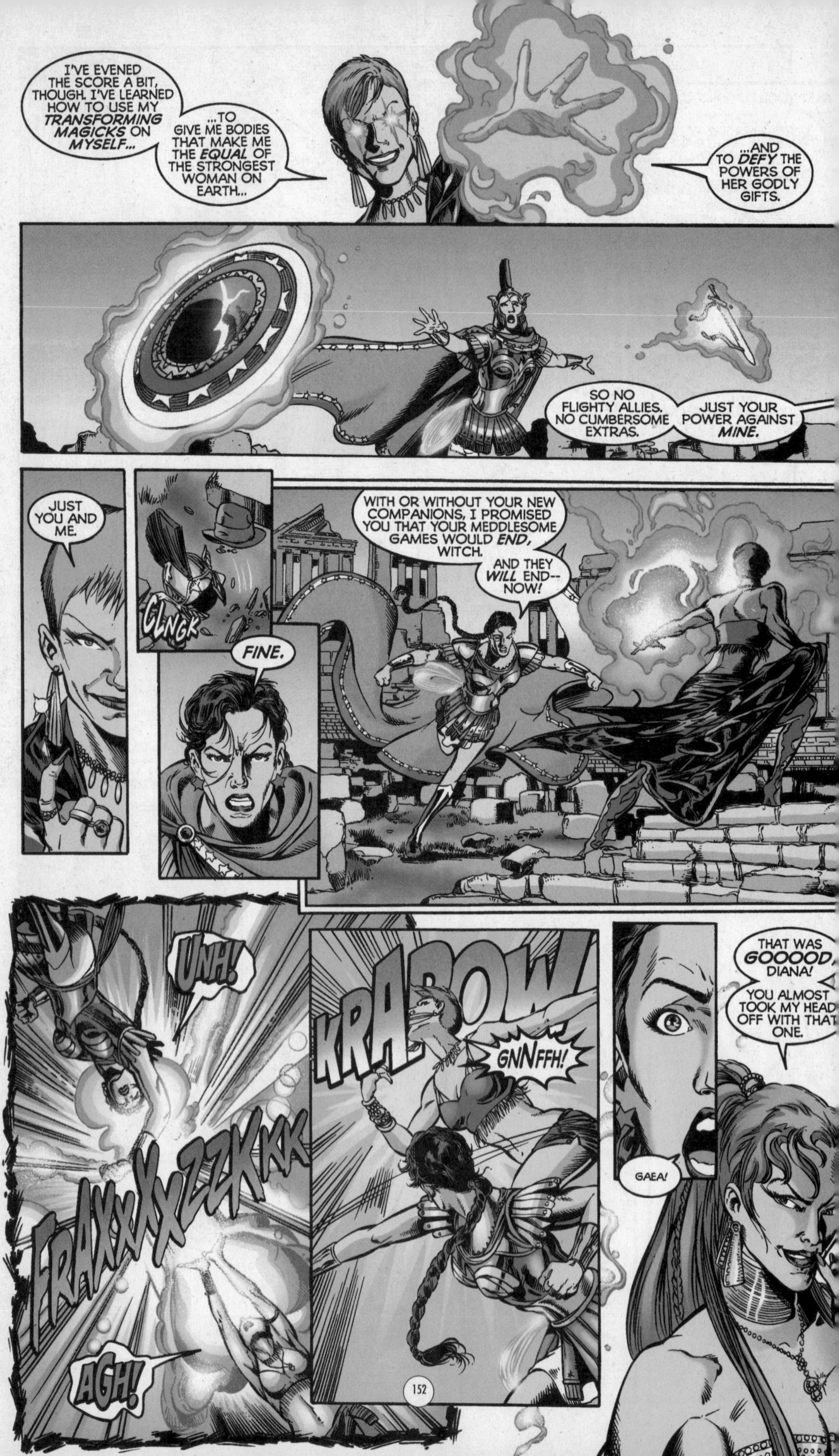
I'VE EVENED THE SCORE A BIT, THOUGH. I'VE LEARNED HOW TO USE MY TRANSFORMING MAGICKS ON MYSELF...
...TO GIVE ME BODIES THAT MAKE ME THE EQUAL OF THE STRONGEST WOMAN ON EARTH...
...AND TO DEFY THE POWERS OF HER GODLY GIFTS.
SO NO FLIGHTY ALLIES. NO CUMBERSOME EXTRAS.
JUST YOUR POWER AGAINST MINE.
JUST YOU AND ME.
CLNGK
FINE.
WITH OR WITHOUT YOUR NEW COMPANIONS, I PROMISED YOU THAT YOUR MEDDLESOME GAMES WOULD END, WITCH.
AND THEY WILL END-- NOW!
UNH!
FRAXXXXZZZKKK
AGH!
KRABOW
GNNFFH!
GAEA!
THAT WAS GOOOOD, DIANA!
YOU ALMOST TOOK MY HEAD OFF WITH THAT ONE.

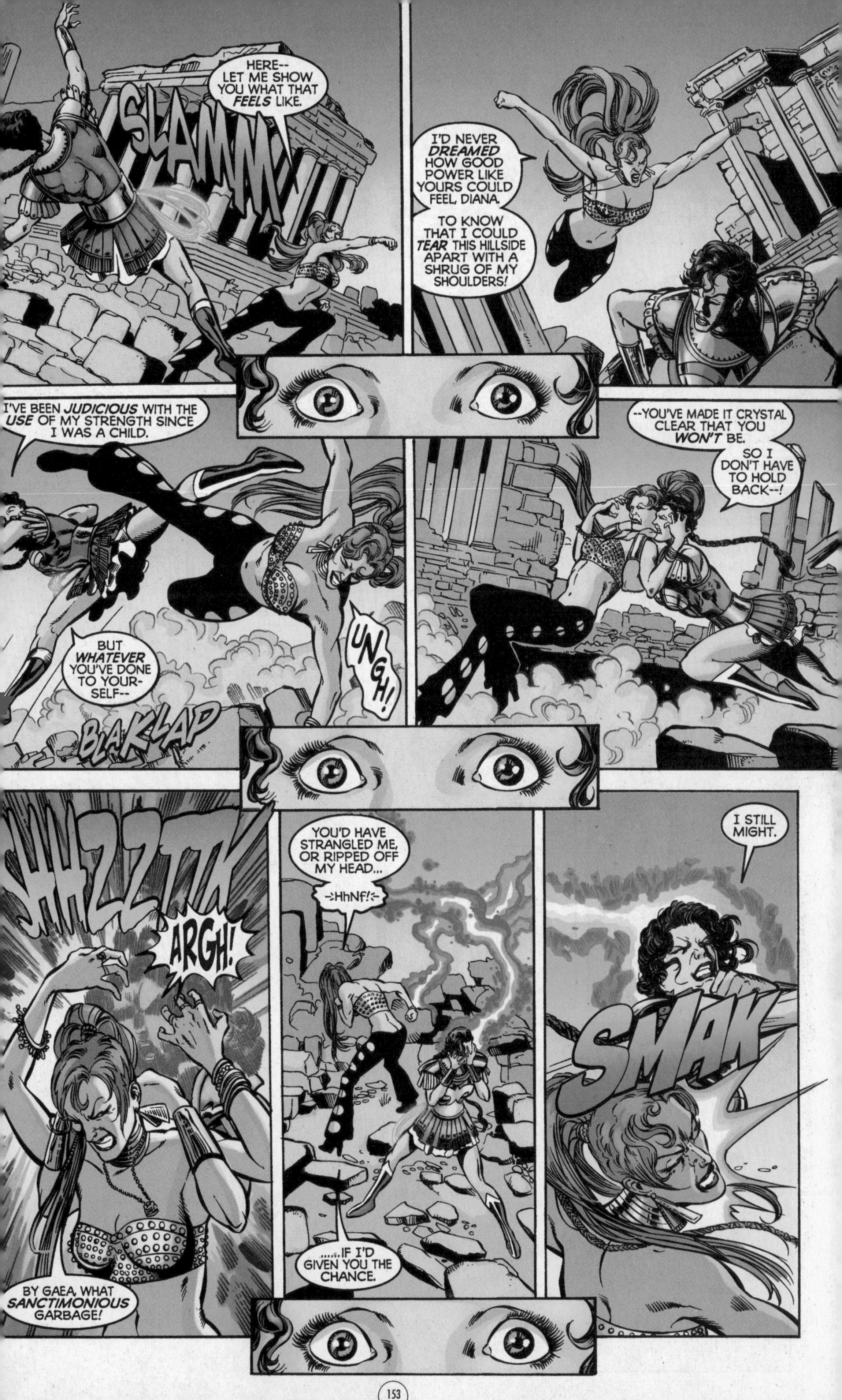
HERE-- LET ME SHOW YOU WHAT THAT FEELS LIKE.
SLAMMM
I'D NEVER DREAMED HOW GOOD POWER LIKE YOURS COULD FEEL, DIANA.
TO KNOW THAT I COULD TEAR THIS HILLSIDE APART WITH A SHRUG OF MY SHOULDERS!
I'VE BEEN JUDICIOUS WITH THE USE OF MY STRENGTH SINCE I WAS A CHILD.
BUT WHATEVER YOU'VE DONE TO YOURSELF--
UNGH!
BLAKLAP
--YOU'VE MADE IT CRYSTAL CLEAR THAT YOU WON'T BE.
SO I DON'T HAVE TO HOLD BACK--!
SHZZTTK
ARGH!
BY GAEA, WHAT SANCTIMONIOUS GARBAGE!
YOU'D HAVE STRANGLED ME, OR RIPPED OFF MY HEAD...
-:HhNf!:-
.....IF I'D GIVEN YOU THE CHANCE.
I STILL MIGHT.
SMAK

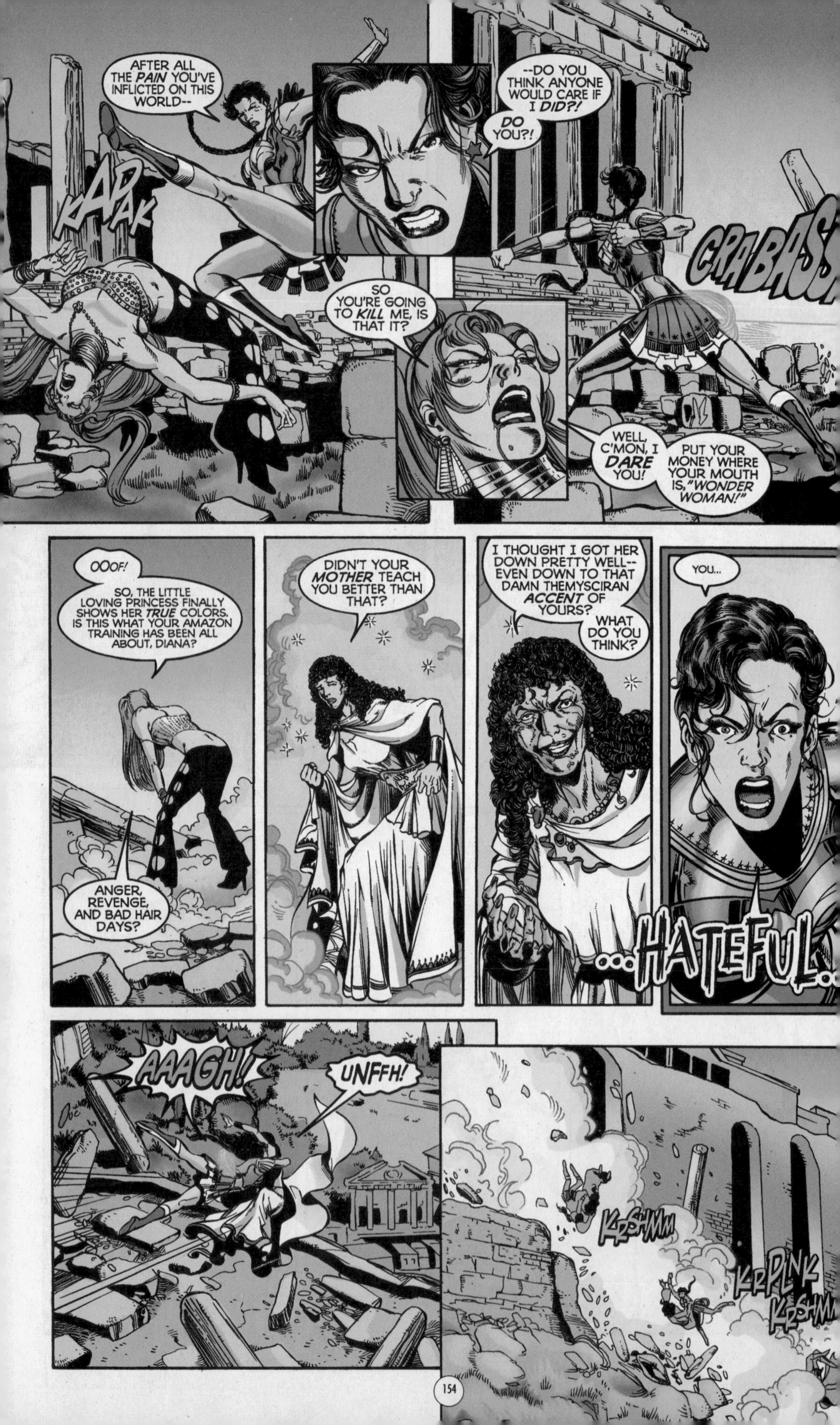

AFTER ALL THE PAIN YOU'VE INFLICTED ON THIS WORLD--
KAPAK
--DO YOU THINK ANYONE WOULD CARE IF I DID?!
DO YOU?!
CRABASS
SO YOU'RE GOING TO KILL ME, IS THAT IT?
WELL, C'MON, I DARE YOU!
PUT YOUR MONEY WHERE YOUR MOUTH IS, "WONDER WOMAN!"
OOOF!
SO, THE LITTLE LOVING PRINCESS FINALLY SHOWS HER TRUE COLORS. IS THIS WHAT YOUR AMAZON TRAINING HAS BEEN ALL ABOUT, DIANA?
ANGER, REVENGE, AND BAD HAIR DAYS?
DIDN'T YOUR MOTHER TEACH YOU BETTER THAN THAT?
I THOUGHT I GOT HER DOWN PRETTY WELL-- EVEN DOWN TO THAT DAMN THEMYSCIRAN ACCENT OF YOURS?
WHAT DO YOU THINK?
YOU...
...HATEFUL...
AAAGH!
UNFFH!
KRSHMM
KRPLNK
KRSHM

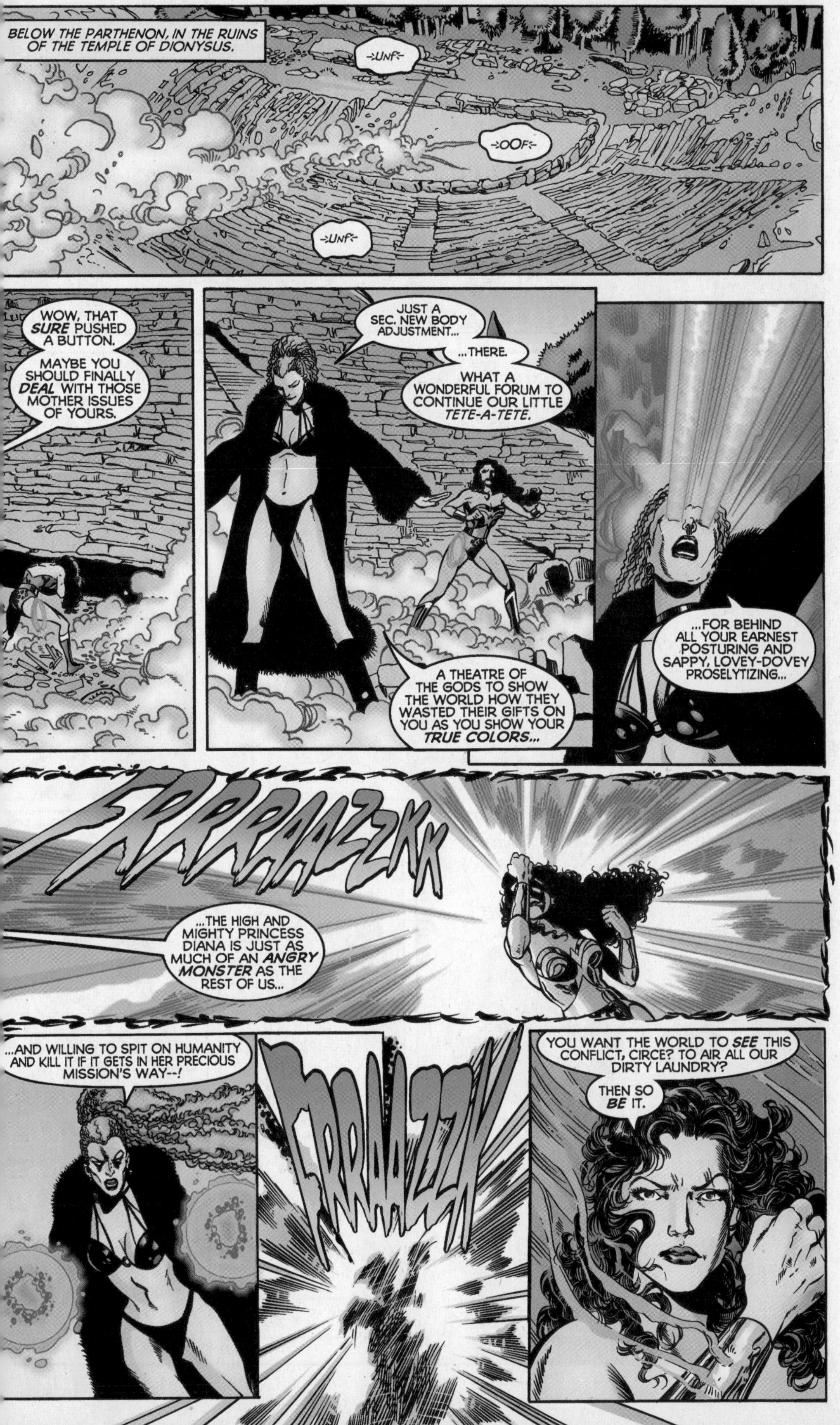
BELOW THE PARTHENON, IN THE RUINS OF THE TEMPLE OF DIONYSUS.
-UNF-
-OOF-
-UNF-
WOW, THAT SURE PUSHED A BUTTON.
MAYBE YOU SHOULD FINALLY DEAL WITH THOSE MOTHER ISSUES OF YOURS.
JUST A SEC. NEW BODY ADJUSTMENT...
...THERE.
WHAT A WONDERFUL FORUM TO CONTINUE OUR LITTLE TETE-A-TETE.
A THEATRE OF THE GODS TO SHOW THE WORLD HOW THEY WASTED THEIR GIFTS ON YOU AS YOU SHOW YOUR TRUE COLORS...
...FOR BEHIND ALL YOUR EARNEST POSTURING AND SAPPY, LOVEY-DOVEY PROSELYTIZING...
FRRRAAZZKK
...THE HIGH AND MIGHTY PRINCESS DIANA IS JUST AS MUCH OF AN ANGRY MONSTER AS THE REST OF US...
...AND WILLING TO SPIT ON HUMANITY AND KILL IT IF IT GETS IN HER PRECIOUS MISSION'S WAY--!
FRRAAZZK
YOU WANT THE WORLD TO SEE THIS CONFLICT, CIRCE? TO AIR ALL OUR DIRTY LAUNDRY?
THEN SO BE IT.

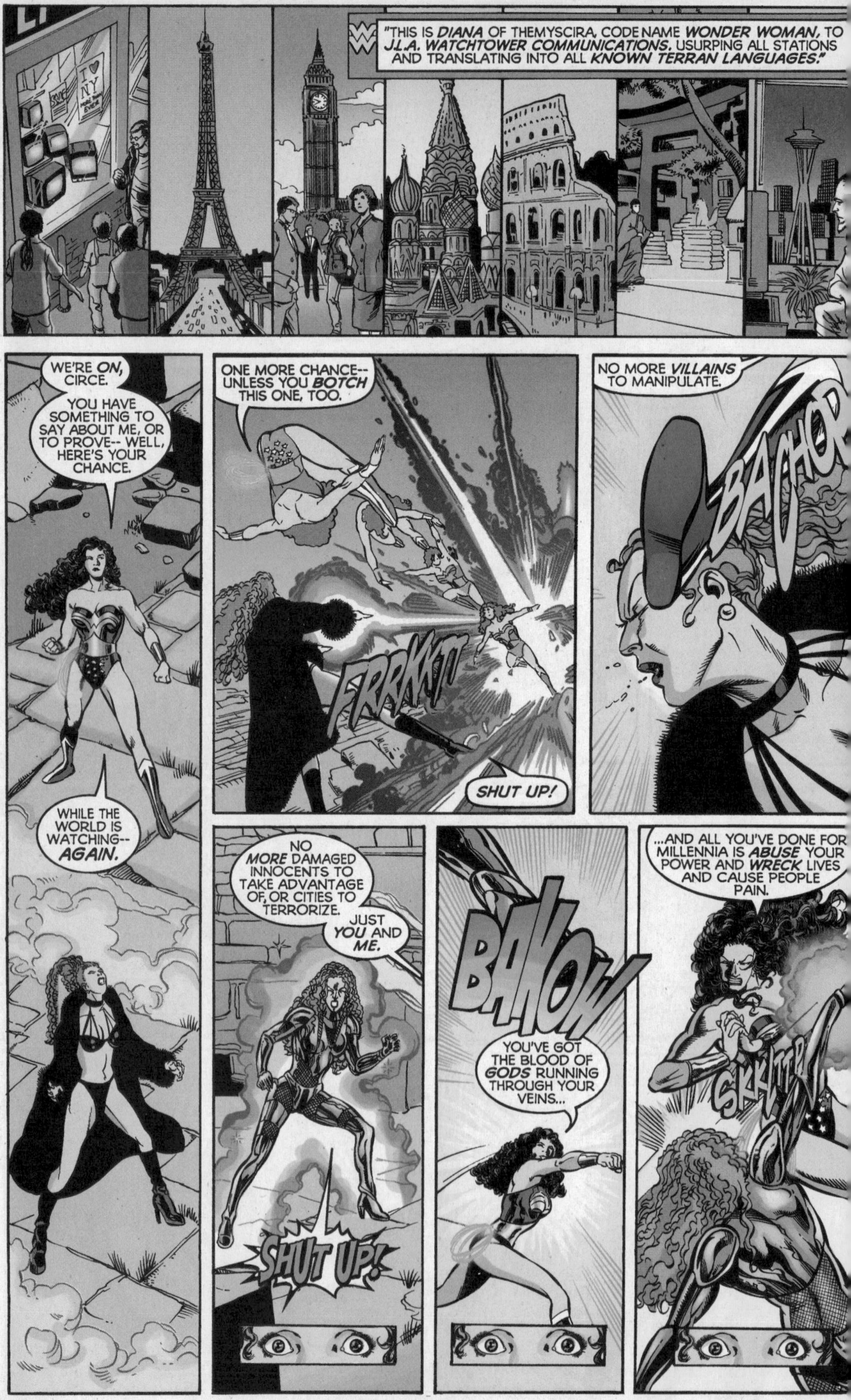
"THIS IS DIANA OF THEMYSCIRA, CODE NAME WONDER WOMAN, TO J.L.A. WATCHTOWER COMMUNICATIONS. USURPING ALL STATIONS AND TRANSLATING INTO ALL KNOWN TERRAN LANGUAGES."
WE'RE ON, CIRCE.
YOU HAVE SOMETHING TO SAY ABOUT ME, OR TO PROVE-- WELL, HERE'S YOUR CHANCE.
WHILE THE WORLD IS WATCHING-- AGAIN.
ONE MORE CHANCE-- UNLESS YOU BOTCH THIS ONE, TOO.
FRRKKT!
SHUT UP!
NO MORE VILLAINS TO MANIPULATE.
BACHOR
NO MORE DAMAGED INNOCENTS TO TAKE ADVANTAGE OF, OR CITIES TO TERRORIZE.
JUST YOU AND ME.
SHUT UP!
BANOW
YOU'VE GOT THE BLOOD OF GODS RUNNING THROUGH YOUR VEINS...
...AND ALL YOU'VE DONE FOR MILLENNIA IS ABUSE YOUR POWER AND WRECK LIVES AND CAUSE PEOPLE PAIN.

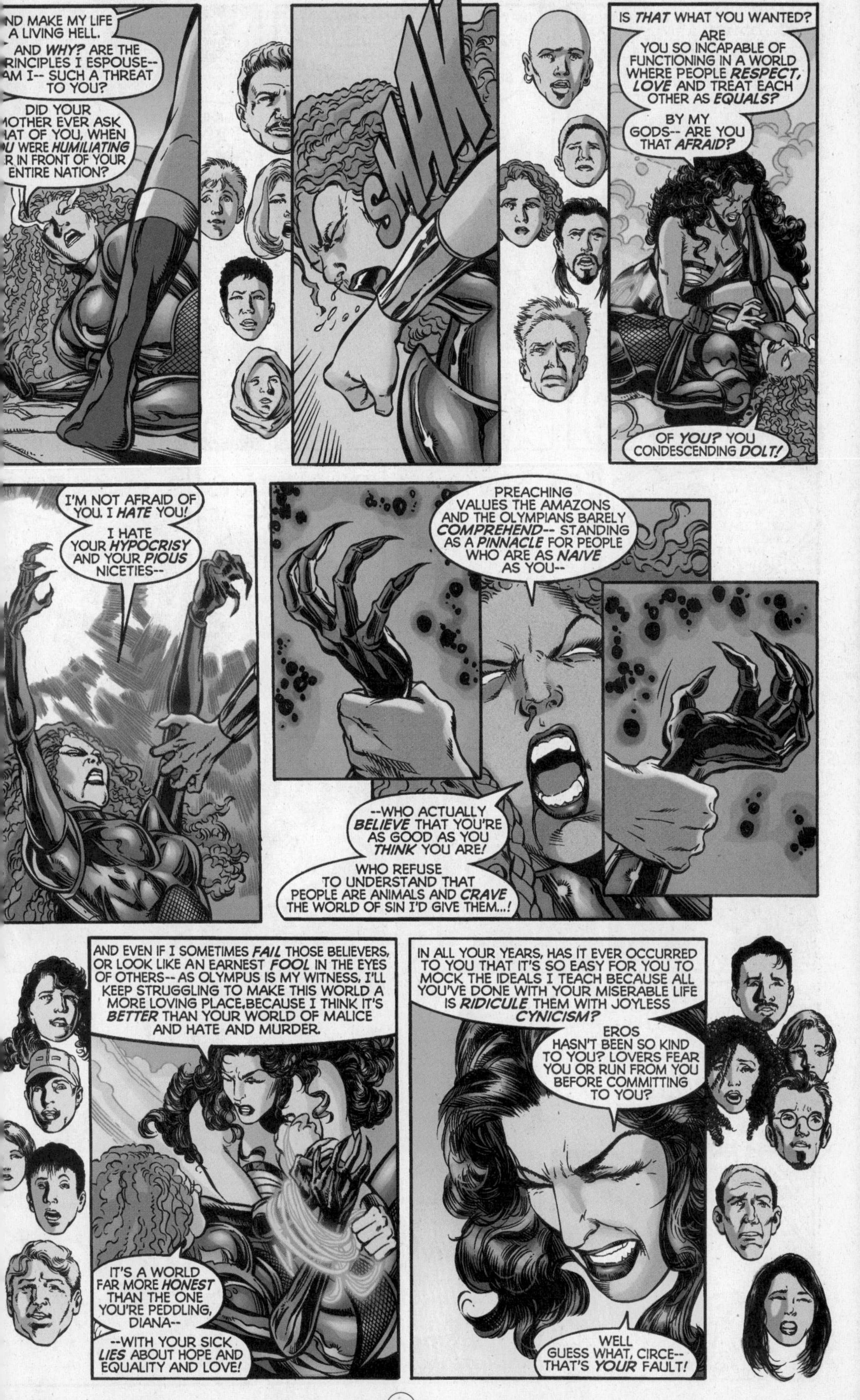
ND MAKE MY LIFE A LIVING HELL.
AND WHY? ARE THE RINCIPLES I ESPOUSE-- AM I-- SUCH A THREAT TO YOU?
DID YOUR MOTHER EVER ASK AT OF YOU, WHEN U WERE HUMILIATING R IN FRONT OF YOUR ENTIRE NATION?
SMAK
IS THAT WHAT YOU WANTED?
ARE YOU SO INCAPABLE OF FUNCTIONING IN A WORLD WHERE PEOPLE RESPECT, LOVE AND TREAT EACH OTHER AS EQUALS?
BY MY GODS-- ARE YOU THAT AFRAID?
OF YOU? YOU CONDESCENDING DOLT!
I'M NOT AFRAID OF YOU. I HATE YOU!
I HATE YOUR HYPOCRISY AND YOUR PIOUS NICETIES--
PREACHING VALUES THE AMAZONS AND THE OLYMPIANS BARELY COMPREHEND-- STANDING AS A PINNACLE FOR PEOPLE WHO ARE AS NAIVE AS YOU--
--WHO ACTUALLY BELIEVE THAT YOU'RE AS GOOD AS YOU THINK YOU ARE!
WHO REFUSE TO UNDERSTAND THAT PEOPLE ARE ANIMALS AND CRAVE THE WORLD OF SIN I'D GIVE THEM...!
AND EVEN IF I SOMETIMES FAIL THOSE BELIEVERS, OR LOOK LIKE AN EARNEST FOOL IN THE EYES OF OTHERS-- AS OLYMPUS IS MY WITNESS, I'LL KEEP STRUGGLING TO MAKE THIS WORLD A MORE LOVING PLACE,BECAUSE I THINK IT'S BETTER THAN YOUR WORLD OF MALICE AND HATE AND MURDER.
IT'S A WORLD FAR MORE HONEST THAN THE ONE YOU'RE PEDDLING, DIANA--
--WITH YOUR SICK LIES ABOUT HOPE AND EQUALITY AND LOVE!
IN ALL YOUR YEARS, HAS IT EVER OCCURRED TO YOU THAT IT'S SO EASY FOR YOU TO MOCK THE IDEALS I TEACH BECAUSE ALL YOU'VE DONE WITH YOUR MISERABLE LIFE IS RIDICULE THEM WITH JOYLESS CYNICISM?
EROS HASN'T BEEN SO KIND TO YOU? LOVERS FEAR YOU OR RUN FROM YOU BEFORE COMMITTING TO YOU?
WELL GUESS WHAT, CIRCE-- THAT'S YOUR FAULT!

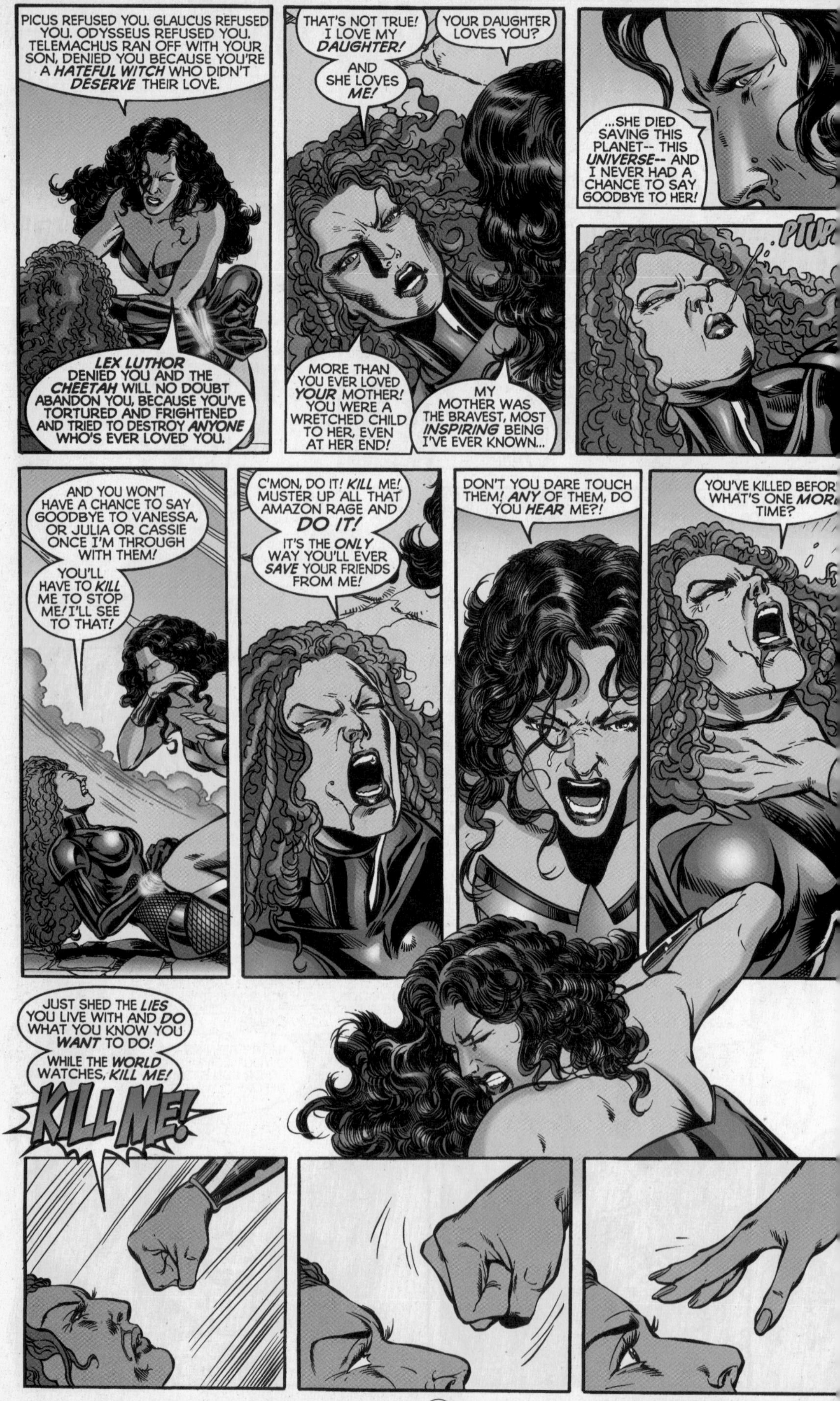
PICUS REFUSED YOU. GLAUCUS REFUSED YOU. ODYSSEUS REFUSED YOU. TELEMACHUS RAN OFF WITH YOUR SON, DENIED YOU BECAUSE YOU'RE A HATEFUL WITCH WHO DIDN'T DESERVE THEIR LOVE.
LEX LUTHOR DENIED YOU AND THE CHEETAH WILL NO DOUBT ABANDON YOU, BECAUSE YOU'VE TORTURED AND FRIGHTENED AND TRIED TO DESTROY ANYONE WHO'S EVER LOVED YOU.
THAT'S NOT TRUE! I LOVE MY DAUGHTER!
AND SHE LOVES ME!
YOUR DAUGHTER LOVES YOU?
MORE THAN YOU EVER LOVED YOUR MOTHER! YOU WERE A WRETCHED CHILD TO HER, EVEN AT HER END!
MY MOTHER WAS THE BRAVEST, MOST INSPIRING BEING I'VE EVER KNOWN...
...SHE DIED SAVING THIS PLANET-- THIS UNIVERSE-- AND I NEVER HAD A CHANCE TO SAY GOODBYE TO HER!
PTUP
AND YOU WON'T HAVE A CHANCE TO SAY GOODBYE TO VANESSA, OR JULIA OR CASSIE ONCE I'M THROUGH WITH THEM!
YOU'LL HAVE TO KILL ME TO STOP ME! I'LL SEE TO THAT!
C'MON, DO IT! KILL ME! MUSTER UP ALL THAT AMAZON RAGE AND DO IT!
IT'S THE ONLY WAY YOU'LL EVER SAVE YOUR FRIENDS FROM ME!
DON'T YOU DARE TOUCH THEM! ANY OF THEM, DO YOU HEAR ME?!
YOU'VE KILLED BEFOR WHAT'S ONE MOR TIME?
JUST SHED THE LIES YOU LIVE WITH AND DO WHAT YOU KNOW YOU WANT TO DO!
WHILE THE WORLD WATCHES, KILL ME!
KILL ME!

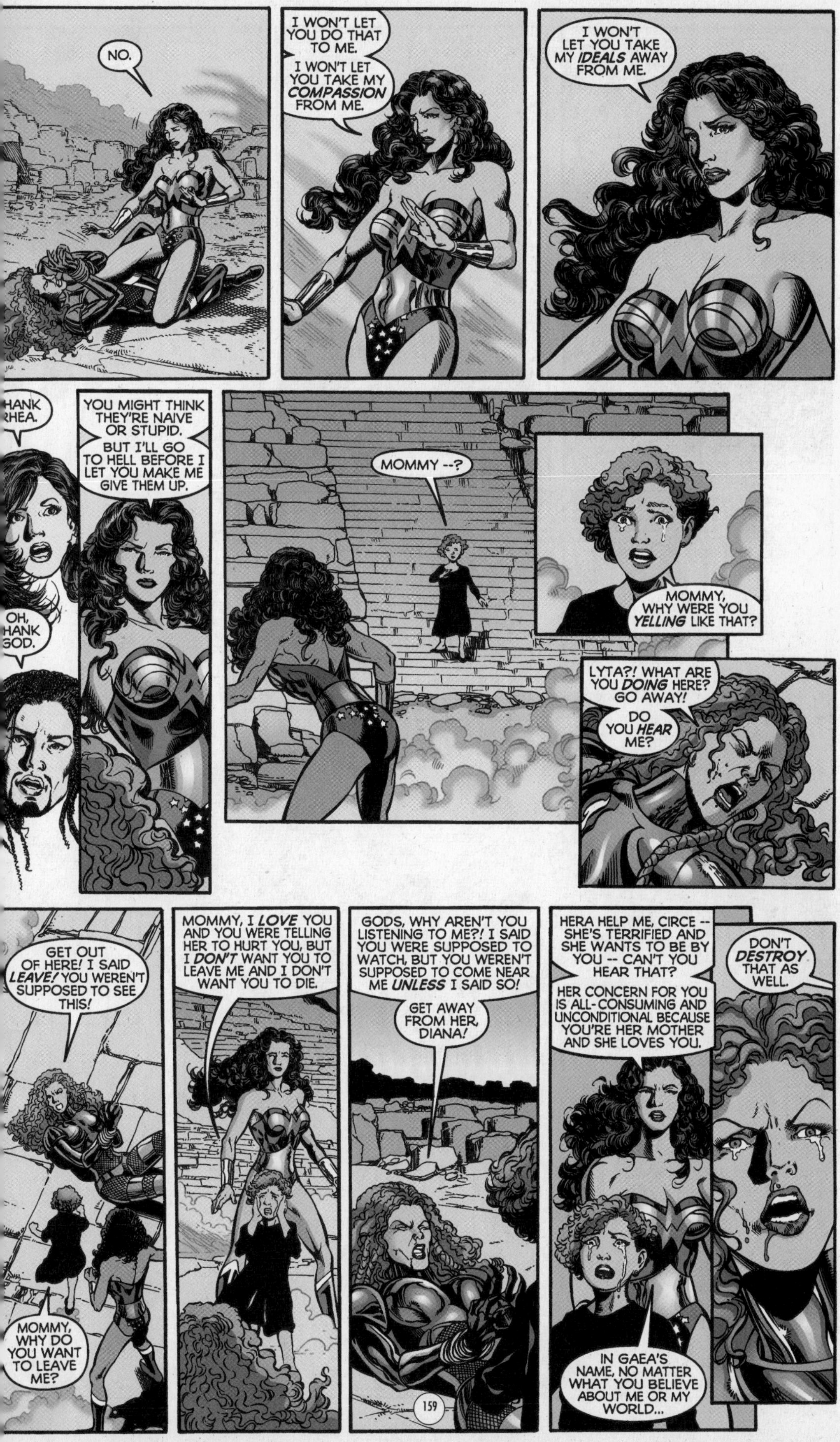

NO.
I WON'T LET YOU DO THAT TO ME.
I WON'T LET YOU TAKE MY *COMPASSION* FROM ME.
I WON'T LET YOU TAKE MY *IDEALS* AWAY FROM ME.
HANK RHEA.
OH, HANK GOD.
YOU MIGHT THINK THEY'RE NAIVE OR STUPID.
BUT I'LL GO TO HELL BEFORE I LET YOU MAKE ME GIVE THEM UP.
MOMMY --?
MOMMY, WHY WERE YOU *YELLING* LIKE THAT?
LYTA?! WHAT ARE YOU *DOING* HERE? GO AWAY!
DO YOU *HEAR* ME?
GET OUT OF HERE! I SAID *LEAVE!* YOU WEREN'T SUPPOSED TO SEE THIS!
MOMMY, WHY DO YOU WANT TO LEAVE ME?
MOMMY, I *LOVE* YOU AND YOU WERE TELLING HER TO HURT YOU, BUT I *DON'T* WANT YOU TO LEAVE ME AND I DON'T WANT YOU TO DIE.
GODS, WHY AREN'T YOU LISTENING TO ME?! I SAID YOU WERE SUPPOSED TO WATCH, BUT YOU WEREN'T SUPPOSED TO COME NEAR ME *UNLESS* I SAID SO!
GET AWAY FROM HER, DIANA!
HERA HELP ME, CIRCE -- SHE'S TERRIFIED AND SHE WANTS TO BE BY YOU -- CAN'T YOU HEAR THAT?
HER CONCERN FOR YOU IS ALL-CONSUMING AND UNCONDITIONAL BECAUSE YOU'RE HER MOTHER AND SHE LOVES YOU.
IN GAEA'S NAME, NO MATTER WHAT YOU BELIEVE ABOUT ME OR MY WORLD...
DON'T *DESTROY* THAT AS WELL.

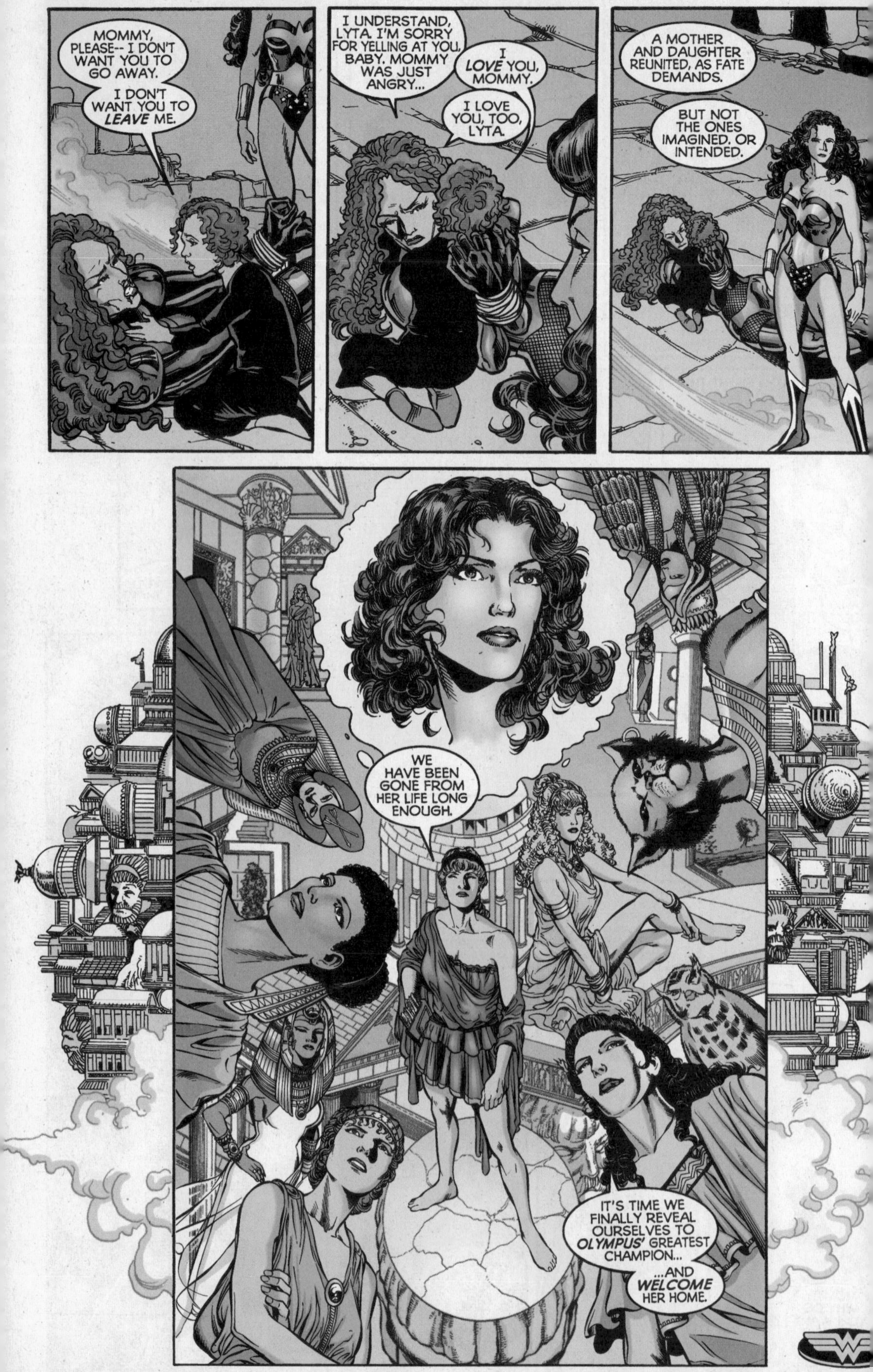
MOMMY, PLEASE-- I DON'T WANT YOU TO GO AWAY.
I DON'T WANT YOU TO LEAVE ME.
I UNDERSTAND, LYTA. I'M SORRY FOR YELLING AT YOU, BABY. MOMMY WAS JUST ANGRY...
I LOVE YOU, MOMMY.
I LOVE YOU, TOO, LYTA.
A MOTHER AND DAUGHTER REUNITED, AS FATE DEMANDS.
BUT NOT THE ONES IMAGINED. OR INTENDED.
WE HAVE BEEN GONE FROM HER LIFE LONG ENOUGH.
IT'S TIME WE FINALLY REVEAL OURSELVES TO OLYMPUS' GREATEST CHAMPION...
...AND WELCOME HER HOME.

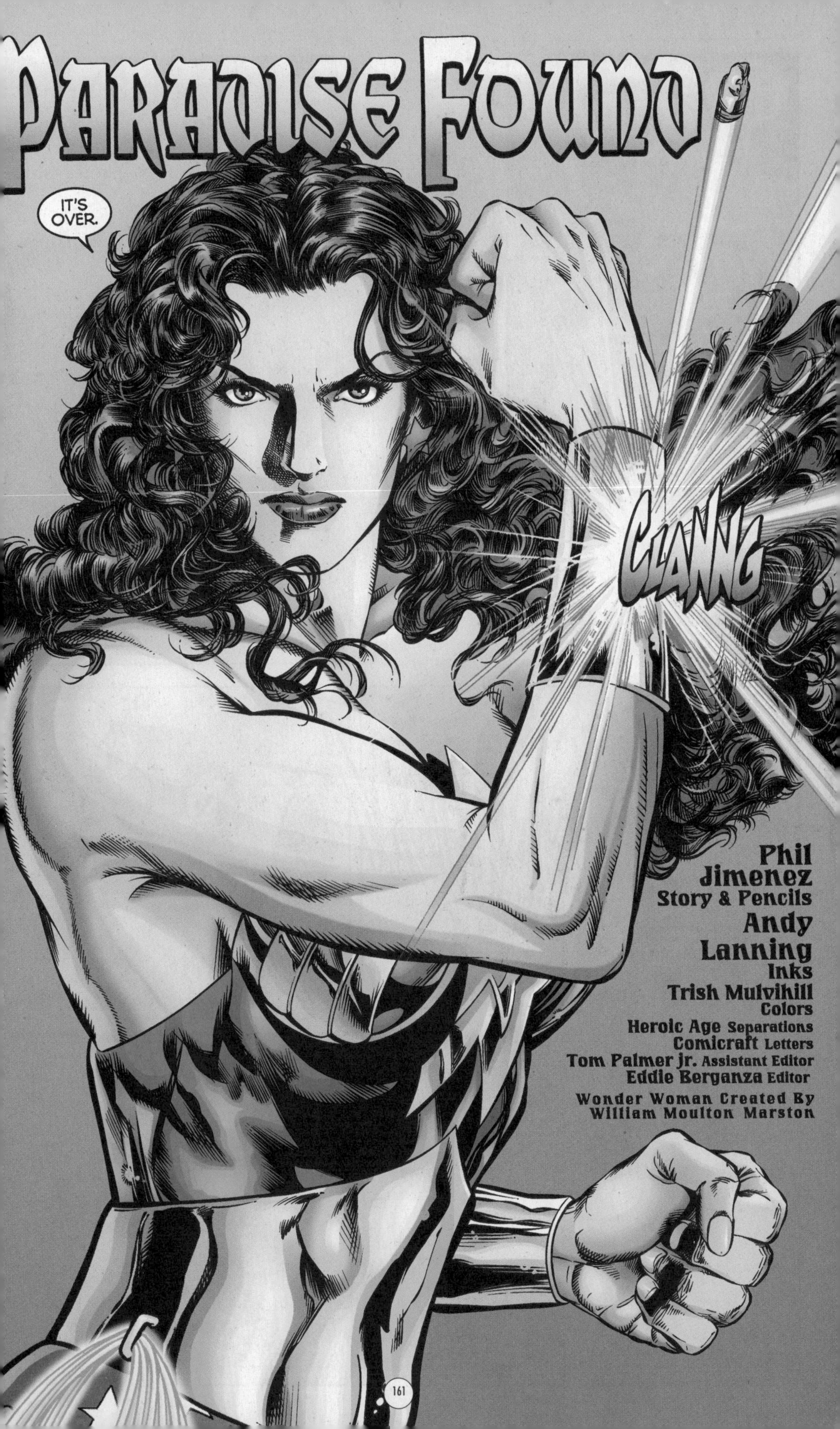
Paradise Found
IT'S OVER.
CLANNG
Phil Jimenez Story & Pencils
Andy Lanning Inks
Trish Mulvihill Colors
Heroic Age Separations
Comicraft Letters
Tom Palmer jr. Assistant Editor
Eddie Berganza Editor
Wonder Woman Created By William Moulton Marston

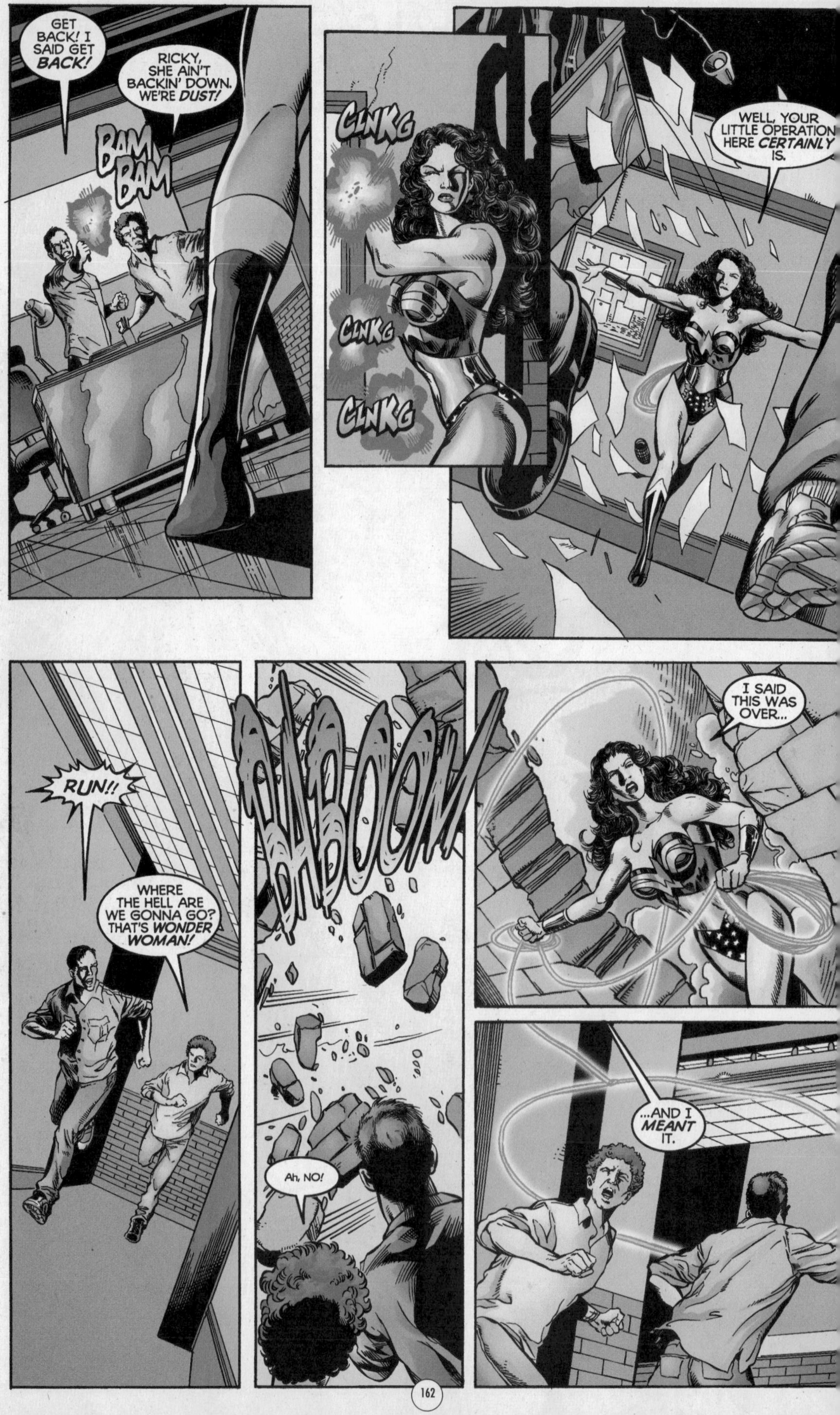

GET BACK! I SAID GET BACK!
RICKY, SHE AIN'T BACKIN' DOWN. WE'RE DUST!
BAM BAM
CLNKG
CLNKG
CLNKG
WELL, YOUR LITTLE OPERATION HERE CERTAINLY IS.
RUN!!
WHERE THE HELL ARE WE GONNA GO? THAT'S WONDER WOMAN!
BABOOM
Ah, NO!
I SAID THIS WAS OVER...
...AND I MEANT IT.

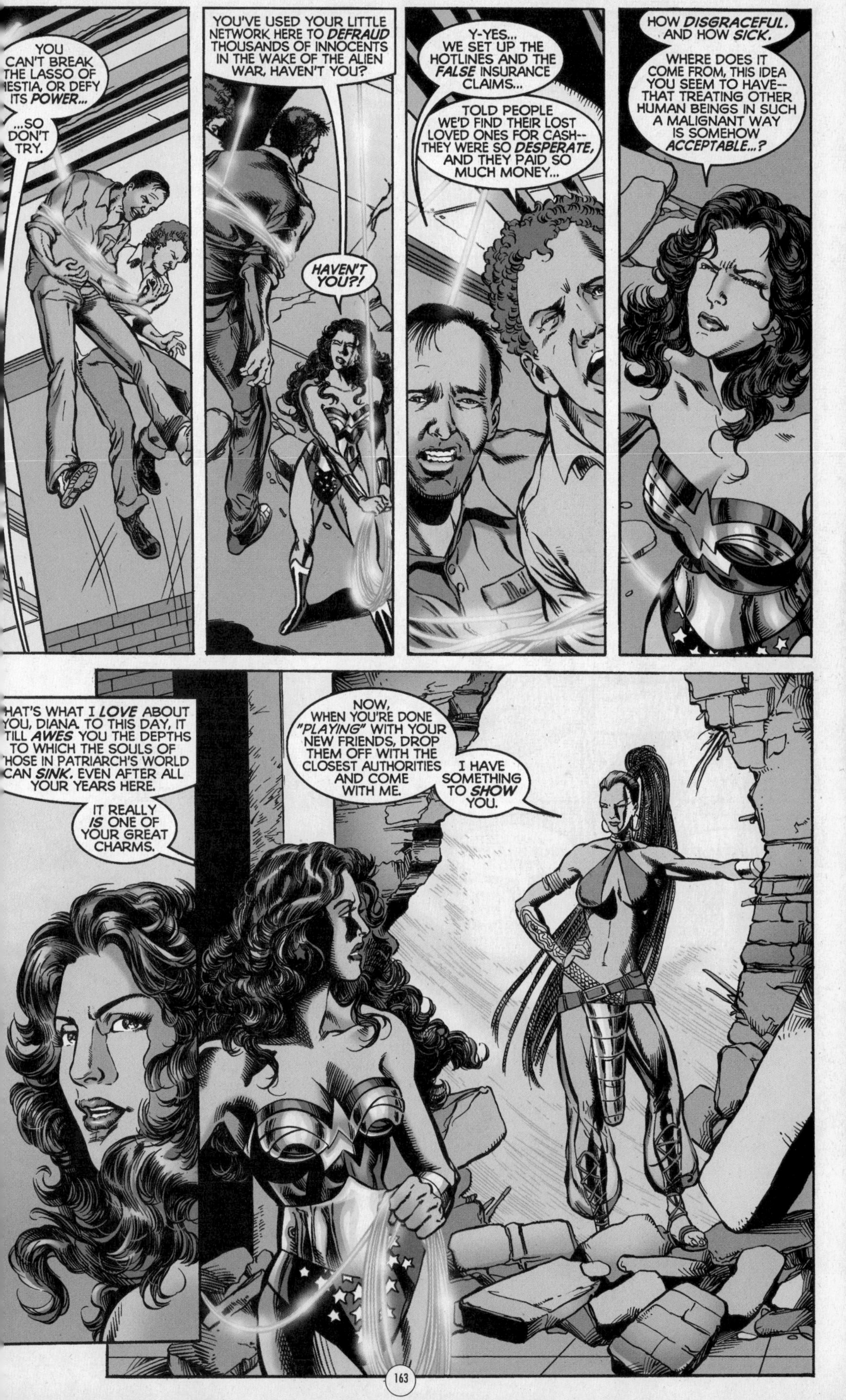
YOU CAN'T BREAK THE LASSO OF HESTIA, OR DEFY ITS POWER...
...SO DON'T TRY.
YOU'VE USED YOUR LITTLE NETWORK HERE TO DEFRAUD THOUSANDS OF INNOCENTS IN THE WAKE OF THE ALIEN WAR, HAVEN'T YOU?
HAVEN'T YOU?!
Y-YES... WE SET UP THE HOTLINES AND THE FALSE INSURANCE CLAIMS...
TOLD PEOPLE WE'D FIND THEIR LOST LOVED ONES FOR CASH-- THEY WERE SO DESPERATE, AND THEY PAID SO MUCH MONEY...
HOW DISGRACEFUL. AND HOW SICK.
WHERE DOES IT COME FROM, THIS IDEA YOU SEEM TO HAVE-- THAT TREATING OTHER HUMAN BEINGS IN SUCH A MALIGNANT WAY IS SOMEHOW ACCEPTABLE...?
HAT'S WHAT I LOVE ABOUT YOU, DIANA. TO THIS DAY, IT TILL AWES YOU THE DEPTHS TO WHICH THE SOULS OF HOSE IN PATRIARCH'S WORLD CAN SINK. EVEN AFTER ALL YOUR YEARS HERE.
IT REALLY IS ONE OF YOUR GREAT CHARMS.
NOW, WHEN YOU'RE DONE "PLAYING" WITH YOUR NEW FRIENDS, DROP THEM OFF WITH THE CLOSEST AUTHORITIES AND COME WITH ME.
I HAVE SOMETHING TO SHOW YOU.

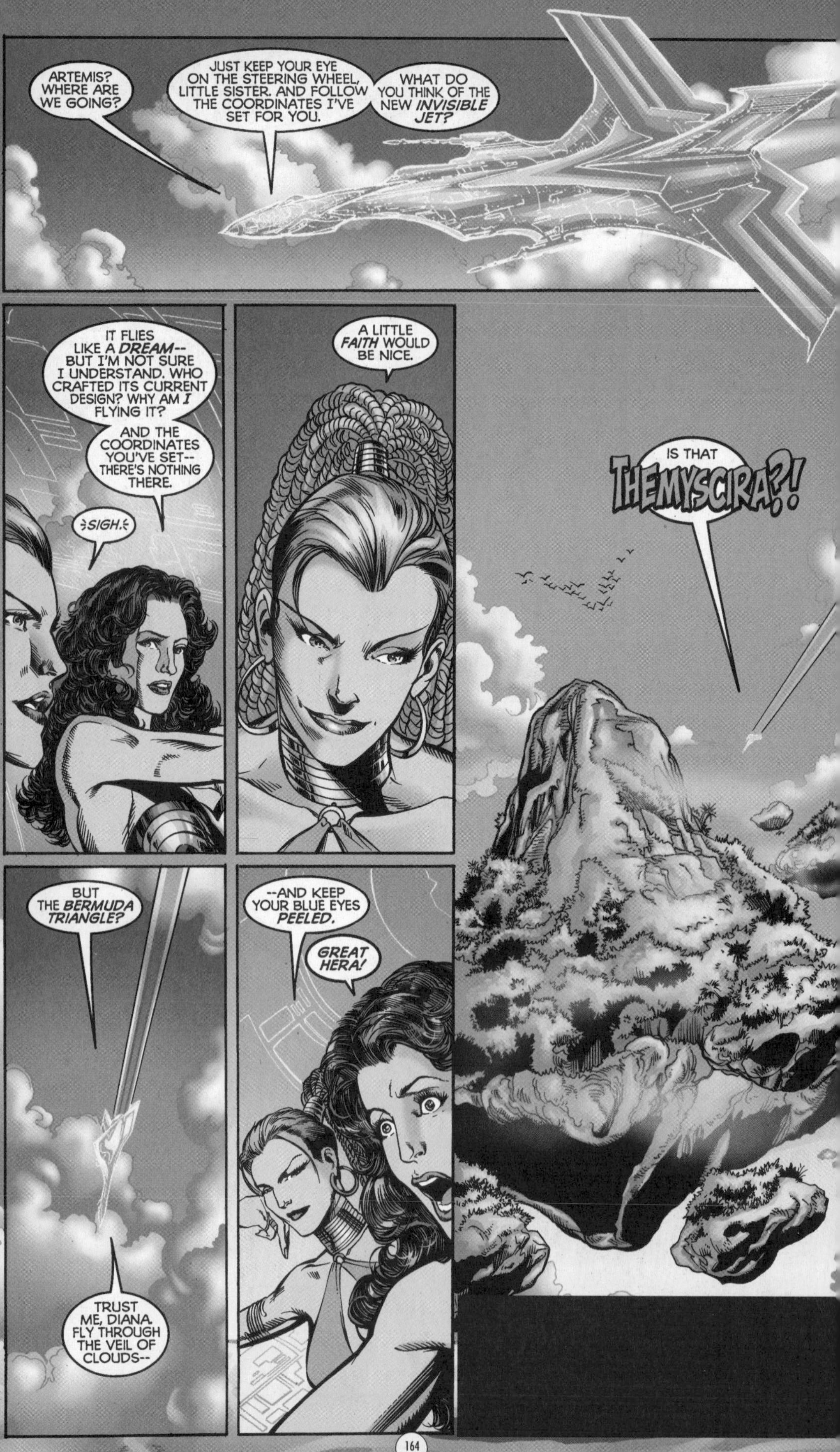
ARTEMIS? WHERE ARE WE GOING?
JUST KEEP YOUR EYE ON THE STEERING WHEEL, LITTLE SISTER. AND FOLLOW THE COORDINATES I'VE SET FOR YOU.
WHAT DO YOU THINK OF THE NEW INVISIBLE JET?
IT FLIES LIKE A DREAM-- BUT I'M NOT SURE I UNDERSTAND. WHO CRAFTED ITS CURRENT DESIGN? WHY AM I FLYING IT?
AND THE COORDINATES YOU'VE SET-- THERE'S NOTHING THERE.
SIGH.
A LITTLE FAITH WOULD BE NICE.
BUT THE BERMUDA TRIANGLE?
TRUST ME, DIANA. FLY THROUGH THE VEIL OF CLOUDS--
--AND KEEP YOUR BLUE EYES PEELED.
GREAT HERA!
IS THAT THEMYSCIRA?!

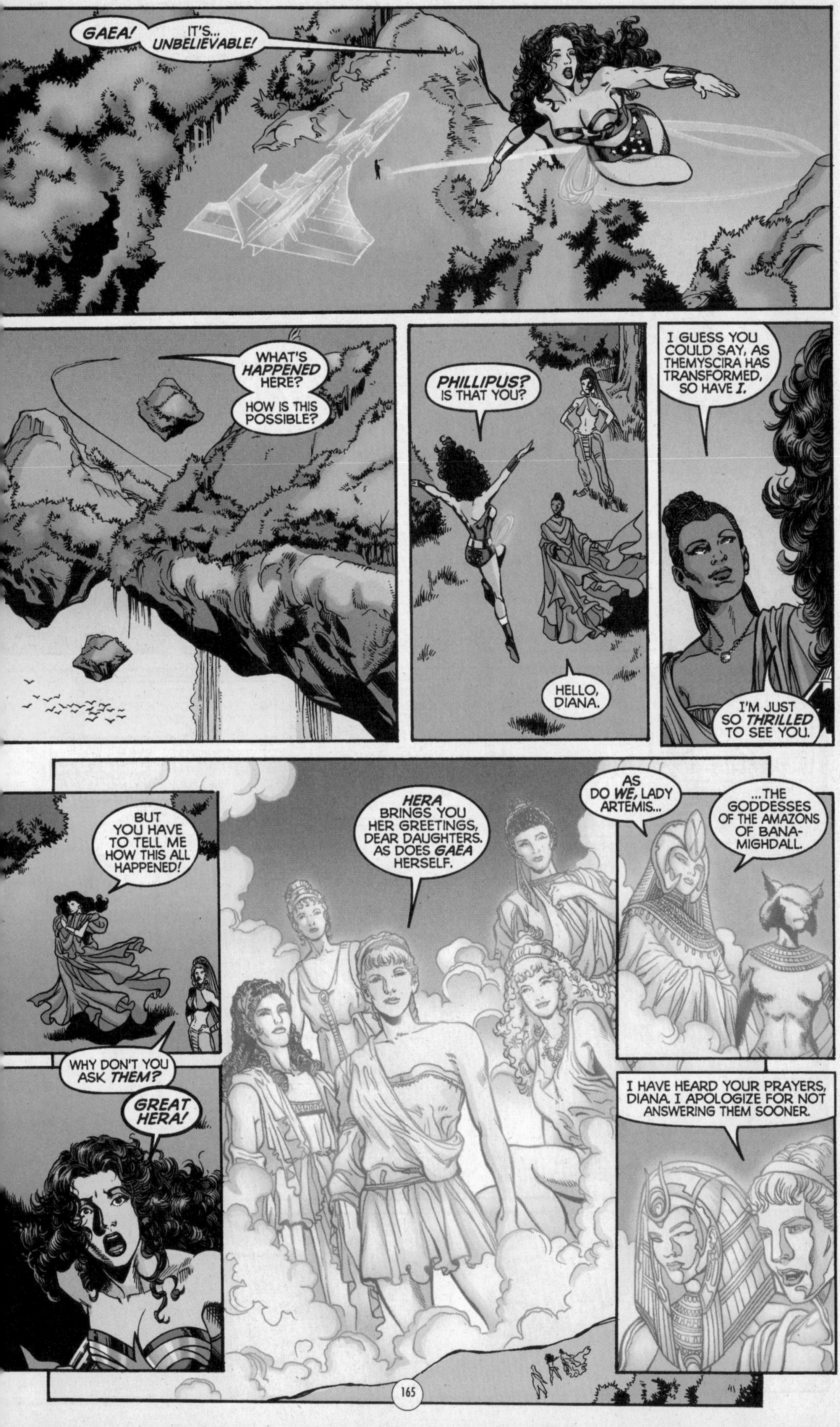
GAEA!
IT'S... UNBELIEVABLE!
WHAT'S HAPPENED HERE?
HOW IS THIS POSSIBLE?
PHILLIPUS? IS THAT YOU?
HELLO, DIANA.
I GUESS YOU COULD SAY, AS THEMYSCIRA HAS TRANSFORMED, SO HAVE I.
I'M JUST SO THRILLED TO SEE YOU.
BUT YOU HAVE TO TELL ME HOW THIS ALL HAPPENED!
WHY DON'T YOU ASK THEM?
GREAT HERA!
HERA BRINGS YOU HER GREETINGS, DEAR DAUGHTERS. AS DOES GAEA HERSELF.
AS DO WE, LADY ARTEMIS...
...THE GODDESSES OF THE AMAZONS OF BANA-MIGHDALL.
I HAVE HEARD YOUR PRAYERS, DIANA. I APOLOGIZE FOR NOT ANSWERING THEM SOONER.

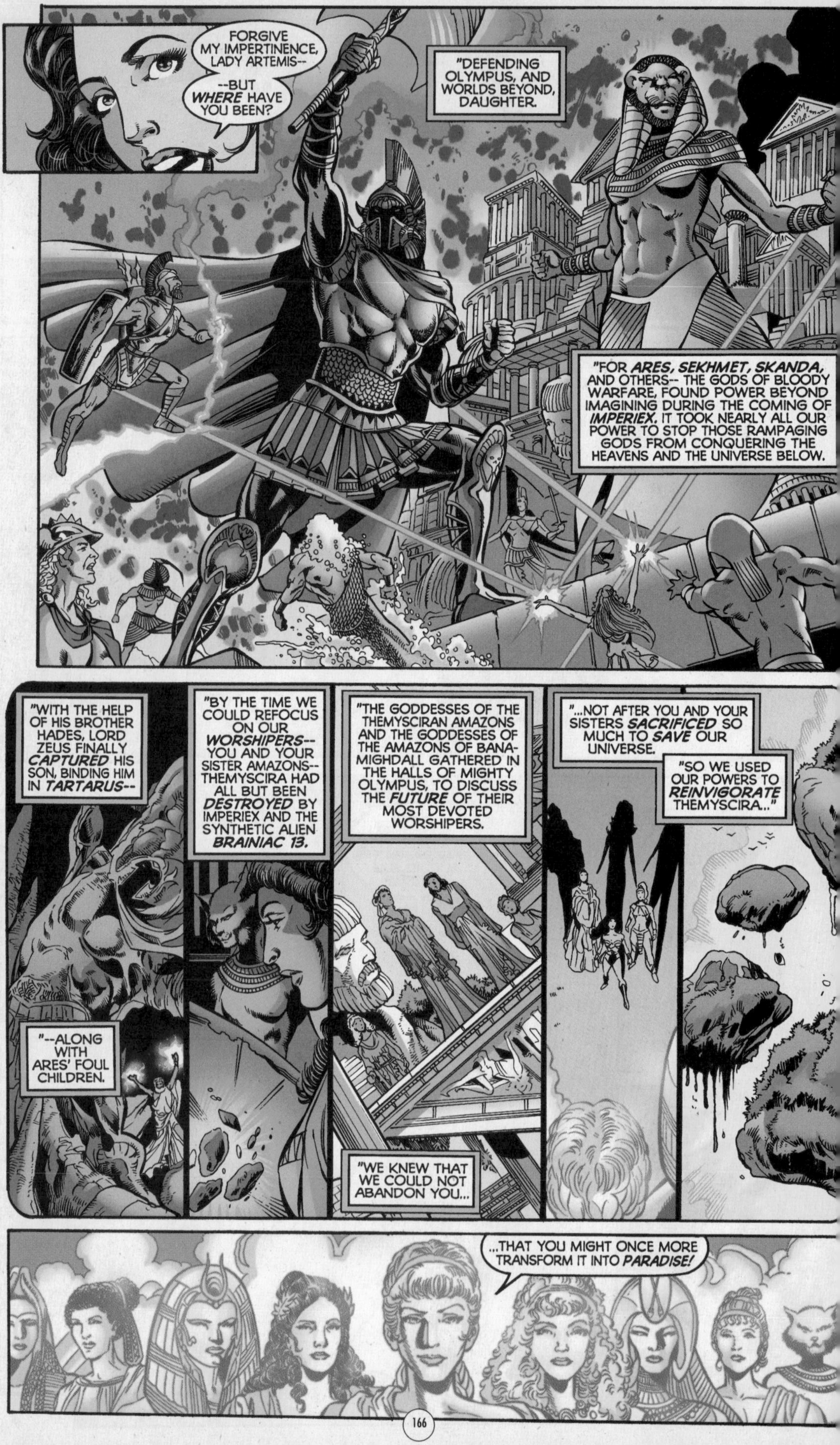

FORGIVE MY IMPERTINENCE, LADY ARTEMIS--
--BUT *WHERE* HAVE YOU BEEN?
"DEFENDING OLYMPUS, AND WORLDS BEYOND, DAUGHTER.
"FOR *ARES, SEKHMET, SKANDA,* AND OTHERS-- THE GODS OF BLOODY WARFARE, FOUND POWER BEYOND IMAGINING DURING THE COMING OF *IMPERIEX.* IT TOOK NEARLY ALL OUR POWER TO STOP THOSE RAMPAGING GODS FROM CONQUERING THE HEAVENS AND THE UNIVERSE BELOW.
"WITH THE HELP OF HIS BROTHER HADES, LORD ZEUS FINALLY *CAPTURED* HIS SON, BINDING HIM IN *TARTARUS*--
"--ALONG WITH ARES' FOUL CHILDREN.
"BY THE TIME WE COULD REFOCUS ON OUR *WORSHIPERS*-- YOU AND YOUR SISTER AMAZONS-- THEMYSCIRA HAD ALL BUT BEEN *DESTROYED* BY IMPERIEX AND THE SYNTHETIC ALIEN *BRAINIAC 13.*
"THE GODDESSES OF THE THEMYSCIRAN AMAZONS AND THE GODDESSES OF THE AMAZONS OF BANA-MIGHDALL GATHERED IN THE HALLS OF MIGHTY OLYMPUS, TO DISCUSS THE *FUTURE* OF THEIR MOST DEVOTED WORSHIPERS.
"WE KNEW THAT WE COULD NOT ABANDON YOU...
"...NOT AFTER YOU AND YOUR SISTERS *SACRIFICED* SO MUCH TO *SAVE* OUR UNIVERSE.
"SO WE USED OUR POWERS TO *REINVIGORATE* THEMYSCIRA..."
...THAT YOU MIGHT ONCE MORE TRANSFORM IT INTO *PARADISE!*

A TRUE **HOME** FOR THE AMAZONS...

WITH A SECOND CHANCE TO FORM ONE MIGHTY **NATION**.

WITH ALL DUE RESPECT, LADY ATHENA -- WILL THIS BE A NATION THE AMAZONS CAN DEVELOP **THEMSELVES**? WITHOUT GODLY LIMITS AS TO DEVELOPMENT OR PROGRESS?

DIANA --!

PHILLIPUS, ARTEMIS -- I HAVE AN **IDEA**. WITH THE GODS' **BLESSING**, I THINK THEMYSCIRA CAN BE TRANSFORMED **UTTERLY**...

...IN A WAY THAT WILL GIVE BACK TO THE AMAZONS FUNCTION... AND **PURPOSE**.

SO?

WHAT DO YOU SAY, GODS OF OLYMPUS AND HELIOPOLIS?

ARE YOU **GAME**?

AND SO, IN THE DAYS AND WEEKS THAT FOLLOW, NEGOTIATIONS BEGIN TO TAKE PLACE BETWEEN THE TWO TRIBES OF AMAZONS AND THEIR GODDESSES...

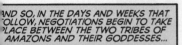

I KNOW IT SOUNDS **TERRIFYING**, BUT MANY OF US HAVE SEEN WHAT PATRIARCH'S WORLD HAS TO OFFER. IT'S NOT SIMPLY WAR AND FILTH...

...BUT SCIENCE AND MEDICINES AND TECH-NOLOGIES MANY OF US HAVE ONLY **DREAMED** ABOUT, FROM THIS WORLD AND A THOUSAND OTHERS.

WE CAN **DO** THIS. WE CAN TAKE THE VERY BEST WE'VE SEEN, AND COMBINE IT WITH THE BEST **WE** HAVE TO OFFER...

AND MAKE A THEMYSCIRA LIKE NONE WE'VE EVER SEEN!

AND SOON, THE INVISIBLE JET GOES FORTH ACROSS THE GLOBE...

...HANDING OUT INVITATIONS TO SOME OF THE GREATEST MINDS AND POWERS ON THE PLANET...

...TO CONTRIBUTE TO THE TRIUMPHANT REBUILDING OF THE AMAZONS' ISLAND HOME.

ARCHITECT HENRI CLAUDE TIBET...

...HARVARD PROFESSOR **JULIA KAPATELIS**, SPIRITUAL DAUGHTER OF THE AMAZON **PYTHIA**...

...**J'ONN J'ONZZ**, THE **MARTIAN MANHUNTER**, AND KIMIYO HOSHI, KNOWN TO SOME AS DOCTOR LIGHT...

DECORATED PILOT AND ENGINEER **STEVE TREVOR**, AFTER WHOSE MOTHER DIANA WAS NAMED...

...ALL COME TOGETHER WITH IDEAS, TECHNOLOGIES, AND POWERS, UNDER THE AMAZON MASTER DESIGNER **KALEEZA FASHED**.

...INCLUDING ONE FINAL BEING:

YOUR *GIFTS* TO ME HAVE ALWAYS BEEN EXTRAORDINARY, *DOME.*

PLEASE -- GRANT THEM TO ME ONCE MORE.

THERE ARE MANY BEYOND THE SHORES OF THEMYSCIRA WHO BELIEVE WE'RE A *DYING* RACE -- PLAGUED BY WAR AND *ANTIQUATED* IDEAS. BEFORE US LIES AN EXTRAORDINARY OPPORTUNITY...

...TO *CHANGE* THAT PERCEPTION.

SO LET'S TAKE IT. FOR THE GLORY OF GAEA.

FOR *ALL* OF US.

USING SECRETS GLEANED FROM THE ALIEN *WONDERDOME'S* TECHNO-BIOLOGY, THE AMAZONS WHO CHOOSE TO STAY ON THEMYSCIRA, ALLIED WITH THEIR OUTWORLD COMPANIONS, BEGIN TO DESIGN THEIR NEW WORLD, INCORPORATING RADICAL ARCHITECTURE, ALIEN SCIENCE, OTHERDIMENSIONAL ENERGIES, AND ANCIENT PHILOSOPHIES ABOUT HARMONY AND NATURE...

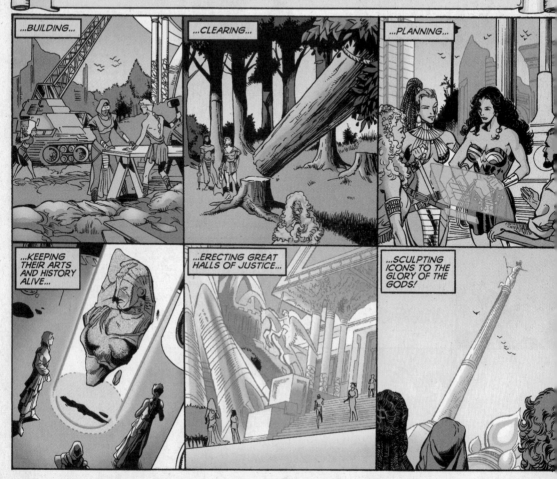

...BUILDING...

...CLEARING...

...PLANNING...

...KEEPING THEIR ARTS AND HISTORY ALIVE...

...ERECTING GREAT HALLS OF JUSTICE...

...SCULPTING ICONS TO THE GLORY OF THE GODS!

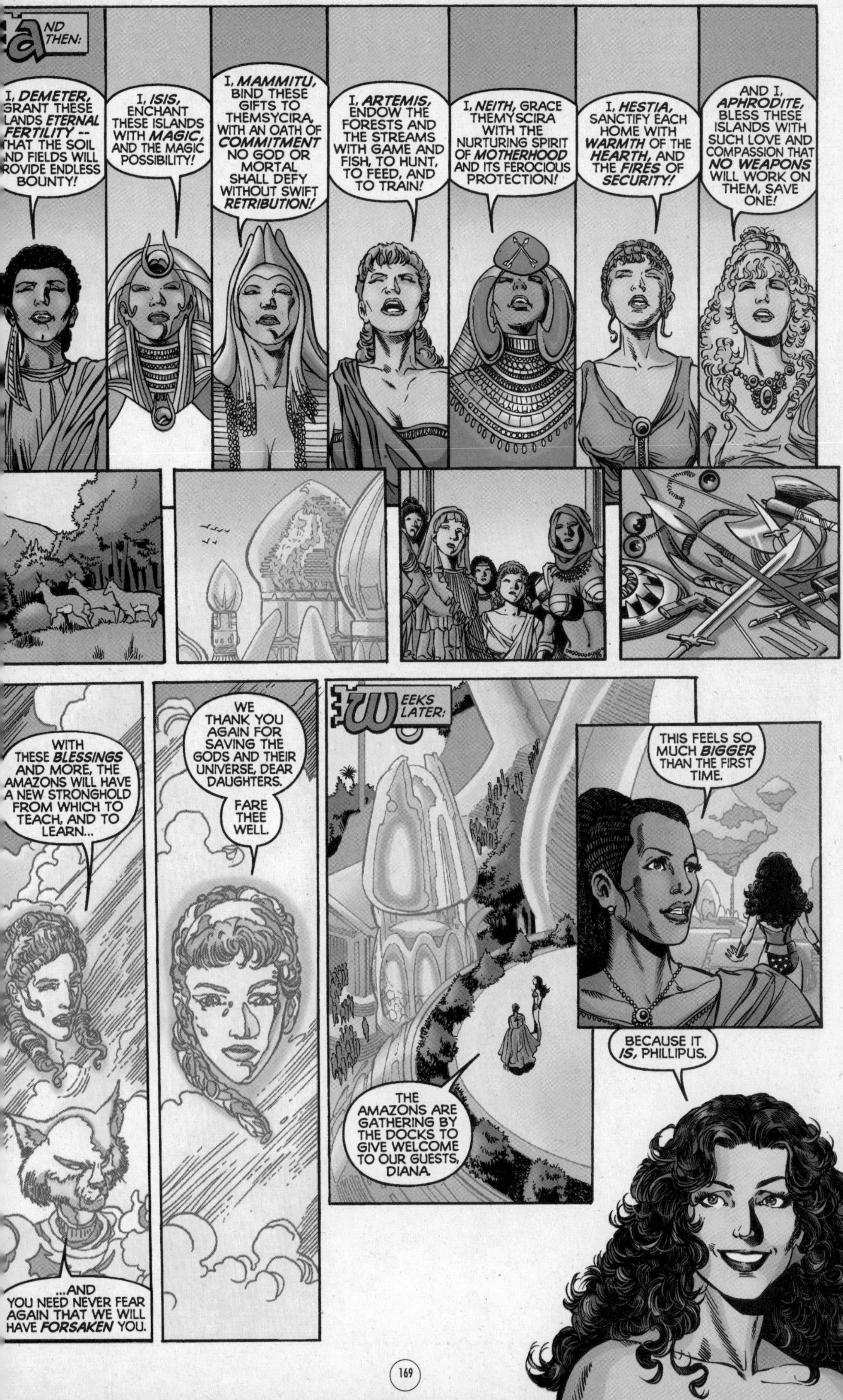
AND THEN:
I, DEMETER, GRANT THESE LANDS ETERNAL FERTILITY -- THAT THE SOIL AND FIELDS WILL PROVIDE ENDLESS BOUNTY!
I, ISIS, ENCHANT THESE ISLANDS WITH MAGIC, AND THE MAGIC POSSIBILITY!
I, MAMMITU, BIND THESE GIFTS TO THEMSYCIRA, WITH AN OATH OF COMMITMENT NO GOD OR MORTAL SHALL DEFY WITHOUT SWIFT RETRIBUTION!
I, ARTEMIS, ENDOW THE FORESTS AND THE STREAMS WITH GAME AND FISH, TO HUNT, TO FEED, AND TO TRAIN!
I, NEITH, GRACE THEMYSCIRA WITH THE NURTURING SPIRIT OF MOTHERHOOD AND ITS FEROCIOUS PROTECTION!
I, HESTIA, SANCTIFY EACH HOME WITH WARMTH OF THE HEARTH, AND THE FIRES OF SECURITY!
AND I, APHRODITE, BLESS THESE ISLANDS WITH SUCH LOVE AND COMPASSION THAT NO WEAPONS WILL WORK ON THEM, SAVE ONE!
WITH THESE BLESSINGS AND MORE, THE AMAZONS WILL HAVE A NEW STRONGHOLD FROM WHICH TO TEACH, AND TO LEARN...
...AND YOU NEED NEVER FEAR AGAIN THAT WE WILL HAVE FORSAKEN YOU.
WE THANK YOU AGAIN FOR SAVING THE GODS AND THEIR UNIVERSE, DEAR DAUGHTERS.
FARE THEE WELL.
WEEKS LATER:
THE AMAZONS ARE GATHERING BY THE DOCKS TO GIVE WELCOME TO OUR GUESTS, DIANA.
THIS FEELS SO MUCH BIGGER THAN THE FIRST TIME.
BECAUSE IT IS, PHILLIPUS.

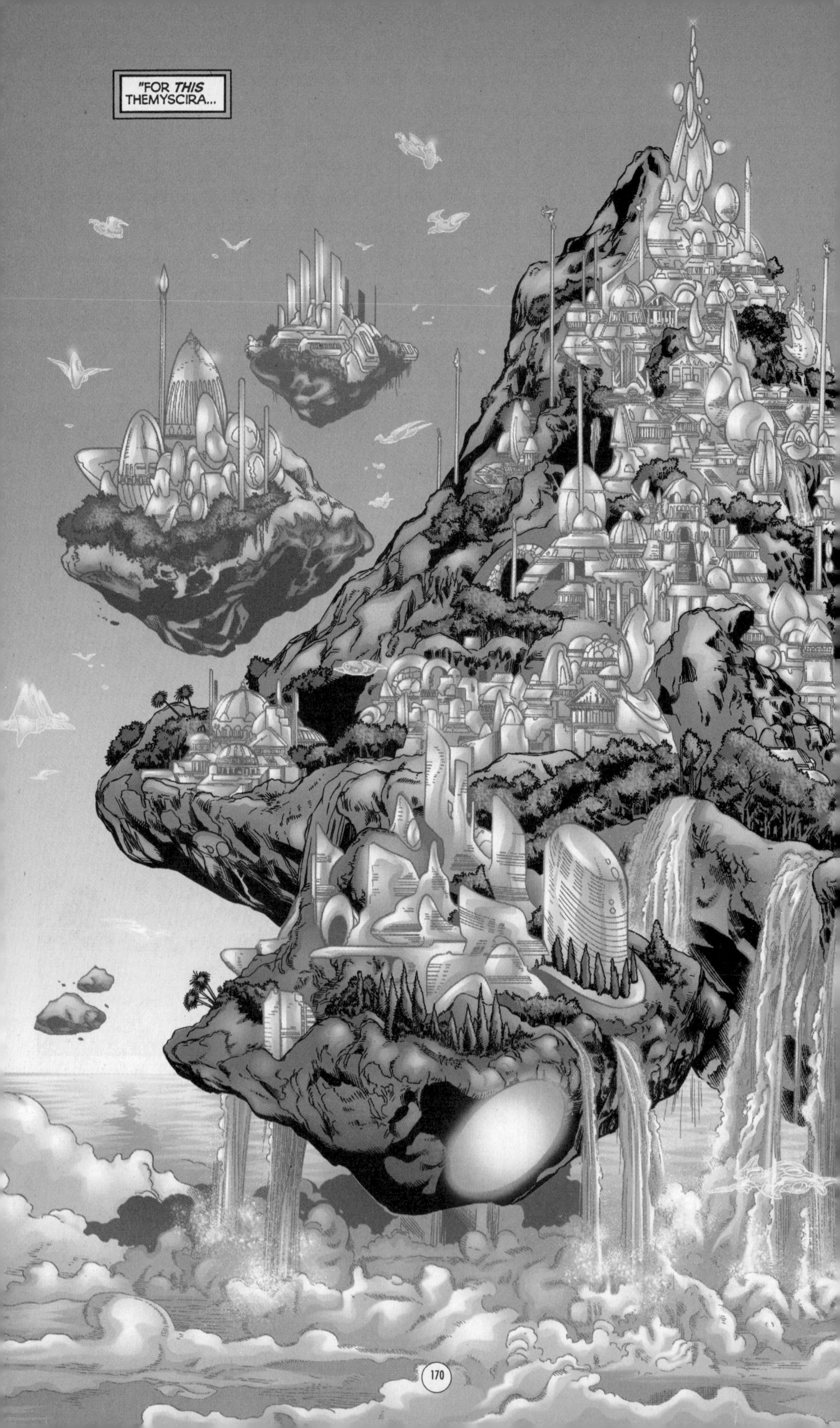
"FOR *THIS* THEMYSCIRA...

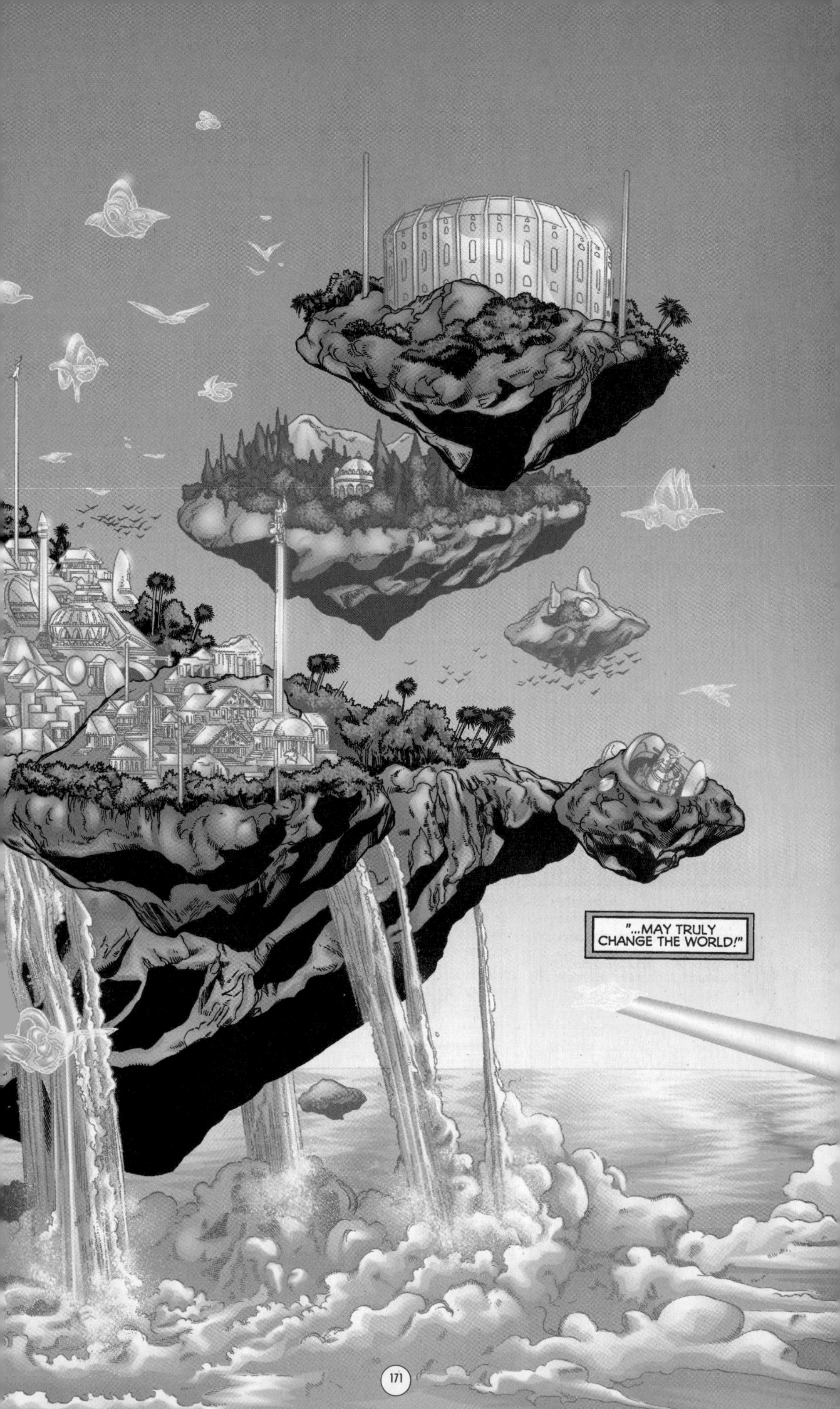
"...MAY TRULY CHANGE THE WORLD!"

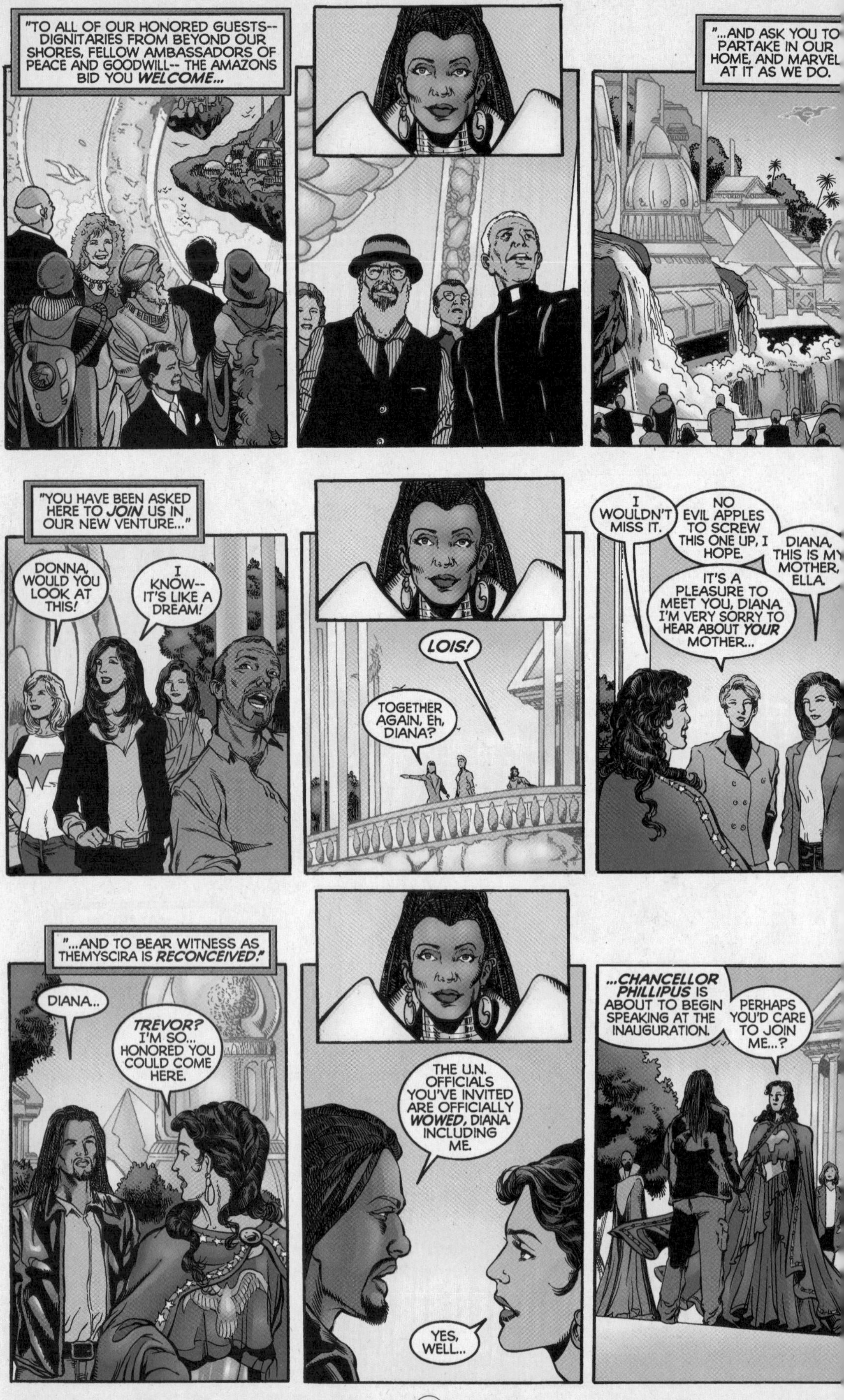
"TO ALL OF OUR HONORED GUESTS-- DIGNITARIES FROM BEYOND OUR SHORES, FELLOW AMBASSADORS OF PEACE AND GOODWILL-- THE AMAZONS BID YOU WELCOME...
"...AND ASK YOU TO PARTAKE IN OUR HOME, AND MARVEL AT IT AS WE DO.
"YOU HAVE BEEN ASKED HERE TO JOIN US IN OUR NEW VENTURE..."
DONNA, WOULD YOU LOOK AT THIS!
I KNOW-- IT'S LIKE A DREAM!
LOIS!
TOGETHER AGAIN, Eh, DIANA?
I WOULDN'T MISS IT.
NO EVIL APPLES TO SCREW THIS ONE UP, I HOPE.
DIANA, THIS IS MY MOTHER, ELLA.
IT'S A PLEASURE TO MEET YOU, DIANA. I'M VERY SORRY TO HEAR ABOUT YOUR MOTHER...
"...AND TO BEAR WITNESS AS THEMYSCIRA IS RECONCEIVED."
DIANA...
TREVOR? I'M SO... HONORED YOU COULD COME HERE.
THE U.N. OFFICIALS YOU'VE INVITED ARE OFFICIALLY WOWED, DIANA. INCLUDING ME.
YES, WELL...
...CHANCELLOR PHILLIPUS IS ABOUT TO BEGIN SPEAKING AT THE INAUGURATION.
PERHAPS YOU'D CARE TO JOIN ME...?

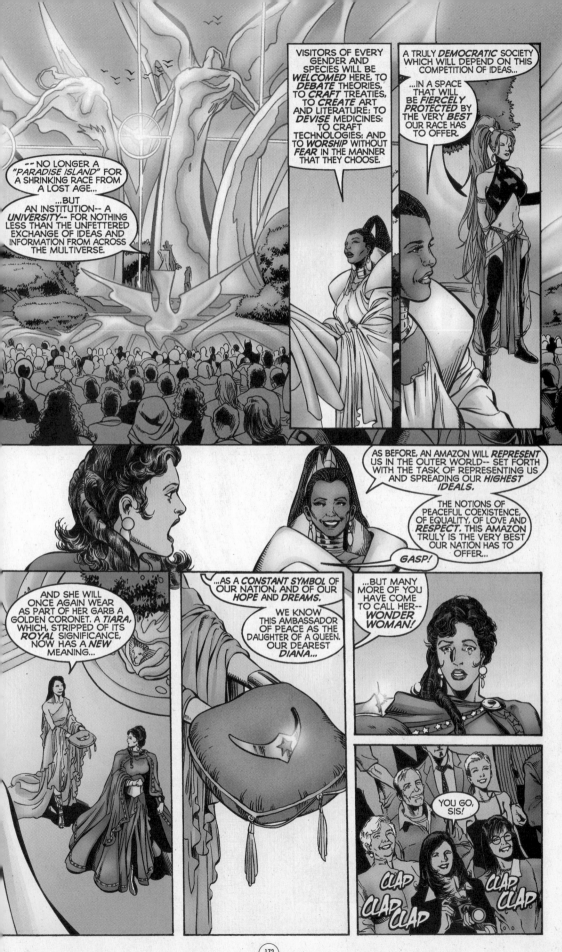

-- NO LONGER A *"PARADISE ISLAND"* FOR A SHRINKING RACE FROM A LOST AGE...

...BUT AN *INSTITUTION*-- A *UNIVERSITY*-- FOR NOTHING LESS THAN THE UNFETTERED EXCHANGE OF IDEAS AND INFORMATION FROM ACROSS THE MULTIVERSE.

VISITORS OF EVERY GENDER AND SPECIES WILL BE *WELCOMED* HERE, TO *DEBATE* THEORIES, TO *CRAFT* TREATIES, TO *CREATE* ART AND LITERATURE; TO *DEVISE* MEDICINES; TO CRAFT TECHNOLOGIES; AND TO *WORSHIP* WITHOUT *FEAR* IN THE MANNER THAT THEY CHOOSE.

A TRULY *DEMOCRATIC* SOCIETY WHICH WILL DEPEND ON THIS COMPETITION OF IDEAS...

...IN A SPACE THAT WILL BE *FIERCELY PROTECTED* BY THE VERY *BEST* OUR RACE HAS TO OFFER.

AS BEFORE, AN AMAZON WILL *REPRESENT* US IN THE OUTER WORLD-- SET FORTH WITH THE TASK OF REPRESENTING US AND SPREADING OUR *HIGHEST IDEALS*.

THE NOTIONS OF PEACEFUL COEXISTENCE, OF EQUALITY, OF LOVE AND *RESPECT*. THIS AMAZON TRULY IS THE VERY *BEST* OUR NATION HAS TO OFFER...

GASP!

AND SHE WILL ONCE AGAIN WEAR AS PART OF HER GARB A *GOLDEN CORONET*. A *TIARA*, WHICH, STRIPPED OF ITS *ROYAL* SIGNIFICANCE, NOW HAS A *NEW* MEANING...

...AS A *CONSTANT SYMBOL* OF OUR NATION, AND OF OUR *HOPE* AND *DREAMS*.

WE KNOW THIS AMBASSADOR OF PEACE AS THE DAUGHTER OF A QUEEN. OUR *DEAREST DIANA*...

...BUT MANY MORE OF YOU HAVE COME TO CALL HER-- *WONDER WOMAN!*

YOU GO, SIS!

CLAP CLAP CLAP *CLAP CLAP*

173

THE TEMPLE OF HIPPOLYTA, ON THE ISLE OF REMEMBRANCE:

THERE ARE *MANY* WAYS TO FIGHT A WAR, DIANA.

AFTER ALL THE *DEATH* I'VE SEEN, THOUGH -- I'M NOT SURE I *EVER* NEED TO WIELD MY SWORD AGAINST ANOTHER.

SO IS IT TRUE, *CHANCELLOR PHILLIPUS?* YOU'VE GIVEN UP YOUR ROLE AS A SOLDIER? AS A *WARRIOR?*

DON'T LET *MOTHER* HEAR YOU SAY THAT. YOU WERE HER *GREATEST GENERAL.*

OH, I WON'T LET HER GO *SOFT* ON US, LITTLE SISTER. I PROMISE YOU THAT. AND DON'T YOU GO SOFT ON US, EITHER.

WE *NEED* YOU OUT THERE IN PATRIARCH'S WORLD AS OUR REPRESENTATIVE. PYTHIA KNOWS *I* WAS NO GOOD AT IT. EVEN YOUR *MOTHER* KNEW IT --

-- AND YES, IT TOOK AMAZONS A LITTLE TIME TO REALIZE IT. BU THINGS WERE SO RA AFTER THE CIVIL WAR...

WE MADE A MISTAKE IN REJECTIN YOU AND YOUR HEL WE'RE TRYING TO *RECTI* THAT NOW.

SO DON'T TAKE TOO LONG DECIDING TO PUT THAT *TIARA* BACK ON YOUR HEAD. THERE'S A WORLD OUT THERE THAT NEEDS YOU.

YOU AND THAT DAMNED *OPTIMISM* OF YOURS.

DID YOU HEAR THAT, MOTHER?

A WORLD THAT NEEDS *ME,* A BEACON OF CIVILITY. A PERFECT EXAMPLE OF HUMANITY.

IF ONLY THEY KNEW HOW *WRONG* THEY WERE.

I NEED YOU SO MUCH, MOTHER.

I *NEED* YOUR HELP.

I NEED TO TELL YOU HOW *SORRY* I AM...

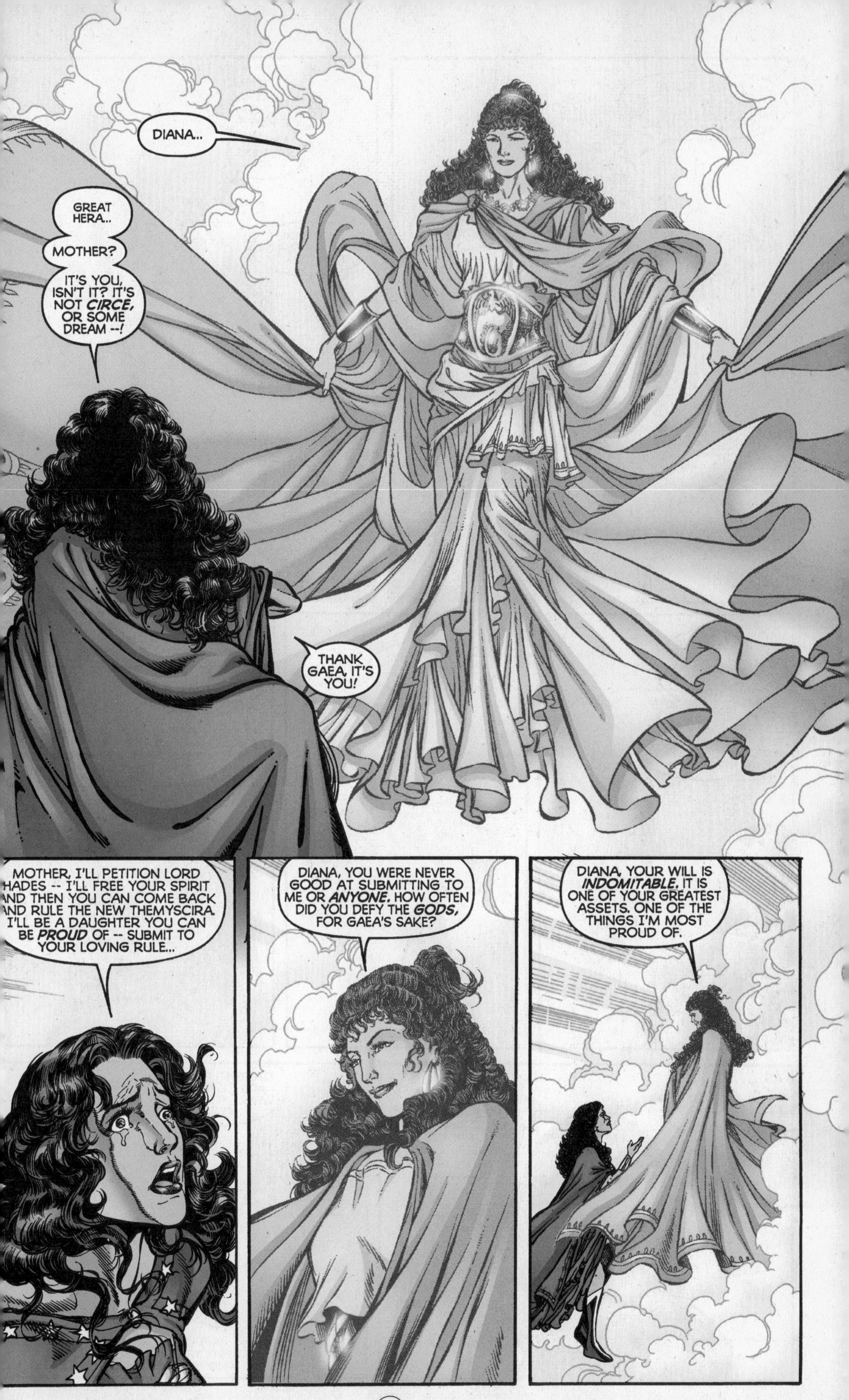
DIANA...
GREAT HERA...
MOTHER?
IT'S YOU, ISN'T IT? IT'S NOT CIRCE, OR SOME DREAM --!
THANK GAEA, IT'S YOU!
MOTHER, I'LL PETITION LORD HADES -- I'LL FREE YOUR SPIRIT AND THEN YOU CAN COME BACK AND RULE THE NEW THEMYSCIRA. I'LL BE A DAUGHTER YOU CAN BE PROUD OF -- SUBMIT TO YOUR LOVING RULE...
DIANA, YOU WERE NEVER GOOD AT SUBMITTING TO ME OR ANYONE. HOW OFTEN DID YOU DEFY THE GODS, FOR GAEA'S SAKE?
DIANA, YOUR WILL IS INDOMITABLE. IT IS ONE OF YOUR GREATEST ASSETS. ONE OF THE THINGS I'M MOST PROUD OF.

INDEED. SOME WOULD SAY IT'S THE STRONGEST TRAIT YOU INHERITED FROM ME.

AUNT ANTIOPE?!

HEY, WHAT AM I, CHOPPED LIVER? NICE TO SEE YOU, DI.

ATHENA HELP ME. DIANA TREVOR--?!

WELL, WE CERTAINLY DO LOOK ALIKE, DON'T WE? HIPPOLYTA HAD TOLD ME AS MUCH, BUT TO SEE IT IN PERSON...

IT'S AN HONOR TO FINALLY MEET YOU, NIECE.

HEY, KIDDO-- HOW YOU DOING? YOU'VE BEEN PUTTING MY NAME TO GOOD USE, EH?

YOUR MOM AND I HA[VE] BEEN PLAYING A LOT [OF] CATCH-UP. YOU KNOW[?] COULDN'T TELL YOU TH[IS] BEFORE, BUT IT WA[S] YOUR MOM WHO INSPIRED ME TO B[E] A PILOT...

I MISS YOU SO MUCH.

IF I CAN'T FREE YOU, THEN I'LL COME WITH YOU. I WANT SO BADLY TO BE WITH YOU.

DAUGHTER, YOU ARE EXACTLY WHERE YOU NEED TO BE.

YOU HAVE A SACRED MISSION. IT'S WHAT YOU WERE BORN TO DO, AND YOU'RE NOT DONE YET.

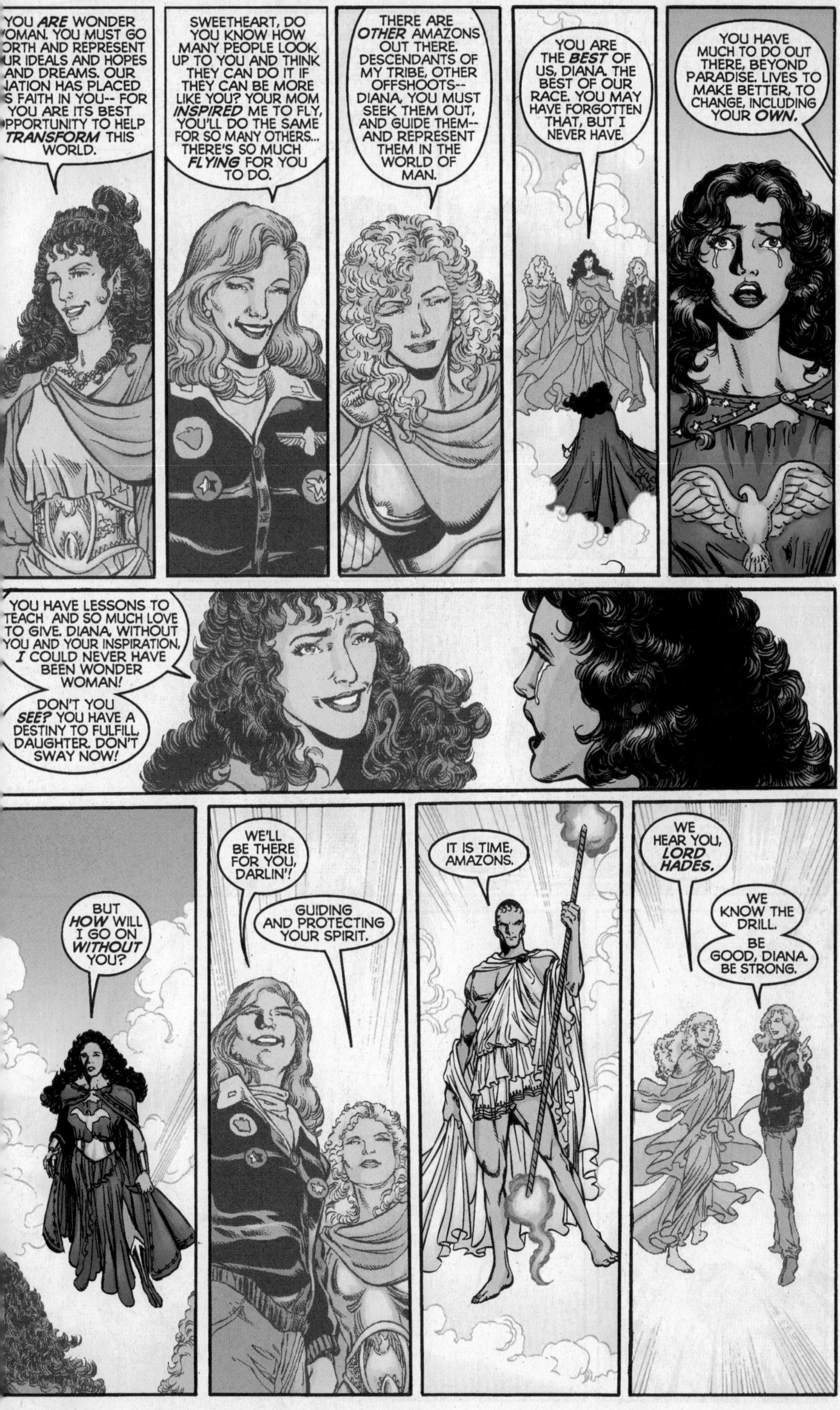
YOU ARE WONDER WOMAN. YOU MUST GO ORTH AND REPRESENT UR IDEALS AND HOPES AND DREAMS. OUR NATION HAS PLACED S FAITH IN YOU-- FOR YOU ARE ITS BEST PPORTUNITY TO HELP TRANSFORM THIS WORLD.
SWEETHEART, DO YOU KNOW HOW MANY PEOPLE LOOK UP TO YOU AND THINK THEY CAN DO IT IF THEY CAN BE MORE LIKE YOU? YOUR MOM INSPIRED ME TO FLY, YOU'LL DO THE SAME FOR SO MANY OTHERS... THERE'S SO MUCH FLYING FOR YOU TO DO.
THERE ARE OTHER AMAZONS OUT THERE. DESCENDANTS OF MY TRIBE, OTHER OFFSHOOTS-- DIANA, YOU MUST SEEK THEM OUT, AND GUIDE THEM-- AND REPRESENT THEM IN THE WORLD OF MAN.
YOU ARE THE BEST OF US, DIANA. THE BEST OF OUR RACE. YOU MAY HAVE FORGOTTEN THAT, BUT I NEVER HAVE.
YOU HAVE MUCH TO DO OUT THERE, BEYOND PARADISE. LIVES TO MAKE BETTER, TO CHANGE, INCLUDING YOUR OWN.
YOU HAVE LESSONS TO TEACH AND SO MUCH LOVE TO GIVE. DIANA, WITHOUT YOU AND YOUR INSPIRATION, I COULD NEVER HAVE BEEN WONDER WOMAN!
DON'T YOU SEE? YOU HAVE A DESTINY TO FULFILL, DAUGHTER. DON'T SWAY NOW!
BUT HOW WILL I GO ON WITHOUT YOU?
WE'LL BE THERE FOR YOU, DARLIN'!
GUIDING AND PROTECTING YOUR SPIRIT.
IT IS TIME, AMAZONS.
WE HEAR YOU, LORD HADES.
WE KNOW THE DRILL.
BE GOOD, DIANA. BE STRONG.

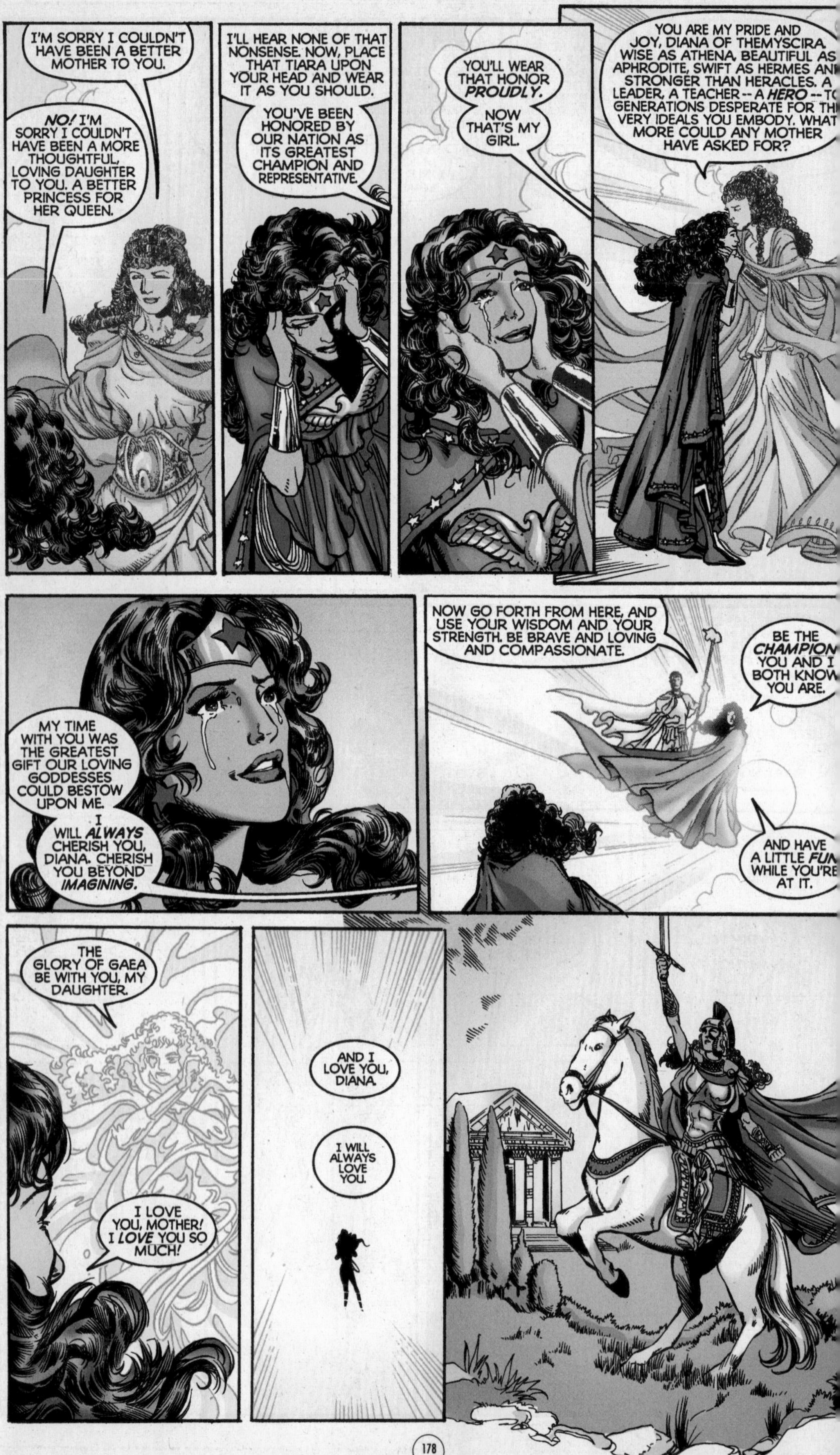

I'M SORRY I COULDN'T HAVE BEEN A BETTER MOTHER TO YOU.
NO! I'M SORRY I COULDN'T HAVE BEEN A MORE THOUGHTFUL, LOVING DAUGHTER TO YOU. A BETTER PRINCESS FOR HER QUEEN.
I'LL HEAR NONE OF THAT NONSENSE. NOW, PLACE THAT TIARA UPON YOUR HEAD AND WEAR IT AS YOU SHOULD.
YOU'VE BEEN HONORED BY OUR NATION AS ITS GREATEST CHAMPION AND REPRESENTATIVE.
YOU'LL WEAR THAT HONOR PROUDLY.
NOW THAT'S MY GIRL.
YOU ARE MY PRIDE AND JOY, DIANA OF THEMYSCIRA. WISE AS ATHENA, BEAUTIFUL AS APHRODITE, SWIFT AS HERMES AN STRONGER THAN HERACLES. A LEADER, A TEACHER -- A HERO -- T GENERATIONS DESPERATE FOR TH VERY IDEALS YOU EMBODY. WHAT MORE COULD ANY MOTHER HAVE ASKED FOR?
MY TIME WITH YOU WAS THE GREATEST GIFT OUR LOVING GODDESSES COULD BESTOW UPON ME.
I WILL ALWAYS CHERISH YOU, DIANA. CHERISH YOU BEYOND IMAGINING.
NOW GO FORTH FROM HERE, AND USE YOUR WISDOM AND YOUR STRENGTH. BE BRAVE AND LOVING AND COMPASSIONATE.
BE THE CHAMPION YOU AND I BOTH KNOW YOU ARE.
AND HAVE A LITTLE FUN WHILE YOU'RE AT IT.
THE GLORY OF GAEA BE WITH YOU, MY DAUGHTER.
I LOVE YOU, MOTHER! I LOVE YOU SO MUCH!
AND I LOVE YOU, DIANA.
I WILL ALWAYS LOVE YOU.

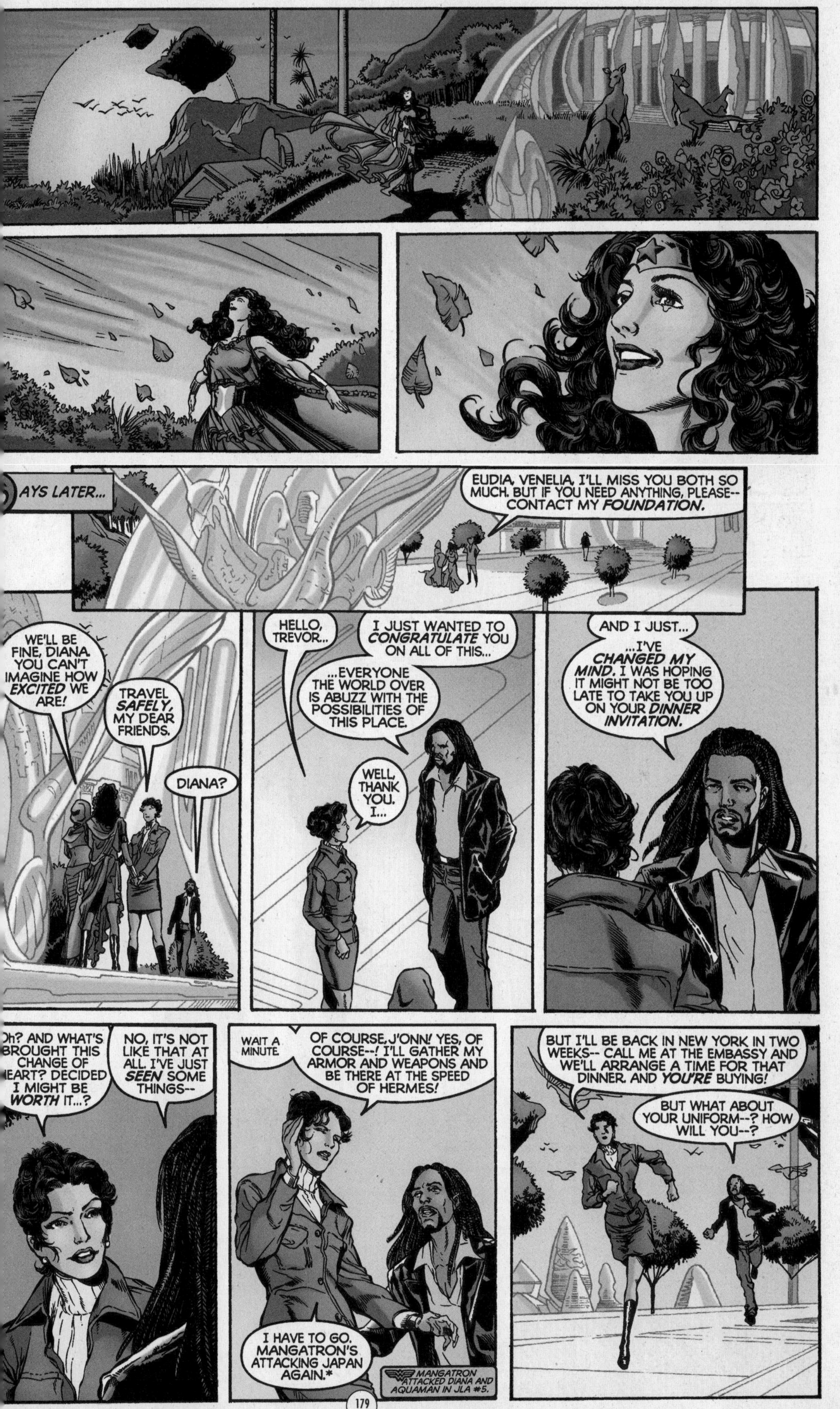
AYS LATER...
EUDIA, VENELIA, I'LL MISS YOU BOTH SO MUCH. BUT IF YOU NEED ANYTHING, PLEASE-- CONTACT MY FOUNDATION.
WE'LL BE FINE, DIANA. YOU CAN'T IMAGINE HOW EXCITED WE ARE!
TRAVEL SAFELY, MY DEAR FRIENDS.
DIANA?
HELLO, TREVOR...
I JUST WANTED TO CONGRATULATE YOU ON ALL OF THIS...
...EVERYONE THE WORLD OVER IS ABUZZ WITH THE POSSIBILITIES OF THIS PLACE.
WELL, THANK YOU. I...
AND I JUST...
...I'VE CHANGED MY MIND. I WAS HOPING IT MIGHT NOT BE TOO LATE TO TAKE YOU UP ON YOUR DINNER INVITATION.
Oh? AND WHAT'S BROUGHT THIS CHANGE OF HEART? DECIDED I MIGHT BE WORTH IT...?
NO, IT'S NOT LIKE THAT AT ALL. I'VE JUST SEEN SOME THINGS--
WAIT A MINUTE.
OF COURSE, J'ONN! YES, OF COURSE--! I'LL GATHER MY ARMOR AND WEAPONS AND BE THERE AT THE SPEED OF HERMES!
I HAVE TO GO. MANGATRON'S ATTACKING JAPAN AGAIN.*
*MANGATRON ATTACKED DIANA AND AQUAMAN IN JLA #5.
BUT I'LL BE BACK IN NEW YORK IN TWO WEEKS-- CALL ME AT THE EMBASSY AND WE'LL ARRANGE A TIME FOR THAT DINNER. AND YOU'RE BUYING!
BUT WHAT ABOUT YOUR UNIFORM--? HOW WILL YOU--?

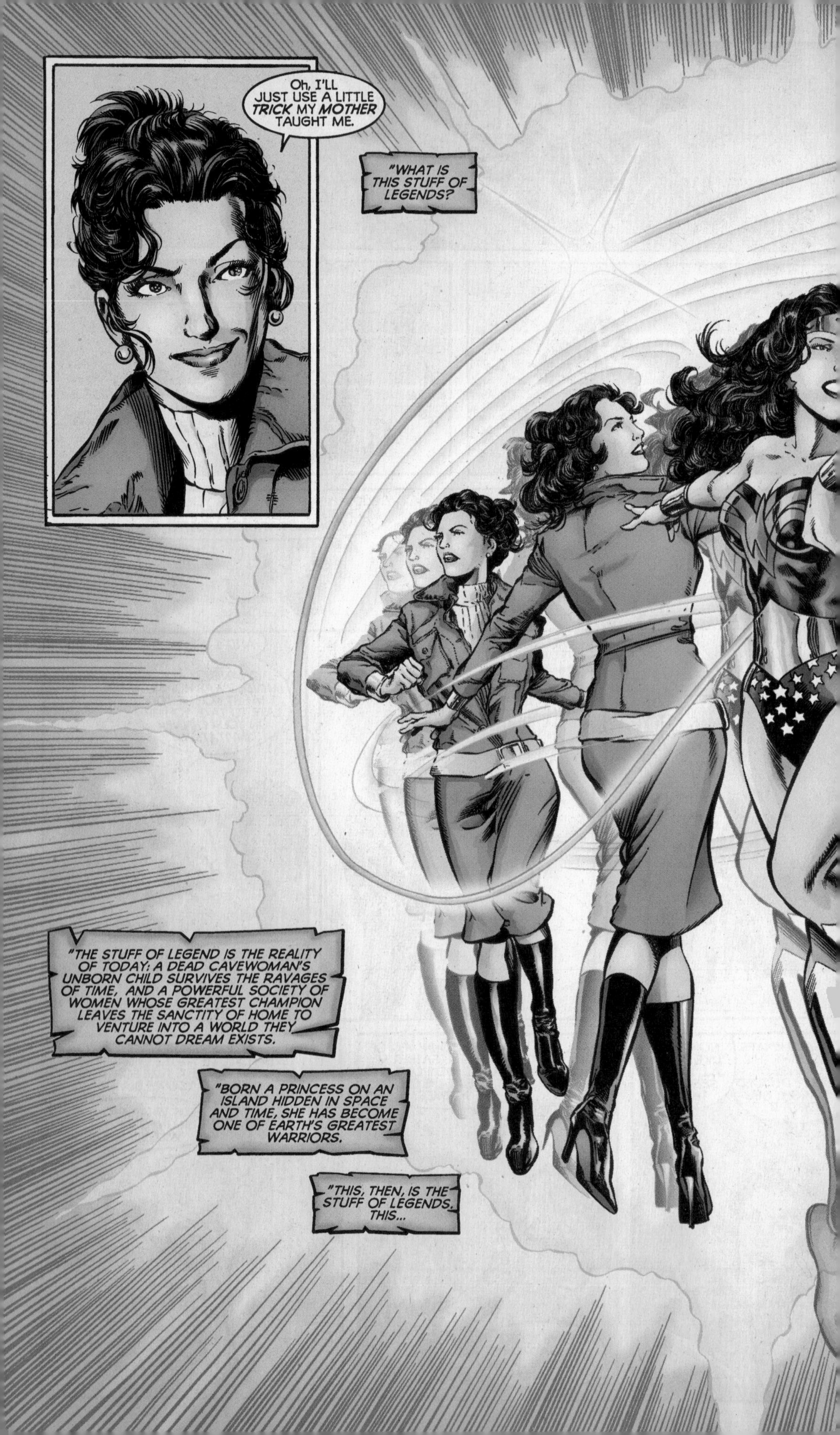

Oh, I'LL JUST USE A LITTLE *TRICK* MY *MOTHER* TAUGHT ME.
"WHAT IS THIS STUFF OF LEGENDS?
"THE STUFF OF LEGEND IS THE REALITY OF TODAY: A DEAD CAVEWOMAN'S UNBORN CHILD SURVIVES THE RAVAGES OF TIME, AND A POWERFUL SOCIETY OF WOMEN WHOSE GREATEST CHAMPION LEAVES THE SANCTITY OF HOME TO VENTURE INTO A WORLD THEY CANNOT DREAM EXISTS.
"BORN A PRINCESS ON AN ISLAND HIDDEN IN SPACE AND TIME, SHE HAS BECOME ONE OF EARTH'S GREATEST WARRIORS.
"THIS, THEN, IS THE STUFF OF LEGENDS. THIS...

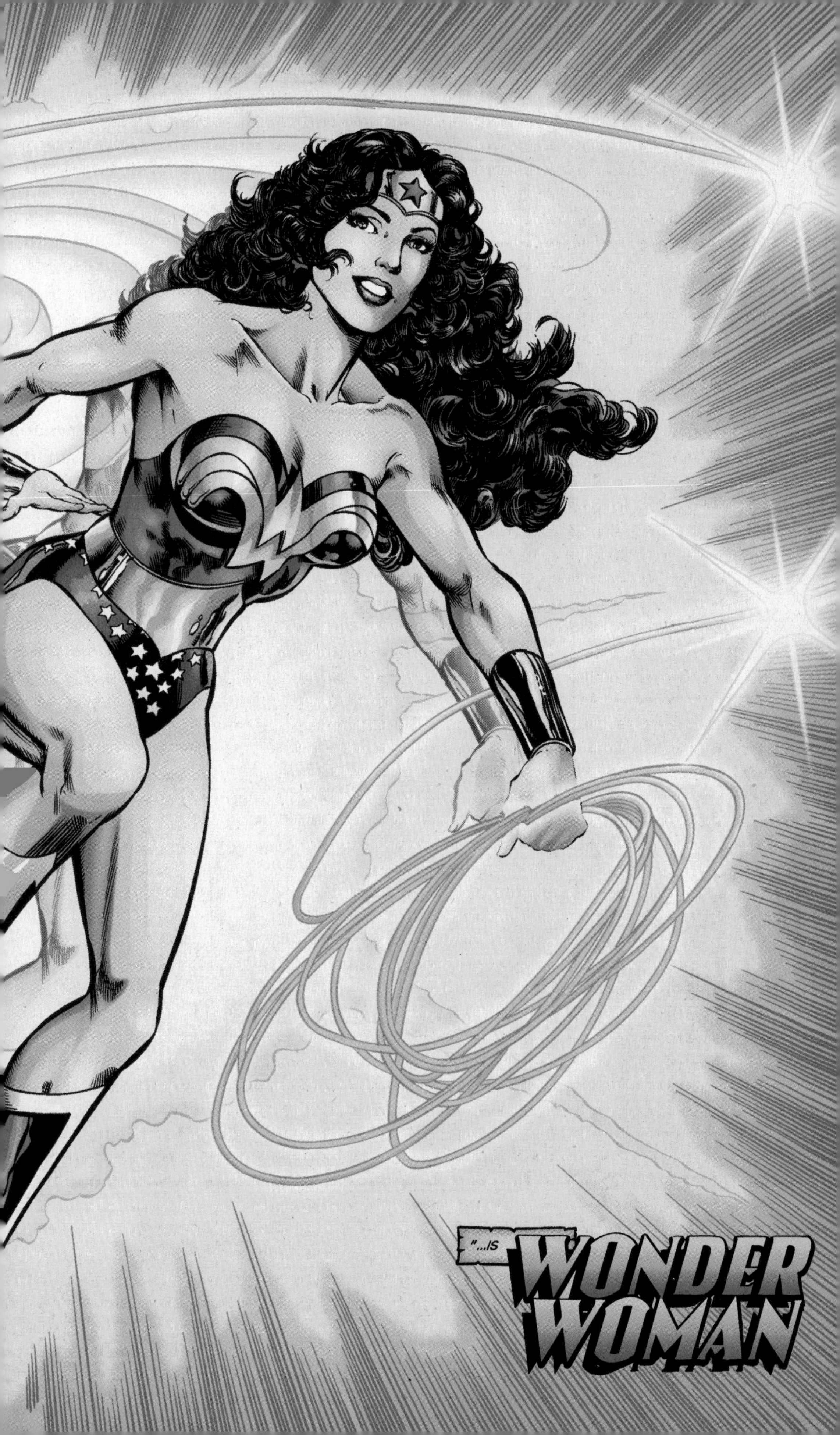
"...IS
WONDER WOMAN

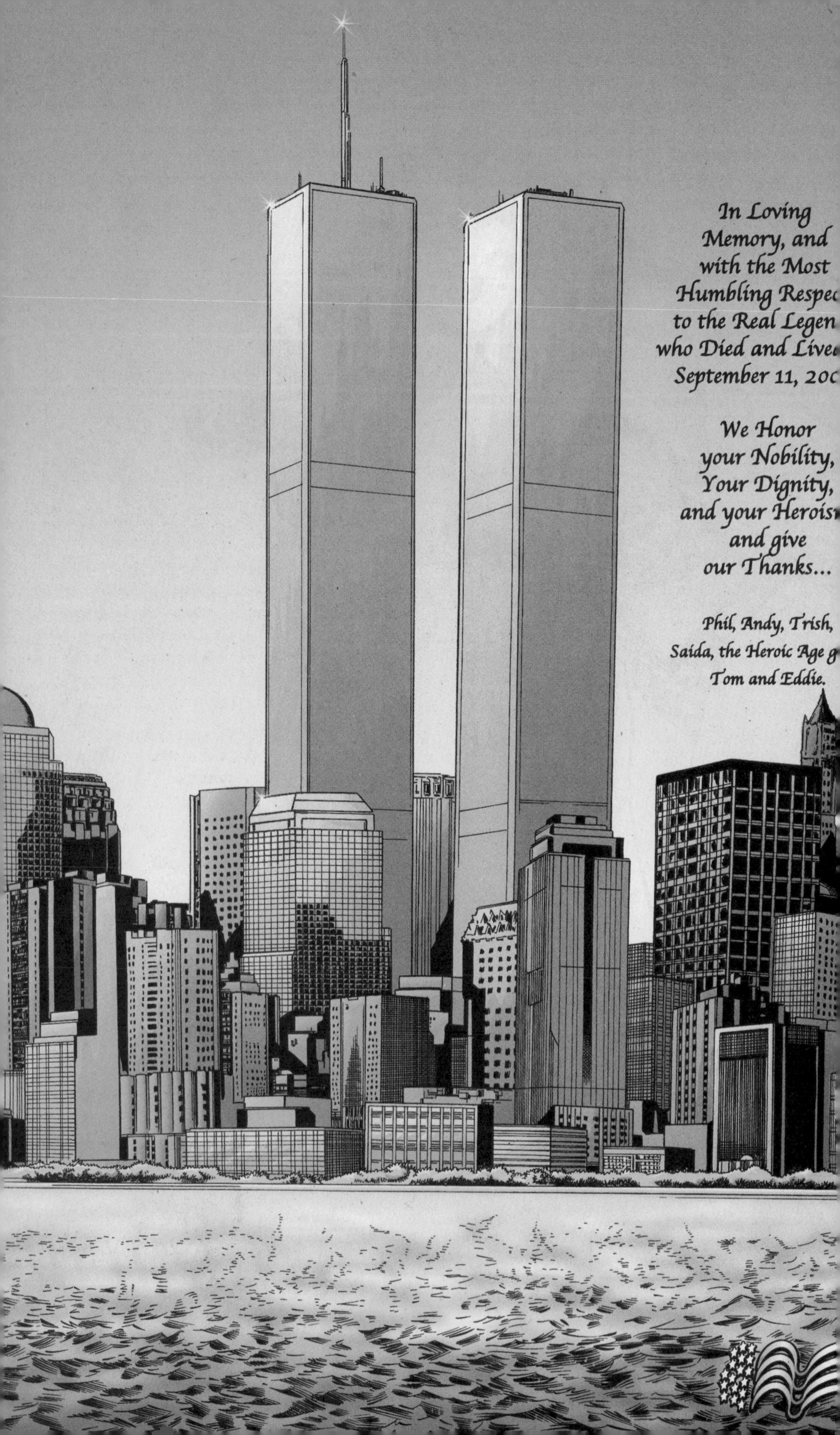
In Loving
Memory, and
with the Most
Humbling Respec
to the Real Legen
who Died and Live
September 11, 20
We Honor
your Nobility,
Your Dignity,
and your Herois
and give
our Thanks...
Phil, Andy, Trish,
Saida, the Heroic Age
Tom and Eddie.

The History of the Amazons

0,000 years ago, a caveman kills his pregnant mate. spirit is taken by the Earth goddess Gaea into the l of Souls — the first of thousands collected over next several centuries — all of women unjustly slain by men.

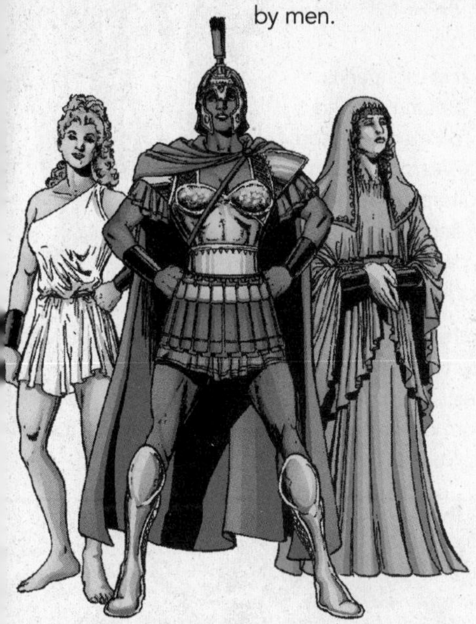

200 B.C. the Amazons are created by five mpian goddesses, who reincarnate the souls ected by Gaea as a tribe of warrior women. se Amazons are decreed a chosen race by the ddesses, teachers of equality, harmony, and justice the ways of Gaea. Under the leadership of Queen polyta and Queen Antiope, the Amazons form the at city-state of Themyscira in Asia Minor.

nder the influence of the war god Ares, Heracles, seus, and their men seduce the Amazons, attack m, rape them, and ransack Themyscira. Hippolyta ys to her goddesses for help and escapes her tors. Two factions of Amazons are formed — one owing Antiope into the hills of Greece seeking enge, the other following Hippolyta and the ddesses to the shores of a remote island hidden yond a veil of impenetrable storm clouds. derneath the island was the gateway to hellish tarus. As penance for their failures, the Amazons come the guardians of Doom's Doorway for eternity.

Granted immortality, Hippolyta's Amazons rebuild ir nation of Themsycira and transform the island a virtual paradise. ey wear

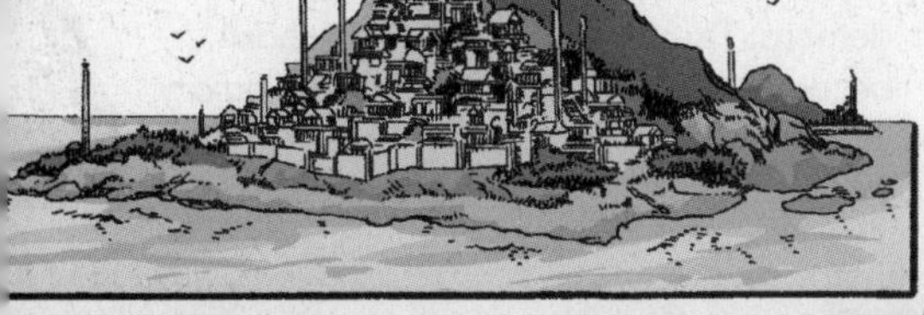

manacles of their captors as constant as reminders of their past and their new responsibility.

Antiope and her Amazons find Heracles and his men in Attica. Before Antiope can slay her attacker Theseus, he humbles himself before her and begs forgiveness. Antiope concedes to Theseus, and the two are married in Athens.

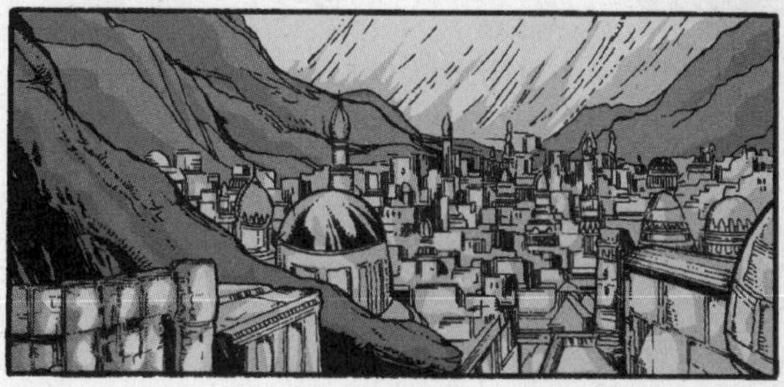

Years later, Antiope is murdered by Ariadne — Theseus's former lover. Phthia, Antiope's foster daughter, is framed for the murder by Theseus's son Menalippus, who hates the Amazons and wants to humiliate them. Phthia becomes an Amazon martyr and her Amazons forsake the ways of Gaea, beginning their campaigns of conquest and war against all men.

Phthia's Amazons eventually settle in Egypt, becoming mercenaries and paid assassins, selling their skills to the highest bidder. With the blessings of goddesses like Isis, Bast, and Neith, these women found the city of Bana-Mighdall, in a valley hidden by swirling sandstorms.

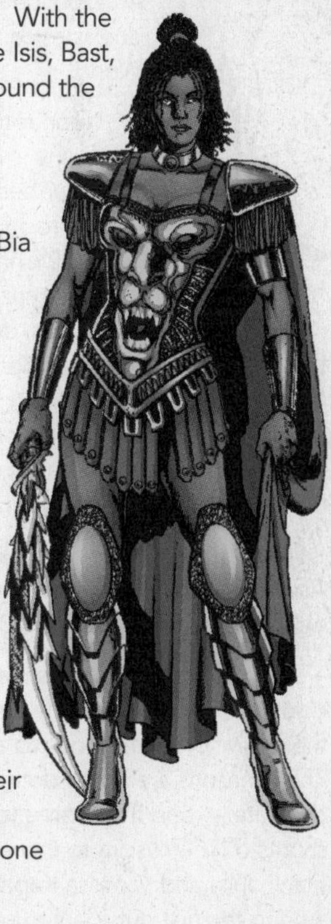

The Amazon warrior Nu'Bia wins the tournament of Grace and Wonder, and is chosen to defend Doom's Doorway from inside the cavern. In a mystic pact with the Gorgons, Nu'bia is given the ability to turn men to stone.

Over the centuries, young children lost at sea are taken to Themyscira and given mystical Amazon training before being returned, unharmed, to their brethren. Julia Kapatelis, a young girl from Greece, is one such child.

For almost 3,000 years, the Amazons of Themyscira live undisturbed by the outside world, perfecting their skills as artisans and warriors. Then, during World War II, Diana Rockwell Trevor crash-lands off the coast of Themyscira, and dies while saving a host of Amazons from the monsters beneath the island. Diana's badges and garb become an Amazon coat-of-arms.

On Themyscira, a lonely Hippolyta carves an infant out of clay. The infant is fused with the final spirit from within the Well of Souls and given powers by the Olympian

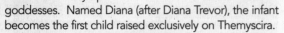

goddesses. Named Diana (after Diana Trevor), the infant becomes the first child raised exclusively on Themyscira.

Years later, the oracle Menalippe learns that the war god Ares has gone mad and plans to destroy the planet in a nuclear war. The gods proclaim that the Amazons' greatest champion shall go forth from Themyscira to defeat Ares.

Against her mother's wishes, a disguised Diana secretly enters the tournament and wins. Donning the sacred Amazon coat-of-arms, she ventures out into Patriarch's World, ending Ares's plans to begin World War III and becoming "Wonder Woman." With the help of Julia Kapatelis and Myndi Mayer, Wonder Woman starts to spread the Amazon ideals of equality and peaceful coexistence to the people of Patriarch's World.

Upon returning to Themyscira, Diana is confronted by Zeus, who wishes to consummate a physical relationship with her. When Diana refuses, Zeus sends the Amazon on a Challenge of the Gods, during which she destroys the monsters of Doom's Doorway. As part of the Challenge, Diana helps free Heracles from his own imprisonment, and after his earnest apology to the Amazons for his treatment of them, becomes the first man to set foot on Themyscira.

Freed of the task of defending Doom's Doorway, the Amazons destroy their warrior garb and lay down their weapons for the first time in 3,000 years.

Soon after, the Amazons learn of the destruction of Olympus by Darkseid and the migration of the gods to a new home. The Amazons are left to determine their own fate — and they agree to open the shores of Themyscira to the world of man. Julia and Vanessa Kapatelis are among the first outsiders to set foot on Paradise Island.

When Diana's magic lasso is stolen by the Cheetah, the Amazon tracks her enemy to Egypt. There, Diana discovers the Amazons of Bana-Mighdall and learns t[heir] origins. After several bloody battles with these Egyptian Amazons and their champion, Shim'Tar, Diana escapes Bana-Mighdall, which disappears into the sands.

The first dignitaries from Patriarch's World travel to Paradise Island, Lois Lane among them. The cultural exchange is nearly destroyed by Ares's daughter Eris, the Goddess of Discord.

Months later, Hippolyta and an entourage of Amazo[ns] journey to New York City under the protection of Hermes. They are greeted at the United Nations with an enormous parade and begin a nationwide tour of [the] United States.

The Amazons' tour is devastated when Circe begins her War of the Gods. Allying herself with the Egyptian Amazons, she frames the Themysciran Amazons for murder and transforms Hippolyta into the warrior que[en] Shim'Tar. The oracle Menalippe and the sculptor Hellene are both slain during the war.

After the War of the Gods, Hippolyta hopes to continue the cultural exchange, but her entreaties are denied and her Amazons ambassadors return to Themyscira humbled and rejected by the outside world.

Later, Circe transports the Amazons of Bana-Mighdall to Themyscira to ambush Hippolyta's Amazons. After days of battle, Circe transports Themyscira into another dimension, where the two tribes of Amazons wind up joining forces against a horde of demons. The Amazons of Bana-Mighdall become staunch guardians of the walled city.

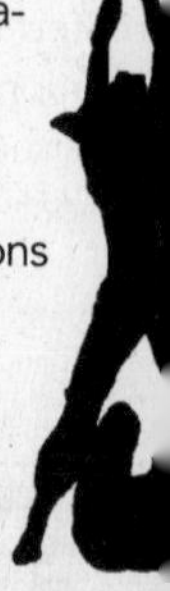

iana helps rescue Themyscira and returns it to our ension. As thanks for the help against the demon de, Hippolyta gives the Egyptian Amazons the far side 'aradise Island — a desolate wasteland — to make r own.

anipulated by the sorceress gala (possessed by the spirit riadne — Antiope's derer), Hippolyta estrates a new contest a new Wonder Woman. emis is chosen to be the ificial lamb, and polyta rigs the Contest hat Artemis will win. red-haired Amazon s, and ventures forth Patriarch's World as new Wonder Woman.

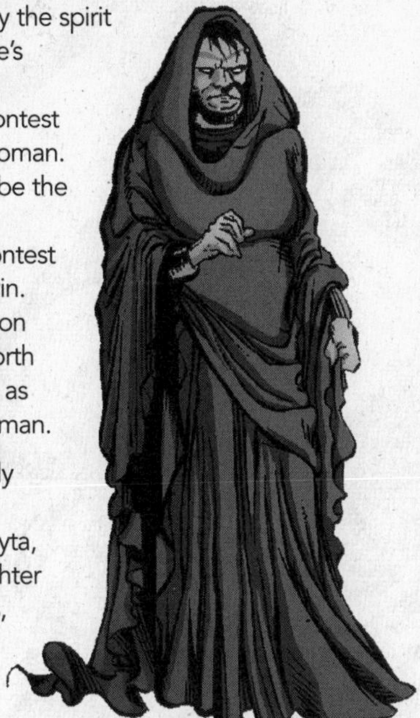

rtemis is eventually by the White gician and Hippolyta, cted by her daughter her manipulations, es Themyscira vander alone in riarch's World.

hemyscira is ravaged by kseid, who has come to the island seeking the secret he gods' location and immortality. Over 1,200 azons are slain by Darkseid's parademons, and the nd is left in ruins.

iana meets Harold Campion, the charming and verful super-hero "Champion." After Campion is ealed to be a revenge-seeking Heracles, Diana begins evert to clay. All of the Amazons begin suffering this , and Heracles deduces it is due to the distance ween the gods and their worshippers.

he Olympian gods return to Earth, transforming their nful followers to normal.

With the help of Diana, Hippolyta, and the Flash, Donna Troy defeats Dark Angel and her secret past as Diana's "sister" is revealed. In a Coronation Ceremony of the Amazons, Donna, once again as Troia, takes her place as royal princess and daughter of Queen Hippolyta.

Hippolyta begins to frequent Patriarch's World more often, fighting alongside the JSA in her own customized Wonder Woman garb.

The sorceress Magala, inhabited by the soul of Ariadne, sparks a civil war between the Themyscirans and the Bana-Mighdall Amazons. Fury slays Magala, and Hippolyta and Diana join forces to end the war by abolishing the matriarchy of Paradise Island forever.

The Amazons join forces with Wonder Woman and the heroes of Earth to defeat Imperiex, a universe-destroying entity. Hippolyta dies and Themyscira is shattered. But both tribes are united as a spiritual force channeling energy into Darkseid, who uses that energy to help Superman destroy Imperiex.

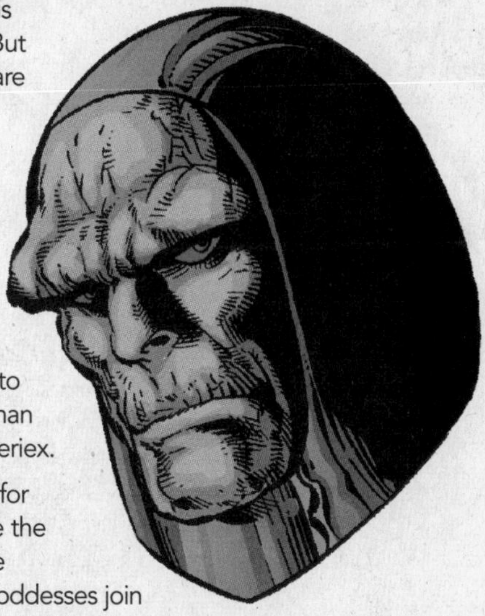

As thanks for helping save the universe, the Olympian goddesses join forces with their Egyptian counterparts to help rebuild Themyscira for all Amazons.

With Diana's guidance, Themyscira is rebuilt, using technologies and insights from across the universe. ocated in the Bermuda Triangle, the new Themyscira is a dimensional gateway, a university devoted to the free xchange of knowledge. Phillipus leads the island as its Chancellor. Artisans, medics, and teachers from across e universe join the Amazons in building this democratic institution and acknowledge Diana as its ambassador.

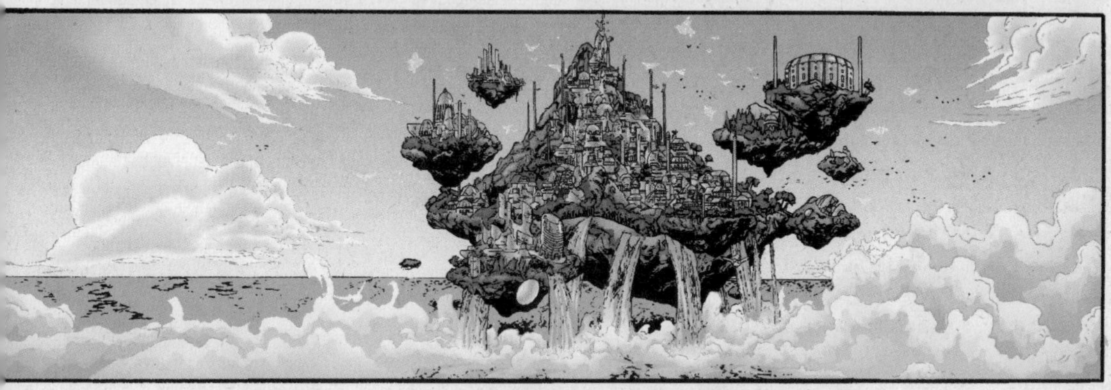

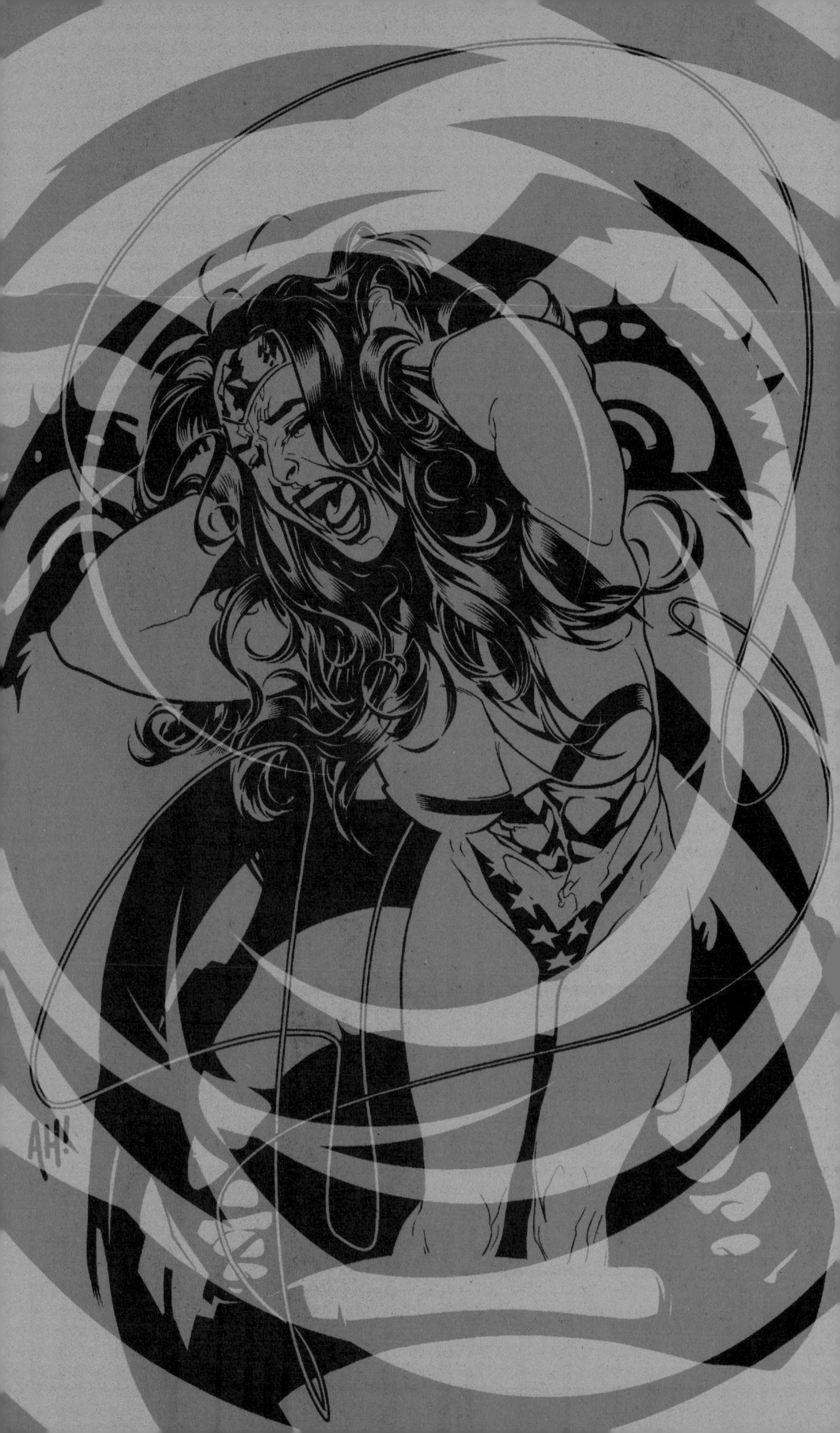
AH!

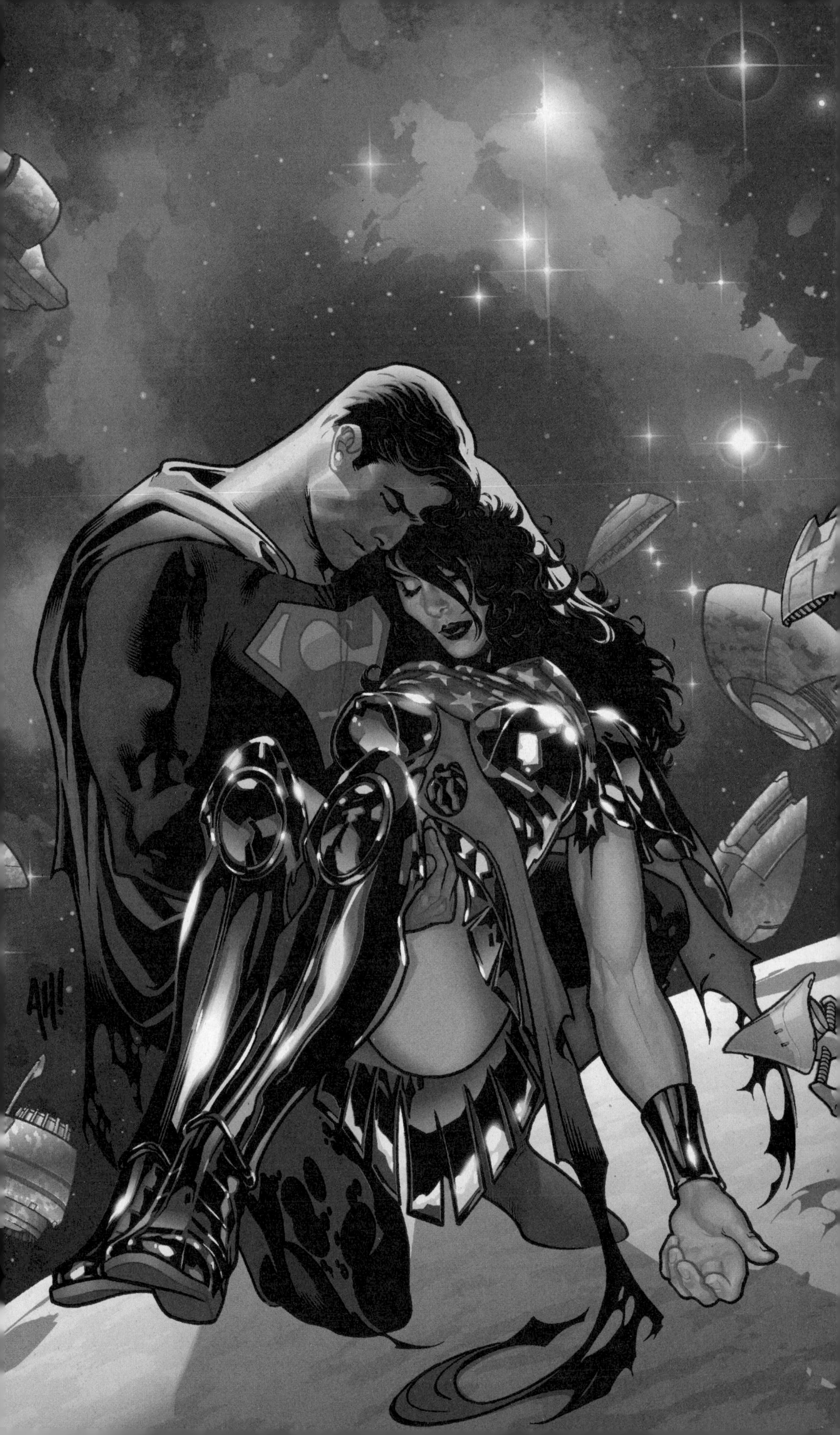
AH!

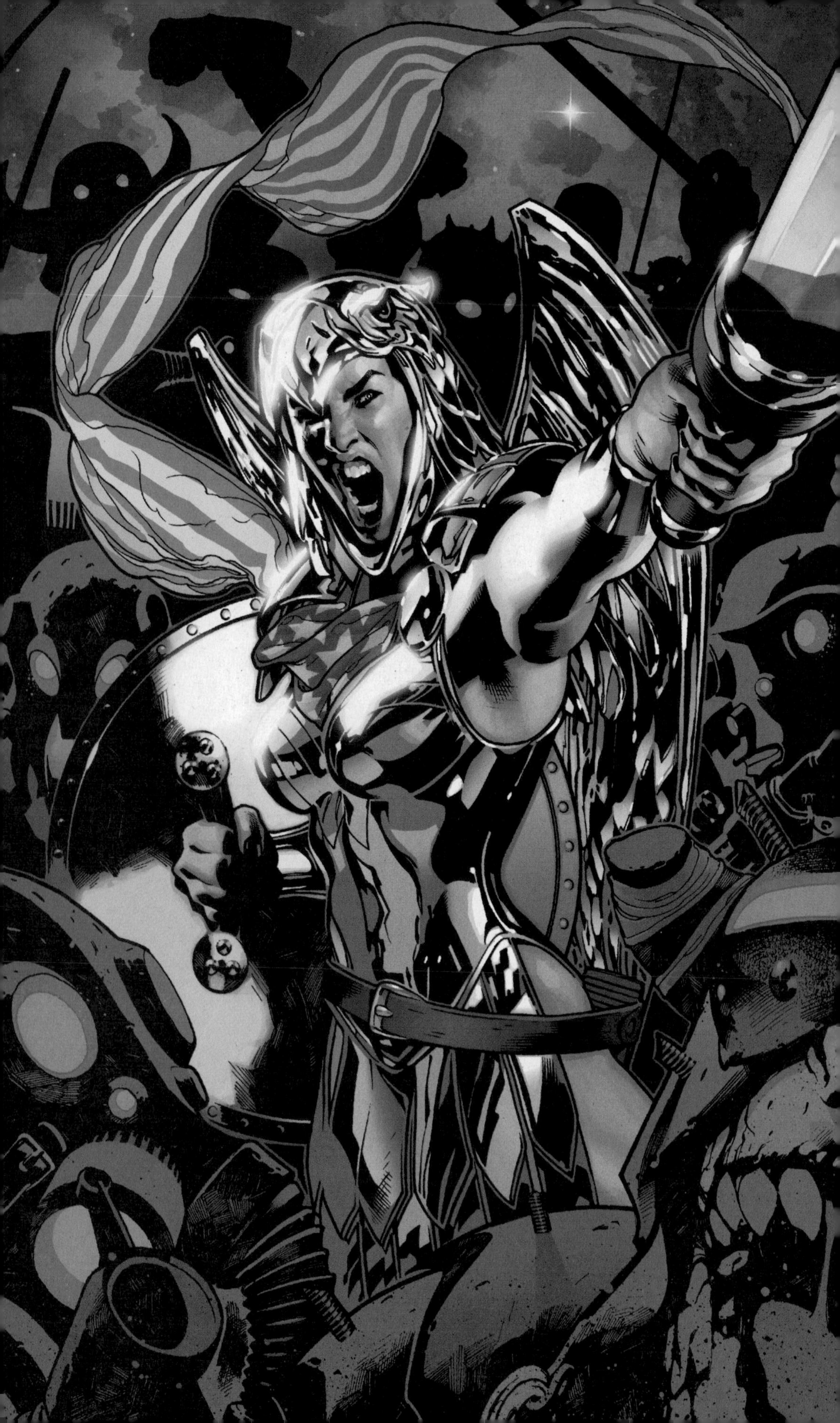

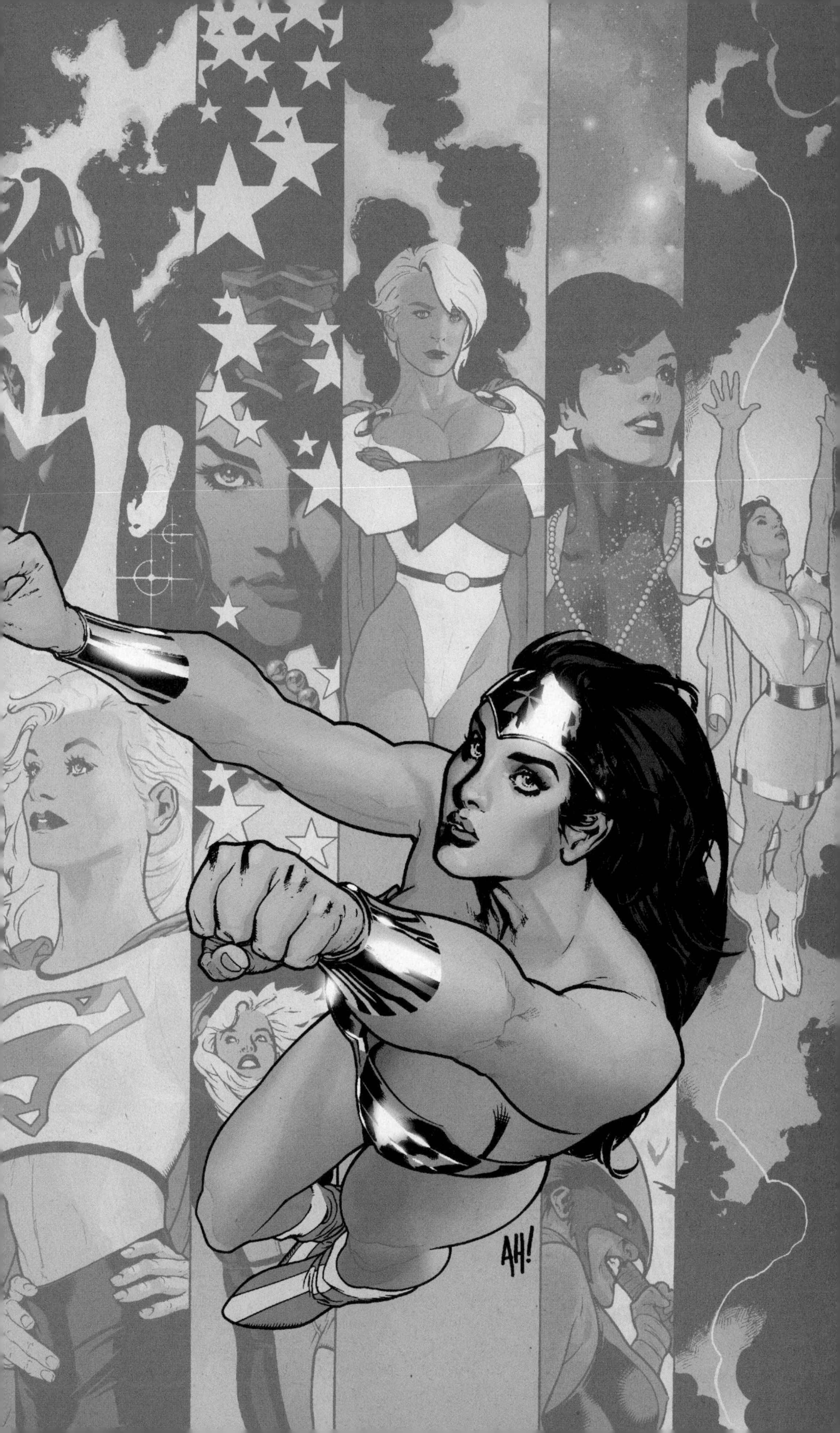
AH!

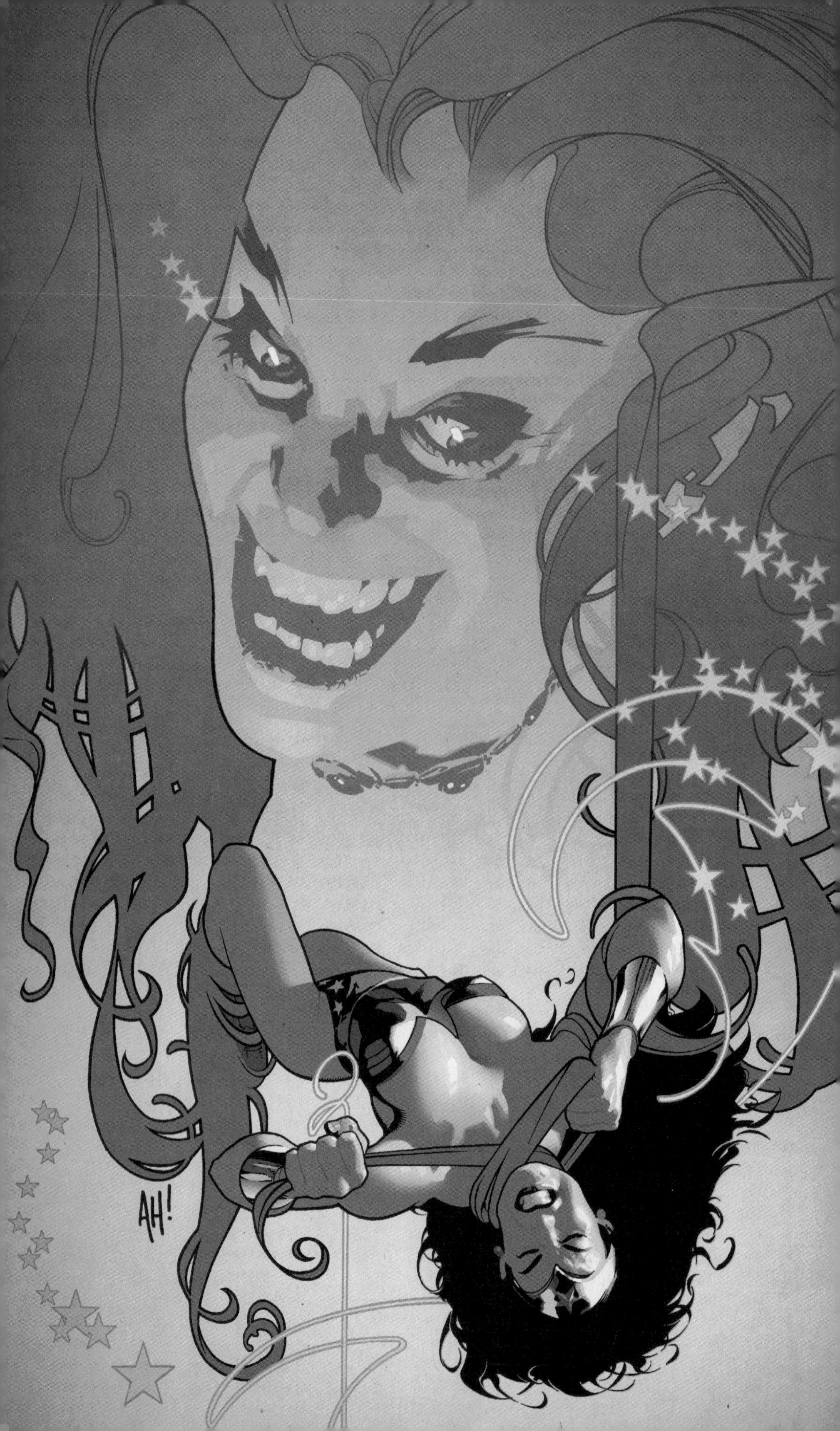
AH!

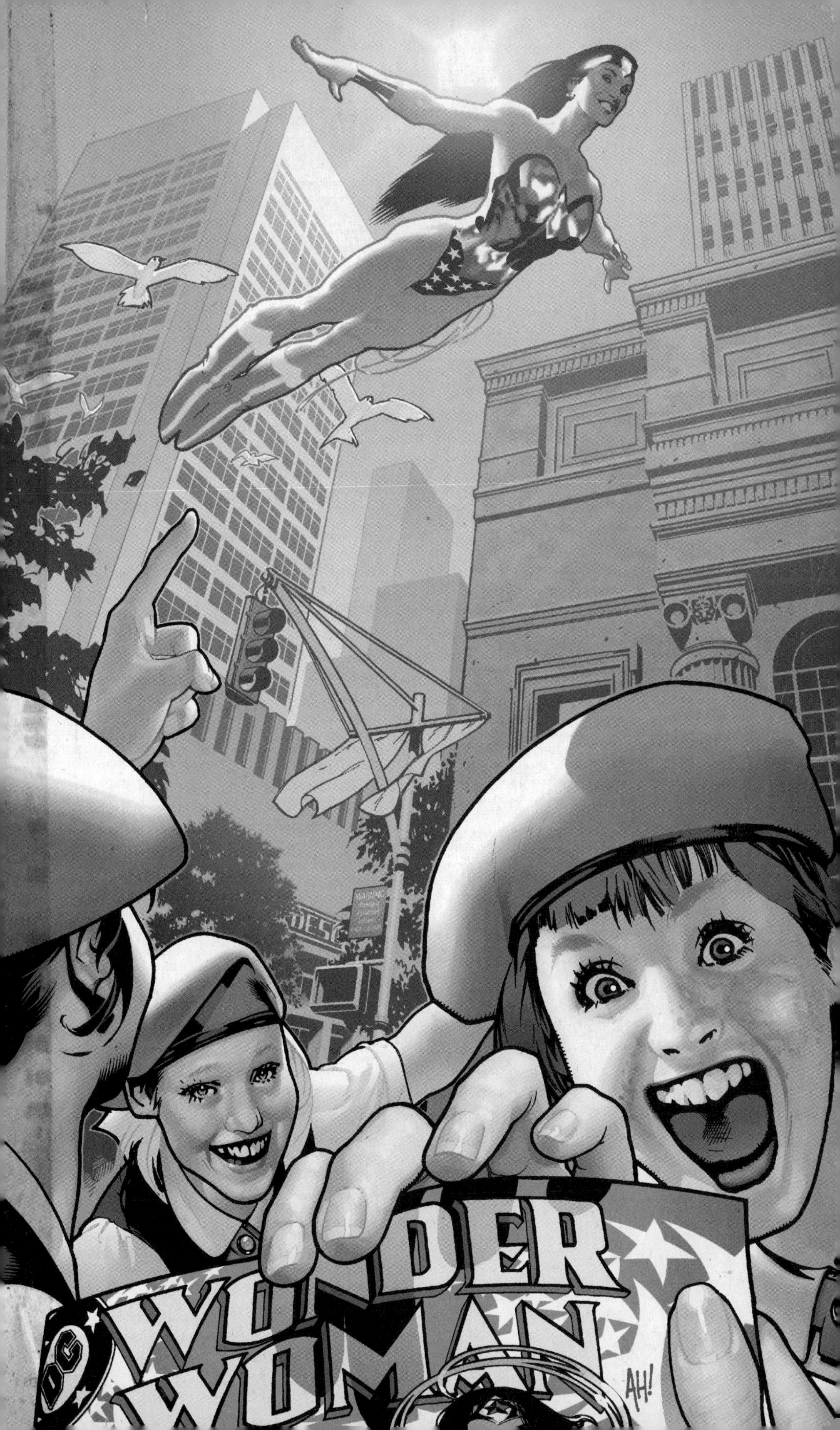
DER
AH!

CAN ALSO BE FOUND IN THESE BOOKS:

GRAPHIC NOVELS

ENEMY ACE: WAR IDYLL
George Pratt

THE FLASH: LIFE STORY OF THE FLASH
M. Waid/B. Augustyn/G. Kane/J. Staton/T. Palmer

GREEN LANTERN: FEAR ITSELF
Ron Marz/Brad Parker

THE POWER OF SHAZAM!
Jerry Ordway

WONDER WOMAN: AMAZONIA
William Messner-Loebs/Phil Winslade

COLLECTIONS

THE GREATEST 1950s STORIES EVER TOLD
Various writers and artists

THE GREATEST TEAM-UP STORIES EVER TOLD
Various writers and artists

AQUAMAN: TIME AND TIDE
Peter David/Kirk Jarvinen/Brad Vancata

DC ONE MILLION
Various writers and artists

THE FINAL NIGHT
K. Kesel/S. Immonen/J. Marzan/various

THE FLASH: BORN TO RUN
M. Waid/T. Peyer/G. LaRocque/H. Ramos/various

GREEN LANTERN: A NEW DAWN
R. Marz/D. Banks/R. Tanghal/various

GREEN LANTERN: BAPTISM OF FIRE
Ron Marz/Darryl Banks/various

GREEN LANTERN: EMERALD KNIGHTS
Ron Marz/Darryl Banks/various

HAWK & DOVE
Karl and Barbara Kesel/Rob Liefeld

HITMAN
Garth Ennis/John McCrea

HITMAN: LOCAL HEROES
G. Ennis/J. McCrea/C. Ezquerra/S. Pugh

HITMAN: TEN THOUSAND BULLETS
Garth Ennis/John McCrea

IMPULSE: RECKLESS YOUTH
Mark Waid/various

JACK KIRBY'S FOREVER PEOPLE
Jack Kirby/various

JACK KIRBY'S NEW GODS
Jack Kirby/various

JACK KIRBY'S MISTER MIRACLE
Jack Kirby/various

JUSTICE LEAGUE: A NEW BEGINNING
K. Giffen/J.M. DeMatteis/K. Maguire/various

JUSTICE LEAGUE: A MIDSUMMER'S NIGHTMARE
M. Waid/F. Nicieza/J. Johnson/D. Robertson/various

JLA: AMERICAN DREAMS
G. Morrison/H. Porter/J. Dell/various

JLA: JUSTICE FOR ALL
G. Morrison/M. Waid/H. Porter/J. Dell/various

JUSTICE LEAGUE OF AMERICA: THE NAIL
Alan Davis/Mark Farmer

JLA: NEW WORLD ORDER
Grant Morrison/Howard Porter/John Dell

JLA: ROCK OF AGES
G. Morrison/H. Porter/J. Dell/various

JLA: STRENGTH IN NUMBERS
G. Morrison/M. Waid/H. Porter/J. Dell/various

JLA: WORLD WITHOUT GROWN-UPS
T. Dezago/T. Nauck/H. Ramos/M. McKone/various

JLA/TITANS: THE TECHNIS IMPERATIVE
D. Grayson/P. Jimenez/P. Pelletier/various

JLA: YEAR ONE
M. Waid/B. Augustyn/B. Kitson/various

KINGDOM COME
Mark Waid/Alex Ross

LEGENDS: THE COLLECTED EDITION
J. Ostrander/L. Wein/J. Byrne/K. Kesel

LOBO'S GREATEST HITS
Various writers and artists

LOBO: THE LAST CZARNIAN
Keith Giffen/Alan Grant/Simon Bisley

LOBO'S BACK'S BACK
K. Giffen/A. Grant/S. Bisley/C. Alamy

MANHUNTER: THE SPECIAL EDITION
Archie Goodwin/Walter Simonson

THE RAY: IN A BLAZE OF POWER
Jack C. Harris/Joe Quesada/Art Nichols

THE SPECTRE: CRIMES AND PUNISHMENTS
John Ostrander/Tom Mandrake

STARMAN: SINS OF THE FATHER
James Robinson/Tony Harris/Wade von Grawbadger

STARMAN: NIGHT AND DAY
James Robinson/Tony Harris/Wade von Grawbadger

STARMAN: TIMES PAST
J. Robinson/O. Jimenez/L. Weeks/various

STARMAN: A WICKED INCLINATION...
J. Robinson/T. Harris/W. von Grawbadger/various

UNDERWORLD UNLEASHED
M. Waid/H. Porter/P. Jimenez/various

WONDER WOMAN: THE CONTEST
William Messner-Loebs/Mike Deodato, Jr.

WONDER WOMAN: SECOND GENESIS
John Byrne

WONDER WOMAN: LIFELINES
John Byrne

DC/MARVEL: CROSSOVER CLASSICS II
Various writers and artists

DC VERSUS MARVEL/MARVEL VERSUS DC
R. Marz/P. David/D. Jurgens/C. Castellini/various

THE AMALGAM AGE OF COMICS: THE DC COMICS COLLECTION
Various writers and artists

RETURN TO THE AMALGAM AGE OF COMICS: THE DC COMICS COLLECTION
Various writers and artists

OTHER COLLECTIONS OF INTEREST

CAMELOT 3000
Mike W. Barr/Brian Bolland/various

RONIN
Frank Miller

WATCHMEN
Alan Moore/Dave Gibbons

ARCHIVE EDITIONS

THE FLASH ARCHIVES Volume 1
(FLASH COMICS 104, SHOWCASE 4, 8, 13, 14, THE FLASH 105-108)
J. Broome/C. Infantino/J. Giella/various

THE FLASH ARCHIVES Volume 2
(THE FLASH 109-116)
J.Broome/C. Infantino/J. Giella/various

GREEN LANTERN ARCHIVES Volume 1
(SHOWCASE 22-23, GREEN LANTERN 1-5)

GREEN LANTERN ARCHIVES Volume 2
(GREEN LANTERN 6-13)
All by J. Broome/G. Kane/J. Giella/various

SHAZAM ARCHIVES Volume 1
(WHIZ COMICS 2-15)

SHAZAM ARCHIVES Volume 2
(SPECIAL EDITION COMICS 1, CAPTAIN MARVEL ADVENTURES 1, WHIZ COMICS 15-20)
All by B. Parker/C.C. Beck/J. Simon/J. Kirby/various

THE NEW TEEN TITANS Volume 1
(DC COMICS PRESENTS 26, THE NEW TITANS 1-8)
Marv Wolfman/George Pérez/various

TO FIND MORE COLLECTED EDITIONS AND MONTHLY COMIC BOOKS FROM DC COMICS,
CALL 1-888-COMIC BOOK FOR THE NEAREST COMICS SHOP OR GO TO YOUR LOCAL BOOK STORE